AN EXALTATION

OF FORMS

AN EXALTATION
OF FORMS

CONTEMPORARY

POETS CELEBRATE

THE DIVERSITY

OF THEIR ART

EDITED BY

Annie Finch
and
Kathrine Varnes

❀

ANN ARBOR

THE UNIVERSITY OF MICHIGAN PRESS

Copyright © by the University of Michigan 2002
All rights reserved
Published in the United States of America by
The University of Michigan Press
Manufactured in the United States of America
♾ Printed on acid-free paper

2005   2004   2003   2002   4   3   2   1

A CIP catalog record for this book is available
from the British Library.

Library of Congress Cataloging-in-
Publication Data applied for

ISBN 0-472-09725-3 (cloth)
ISBN 0-472-06725-7 (paper)

To my very first teacher of poetry,
Maggie Finch—
and
to Penelope Laurans
who first taught me form
and the patience to love form—A.F.

To Robyn Bell
who gave me my first *Book of Forms,* and
to John Ridland
who taught me how to scan—K.V.

Acknowledgments

This book came to fruition with the help of numberless poets, critics, and teachers, who wrote with queries and offered suggestions, poems, and names. We are indebted to all, even those whose work did not end up in these pages.

For helping inspire the original idea for the book, we offer our thanks to Marilyn Hacker. We are also happily grateful for the networking genius of Fleda Brown, Alfred Corn, Peter X. Feng, Vince Gotera, Rob Hardin, Bob Holman, Carolyn Kizer, Phillis Levin, E. Ethelbert Miller, the Poetics listserv at SUNY Buffalo, Mike Piech and the Exploring Form and Narrative conference at West Chester University—where, incidentally, we also first met each other.

The publication of this book would not have been possible without the generous support of Miami University in Oxford, Ohio. We would especially like to thank the following people and departments at Miami: John Hughes, the College of Arts and Sciences, Carol Willeke, the Office for the Advancement of Scholarship and Teaching, Dianne Sadoff, and the Department of English. We are also grateful to the Delaware State Arts Council, the University of Delaware's Department of English, the University of Missouri-Columbia's Department of English, and LeAnn Fields and the University of Michigan Press for their support of this book when it was still a fledgling project. Thanks also to Sherod Santos and Bob Watts. And for invaluable editorial assistance in the harried final stages, we thank Erick Kelemen, Karen Powell, Anne Thalheimer, Sara Triller, and Greg Winston. Special thanks go to Fred Courtright and the Permissions Company.

We would like to thank Agha Iqbal Ali for his assistance during his brother's illness. Agha Shahid Ali passed away while these pages were in proof. We are honored to have his work in our book, and we mourn his passing.

Finally, we are deeply grateful to our families: Glen Brand, Julian and Althea Finch-Brand, Erick Kelemen, Dee Barlow, and Richard Varnes.

Contents

II.
STANZAS

III.
RECEIVED FORMS

IV.
PRINCIPLES FOR FORMAL EXPERIMENTATION

Introduction

An Exaltation of Forms grew out of our desire to celebrate contemporary poetry's shapes and materials through the words of the poets who know and love them. Over several years, we asked numerous poets to write brief introductory histories and how-tos for a particular form, meter, stanza, or principle for formal experimentation. We also asked each of them to assemble a mix of poems, showing some of the directions possible for that particular mode of embodying language. We were delighted that so many of our favorite poets agreed to help us with the project.

We look at this exaltation of poetics as we might at a flock of birds: less a historical anthology or handbook detailing rules than a grouping of modes of flight. Passionate interest in poetics brings poets together across different poetic schools, and we believe that an intermingling of styles is a strength. For this reason, we have gathered a great range of approaches to poetic form in one volume, whether form is defined in terms of rhythm, rhyme, repetition, numbering, lineation, spatial arrangement, or other ordering principles. The forms included in this book cover large territories of time, space, and aesthetic inclination, from ancient litany and ghazal to contemporary fractal verse and hip-hop; Eastern haiku and pantoum to Western sonnet and rondeau; familiar ballad and blues to arcane hendecasyllabics and procedural verse.

Our book aims to facilitate an understanding of the true diversity of American poetry today fuller than that available in any other book. In order to accomplish this goal, we chose contributors influenced by sometimes warring schools of contemporary poetics: Language and avant-garde, free verse and mainstream, formalist and traditional, Beat and performance. In order to accommodate such a mix of poetic viewpoints, we made three conscious decisions that may inspire some controversy.

First, we refuse to accept a simplistic dichotomy between "free" and "formal" verse. Instead, we emphasize the continuity of language elements, such as the line break, that these two types of poetry hold in common. We hope the sections on free verse in this book will clarify the way that free verse participates in a continuum of poetic patterning.

Second, this book includes sections on other forms recently imported into literary English from American oral traditions and other oral and written cultures, side by side with older imports. Most previous poetry handbooks omit thorough discussion of the new forms that have claimed increasingly central roles in our poetry. Our book's communal authorship encompasses American poets of many traditions and backgrounds who enable us to include expert sections on forms including blues, *décima*, ghazal, haiku, hip-hop, pantoum, rap, and renku.

Our third decision may require some background explanation. For the past few decades, many poets and critics, both traditional and experimental, have suggested that to write in certain forms is incompatible with postmodern insights about the contingency and fragmentariness of the self. According to this assumption, to write in form implies both a coherent self and a hegemonic way of thinking, and is therefore a nostalgic throwback to the pre-postmodern era. We disagree. In fact, some critics (see Emanuel, Finch, and Schultz) have recently begun to explore the fact that poetic form, in different guises, was a commonly shared passion of both new formalists and of exploratory/experimental poets during the late twentieth century. By including both exploratory and traditional forms in one volume, we hope to open a discussion about form that cuts across poetic movements, which have for too long either ignored or distorted each others' insights and expertise. We want readers to consider for themselves the depth and degree of the contrast between the formal devices of avant-garde and traditional poetics.

Having devoted many years to constructing what we believe to be the most comprehensive portrait of the state of contemporary poetics in the United States to date, we have naturally found ourselves thinking, long and hard, about a question that has divided the poetry world now for several decades. How can we make sense of the many different and apparently conflicting models of poetry available today? In the end, we find ourselves most comfortable with the model presented by literary critic David Kellogg.

> In a poetry culture as diverse in practice and theory as that of
> contemporary America, the concept of the establishment may
> be necessary, allowing as it does for resistance to take the form
> of opposition to a perceived "center." In my model, however,
> the center is a function of the poetic field itself, and an emer-
> gent property of the interaction of all its poles; there is no one
> site for resistance or authenticity.

HOW TO USE THIS BOOK

This book is divided into four sections covering four of the basic tools of poetic form in English, and each section is organized according to its own logic. The section on meter, which we define as the counting of units within poetic lines, moves from the simplest countable entities, accent and word, to more complex patterns. The section on stanzas moves from shorter to longer stanzas. The section on specific poetic forms, the longest, is organized alphabetically by the name of the form, and the section on principles for formal experimentation by increasing complexity of the principle. To make it easier to consult the book, we have also included an index of names.

For the dedicated writer and reader of poetry, this anthology will serve as a supplement and as a way of gaining guidance from many poets in one volume. But we also provide a simple primer of prosody at the end of this introduction, so that beginners can hold their own. This book can stand alone as a text for a poetry writing class, by reading straight through each essay in order, or by assigning sections to students based on interest. It also provides a resource for a workshop leader who discovers a student pursuing a form—such as the rondeau or rap—with which he or she is not familiar. *An Exaltation of Forms* will also complement a large anthology in an introduction to poetry class, answering the perennial question, "Do poets really think about all this when they write poetry?" For scholars and critics, this book can explain the forms thoroughly, offer an eclectic sampling of examples, and provide insight into the writing lives of contemporary poets.

Although technical wisdom certainly abounds in this volume, a less obvious thread also holds the essays together: creative vision. These essays reveal the interweaving of form with imagination, political identity, and worldview. But the link between form and vision is an ever-shifting, ever-slipping one, as we see when Paul Hoover explores counted verse as a visual flaunting of poetry's artificiality, when Margaret Holley describes the subliminal power of syllabic verse, when Dana Gioia praises accentual verse for its ability to "capture speech rhythms without sounding conventionally literary," and when Anthony Hecht remarks that blank verse, "poetry's tool-of-all-trades," at its best "should observe the directness and expediency of prose discourse, yet at the same time contrive to make itself manifestly distinguishable from prose." Such an accomplishment cannot merely be technical. We see the intricacy of the connection between form and vision again when Charles Hartman warns against the "blithe shallowness" of too much rhythm in anapestics, when Carl Phillips speculates that the paucity of perfectly trochaic poems written in English might have something to do with a "suspicion of open-endedness," when Annie Finch associates dactylic rhythms with "the unconscious, the body, femininity, and wild natural power," and when Rachel Hadas considers hendecasyllabics a good meter for meditative thought. And that's only a peek at some essays in the first section on meters.

Reading through these essays will reveal how deeply poetic form and culture reflect and require each other. W. D. Snodgrass notes the centrality of the folk ballad's story to its culture; Agha Shahid Ali explores the lessons for a Western reader of the ghazal, which demands formal adherence alongside a substantive "disunity"; Vince Gotera reinvests the pantoum with its Malay origins and asserts that, together, the two halves of the quatrain "portray ineffable cultural and universal truths." We get a sense for the vital connection between form and content when Pat Mora tells the story of recovering the *décima* and its oral tradition in her search for a form to hold "the voice of an older woman in New Mexico."

So much of good writing matches the right form to the right occasion. Remembering his composition of a poem set in Los Angeles, Timothy Steele expresses his desire to convey the place's multiplicity while still maintaining the "preservative power of the couplet." Explaining the genesis of haiku, Jean Hyung Yul Chu describes a form developing from the conditions of Bashō's travels, reflecting "the spareness required by his itinerant life." Tracie Morris reminds us of the crucial role of community to hip-hop, where performance "flow" is just as essential as word choice when poets test their new works. Likewise, Bob Holman's essay makes clear that performance poetry would be unheard of without a venue, and each venue encourages its own style. Detailing the elaborate rules for writing Japanese-style linked poems, William Higginson and Penny Harter emphasize that social mores—such as a guest complimenting a host—are an integral part of the poem's form.

Some of our contributors sketch out a poetics triggered by a desire to bridge disciplines; others explain their form as steeped in conversation. Rob Hardin refuses the division between prosody and music, while Alice Fulton reaches across to theories of science and proposes a fractal poetics as an aesthetic "between set forms and aimlessness" that relies on "interruption, artifice, discontinuity, and raggedness" to provide a deep structure akin to events such as earthquakes in the natural world. Connecting blues to daily living, Raymond Patterson explains blues repetition "as a means of gaining time to improvise a response to a life situation." Marilyn Hacker, foreshadowing her own essay's richness, describes the sonnet as "a form that invites close engagement" and "often becomes a kind of dialogue with its past and present uses and connotations." Suggesting an ever-present poststructuralist discourse, Mark Wallace sees the act of creating predetermined avant-garde forms as an acknowledgment that language already imposes a control over expression. Later, Aldon Nielsen on Oulipo and Jena Osman on procedural verse both consider the relationship between mechanical processes and the writer's unconscious, valuing the semantic surprises that avant-garde methods can uncover in language. Osman even enticingly suggests that such poems function as "utopian mediations" that hint toward not just an alternative life of language but even, perhaps, the hope for an alternative means of living.

Never unadulterated patterns, forms carry rich associations. Defending the epigram, X. J. Kennedy pokes fun at editors who "mistake length in poetry for importance," and Gail White refuses to look askance as she details the sometime scandalous history of the limerick. Kathleene West warns would-be triolet writers of the form's tendency toward "vapid description—nature and love often being the culprits," and Thomas M. Disch warns those attempting roundels and rondeaux in English that the poems "are apt to come across as greeting cards." These are sobering but invaluable cautions. In a more laudatory strain, Jacqueline Osherow praises the "all-encompassing capaciousness" of ottava rima to support lyricism as well as narrative, while Nancy Willard asks why the litany has the power to "leave us spellbound." Lewis Turco, sounding a psychotherapeutic note, explains how he turned the "obsessive quality" of the sestina to his advantage, while Maxine Kumin characterizes the refrains of the villanelle as "hypnotic."

The relationships between form and meaning are historical, changing and shifting with time. None of the above connections is necessarily paradigmatic, but writers derive strength from such associations, adapting them as required. We feel especially blessed to have the careful words of three masters of adaptation, the late Hilda Morley, the late John Frederick Nims, and the late Raymond Patterson, three generous poets whose aesthetic choices inextricably blended vision with form, whether they took shape in an archaeology of the self or in the sound of ancient meters.

All anthologies require many hard decisions, and we had to omit much material we would rather have included. Two particular absences deserve mention. Although we had initially hoped to include a section on Native American chant forms, the most expert practitioners whom we contacted discouraged our interest, arguing that the forms could not be taken out of their ritualistic cultural context. Not able to see a way to include these forms while still respecting such a link between vision and form, we deferred to their judgment. We are also particularly sorry not to have a section on the internal rhyme schemes of Celtic verse forms but encourage those intrigued to look them up in Lewis Turco's *New Book of Forms*, Miller Williams's *Patterns of Poetry*, and elsewhere. As abundant as our book is, the selected bibliographies offered by our contributors point toward even more resources for exploration, and we hope our readers will follow their leads.

THE BASIC TERMS OF PROSODY
USED IN THIS BOOK

If you have a shelf of books on prosody, or even one dog-eared poetics handbook, this section is probably not for you. However, if a good number of the words appearing in the table of contents strike you as odd or unfamiliar, if you are new to prosody, or if you just prefer a quick overview of terms before you plunge in, the next few pages should provide enough basic information to get you going. Though advanced prosody abounds in complex theories and intricate arguments, the simple definitions that follow are not usually sites of contention among poets.

Traditional metrical systems in English can be classified as accentual, syllabic, and accentual-syllabic. Accentual verse, as the name suggests, has a regular number of accents, or beats, per line, with any number of unaccented syllables running between. Syllabic verse, logically enough, is guided by the number of syllables in a line, without any particular regard to how many beats may occur. Often syllabic verse poems vary the syllable count from line to line (three, five, seven, nine) but maintain the first stanza's pattern variation in the following stanzas. Accentual-syllabic verse, which has dominated poetry written in English roughly from the early Renaissance to the mid–twentieth century, is also referred to generically as *meter*. Accentual-syllabic verse pays attention to both accented and unaccented syllables in particular patterns that poets call *feet*. The feet are designated by marks in a process called *scansion*. The most common metrical feet appear below, with unaccented syllables indicated by a breve (˘) and accented syllables indicated by an acute accent ('). These marks belong over the vowels of the corresponding syllables.

Foot	Marking	Example	Adjectival Form
Iamb	˘ ′	*Annoy* is a natural iamb because it sounds awkward to stress the first syllable.	Adjectivally a line of iambs is referred to as *iambic.*
Trochee	′ ˘	*Retro* is a natural trochee.	A line of trochees is called *trochaic.*
Anapest	˘ ˘ ′	*On the top* will usually scan as an anapest because nouns tend to bear more weight than articles or prepositions.	A line primarily comprised of anapests, or one foot appearing in a line dominated by other feet, is *anapestic.*
Dactyl	′ ˘ ˘	*Wonderful* will scan as a dactyl if the last syllable gets swallowed as it usually does in normal conversation. *Wilderness* and *adjective* are less ambiguous dactyls.	As you may expect, the adjectival form is *dactylic.*

When naming a poem's meter, we generally use a two-word designation: an adjective describing the type of foot (given above) and a noun indicating the line length. A line of verse with one foot is called monometer; two feet are called dimeter; three feet are trimeter; four are tetrameter; five pentameter; six hexameter; seven heptameter; eight octameter. In scansion we show the separation of feet with a vertical line. Thus, a line of four feet, consisting mainly of iambs, is called iambic tetrameter, as with the first line of Robert Frost's "Stopping by Woods on a Snowy Evening":

$$\breve{} \quad ′ \quad | \quad \breve{} \quad ′ \quad | \breve{} \quad ′ \quad | \breve{} \quad ′$$
Whose woods these are I think I know.

If you have been noting the qualifiers above, you may have already surmised that scansion is an inexact science. The same word or phrase may scan differently in a new context. Indeed, the same poem scanned by two readers may not produce identical results, especially if one emphasizes a particular word in favor of an alternative meaning. In order to guard against too much mushiness, most poets and readers agree on the following principles:

1. Assume at first the poem is iambic (by far the most common meter), until it tells you otherwise.
2. If a poem begins strongly in one meter, give later lines some credit of momentum.
3. Distinguish between natural speech stress (which correlates to the accent marks in your dictionary) and accent, which is relative within a foot. Lightly stressed syllables can become promoted in a musical context and carry a metrical accent, as we see in the last line of an Edna St. Vincent Millay sonnet, "I shall be gone—and you may whistle for me." We might not expect heavy accent on the preposition *for*, yet when snug against the last syllable of *whistle* in an iambic pentameter line, *for* carries a beat. While in another poem, one might argue to emphasize *me* instead, this particular line rhymes with a previous that ended with "not too stormy," which encourages us to replicate a similar accentual pattern in "whistle for me."
4. When torn between complicated and simple ways of scanning a poem, choose the simpler.
5. Be careful not to distort pronunciation just to claim a perfect meter. Well-placed variance adds suspense and texture to a poem.

Metric variance, when not all syllables adhere to the prevailing pattern, is called *substitution*. In other words, we account for variance by identifying specific feet as having been replaced with another type. For instance, if Frost had spent more time in cities, he might have written

> Whose gardens these are I think I know.

Writing "gardens" instead of "woods" introduces an extra unaccented syllable into an otherwise iambic line. We could understand this extra syllable as creating an anapest *(= ens these are),* since most readers, as a way of straightening out the reversed syntax (i.e., toward "I think I know whose gardens these are"), would pause after "are" and give it a bit more emphasis than "these." If, however, the speaker's indecision turned out to be crucial for the poem's meaning, someone might make a reasonable case for putting an accent on "these" and delaying the anapest until "are I think." Then again, if we understood there to be a contest between the speaker and someone else, we might argue for an emphasis on "I," but that creates more rather than less metrical havoc. Caught by all these possibilities, one might turn again to principle 4 above, and finally select the first option, which doesn't require an explanation hinged on meaning.

Trochaic substitutions in iambic poems (called also Miltonic substitutions, since John Milton was so fond of them) usually occur in the first foot or after a pause (often though not always signaled by punctuation) in the line. A pause in a line of poetry is also called a *caesura,* which is indicated in scansion by double vertical lines. We see dactylic substitution less frequently in iambic verse, but no rules bar it. Anapestic, trochaic, and dactylic poems tend to rely even more on substitution, dropping unaccented syllables as necessary. For detailed discussions with illustrations of all four meters, see Ridland, Hartman, Phillips, and Finch.

Two other feet mentioned repeatedly in this book are the *spondee* (scanned ′ ′; adjective: *spondaic*) and the *pyrrhic* (scanned ˘ ˘; adjective also *pyrrhic*). These feet are unusual in that they occur only as substitutions in lines made up primarily of other meters. Depending on context, an example for the spondee might be *hogwash,* since both heavy syllables bear equal or nearly equal weight. "These are" in Frost's poem could arguably be pyrrhic, again depending on context, since the syllables could come across as equally lightweight. Because these two feet function only as substitutes, some prosodists argue that they are not true metrical feet. The position gains merit when we remember that accent is relative within a foot, and that, in the human voice, one syllable would inevitably take more accent than the other. (For more on substitution and scansion, see Ridland on iambic meter, Hartman on anapestic meter.) Still, the spondee and pyrrhic are terms much in use, as are the *amphibrach* (scanned ˘ ′ ˘) and many other terms borrowed from Greek quantitative verse, which measures vowel duration rather than accent (a nearly impossible enterprise in English, although some poets have trained their ears to manage it). When indicating quantitative meter, scansion marks are placed in the same manner, except that where we would note accent, instead poets use a dash or *macron* (˘ —). For a thorough discussion of the trickiness of translating such meters, see especially Warren, Hadas, and also Schulman. For more on discovering unusual meters in ancient poetry, see Nims. For verse that counts words instead of syllables, see Hoover.

Free verse, or open verse, describes a huge variety of poetic rhythms that cannot be adequately described with the tools adapted to accentual, syllabic, and accentual-syllabic meters. While a relatively new category in poetry, free verse partakes in many well-established modes and traditions, several of which appear in this book, including the found poem, the list poem, and organic poetry (see Tuma, Lehman, and Morley). In free verse, the lines may be of any length the poet deems necessary. Often this generates interest in where the line breaks occur and whether the break comes with or against the sentence syntax, with or against an expected meaning. Two invaluable adjectives describing any poetry written in lines are *enjambed* and *end-stopped*. Running a sentence over the line break and into the next line without pause is called *enjambment*. A line that ends with punctuation is referred to as *end-stopped*. (For a more complete discussion of free verse, see Boisseau.)

Whereas prose is written in paragraphs, lines of verse grouped together are called stanzas. Two lines are a couplet; three make up a tercet; four a quatrain; five a quintet; six a sestet; seven a septet; eight an octave. Each stanza length has developed a history, sometimes several, as our contributors on stanzaic traditions suggest (see especially Steele, Hollander, and Schulman). Some formal poets cultivate a favorite stanza for a long while; others spend a great deal of time researching stanzaic possibilities. The exception to the stanza's domain is the prose poem, which is written in paragraphs (see Delville and Chernoff).

Over the years, poets have developed names not only for meters, lines, and stanzas but also for specific patterns, whether chiefly rhythmical (such as the sapphic stanza), rhyming (as with the limerick), deliberately repetitive (the sestina), or linguistic/numerical (as with the S + 7 process described by Osman). Most, though certainly not all, traditional forms are recognized first by their signature rhyming patterns, second by an expected meter. Rhymes are designated with lowercase vowels, with *x* frequently reserved to indicate an unrhymed line. Thus, a quatrain labeled *abab* would mean that the final words of the first and third lines rhymed together, as did the second and fourth lines. These are called *end rhymes*. A pair of quintets labeled *abbxa cddxc* would mean that the fourth line consistently went unrhymed even though the poet introduced new rhymes as the poem continued (as opposed to, say, an interlocking scheme of *abbca cddec effge*). Capital letters signal refrains, entire (or partial) lines that repeat in the poem. This is particularly common in the blues (see Patterson) and in forms imported from the French, as in the ballade, roundel, rondeau, triolet, and villanelle (see Barrington, Disch, West, and Kumin). If a poem requires different refrains that rhyme together, as in the villanelle, superscript numbers, A^1, A^2, distinguish them. The most established rhyming patterns connote an expected logic or attitude, although poets respond to these expectations variously—by ignoring, embracing, or deliberately breaking them. And each choice is, of course, limited by the rhyme-sounds in question. Some poets will take advantage of a shift from, say, soft *ish* and *eese* rhymes to hard-sounding *at* and *ock* rhymes as an opportunity to turn the mood or subject of a poem, but if changes in rhyme-sounds don't offer some dramatic difference, there's less advantage to take.

Rhyme takes various forms, indicated most simply as either perfect *(won/done)* or imperfect *(spies/trite)*. Perfect rhyme is also known as *full, pure,* or *true.* Imperfect rhyme, popular in contemporary poems for its dissonant effect, also answers to *half, near, off,* or *slant. Eye rhyme,* a subcategory to imperfect, sounds off to the ear even if it looks perfect on the page *(ear/bear).* A second subcategory worth noting, *pararhyme,* indicates words with the same consonant sounds but different vowels *(case/kiss).* While our examples thus far have been single or monosyllabic rhymes, double, triple—or more generically, polysyllabic—rhymes can have a delightful effect frequently found in jazz standards and light, or humorous, verse *(rhapsody/can't you see; between us/Venus).*

With the exception primarily of Celtic verse forms, internal rhyming—rhyme within a line rather than at its end—is usually not part of a named pattern, but an embellishment. Internal rhyme includes *assonance* (words sharing the same vowel sounds—hot/modern/odd), *consonance* (words containing the same-sounding consonants—cat/bike/attic), and *alliteration* (words beginning with the same sounds—*w*ide/*w*aters/*w*ithout). In free verse, prose poetry, or some of the avant-garde and Oulipian forms that are not defined by a particular rhyming shape in the traditional sense, the sounds created by the words may be less immediately apparent. It may take some marking—color-coding certain vowels or consonants, circling rhymes wherever they appear—to uncover the subtler melodies at first.

We hope that our readers, having become familiar with the terms and forms covered in this book, will feel encouraged to use the book as a point of entry for continued explorations of poetic form. We like to think that you will take up where we left off, venture into the spaces between the forms included here, and resurvey the boundaries we have sketched out. To edit this book was an unforgettable lesson in the immense richness of contemporary poetics and the strength of poets' passion for the forms of their art. We hope that you, in using this book, will be as heartened, amazed, and delighted as we have been during our editorship.

Meters

Accentual Verse

DANA GIOIA

Accentual meter is the simplest and oldest poetic measure in English. Its origins date back to the beginnings of our language. In one form or another it has been a constant presence in English poetry from *Beowulf* and *Piers Plowman* to the present. Perennially popular, it is the meter of most nursery rhymes and playground chants as well as many folk ballads. Even today stress meter provides the underlying structure for such forms as rap and cowboy poetry.

The traditional prosody of a language always selects phonetic features immediately audible to native speakers—such as pitch, quantity, syllable counts, accent, assonance, alliteration—and arranges one or more of them in expressive patterns. Compared to most other languages, English is very strongly stressed. Speech stress in English conveys meaning. The more meaningful a word, the stronger speech stress it receives. It was, therefore, almost inevitable that stress would provide the basis for most English meters—first in purely accentual form, then in later accentual-syllabic developments.

The basic principles of accentual verse are stunningly simple. There is, in fact, only one steadfast rule: there must be an identical number of strong stresses in each line. (If the poem is stanzaic in structure like a ballad, then there must be the same number of strong stresses in, say, the second line of the stanza.) All other rules of stress meter are only qualifications of this single principle. Stress verse does not require any set number of syllables per line or any set arrangement between stressed and unstressed syllables. Accentual verse demands only an audible and regular number of natural speech stresses per line. The direct and simple nature of accentual verse explains its central importance for oral poetry. Even a child can master the meter without recourse to pen and paper. No wonder most nursery rhymes are written in accentual measures. Nursery rhymes can have between one and seven stresses per line, but the most popular form—and indeed the most common measure for all English accentual verse—is the four-beat line with a medial caesura.

Stár líght ‖ Stár bríght,   (four syllables)

Fírst stár ‖ I sée tonight   (six syllables)

I wísh I máy ‖ I wísh I míght   (eight syllables)

Háve the wish ‖ I wish tonight   (seven syllables)

Although every line in this famous folk charm has a different syllable count, the meter is constant—four strong beats per line.

Prosodists, like all literary theorists, adore complexity, and they are liable to make distinctions where meaningful differences do not exist. Consequently, they have often been flummoxed and outwitted by the simple country sense of strong stress meter. Frequently they try to analyze accentual verse in terms of metrical feet, but the concept of the foot, which is derived from Greek and Latin verse, has no relevance to this Germanic form. The structural unit of accentual verse is the line or half line. Dividing accentual verse into metrical feet can be done (just as it can be done to prose), but it reveals nothing essential about the generative principles of the form. Let's analyze the same nursery rhyme in the conventional accentual-syllabic manner.

Stár | líght | Stár | bright

fírst | stár | I sée | tonight

I wísh | I máy | I wísh | I míght

Háve the | wish I | wish to | night

This analysis would suggest that the poem is metrically incoherent. In accentual-syllabic terms, the meter seems to change in every line. By seeking too much metrical organization, an accentual-syllabic scansion misconstrues what is there. Yet the English-speaking ear immediately hears the underlying and unifying form, which is created by stress alone without regard to syllables.

Anglo-Saxon poets added two important acoustic elements to the basic rule of accentual verse—alliteration and the medial pause. They heightened the central sonic effect of their basic meter, the four-beat lines, by pausing slightly midway and alliterating three of the four stressed syllables. One significant and often overlooked purpose of meter is to stylize poetic speech in a way that immediately differentiates it from ordinary speech. Such stylization is essential to oral poetry since meter must endow what is being said with the special status of art. Anglo-Saxon verse used alliterative stress to accomplish this stylization. In *The Age of Anxiety* (1947), a long poem written in the Anglo-Saxon measure, W. H. Auden demonstrates how even a wartime radio newscast can be transformed into poetry:

> Now the news. Night raids on
> Five cities. Fires started.
> Pressure applied by pincer movement
> In threatening thrust. Third Division
> Enlarges beachhead. Lucky charm
> Saves sniper. Sabotage hinted
> In steel-mill stoppage. Strong point held
> By fanatical Nazis. Canal crossed . . .

Auden's example also illustrates the three standard variations of alliterative verse. First, he substitutes two paired alliterations (as in "Five cities. Fires started.") for the usual triple alliteration per line. Second, Auden's alliterations in "Pressure applied by pincer movement" demonstrate that alliteration does not necessarily fall on the first syllable of a word but rather the first strongly stressed syllable. Finally, even the ambiguous alliterations of line 5 (in which bea*ch* perhaps alliterates with *ch*arm) remind one that Anglo-Saxon poets sometimes included only two alliterations per line—one on each side of the caesura.

Anglo-Saxon poets sometimes added other elements. There often were pervasive syllabic and quantitative elements in Old English verse. (Anglo-Saxon poets especially loved to arrange the second half of the line in particular shapes.) Those features, however, have not been adopted by modern poets using alliterative stress meter. Contemporary poets have generally followed only three basic rules:

1. There should be four strong stresses per line.
2. The line should have an audible medial pause or caesura with two strong stresses on each side.
3. Three of the four strong stresses should alliterate (or there should be two pairs of alliterated stressed syllables).

In all accentual verse there is also an implied fourth rule—avoid metrical ambiguity by reducing or eliminating secondary stresses that might confuse where the beat falls. The passage from *The Age of Anxiety* shows how extreme this reduction of secondary stresses can be; Auden has eliminated almost all possibly ambiguous secondary stresses. (He also avoids letting the lines consistently fall into any regular accentual-syllabic rhythms, though any individual line might be entirely iambic, trochaic, anapestic, or dactyllic.)

English accentual poetry grew out of the oral tradition of pre-Christian Teutonic tribes, and the metrical practice was strikingly homogeneous from Germany and Scandinavia to Iceland and Britain. Accentual alliterative verse was the dominant English form until the Norman invasion, and it maintained a strong hold on native speakers for centuries afterwards. In some sense accentual verse still represents the core Germanic rhythm of basic English as opposed to the more cosmopolitan hybrid of French, Latin, and Anglo-Saxon that characterizes modern English. Only after the principles of accentual-syllabic verse were codified in the Elizabethan age did literary poets mostly abandon the purely accentual system. A great split then occurred in English-language poetry. For the next three hundred years literary poets worked almost exclusively in accentual-syllabic meters, while accentual meters survived in popular oral poetry.

Most of this oral poetry has been lost. Only what was transcribed into writing (and perhaps thereby changed) has been preserved. The greatest single source of this popular oral poetry is probably *Mother Goose's Melody* (c. 1765). This volume, which goes unmentioned in many standard histories of English poetry, remains an indispensable classic of the language. The appearance of this rambunctious volume at the height of the Augustan Age also demonstrates how the oral tradition preserved the older accentual meters that literary poets had discarded. Even today accentual verse survives in verse composed for oral presentation like cowboy poetry and rap. It remains a natural medium for spoken verse.

Accentual meter has proved influential among modern poets. In both its basic and alliterative forms, it provided innovative writers with a potent, audible measure that was immediately distinct from the traditional accent-syllabic meters that had dominated literary poetry since Sir Philip Sidney. Syllabic meters offered a similar novelty, but they could not be easily heard in English. (See Margaret Holley on syllabics.) Accentual measures gave poets auditory patterns that could easily capture speech rhythms without sounding conventionally literary. Coleridge, Tennyson, Longfellow, Dickinson, Kipling, Hardy, and others employed stress verse on occasion, though almost never with alliteration, but the great nineteenth-century pioneer was Gerard Manley Hopkins. While his personal practice of "sprung verse" proved too idiosyncratic to serve as a general paradigm, his work suggested the broad artistic possibilities of the method. Modern poets who have commonly employed accentual verse include William Butler Yeats, W. H. Auden, T. S. Eliot, Robinson Jeffers, Edith Sitwell, Theodore Roethke, Charles Causley, Gwendolyn Brooks, and Donald Justice. A few have revived the Anglo-Saxon alliterative line, but most have preferred the basic measure. Among contemporary poets three-beat and four-beat lines remain the most common measures, although longer and shorter lines sometimes appear. Used with skill and imagination, accentual verse sounds perpetually fresh.

ANONYMOUS AUTHOR OF BEOWULF

Beowulf's Funeral

Translated by Tim Murphy and Alan Sullivan

His people prepared him

        a funeral pyre

hung with helmets

        shields and hauberks.

Lamenting the hero,

        their beloved lord,

they laid him lengthwise

        laden with spoils.

His warriors woke

        the woefullest fire

to blaze on the bier.

        Loud was the burning,

woven with weeping,

        and woodsmoke rose

black over the barrow,

        blown with a roar.

The firewind faltered

        and flames dwindled,

hot at their heart

        the broken bonehouse.

Her hair waving,

        a Geatish woman

sang for the Stalwart

        a sorrowful dirge

foretelling a future

      fraught with misfortune,

kinfolk sundered,

      slaughter and slavery

even as heaven

      swallowed the smoke.

High on a headland

      they heaped his barrow

which seafaring sailors

      would spy from afar.

                  Eighth century

MOTHER GOOSE

Rich Man, Poor Man

Rich man,
Poor man,
Beggarman,
Thief.
Doctor,
Lawyer,
Merchant,
Chief.
Tinker,
Tailor,
Soldier,
Sailor,
Gentleman,
Apothecary,
Ploughboy,
Thief.

                        c. 1765

If Wishes Were Horses

If wishes were horses
Beggars would ride;
If turnips were watches
I would wear one by my side.

                        c. 1765

RUDYARD KIPLING

Harp Song of the Dane Women

What is a woman that you forsake her,
And the hearth-fire and the home-acre,
To go with the old grey Widow-maker?

She has no house to lay a guest in—
But one chill bed for all to rest in,
That the pale suns and the stray bergs nest in.

She has no strong white arms to fold you,
But the ten-times-fingering weed to hold you—
Out on the rocks where the tide has rolled you.

Yet, when the signs of summer thicken,
And the ice breaks, and the birch-buds quicken,
Yearly you turn from our side, and sicken—

Sicken again for the shouts and the slaughters.
You steal away to the lapping waters,
And look at your ship in her winter-quarters.

You forget our mirth, and talk at the tables,
The kine in the shed and the horse in the stables—
To pitch her sides and go over her cables.

Then you drive out where the storm-clouds swallow,
And the sound of your oar-blades, falling hollow,
Is all we have left through the months to follow.

Ah, what is Woman that you forsake her,
And the hearth-fire and the home-acre,
To go with the old grey Widow-maker?

                                        1913

GWENDOLYN BROOKS

We Real Cool

The Pool Players.
Seven at the Golden Shovel.

We real cool. We
Left school. We

Lurk late. We
Strike straight. We

Sing sin. We
Thin gin. We

Jazz June. We
Die soon.

1960

DAVID MASON

Song of the Powers

Mine, said the stone,
mine is the hour.
I crush the scissors,
such is my power.
Stronger than wishes,
my power, alone.

Mine, said the paper,
mine are the words
that smother the stone
with imagined birds,
reams of them, flown
from the mind of the shaper.

Mine, said the scissors,
mine all the knives
gashing through paper's
ethereal lives;
nothing's so proper
as tattering wishes.

As stone crushes scissors,
as paper snuffs stone
and scissors cut paper,
all end alone.
So heap up your paper
and scissor your wishes
and uproot the stone
from the top of the hill.
They all end alone
as you will, you will.

1996

DANA GIOIA

Nosferatu's Serenade

I am the image that darkens your glass,
The shadow that falls wherever you pass.
I am the dream you cannot forget,
The face you remember without having met.

I am the truth that must not be spoken,
The midnight vow that cannot be broken.
I am the bell that tolls out the hours.
I am the fire that warms and devours.

I am the hunger that you have denied,
The ache of desire piercing your side.
I am the sin you have never confessed,
The forbidden hand caressing your breast.

You've heard me inside you speak in your dreams,
Sigh in the ocean, whisper in streams.
I am the future you crave and you fear.
You know what I bring. Now I am here.

2001

Syllabics: Sweeter Melodies

MARGARET HOLLEY

> Heard melodies are sweet, but those unheard
> Are sweeter.

Keats's claim in "Ode on a Grecian Urn" will be dear to lovers of syllabic verse. The syllable, that smallest segment of speech, is the variable grid on which all our words and sentences are built. *I* is a syllable, and *squelch* is a syllable, but the voice dances quite differently through each of them. Nevertheless, in a syllabic poem the lines are measured by syllable count only and not by accents or metrical feet. Most English-language poetry prior to the twentieth century was measured by syllables and accents together, the combination that forms our accentual-syllabic meters (iambic, anapestic, etc.). And since English is a heavily accented language, the accents have naturally gleaned most of our attention. But verse that is measured by syllables only need not adhere to any audible pattern of stresses. Its counterpoint is subtler. What is heard are the rhythms of prose; what is known and subliminally registered is the precision of the silent pattern.

Purely syllabic verse, free of underpinnings of stress meter, is largely a twentieth-century phenomenon in English-language poetry. Its creators are Robert Bridges, his daughter Elizabeth Daryush, and Marianne Moore. Bridges spoke of syllabic verse in his 1901 study *Milton's Prosody*, and it has been suggested that Milton's prosody owes its syllabic tendencies to its Italian background.[1] My own hunch is that Bridges's early suggestions about Milton fell like seeds on Marianne Moore's fertile and original mind and bloomed there, as she gradually freed herself from the stress pattern, into "The Fish," first published in 1918. Bridges's long efforts to write quantitative verse on classical models surely hovers in some indefinite way behind his daughter's use of syllabic measure in her wonderful sonnet "Still-Life" and others of her poems of the 1930s. This versatile measure—strict but inaudible—can accommodate a wide variety of tones from the playfulness of Thom Gunn's "Blackie, the Electric Rembrandt" to the grandeur of W. H. Auden's syllabically based alcaic stanzas in his elegy "In Memory of Sigmund Freud."

The syllabic poem may be written in a single repeated measure, as is Sylvia Plath's "Metaphors." "I'm a riddle in nine syllables," she begins, and her catalog of images for the pregnant woman proceeds through nine identically measured lines. Among her several syllabic poems from 1958 and 1959, "Mushrooms" uses five-syllable lines in triplets to detail the nocturnal emergence of the new white blooms. This pattern is called *normative syllabic verse* in the anthology *Strong Measures,* which offers a rich selection. Another practitioner, Donald Justice, remarks in his essay "Bus Stop: Or, Fear and Loneliness on Portrero Hill" on one of the challenges of writing identically measured syllabic lines: "It was the possibility of keeping the number of accents *and* the number of syllables the same from line to line, but without letting them fall together into the regular foot-patterns, iambs and the like, too often and too familiarly."[2] He notes that an odd number of syllables are "a help in avoiding iambics." In "Bus Stop," however, he sets himself the challenge of using the two-beat, four-syllable line throughout in such a way that it resists a regular iambic pattern.

Another kind of syllabic measure is the repeated stanza pattern of varied line-lengths—this is called *quantitative syllabic verse* in *Strong Measures* and *line mating* by Robert Beum.[3] Marianne Moore, a master of syllabic grace, often combines accented and unaccented end-rhymes with repeated syllabically patterned stanzas. One can see in just the two opening stanzas of "The Mind Is an Enchanting Thing" how the lines of six, five, four, six, seven, and nine syllables create a flowing, syncopated composition that enhances the subject.

> is an enchanted thing
>   like the glaze on a
> katydid-wing
>   subdivided by sun
>   till the nettings are legion.
> Like Geiseking playing Scarlatti;
>
> like the apteryx-awl
>   as a beak, or the
> kiwi's rain-shawl
>   of haired feathers, the mind
>   feeling its way as though blind,
> walks along with its eyes on the ground.

1944

Another master of syllabic composition, Dylan Thomas, shows us that variations in the syllabic-counted stanza can be as eloquent as those in the accentual-syllabic meters. One of Thomas's richest, most resonant poems, "Fern Hill," using a 14-14-9-6-9-14-14-7-9 pattern, introduces a variation in the very first stanza, the fifteen-syllable sixth line "And honoured among wagons I was prince of the apple towns." Couldn't the poet have simply omitted the opening "And" from that line and produced a more regular pattern? Yes, but he was also beginning a long series of echoing sentence openings on that phrase "And . . . I . . ." One could write a rather long essay on his use of *and* in this poem, but suffice it for now to say that the building of that anaphora was rhetorically and rhythmically more urgent than the perfection of the syllabic schema. Likewise, Thomas inverted his 7-9 closing couplet in three of the inner stanzas of "Fern Hill." These more suspended 9-6 couplets give added power to the returning 7-9 couplet at the poem's end.

A third compositional possibility for the syllabic poet is to use a traditional syllabic form, such as the Japanese haiku or tanka, as a stanza form. Richard Wilbur's elegant "Thyme Flowering among Rocks" adds rhyme to the 5-7-5 pattern of the haiku, as it draws the haiku master Bashō into this poem's meditation on thyme and time. Repeated syllabic stanzas also appear in many of the French forms, like the cinquain, the kyrielle, and the rondel and its variations, and in Welsh forms with interesting names like the *awdl gywydd,* the *cyhydedd naw ban,* the *englyn proest dalgrom,* the *clogyrnach,* and many others nicely documented by Miller Williams in *Patterns of Poetry* and by Lewis Turco in *The New Book of Forms.*

Composing with a syllabic measure presents several challenges that are quite familiar to metrical poets. First, it is not always clear whether certain words have one syllable or two. In "The Mind Is an Enchanting Thing" Marianne Moore counts *fire* as one syllable; in "Fern Hill" Dylan Thomas counts it as two. Thomas counts *shower* as two syllables in "Poem in October," while Donald Justice in "Bus Stop" counts *flowers* as one. Clearly there is some leeway here, just as in accentual-syllabic meters.

A second challenge is that checking the number of syllables in each line can be inimical to hearing the sense of the words, since counting each syllable equally flattens the natural stresses and tends to dim the import of the words. For this reason, it helps greatly to develop one's ear for the shorter clusters of two, three, and four syllables before moving on to their combinations. The poetic line will tend to fall naturally into clusters of two-, three-, and four-syllable words and phrases. And if longer lines do not seem easily added up, counting on one's fingers is a time-honored method of checking one's ear and intuition. Perhaps the prize for elaborate complexity in syllabic patterning goes to Miss Moore for her uncollected poem "Pigeons," which adheres to a strict twenty-four-line stanza pattern of 8, 11, 6, 8, 4, 12, 7, 8, 9, 8, 8, 5, 9, 10, 8, 6, 6, 5, 7, 8, 8, 12, 6, and 9 syllables repeated five times over without variations.[4] At the other end of the spectrum, Rosellen Brown adopted syllabics as "a tight cinch against excess" for her book-length sequence of spare and slender syllabic poems, *Cora Fry,* a practice she illuminates in her statement "On Syllabics and *Cora Fry*" in *A Formal Feeling Comes.*[5]

It makes good sense that the syllabic method has gained popularity in English during a century that opened with a rebellion against traditional meters and that is closing with a renewed interest in formal design. Metrical poets seeking freedom and free verse poets seeking stricter forms meet in the middle ground of the syllable's subtle but countable presence. Syllabic measure, like the many silent rhythms of nature, is there when you look for it, a governing principle that calls no special attention to itself.

MARIANNE MOORE

The Fish

wade
through black jade.
   Of the crow-blue mussel-shells, one keeps
   adjusting the ash-heaps;
      opening and shutting itself like

an
injured fan.
   The barnacles which encrust the side
   of the wave, cannot hide
      there for the submerged shafts of the

sun
split like spun
   glass, move themselves with spotlight swiftness
   into the crevices—
      in and out, illuminating

the
turquoise sea
   of bodies. The water drives a wedge
   of iron through the iron edge
      of the cliff; whereupon the stars,

pink
rice-grains, ink-
   bespattered jelly-fish, crabs like green
   lilies, and submarine
     toadstools, slide each on the other.

All
external
   marks of abuse are present on this
   defiant edifice—
     all the physical features of

ac-
cident—lack
   of cornice, dynamite grooves, burns, and
   hatchet strokes, these things stand
     out on it; the chasm-side is

dead.
Repeated
   evidence has proved that it can live
   on what can not revive
     its youth. The sea grows old in it.

                                        1918

ELIZABETH DARYUSH

Still-Life

Through the open French window the warm sun
lights up the polished breakfast-table, laid
round a bowl of crimson roses, for one—
a service of Worcester porcelain, arrayed
near it a melon, peaches, figs, small hot
rolls in a napkin, fairy rack of toast,
butter in ice, high silver coffee-pot,
and, heaped on a salver, the morning's post.

She comes over the lawn, the young heiress,
from her early walk in her garden-wood
feeling that life's a table set to bless
her delicate desires with all that's good,

that even the unopened future lies
like a love-letter, full of sweet surprise.

                                        1976

RICHARD WILBUR

Thyme Flowering among Rocks

This, if Japanese,
Would represent grey boulders
Walloped by rough seas

So that, here or there,
The balked water tossed its froth
Straight into the air.

Here, where things are what
They are, it is thyme blooming,
Rocks, and nothing but—

Having, nonetheless,
Many small leaves implicit,
A green countlessness.

Crouching down, peering
Into perplexed recesses,
You find a clearing

Occupied by sun
Where, along prone, rachitic
Branches, one by one,

Pale stems arise, squared
In the manner of *Mentha,*
The oblong leaves paired.

One branch, in ending,
Lifts a little and begets
A straight-ascending

Spike, whorled with fine blue
Or purple trumpets, banked in
The leaf-axils. You

Are lost now in dense
Fact, fact which one might have thought
Hidden from the sense,

Blinking at detail
Peppery as this fragrance,
Lost to proper scale

As, in the motion
Of striped fins, a bathysphere
Forgets the ocean.

It makes the craned head
Spin. Unfathomed thyme! The world's
A dream, Basho said,

Not because that dream's
A falsehood, but because it's
Truer than it seems.

1988

MARGARET HOLLEY

Other Countries

Rose cockles, a box of coquina shells.
From the Chiesa degli Angeli
next door, the hourly counting of the bells,
answered faintly further down the valley.
Waking inside the dream. Waking to smells
of baking bread and oranges and tea.
Yeats's version of Ronsard's poem "When you
are old and grey and full of sleep." Fresh-mown
grass. Blue iris. Blue herons. Twilight blue.
Fire in the fireplace. *Deutsche Grammaphon*'s
recording of Brahms' *Requiem* played through
endlessly. Your voice on the telephone.
Lilac scent. Evening star. Relief of tears.
Time, leisure, laughter. Future. Years.

NOTES

1. See Robert Bridges, *Milton's Prosody* (Oxford: Clarendon, 1901), 29 and 111; also see Roy Fuller, *Owls and Artificers: Oxford Lectures on Poetry* (London: Andre Deutsch, 1971), 66.

2. See Martin Lammon, ed., *Written Water, Written in Stone: Twenty Years of Poets on Poetry* (Ann Arbor: University of Michigan Press, 1996), 253.

3. See Philip Dacey and David Jauss, eds., *Strong Measures: Contemporary American Poetry in Traditional Forms* (New York: HarperCollins, 1986), 447; and Robert Beum, "Syllabic Verse in English," *Prairie Schooner* 31 (1957): 262.

4. Marianne Moore's "Pidgeons" appeared in *Poetry*, November 1935, 61–65.

5. Annie Finch, ed., *A Formal Feeling Comes* (Ashland, Ore.: Story Line Press, 1994), 27–29.

Counted Verse:
Upper Limit Music

PAUL HOOVER

Counted verse operates by the number of words rather than the number of syllables and stresses to the line. It is not primarily syllabic and accentual, though it obviously has those features. As Dana Gioia suggested in conversation, it reminds us that there are two kinds of lines, the visual and the aural. Often the appearance of a poem on the page is the first information we have of it. In this respect, counted verse has a designed look similar to shaped or patterned poetry. Counted verse does not make the shapes of objects in words like Apollinaire's calligrammes ("Il Pluet" is written vertically to give the appearance of rain falling). Rather, it announces the physical reality of words as objects. They fill actual, intellectual, and sonic space. George Herbert's shaped poem "Easter Wings" has aspects of counted verse, rising and falling in number as the visual pattern is served. This is especially apparent at the pinched center of each stanza, where two words ("Most poore" and "With thee," for instance) provide stable connective tissue. While the words per line in Herbert's "Paradise" vary between six and eight, the first tercet contains only seven-word lines and the concluding tercet six. But the poem's main feature is that the final word of the first line of each tercet holds within it the next two end words, with which it also rhymes. Counting by subtraction, the end words of the second stanza are *charm, harm,* and *arm.* Reminiscent of Russian nesting dolls, the project is sculptural as much as musical.

Counted verse reminds us of the arbitrariness of all poetic forms. Such willed orderliness has elements of absurdity. Why two words to the line, or three? On the other hand, if the poet has wit, strictness of the poetic line adds pleasure to the formal game. *The Princeton Encyclopedia of Poetry and Poetics* states that meter "establishes a sort of distance between both poet and subject and reader and subject by interposing a film of unaccustomed rhythmical ritual between observer and experience." At the same time, meter "reminds the apprehender unremittingly that he is not experiencing the real object of the 'imitation' . . . but is experiencing instead that object transmuted into symbolic form." It is foolish therefore to speak of "natural" rhythms in poetry. Even heart-beats have irregular stress and duration. Poetry is a *thing made,* an artificial object constructed of sound, image, thought, and intention (though its meanings are often unintended). It is important to remember, of course, that symbolic meanings often have as much or more power than the experiences they represent. Poems are "complete" even when indeterminate. Ron Silliman's book-length prose poem *Tjanting* is structured according to the Fibonacci number sequence, an arithmetic progression of 1, 1, 2, 3, 5, 8, 13, 21, and so on, seen in natural objects such as seashells. But the poem itself is far from "natural" in its formal mania and artifice.

As preordained shape, all poetic form is conceptual, presenting a dubious "What if?" to which the text then adheres. This is especially true of counted verse, which gently parodies poetic meter but also faithfully serves the cause of compression. Once a concept is created, word choice is central to the integrity of the line. The poet becomes conscious of how much weight the words in a given line should have. Given that the line in counted verse is generally narrow—two to four words—it is less the sentence than the word group ("blueing to translucent," Zukofsky) where the drama of relation occurs. In May Swenson's "Four-Word Lines," generally two of the four words in each line have relational weight. In the line "I wish we were," alliteration and mirroring (the "we" in "were") are barely enough to sustain the line, and it feels thin. But the sentence "When your / lashes ride down and / rise like brown bees' / legs, your pronged gaze / makes my eyes gauze" is weighty and resonant line by line. The parallelism of "pronged gaze" and "eyes gauze" is reminiscent of Gwendolyn Brooks's "We Real Cool." Written in counted verse of mostly three-word lines, Brooks's poem contains a "boxed set" of internal rhymes: "sing sin. We / thin gin. We" It also contains identical end rhyme (coupled with enjambment), caesura, internal rhyme, alliteration, and a choral point-of-view. Except for its stage direction, the poem is entirely monosyllabic. Shakespeare's sonnets contain numerous monosyllabic lines ("If snow be white, why then her breasts are dun"); their frequency shows the poet's pleasure in formal gamesmanship, central to which is a primitive delight in counting-as-utterance.

Like "We Real Cool," William Carlos Williams's "The Red Wheelbarrow" is written in counted verse; it is also formally replete despite being only eight lines long. The first line of each stanza contains three words and the second line, one. The poem is just as orderly in its syntax, as modifying phrases like "glazed with rain" fall from the first line of each stanza onto the hard surface of the noun in the second line.

Williams's friend Louis Zukofsky made major use of counted verse in his encyclopedic poem *A,* especially section 14. He begins the section with one-word lines, moves quickly to couplets, each of which contain two-word lines, and takes up the bulk of the poem with tercets consisting of three-word lines. The poem concludes by reversing the same pattern. The mathematic balance is perfect—one by one, two by two, and three by three. The use of three-word lines is especially successful, as it allows for relation and difference within the line itself. The number three is stable (a stool can be made with three legs) but more inviting of "indeterminacy" than two or four. Compositionally, it encourages weaving and folding and lends excitement to the line break. "A-14" contains the often-quoted lines "lower limit speech / upper limit music," part of a hierarchy that concludes with "lower limit music / upper limit *mathemata.*" In Zukofsky's cosmology, dance is superior to the body, speech superior to dance, music superior to speech, and mathematics superior to music.

My own attraction to counted verse is not its superiority as *mathemata,* but to the basic animal pleasure of striking your hoof in the dirt. I use a "squared" form of counted verse (two by two) in the love poem "Theoretical People." My long poem "South of X" uses a three-by-three counted verse stanza. (A four-by-four or five-by-five stanza has little formal attraction, perhaps because the line break ceases to be of interest.) Discovering counted verse changed the tenor of my work. Often relying on a "reading through" of other texts, usually prose, I let the conjunction of words come as a surprise. Despite the arbitrariness of this procedure, my poems took on a starker, more elegiac character, and the act of naming took precedence over predetermined themes. In allegiance to a shape, I stopped paying attention to the sentence and any necessary connection between sentences.

Bob Perelman's poem "Chronic Meanings" contains lines of five words. The great majority of the lines are sentence fragments and therefore indeterminate. But indeterminacy is also used lyrically in the poem, which was written in memory of Leland Hickman, who died of AIDS. I first encountered "Chronic Meanings" when the author read it at New York's Ear Inn poetry series. Informed that the poem was about a specific death, the patrons at the crowded bar became quietly attentive despite the work's lack of resolution. Once we are accustomed to the rule of discontinuity, we chafe at complete sentences such as "The train seems practically expressive." The last five stanzas contain no complete sentences, as incompletion is central to the poem's drama.

Traditionalists and avant-gardists have more interest in poetic form than practitioners of confessional free verse. Both admire intelligence, irony, and formal play. Well-educated, they are tolerant of difficulty and suspicious of personal subject matter. Both the traditionalist and the van-guardist are good readers of history, especially the history of poetry, and their work often comments, directly or implicitly, on it. With their love of pantoums, sestinas, and sonnets, the poets of the New York School generally and John Ashbery especially have provided a bridge between experimentation and tradition. In every avant-gardist, a traditionalist lies in hiding, for he or she has shaped a practice in reaction to the estab-lished dominant. Once this reaction becomes the new dominant, he or she must protect it from the depradations of change.

MAY SWENSON

Four-Word Lines

Your eyes are just
like bees, and I
feel like a flower.
Their brown power makes
a breeze go over
my skin. When your
lashes ride down and
rise like brown bees'
legs, your pronged gaze
makes my eyes gauze.
I wish we were
in some shade and
no swarm of other
eyes to know that
I'm a flower breathing
bare laid open to
your bees' warm stare.
I'd let you wade
in me and seize
with your eager brown
bees' power a sweet
glistening at my core.

1967

GEORGE HERBERT

Paradise

I bless thee, Lord, because I GROW
Among thy trees, which in a   ROW
To thee both fruit and order   OW.

What open force, or hidden   CHARM
Can blast my fruit, or bring me HARM,
While the inclosure is thine   ARM?

Inclose me still for fear I   START.
Be to me rather sharp and   TART,
Then let me want they hand & ART.

When thou dost greater judgments SPARE,
And with thy knife but prune and   PARE,
Ev'n fruitfull trees more fruitfull   ARE.

Such sharpnes shows the sweetest FREND:
Such cuttings rather heal than   REND:
And such beginnings touch their   END.

1593–1633

BOB PERELMAN

From Chronic Meanings

The single fact is matter.
Five words can say only.
Black sky at night, resonably.
I am, the irrational residue.

Blown up chain link fence.
Next morning stronger than ever.
Midnight the pain is almost.
The train seems practically expressive.

A story familiar as a.
Society has broken into bands.
The nineteenth century was sure.
Characters in the withering capital.

The heroic figure straddled the.
The clouds enveloped the tallest.
Tens of thousands of drops.
The monster struggled with Milton.

On our wedding night I.
The sorrow burned deeper than.
Grimly I pursued what violence.
A trap, a catch, a.

Fans stand up, yelling their.
Lights go off in houses.
A fictional look, not quite.
To be able to talk.

The coffee sounds intriguing but.
She put her cards on.
What had been comfortable subjectivity.
The lesson we can each.

Not enough time to thoroughly.
Structure announces structure and takes.
He caught his breath in.
The vista disclosed no immediate.

Alone with a pun in.
The clock face and the.
Rock of ages, a modern.
I think I had better.

Now this particular mall seemed.
The bag of groceries had.
Whether a biographical junkheap or.
In no sense do I.

These fields make me feel.
Mount Rushmore in a sonnet.
Some in the party tried.
So it's not as if.

That always happened until one.
She spread her arms and.
The sky if anything grew.
Which left a lot of.

No one could help it.
I ran farther than I.
That wasn't a good one.
Now put down your pencils.

They won't pull that over.
Standing up to the Empire.
Stop it, screaming in a.
The strong smell of pine needles.

Economics is not my strong.
Until one of us reads.
I took a breath, then.
The singular heroic vision, unilaterally.

Voices imitate the very words.
Bed was one place where.
A personal life, a toaster.
Memorized experience can't be completely.

The impossibility of the simplest.
So shut the fucking thing.
Now I've gone and put.
But that makes the world.

1993

Iambic Meter

JOHN RIDLAND

After the English language was infiltrated by French following the Norman Conquest in 1066, poets began to discover that the sprawl of unaccented syllables that the Germanic alliterative or strong-stress tradition had accommodated could be more tightly regulated (see Gioia on accentual verse). Learning to measure a line by counting syllables, however, English verse, unlike the French syllabic meter (see Holley on syllabics) kept counting its beats or accents as well, establishing the system we call *accentual-syllabic* or *syllable-stress* meter. We don't know how heavily Chaucer (d. 1400) stressed his beats or metrical accents when he recited or chanted his poems in court, but we can see and hear his intended pattern clearly:

> And for there is so gret diversitie
> In Englissh and in writyng of oure tonge,
> So prey I God that non myswrite the,
> Ne the mysmetre for defaute of tonge.
> And red wherso thow be, or elles songe,
> That thow be understonde, God I biseche!
>> *Troilus and Criseyde*, V, 1793–98

Chaucer's meter alternates lightly and more heavily stressed syllables; if ˘ = lighter, and ′ = heavier, and the metrical beats are underlined, the third line can be scanned:

> ˘ ′ ˘ ′ ˘ ′ ˘ ′ ˘ ′
> So prey I God that non myswrite the

Most poets in the English accentual-syllabic tradition have been taught to think of metrical verse as written in feet (and most discussions in this book employ that concept). Since iambic lines normally begin on an offbeat and end on a beat, with beats and offbeats alternating throughout the line, Chaucer's is taken as a prime example: ˘ ′ ˘ ′ ˘ ′ ˘ ′ ˘ ′. But during the fifteenth century the loss of final *-e* and other linguistic changes from Middle to Modern English upset that metrical apple cart.

39

If "myswrite" drops its third syllable, an offbeat between "writ" and "the," then the last two beats collapse on themselves.

So prey I God that non myswrite the,

When the poets of the late sixteenth century reinvented this pattern, they added a further defining element, the *foot*.[1] With ˘ = an unaccented syllable and ′ = a metrical accent, the iambic foot becomes |˘ ′|, and five feet in this pattern make the famous and predominant iambic pentameter, whether rhymed or unrhymed (see Hecht on blank verse, Steele on couplets, and other stanza forms). Structural linguists confirm the poets' hunch that English inflections tend naturally toward the rising stress pattern of iambics, and therefore that iambic meter fits the language better than any other accentual-syllabic meter. J. V. Cunningham and John Frederick Nims plucked dozens of regular iambic pentameter lines (with | indicating foot divisions) from common American speech, such as

I'd like to introduce a friend of mine.

You ever been in Albuquerque, hey?

In the twentieth century, however, iambic meter has been charged with monotony, as if a steady series of dips and rises, with pauses after every pair, were its actual rhythm: *te-dumm, te-dumm, te-dumm, te-dumm, te-dumm*. But "Unvarying regularity is not the ideal towards which English verse aspires," James McAuley cautioned, and iambic rhythms can be varied in several ways, including these:

   1. *By breaking the phrases and clauses of syntax across the invisible, inaudible, and in fact nonexistent "dividers" between the feet,* rather than aligning them mechanically with one- or two-syllable words, as beginners often do—and even the greatest poets, sometimes.

And swims or sinks, or wades, or creeps, or flies
                    John Milton, *Paradise Lost*, book II, 950

"Musically," George R. Stewart wrote, "such a line corresponds to the unvaried beating of a drum." Alexander Pope's virtuoso variations in the self-reflexive explanations of *An Essay on Criticism* are often cited in this regard. (Note how lines 338 and 347, though monosyllabic, neatly slip the drumbeat trap; "ear/repair" and "join/line" were true rhymes in Pope's time.)

But most by numbers judge a poet's song,
And smooth or rough, with them, is right or wrong;
In the bright Muse though thousand charms conspire,
Her voice is all these tuneful fools admire,   (340)
Who haunt Parnassus but to please their ear,
Not mend their minds; as some to church repair,
Not for the doctrine but the music there.
These, equal syllables alone require,
Though oft the ear the open vowels tire,   (345)
While expletives their feeble aid do join,
And ten low words oft creep in one dull line,
While they ring round the same unvaried chimes,
With sure returns of still expected rhymes.
Where'er you find *the cooling western breeze,*   (350)
In the next line, it *whispers through the trees,*
If crystal streams *with pleasing murmurs creep,*
The reader's threatened (not in vain) with *sleep.*
Then, at the last and only couplet fraught
With some unmeaning thing they call a thought,   (355)
A needless Alexandrine ends the song,
That, like a wounded snake, drags its slow length along.

2. *By varying the relative weights of the beats and offbeats,* within
each iambic foot, and between one foot and the others—"breaking the
sounds of sense with all their irregularity of accent across the regular
beat of the metre," as Frost said. And by adjusting the lengths of the
pauses within the lines that are called for by the phrasing. The main
midline pause is often called a *caesura,* a term borrowed from French
prosody, where it denotes an obligatory structural rest after the sixth of
twelve syllables in the classical alexandrine (as in Pope's line 357). The
entire passage illustrates many of these options in pentameter; Pope ad-
vocated caesuras after the fourth to sixth syllables, but not for more
than three successive lines in the same position: the parodic lines 348–52
illustrate how this gets boring, while the next five show how to move
the pause around.

3. *By varying the speed with which the plow turns at the end of
each furrow of words*—this *versus* lies at the root of the word *verse* and
sets it off from prose, in which nothing slows or stops the voice except
phrase ends, clause ends (punctuated or not), and periods. Even in
Pope's heroic couplets, which generally are end-stopped syntactically,
variants are found: note the unusual arrangement of mid- and end-line
pauses in the triplet rhyming lines 341–43.

Run-on or enjambed lines, in which the syntax forces the reader to hurry past the end of the line, are virtually a prerequisite of much free verse. They are also extremely frequent in iambic pentameters and trimeters, though perhaps less so in tetrameters, with their even numbers of beats. Ben Jonson's elegy "To the Immortal Memory and Friendship of That Noble Pair, Sir Lucius Cary and Sir H. Morison," punctuated rhetorically as in Jonson's time, employs enjambment discretely and effectively at two critical points (lines 1 and 5):

> It is not growing like a tree
> In bulk, doth make man better be;
> Or standing long an oak, three hundred year,
> To fall a log at last, dry, bald, and sere:
> A lily of a day   (5)
> Is fairer far, in May,
> Although it fall, and die that night;
> It was the plant, and flower of light.
> In small proportions, we just beauty see,
> And in short measures, life may perfect be.   (10)

Shakespeare increased the freedom of his enjambments steadily through the course of his plays, and Milton sprang the line ends loose to the extent that the Augustans had to cage them again within heroic couplets—only for the eighteenth-century Milton imitators, and later for Wordsworth and the Romantics, to set them free again. Shakespeare also increasingly freed his blank verse lines from closure with an extra unaccented syllable at the end, the so-called "feminine" or hypermetrical ending, which can occur mid-line:

> To be or not to be, that is the question.
> Whether 'tis nobler in the mind to suffer
> The slings and arrows of outrageous fortune
> Or to take arms against a sea of troubles
> And by opposing end them.
>
> *Hamlet* III.i.56–60

4. *By varying the metrical lengths of the lines,* not arbitrarily but for good cause, as Jonson does above, or George Herbert in "Easter Wings." In "The Collar" Herbert varies the line lengths and rhyme

scheme erratically, while running many lines on with astonishing free-
dom for his times, enacting the tantrum his speaker is throwing, before
bringing the last four lines back into order as God the Father calms
down the wayward child.

5. *By grouping lines variously rather than repetitiously,* in rhyming
stanzas or irregular verse paragraphs. The sentences can overlap the
metrical lines either to play up the recurrences of rhyme (as in much
comic verse like Byron's *Don Juan*), or to downplay them (as in the Alan
Stephens poem cited below).

6. *By substituting other feet for iambic ones.* Understanding this all
but universal technique involves turning meter, an auditory event, into
a visual one, by means of *scansion*—a subject fraught with confusion
and controversy. One distinction is fundamental; as McAuley writes:
"Speech uses a wide gamut of stress; but metre deals in only two values:
accented and unaccented." Although four levels of speech stress are sig-
nificant in English, practice is needed to rank these with certainty, and
Derek Attridge simplifies matters by marking only three levels: ˘ = un-
stressed syllables (in this book marked with a breve), ′ = stressed ones,
and ˋ = those with secondary stress. Thus we can see the *speech stresses*
in a Shakespeare line as:

<blockquote>
ˋ ˘ ˘ ′ ˘ ˘ ′ ′˘ ′
When to the sessions of sweet silent thought
</blockquote>

("sweet" and "si-" might be marked ˋ ˋ.) We can mark the *metrical ac-
cents* indicating the foot divisions as |.

<blockquote>
ˋ ˘| ˘ ′| ˘ ˘ | ′ ′|˘ ′
When to the sessions of sweet silent thought
</blockquote>

This example presents the basic iambic pattern in its second and fifth
feet, and three of the commonest variations, often called *substitutions*:
in the first foot, the inversion of accented and unaccented syllables (a
trochee; see also Phillips on trochaic meter); in the third the promotion
of the unstressed "of" to take the beat (often called a *pyrrhic*); in the
fourth the demotion of the strongly stressed "sweet" to an unaccented
position (a *spondee*). The third and fourth feet taken together form a
very common variation from the steady iambic pattern, which Attridge
calls a *rising inversion* and others a *double foot*. Another common sub-
stitution is to add an unstressed or lightly stressed syllable, turning an
iamb into an anapest, as in the third foot of Frost's:

<blockquote>
˘ ′ | ˘ ′ |˘ ˘ ′|˘ ′ |
Two roads diverged in a yellow wood
</blockquote>

Frost said there were only two or three meters worth anything in English—"strict iambics," containing few if any variant feet (as in "Stopping by Woods on a Snowy Evening" and "Fire and Ice"), and "loose iambics," with more anapests, trochees, and spondee-like feet (as in "The Road Not Taken"). Blending anapests into iambic feet, or vice versa, produces a mixture the Greeks called *logaoedic,* and claiming such mixes as primarily one or the other quickly becomes a quibble—hence the usefulness of Frost's term loose iambics, which characterizes the effect while describing the technique. (See also Hartman on anapestics.) Emily Dickinson wrote always iambically, though sometimes breaking her lines as unconventionally as she slanted her rhymes. Free verse like William Carlos Williams's, which became the standard layout for most modern American poems, must be analyzed on its own prosodic terms (which are, it should be noted, still quite unfixed), and not as would-be iambic or other meters. Iambic meter, which has long been known to conspire most effectively with the rhythms of the English language, sustains itself through examples as various in their play with line lengths and with stress patterns as the following recent American poems from writers and publishers out of the mainstream.

ROBYN BELL

Visitation

Inside Ukiah's chronic ward
sit older women playing cards
on tables in the center square.
Against the wall you pat your hair.

Technicians fixed you up, I guess.
They starched you in somebody's dress
and cleaned out all ten fingernails
that tap your armchair's silver rails.

You lead me to a snack machine
then feed it quarters chattering
your teeth as if to mimic talk.
The mockingbird knows what to mock.

But nothing much can agitate
the quiet catatonic air
two flat warm sodas celebrate
this winter of your eighteenth year.

1996

JANET LEWIS

A Cautionary Note

We have long known
His eye is on the sparrow
But let us not be narrow
Let us remember, and remembering smile,
His eye is also on the crocodile.

1994

ALAN STEPHENS

The Morning of Glenn Gould's Funeral

Hearing him now on the car stereo—
        That's as he wished it when alive—
        I look for browsing deer, and slow
        For the tight down-curves as I drive
                Through deep oak shadows
        Over the back way to Ojai.
The October day burns quiet bright and dry
                In the brown meadows.

The thing he's playing's a rocky-riffled clear
        Mountain stream of a piece by Bach:
        The bright quick-moving length of it's here
        Along with sun and oak and rock
                O brief survival
                Glittering in the light and air,
And in the dark unbreakable silence there
                The new arrival.

1995

NOTE

1. See Thomas Cable, *The English Alliterative Tradition* (Philadelphia: University of Pennsylvania Press, 1991), and John Thompson, *The Founding of English Metre* (New York: Columbia University Press, 1961).

Blank Verse

ANTHONY HECHT

Blank verse in English (unrhymed iambic pentameter) seems to have been the virtually simultaneous discovery or invention of two poets engaged in translating Latin verse. Nicholas Grimald (1519?–1562?) turned the Latin poem of a contemporary French poet, Theodore Beza, on the life of Cicero, into the English meter at roughly the same time that Henry Howard, earl of Surrey (1517–1547) translated the second and fourth books of the *Aeneid* of Virgil into the same form. The Latin poems had been composed in unrhymed heroic hexameters, but something about the native rhythms of English speech seems antipathetic to, or distrustful of, hexameters, which to our ears tend to fold in the middle and sound instead like two trimeter lines. Once blank verse had been introduced, it was found infinitely serviceable, and by dint of its adaptability and versatility became the most familiar pattern for poetic discourse in the English language. It is, for example, the meter of Shakespeare's and Marlowe's plays, major poems of Milton, Wordsworth, Keats, Tennyson, and Robert Browning; and even in the elegant eighteenth century it was employed by Joseph Warton and James Thomson. As for the moderns, it has proven invaluable to Frost, Stevens, Nemerov, Wilbur, and Derek Walcott.

Adaptability or flexibility is dramatically evident in the late Shakespeare plays, in which the text slips seamlessly from verse to prose and back within the compass of a very few lines *(The Tempest,* III.ii; *Lear,* II.ii.)* Pages of analysis could be devoted to the tensions created by this practice. But something of the form's variety may be illustrated as well by the pronounced rhythmic differences of the following lines, all from works in blank verse.

> Fortune, good night; smile once more, turn thy wheel
> —Shakespeare, *King Lear*

> Of something far more deeply interfused
> —Wordsworth, "Tintern Abbey"

> See see where Christ's blood streams in the firmament
> —Marlowe, *Dr. Faustus*

> Paint the soul, never mind the legs and arms
> —Browning, "Andrea Del Sarto"

> Back out of all this now too much for us
> —Frost, "Directive"

> The youth in life's fresh spring, and he who goes
> —William Cullen Bryant, "Thanatopsis"

Some curious observations may be made about these juxtaposed lines. The Frost and Bryant lines are composed of ten single-syllable words, while Browning's and Shakespeare's deviate from this only by the inclusion of the trochaic disyllabics "never" and "Fortune." Yet for all their similarities, the differences are remarkable. Bryant's is the most conventional, Browning's the most eccentric, and Frost's the most equivocal. Ten monosyllabic words sometimes present puzzles about the distribution of accents, and the relative weight they are to be given; the ear is alerted to large possibilities. Frost's line is the most enigmatic, as befits the teasingly mysterious poem ("Directive") of which it is the first line. Shakespeare's is the most densely packed or heavily loaded, while Marlowe's, depending on whether one or two accents are assigned to "firmament," may be scanned as having either six or seven strong beats; and yet for all that it is a part of a blank verse drama.

The standard definition of blank verse—unrhymed iambic pentameter—conceals almost as much as it reveals, because it can be, and has been, employed for so many different purposes, and must accordingly be treated in different ways. Though Shakespeare and Marlowe may sound archaic (and therefore poetic) to us, we must imagine that a great deal of what they wrote must have seemed almost straightforward to an Elizabethan audience who, in large numbers, were obliged to stand throughout the play's performance, and whose patience could not be unduly imposed upon. Milton, with Virgil and Homer lurking in his memory, felt that an epic demanded elevated diction and elaborate syntax such as neither Wordsworth nor Frost would wish to employ. Blank verse is consequently poetry's tool-of-all-trades, and its nature and uses cannot be construed by examining any *single line* because iambic pentameter (rhymed) is used in many stanzaic verse forms from Chaucer to this day; and the way we evaluate any single line is inevitably determined by *context:* certain poetic voices insist on colloquial directness, others on impersonal grandeur. The liberties permitted in a long poem might seem conspicuous blemishes in a short one. And further expectations appear when the line is used specifically for musical setting: "Slow,

slow, fresh fount, keep time with my salt tears," the first line of a song by Ben Jonson (nominally iambic pentameter, employed in a rhyming context) has technically only two unaccented syllables ("with my"), which normally would seem a grave flaw. But we can assume that the composer who set Jonson's words was able to take the richest advantage of the slow, relentless piling up of strongly accented monosyllabic words, making the slow, insistent monotony suitable to the expression of grief.

The chief virtue, as well as peril, of blank verse, is that it can slip so imperceptibly into the rhythms of ordinary prose and casual speech as to become virtually unnoticeable, and in some of his heightened and ennobled passages, Herman Melville, trying to attain to a Shakespearean sonorousness in *Moby Dick*, deliberately evokes the rhythms of the great tragedies, as in these lines from chapter 38:

> My soul is more than matched; she's overmanned; and by a madman! Insufferable sting, that sanity should ground arms on such a field! But he drilled deep down, and blasted all my reason out of me! I think I see his impious end; but feel that I must help him to it, willy nilly, the ineffable thing has tied me to him; tows me a cable I have no knife to cut. . . . He would be a democrat to all above; look, how he lords it over all below!

The close kinship of prose to certain kinds of verse, mockingly described by Alexander Pope as "Prose swell'd to verse, verse loit'ring into prose," provoked some serious, strategic thought in Wordsworth when he was about to embark on his magnum opus, *The Prelude*. He wrote a memorandum to himself concerning the dangers incident to the writing of blank verse:

> Dr. Johnson observed, that in blank verse, the language suffered more distortion to keep it out of prose than any inconvenience to be apprehended from the shackles and circumspection of rhyme. This kind of distortion is the worst fault that poetry can have; for if once the natural order and connection of the words is broken, and the idiom of the language violated, the lines appear manufactured, and lose all that character of enthusiasm and inspiration, without which they become cold and insipid, how sublime soever the ideas and the images may be which they express.

Wordsworth is very cunning here. He posits an idiom of language that is distinct from the ideas and images it is used to express; and that idiom must avoid any distortions of "the natural order and connection of the words," which is to say, it should observe the directness and expediency of prose discourse, yet at the same time contrive to make itself manifestly distinguishable from prose. A skill of enormous delicacy as well as strength is being proposed, and not least when we consider that "the natural order and connection of the words" and the "idiom of the language" are by no means constant and unvarying factors. Being, as he was, a poet of genius, he was able to write a blank verse of distinction, originality, and flexibility, and, most impressively, of both naturalness and grandeur. But the problem for any given poet remains, and a new idiom must be found by each new poet, allowing for the changes in prose as well as poetic conventions.

FOUR SPECIMENS OF BLANK VERSE: EARLY, MIDDLE, AND LATE

The first, by Henry Howard, earl of Surrey, may be the earliest blank verse in English, and is intended to approximate the dignity of Virgil's Latin epic, which was written in hexameters, a meter that becomes ungainly in English. Surrey sought for a language that would convey grandeur, tragic resolve, and heroic endeavor. To be sure, his Tudor vocabulary is very dated from our point of view, and sounds archaic, stilted, and unnatural to our ears. But Virgil, too, wrote in an idiom that was far from colloquial, with a formality he deemed appropriate to the grandeur of his subject: the founding of the Roman Empire.

Translation from Book II of *The Aeneid*

> They whistled all, with fixed face attent
> When prince Aeneas from the royal seat
> Thus gan to speak: O Queen, it is thy will
> I should renew a woe cannot be told!
> How that the Greeks did spoil and overthrow
> The Phrygian wealth and wailful realm of Troy.
> Those ruthful things that I myself beheld
> And whereof no small part fell to my share,
> Which to express, who could refrain from tears?

1557

Before John Milton selected the story of the Fall from Grace in Eden as his subject for *Paradise Lost* he had dallied with some other tales, the

life of King Arthur among them. It, like *The Aeneid,* was to have been
a national epic, composed in heroic language. Instead, Milton used his
art to fashion a still more universal epic, the origins and condition of all
mankind, in a language no less elevated, dignified, and heroic than his
classical predecessor. This poetry is consciously raised above ordinary
speech, because it deals with sacred materials, from which the heroic el-
ement, including a war in heaven, is not free. There are important par-
allels between Milton, Virgil, and Homer that the English poet meant to
be recognized, and to which the formality of his language contributed.

From *Paradise Lost,* Book IV, ll. 223–35

> Southward through Eden went a river large,
> Nor changed his course, but through the shaggy hill
> Passed underneath ingulfed, for God had thrown
> That mountain as his garden mold, high raised
> Upon the rapid current, which through veins
> Of porous earth with kindly thirst updrawn
> Rose a fresh fountain, and with many a rill
> Watered the garden; thence united fell
> Down the steep glade, and met the nether flood,
> Which from his darksome passage now appears,
> And now divided into four main streams
> Runs diverse, wand'ring many a famous realm
> And country whereof here needs no account.

1665

The raw material of much of William Wordsworth's poetry is drawn
from his inward thoughts and meditations, his feelings and reflections
about his feelings. The focus of such poetry is largely inward, even when
the inward thoughts are prompted by something external. In composing
one's thoughts, one is not trying to impress anyone, not even oneself.
The chief task is to be honest and accurate. So there is no attempt at the
heroic, the artificial, the stately, in these lines. But there is a simple dig-
nity of thought and feeling, a quiet identification with the most secret
aspects of the natural setting.

Lines Composed a Few Miles above
Tintern Abbey, *opening passage*

> Five years have past; five summers, with the length
> Of five long winters! and again I hear

These waters, rolling down their mountain-springs
With a soft inland murmur.—Once again
Do I behold these steep and lofty cliffs,
That on a wild secluded scene impress
Thoughts of a more deep seclusion; and connect
The landscape with the quiet of the sky.

July 13, 1798

Robert Frost, too, is careful to avoid the posture of grandeur and heroic enterprise; and, like Wordsworth, he is writing about a natural setting. But he is even more inward, the very colloquial debate with himself about whether to go on is couched in the plainest language, and is the signal of an uncertainty that will, ultimately, become the subject of this entire poem. Getting lost in woods is the way Dante begins his epic, *The Divine Comedy*, and Frost is cunning enough to allude to it in his very plain, understated way. The very plainness allows his effects to reveal themselves to us in utterly unexpected ways—sometimes not until we've read the poem over a good number of times.

The Wood Pile, *opening lines*

Out walking in the frozen swamp one gray day,
I paused and said, "I will turn back from here.
No, I will go on farther—and we shall see."
The hard snow held me, save where now and then
One foot went through. The view was all in lines
Straight up and down of tall slim trees
Too much alike to mark or name a place by
So as to say for certain I was here
Or somewhere else: I was just far from home.

1914

Anapestics

CHARLES O. HARTMAN

An important minority of English poems are in anapestic meters, most often trimeters and tetrameters. Anapestics offer the main triple-meter alternative to the dominant iambic meters. Surveying an anthology chosen at random (Bate and Perkins's *British and American Poets*) suggests that about 1 percent of poems from Chaucer onward are anapestic.[1] This may be misleading, since these meters are more often used in lighter poems, which synoptic anthologists are less likely to choose.

Both the strength and the risks of anapestics lie in the extreme catchiness of a regular triple rhythm. It's worth speculating where this headlong feel comes from. The usual rhythms of English speech, at least when closely listened to, seem to put one or two unstressed syllables between stresses—stresses that tend to become isochronous, or equal in time. Iambics (and trochaics) compress these speech rhythms, and make the poems that use them feel more weighty than speech, more intense and incisive. Anapestics, on the other hand, expand and regularize the speech rhythms, and make us more aware of the regular recurrence of the stresses. A little more than in iambic meter, the stresses take on the character of a *beat*, a "meter" in the musical sense of that word. As a result, the lines can seem "light" or "quick" or, above all, unstoppable. Robert Browning isn't the only poet to have associated the movement of anapests with that of horses:

> And into the midnight we galloped abreast.
>> "How They Brought the Good News
>>> from Ghent to Aix"

This kind of relentless motion can be exhilarating, but it can also seem crude, and it can wear us out. The pitfall of regular anapestics is blithe shallowness. They are "rhythmic," but too obviously so for many ears. If the poet wants to use an anapestic meter for serious, delicate, or meditative tones, then substitutions become even more important than they are in iambics. Strict regularity in the iambic pentameter can, at its best, lend a kind of stateliness to the verse; in anapestics, it can be the kiss of swift death. Substituted feet add rich flexibility to iambics; the same is more urgently true of anapestics.

The substitutions used in anapestic meters, however, differ from the standard variations in iambics. Abstractly, we can think of all foot-substitutions as ways for the poet to do one (or more) of four things to the foot: stretch it, trim it, load it, or reverse it. In iambics, this produces the anapest (or the ˘ ′ ˘ of the amphibrach), the *defective foot* or single stress, the spondee, and the trochee. (Other substitutions are more complicated combinations, such as the reversal across two consecutive feet that generates the so-called *double iamb* or pyrrhic-spondee pair.) In anapestic meters, the same four actions produce a different range of possibilities, and they're complicated enough to invite detailed scrutiny.

Stretching the anapest can mean adding a slack syllable to the end, producing the third *paeon* (˘ ˘ ′ ˘). This happens almost exclusively at the ends of lines, where it's often part of a rhyme pattern, like the amphibrach in iambic poems. The reason it doesn't happen elsewhere is the same reason why the other possible stretching action—adding a slack before the stress to produce the fourth paeon (˘ ˘ ˘ ′)—is almost unusable. In either case, three unstressed syllables intervene between stresses, and the verse becomes too loose to feel rhythmically controlled, looser even than most speech.

Trimming, on the other hand, is far more common in anapestics than in iambics. This is probably a gesture toward the one-to-two-slack average of intense speech, just as the substitution of anapests is in iambic pentameter. The effect is the opposite, though; anapests loosen the iambic line, while iambs tighten the anapestic. Even doubly trimming the anapest to a single-stress foot is not uncommon at the beginnings of lines.

The most interesting variations come from loading the anapest. There are two good candidates: the *bacchius* (˘ ′ ′) and the *cretic* (′ ˘ ′, also called *amphimacer*). These substitutions slow and complicate the line even more subtly than the spondee does in iambics. This feeling of rhythmic complexity arises from the same force that makes the fourth possible alteration, reversing the anapest to a *dactyl* (′ ˘ ˘), more or less impossible: the need to preserve the "beat" so characteristic of anapestics, even while taming it. To stay rhythmically oriented, the reader needs to know when to expect the main stress of the foot. (We know the variations of iambic pentameter so thoroughly that the poet can hardly throw us.) A dactyl, substituted for an anapest, would put the beat too early for a reader to be prepared to hear it, and would also create a bewildering run of four slack syllables, one of which the reader would try to "promote" to stress. The bacchius and the cretic, on the other hand, make the game interesting while keeping it fair. The final stress is where we expect it; the earlier stress is a bonus, an unexpected emphasis. Especially by using these two substitutions, the poet can keep the reader slightly off-balance, and so intrigued. The reader slows down to pay attention, yet continues to feel the forward momentum of the anapestic norm.

Here, as a candidate for the best anapestic poem in English, is Blake's "Ah! Sun-flower":

Ah, Sun-flower! weary of time,
Who countest the steps of the Sun,
Seeking after that sweet golden clime
Where the traveller's journey is done:

Where the youth pined away with desire,
And the pale Virgin shrouded in snow
Arise from their graves and aspire
Where my Sun-flower wishes to go.

The three regular lines in the poem (a single initial iamb hardly registers for us as irregularity) occupy strategic positions. The second line clearly establishes the unusual meter, after an opening line that—given our iambic assumptions—may have left us in doubt. The fourth line rounds out its stanza, resolving and anchoring it in the meter. The seventh line does the same for its stanza, but ingeniously just before the end, so that the last line can repeat the celebratory emphasis on the sunflower.

The poem does not use the bacchius, which may be a slightly more destabilizing substitution than the cretic. (A bacchius does come in if we stress the demonstrative pronoun "that" in the third line.) Cretics occur six times, and they are carefully deployed in pairs. One begins in the middle of each mention of the "Sun-flower," framing the beginning and end of the poem. Two cretics combine to make the third line the most labored in the poem, mirroring its image of arduous quest. In the first two lines of the second stanza, the identical placement of the cretics underscores the parallel between the paired images of "youth" and "Virgin." At the same time, by laying the syntax across the feet at a different angle, Blake keeps the parallelism from feeling rigid: "pined away" matches "shrouded," but the second participle is delayed by the adjective "pale" and the two-syllable noun "Virgin," while the final prepositional phrase is shortened in compensation.

Only fifteen out of twenty-four feet in the poem are anapests, though all but three feet are trisyllables of some kind. The two-syllable feet (a spondee and two iambs) all begin lines. All but one of the poem's lines end with a regular anapest. These characteristics are common to many anapestic poems, and reflect the requirements of the meter outlined earlier.

The Romantic period was probably the heyday for anapestics. Shelley's "The Cloud" (1820), over eighty lines of anapestic tetrameter and trimeter (with some dimeters), displays the full catalog of substitutions, especially spondees. In "Annabel Lee" (1849), Poe combines the tetrameters and trimeters with pervasive repetition of words, and so exploits the anapestic beat for an hypnotic effect. In Swinburne's "Before the Beginning of Years" (from *Atlanta in Calydon*, 1865) the form has become more mechanical, as if from anxiety that we might not recognize it. In the twentieth century, anapestics have been relegated almost entirely to comic or ironic use, as in Hardy's "The Ruined Maid." It may be difficult for us now to hear old anapestics, such as John Skelton's, as serious. (Skelton's enthusiasm for rhyme doesn't help.)

So pervasive is substitution in anapestic poems, that it's worth asking how we recognize them. *Logaoedic* poems—poems with a nearly equal mix of anapests and iambs—present the toughest challenge. For some critics, they belong logically to the dominant iambic regime, and are merely excessive in anapestic substitutions. I suggest, though, that what I have said about the hard-to-bridle insistence of the anapestic beat gives it a perceptual edge, so that if all of a poem's lines contain at least one trisyllabic foot, and the lines are short, we readily hear it as anapestic. Dryden's "Chorus on the New Year," from *The Secular Masque*, would sound metrically unstable if we read it as basically iambic; heard within an anapestic framework, it satisfies:

All, all, of a piece throughout:
Thy chase had a beast in view;
Thy wars brought nothing about;
Thy lovers were all untrue.
'Tis well an old age is out,
And time to begin a new.

Masefield's "Sea-Fever" uses a similar mixture of feet, if less adroitly.

If the Romantic poets revived anapestics, as part of a reaction to neoclassical canons, the Victorians more thoroughly developed and explored the literary-ballad associations of the meter. Two examples, both deft and various in their handling of substitution, show the range poets could find within this apparently stereotyped form. Emily Jane Brontë's Gondal poem, "M.A. Written on the Dungeon Wall—N.C.," composed in 1845, demonstrates the surprising darkness of which a triple meter is capable:

> I know that tonight, the wind is sighing,
> The soft August wind, over forest and moor
> While I in a grave-like chill am lying
> On the damp black flags of my dungeon-floor—
>
> I know that the Harvest Moon is shining;
> She neither will wax nor wane for me,
> Yet I weary, weary, with vain repining,
> One gleam of her heaven-bright face to see!
>
> For this constant darkness is wasting the gladness
> Fast wasting the gladness of life away;
> It gathers up thoughts akin to madness
> That never would cloud the world of day
>
> I chide with my soul—I bid it cherish
> The feelings it lived on when I was free,
> But, shrinking it murmurs, "Let memory perish
> Forget for thy Friends have forgotten thee!"
>
> Alas, I did think that they were weeping
> Such tears as I weep—it is not so!
> Their careless young eyes are closed in sleeping;
> Their brows are unshadowed, undimmed by woe—
>
> Might I go to their beds, I'd rouse that slumber,
> My spirit should startle their rest, and tell
> How hour after hour, I wakefully number
> Deep buried from light in my lonely cell!
>
> Yet let them dream on, though dreary dreaming
> Would haunt my pillow if *they* were here
> And *I* were laid warmly under the gleaming
> Of that guardian moon and her comrade star—

Better that I my own fate mourning
Should pine alone in the prison-gloom
Than waken free on the summer morning
And feel they were suffering this awful doom

Details the connoisseur might savor are the pair of cretics in the middle of line 2, and the wholly plausible *palimbacchius* (´ ´ ˘) at the end of the last stanza's first line. More generally, the poem substantiates our sense of how anapestics work: Brontë signals the seriousness of her mode by reining in the foot with a high proportion of two-syllable substitutions. Lines like "That never would cloud the world of day" or the difficult "Such tears as I weep—it is not so!" would hardly stand out among iambic tetrameters.

Later in the century (1876) Lewis Carroll brought the faux ballad to a different apotheosis in *The Hunting of the Snark*. Here is Fit the Seventh, the shortest of the eight, "The Banker's Tale":

They sought it with thimbles, they sought it with care;
    They pursued it with forks and hope;
They threatened its life with a railway-share;
    They charmed it with smiles and soap.

And the Banker, inspired with a courage so new
    It was matter for general remark,
Rushed madly ahead and was lost to their view
    In his zeal to discover the Snark.

But while he was seeking with thimbles and care,
    A Bandersnatch swiftly drew nigh
And grabbed at the Banker, who shrieked in despair,
    For he knew it was useless to fly.

He offered large discount—he offered a cheque
    (Drawn "to bearer") for seven-pounds-ten:
But the Bandersnatch merely extended its neck
    And grabbed at the Banker again.

Without rest or pause—while those frumious jaws
    Went savagely snapping around—
He skipped and he hopped, and he floundered and flopped,
    Till fainting he fell on the ground.

The Bandersnatch fled as the others appeared
    Led on by that fear-stricken yell:
And the Bellman remarked "It is just as I feared!"
    And solemnly tolled on his bell.

He was black in the face, and they scarcely could trace
  The least likeness to what he had been:
While so great was his fright that his waistcoat turned white—
  A wonderful thing to be seen!

To the horror of all who were present that day,
  He uprose in full evening dress,
And with senseless grimaces endeavoured to say
  What his tongue could no longer express.

Down he sank in a chair—ran his hands through his hair—
  And chanted in mimsiest tones
Words whose utter inanity proved his insanity,
  While he rattled a couple of bones.

"Leave him here to his fate—it is getting so late!"
  The Bellman exclaimed in a fright.
"We have lost half the day. Any further delay,
  And we sha'n't catch a Snark before night!"

(The meter reminds us to stress the second syllable of "grimaces.") In this mock-heroic mode Carroll is obviously far more willing than Brontë to rollick. Yet a line like "Led on by that fear-stricken yell" (an anapest flanked by spondee and cretic) reminds us that the mockery would have no point if the gothic-heroic tone were inaudible to us. Echoing within such a double consciousness, these anapestics are funny, but never fatuous.

NOTE

  1. See *British and American Poets: Chaucer to the Present,* ed. W. Jackson Bate and David Perkins (New York: Harcourt Brace, 1986).

Running with Abandon:
Some Notes on Trochaic Meter

CARL PHILLIPS

Purely trochaic verse—that is, verse in which a regular pattern of trochees (′ ˘ , as in *hunger*) appears throughout not just the line but the entire poem—is relatively rare in English. The possibilities as to why this is so—and as to what is consequently implied about the human condition (at least in English-speaking cultures)—are where the trochaic becomes my choice for the most intriguing of metrical options.

The terms *trochee* and *trochaic* come from the Greek for *to run,* and the meter is indeed a running, lilting one, for which reason it is often referred to as a falling meter (as opposed to the way in which the intonation rises in iambic words, such as *bizarre*). Because the trochee must always end on an unaccented syllable, it has an open-ended, unfinished sound, suggestive of a falling away that goes on indefinitely, lacking as it does the stressed ending that would suggest finality, conclusion ("Why so dull and mute, young sinner?" for example, from Suckling's "Song"). What becomes clear when we look for verse whose lines are trochaic throughout is that such verse is rare. More commonly, trochaic verse consists of lines that are trochaic until the last foot, where the unstressed ending is simply omitted. The result is what is known as a *catalectic* line: "Many times man lives and dies" (Yeats, "Under Ben Bulben"). The audible effect is of a rocking motion that is, after some time, abruptly halted.

It is true enough that English has fewer trochaic word-options than do more inflected languages such as Italian or German, but I hold this fact less responsible for the scarcity of purely trochaic lines than do some. Rather, I suspect that this metrical "situation" has to do with the English-speaker's preference for closure at the ends of things and a concomitant suspicion of open-endedness, where the possibilities remain endless because never fully accounted for. A poem that exemplifies this idea metrically is the madrigal "What Is Life," by an unknown author.

What is life or worldly pleasure?
Seeming shadows quickly sliding.
What is wealth or golden treasure?
Borrowed fortune never biding.
What is grace or princes' smiling?
Hopëd honor, time beguiling.

What are all in one combined,
Which divided so displease?
Apish toys and vain delights,
Mind's unrest and soul's disease.

Late sixteenth/early seventeenth c.

The first stanza, entirely trochaic, is the one whose focus is on the pleasures and vices presumably to be guarded against in a life. The second stanza, however, is where the sound is less melodic, each line ends with finality and closure because each is catalectic; and, not coincidentally, it is in this stanza that all of the vices and temptations considered individually—and more infectiously, in terms of sound—in stanza 1 are now corralled, as it were, and finally dismissed as "apish toys and vain delights," likely to lead to the "soul's disease."

    The general association of trochaic meter with abandon and play (both aural and moral) is probably why we most often encounter this meter in songs ("Where the Bee Sucks, There Suck I" and "Fear No More the Heat o' the Sun" from Shakespeare's *The Tempest* and *Cymbeline*, respectively), nursery rhymes ("Jack be nimble, Jack be quick"), and other genres in which playfulness is the point (or a kind of innocence, as in the refrain of Blake's "The Lamb": "Little Lamb, who made thee? / Dost thou know who made thee?"). It is also the likeliest reason for there being few examples of trochaic meter in lines of greater length than tetrameter; more than four feet of trochees, and things begin to sound, more than playful, downright silly, at least to the English-speaker's ear. Some exceptions are Swinburne's "The Last Oracle" (trochaic hexameter) and Robert Browning's "A Toccata of Galuppi's" (trochaic octameter, though all lines are catalectic). Likewise—doubtless because it requires at least three feet, preferably four, to establish and solidify a pleasing rhythm, we rarely see lines shorter than tetrameter. But—again, for exceptions—see Shelley's "To a Skylark," where, except for each stanza's last line, all lines are in trochaic trimeter; or Campion's "Rose-Cheeked Laura," each of whose stanzas includes two lines of purely trochaic tetrameter and a line of the trochaic dimeter so rarely seen that it is worth including a stanza here:

Rose-cheeked Laura, come,
Sing thou smoothly with thy beauty's
Silent music, either other
    Sweetly gracing.

    The challenge in using trochaic meter—as with any meter—is to look squarely at its virtues and flaws and to employ both to the poem's advantage. The rollicking aspect of trochaic meter captures well the levity of the Apollo pub in Jonson's "Over the Door at the Entrance into the Apollo." And what better way to underscore the tension between the pious, restrained Brother Lawrence and the morally abandoned narrator of Browning's "Soliloquy of the Spanish Cloister" than to alternate purely trochaic lines with the more reined-in—because catalectic—version of those lines?

    Gr-rr—there go, my heart's abhorrence!
      Water your damned flower-pots, do!
    If hate killed men, Brother Lawrence,
      God's blood, would not mine kill you!
    What? your myrtle-bush wants trimming?
      Oh, that rose has prior claims—
    Needs its leaden vase filled brimming?
      Hell dry you up with its flames!

                    1842

Dickinson uses a similar technique of alternation in her "Publication—is the Auction" (in the anthology that follows) in order to argue that a lack of modesty is inferior to the restraint that is patience. The playful motion of trochees suddenly brought to a halt—again, via catalexis—is grimly appropriate for Gunn's elegy to a rich life now reduced to scattered ash ("Words for Some Ash"). It's a strange meter, but strangely versatile, as useful a tool in the writing of satire and stinging epigram as in the writing of high lyric, whether its purpose is to elegize or to pitch intellectual argument. In the poems included here we can see that, when handled well, trochaic meter—in its ability to lend variously humor, grace, and poignancy (of sound and of mood)—is an essential part of that particularly human music we call poetry.

EMILY BRONTË

Hope

Hope was but a timid friend—
She sat without my grated den
Watching how my fate would tend
Even as selfish-hearted men.

She was cruel in her fear.
Through the bars, one dreary day,
I looked out to see her there
And she turned her face away!

Like a false guard false watch keeping
Still in strife she whispered peace;
She would sing while I was weeping,
If I listened, she would cease.

False she was, and unrelenting.
When my last joys strewed the ground
Even Sorrow saw repenting
Those sad relics scattered round;

Hope—whose whisper would have given
Balm to all that frenzied pain—
Stretched her wings and soared to heaven;
Went—and ne'er returned again!

1843

WILLIAM BLAKE

Never Pain to Tell Thy Love

Never pain to tell thy love
Love that never told can be
For the gentle wind does move
Silently invisibly

I told my love I told my love
I told her all my heart
Trembling cold in ghastly fears
Ah she doth depart

Soon as she was gone from me
A traveller came by
Silently invisibly
O was no deny

1793?

COUNTEE CULLEN

From Heritage

Africa? A book one thumbs
Listlessly, till slumber comes.
Unremembered are her bats
Circling through the night, her cats
Crouching in the river reeds,
Stalking gentle flesh that feeds
By the river brink; no more
Does the bugle-throated roar
Cry that monarch claws have leapt
From the scabbards where they slept.

1927

BEN JONSON

Over the Door at the Entrance into the Apollo

Welcome all that lead or follow,
To the oracle of Apollo—
Here he speaks out of his pottle,
Or the tripos, his tower bottle:
All his answers are divine,
Truth itself doth flow in wine.
Hang up all the poor hop-drinkers,
Cries old Sym, the king of skinkers;
He the half of life abuses,
That sits watering with the muses.
Those dull girls no good can mean us,
Wine, it is the milk of Venus,
And the poet's horse accounted:

Ply it, and you all are mounted.
'Tis the true Phoebian liquor,
Cheers the brains, makes wit the quicker,
Pays all debts, cures all diseases,
And at once three senses pleases.
Welcome, all that lead or follow,
To the oracle of Apollo.

1573–1637

THOM GUNN

Words for Some Ash

Poor parched man, we had to squeeze
Dental sponge against your teeth,
So that moisture by degrees
Dribbled to the mouth beneath.

Christmas Day your pupils crossed,
Staring at your nose's tip,
Seeking there the air you lost
Yet still gaped for, dry of lip.

Now you are a bag of ash
Scattered on a coastal ridge,
Where you watched the distant crash,
Ocean on a broken edge.

Death has wiped away each sense;
Fire took muscle, bone, and brains;
Next may rain leach discontents
From your dust, wash what remains

Deeper into damper ground
Till the granules work their way
Down to unseen streams, and bound
Briskly in the water's play;

May you lastly reach the shore,
Joining tide without intent,
Only worried any more
By the currents' argument.

1992

EMILY DICKINSON

709

Publication—is the Auction
Of the Mind of Man—
Poverty—be justifying
For so foul a thing

Possibly—but We—would rather
From Our Garret go
White—Unto the White Creator
Than invest—Our Snow

Thought belong to Him who gave it—
Then—to Him Who bear
Its Corporeal illustration—Sell
The Royal Air—

In the Parcel—Be the Merchant
Of the Heavenly Grace—
But reduce no Human Spirit
To Disgrace of Price—

c. 1863

Dactylic Meter:
A Many-Sounding Sea

ANNIE FINCH

Since Homer and perhaps much earlier, before written poetry, the dactylic meter has rolled through Western literature like a "polyphlosboiou thalassa" (many-sounding sea), to use a phrase of Homer's. The ancient dactylic poems have been a touchstone for poets for centuries, yet few have attempted the meter in English. Rarer in English poetry than the trochee or anapest, the dactyl is the furthest common metrical foot from the familiar iamb. Because of this as well as its beauty, to write in dactyls can be a liberating, if challenging, experience for the contemporary poet.

A triple instead of a double foot, falling instead of rising, the dactyl acts rhythmically as the iamb's shadow, the alter ego of the dominant meter. The rarity of the dactyl in English-language poetry has led many to regard it as "unnatural and abhorrent" in English, as Swinburne claimed. However, dactylic rhythm is as natural to our language as iambic, and the proof is clear to anyone with open ears: people speak in dactylic rhythm all the time. Even the poet who once told me that "English falls naturally into iambics" was speaking in dactyls.

Like other meters, dactyls have been claimed to be the perfect vehicle for a range of moods, from somber to facile. George Puttenham, in 1589, singled out "comicall verses" to illustrate dactyls, while others have heard in the meter a sonorous and imposing authority. In my own reading, I observed that dactylic passages in free verse ranging from Whitman to Audre Lorde carry compelling connotations of the unconscious, the body, female energy, and the power of nature (for more on these metrical connotations, see my book *The Ghost of Meter*). Whatever connotations one hears or does not hear in the dactylic meter, it is easy to be caught up in its crashing rhythmic beauty and cascading momentum.

The quantitative version of the dactylic foot was key not only to the dactylic hexameter of Homer's and Virgil's epics, but also to the elegiac couplet and the Sapphic stanza. However, the classical dactylic hexameter includes two or more spondees (feet of two equal stresses). Since English does not have the mathematically exact stress equivalences assumed of classical verse (see Warren on quantitative meter), spondees are either rare or impossible in English, depending on one's ear. As a result, nineteenth-century poets who wanted to imitate classical meters by writing accentual-syllabic dactyls in English gave up in frustration. Walter Savage Landor wrote, in ironic dactylic hexameters,

> Much as old meters delight me, 'tis only where first they were
>   nurtured,
> In their own clime, their own speech; than pamper them here,
>   I would rather
> Tie up my Pegasus tight to the scanty-fed rack of a sonnet.

Probably because the dactyl is such an irrepressibly captivating rhythmic pattern, however, poets did continue to use it. Tennyson, Hardy, Browning ("Misconceptions"), and E. A. Robinson ("Pasa Thalassa Thalassa") treated dactyls as a metrical curiosity, each writing one dactylic poem. Longfellow, perhaps freer than the English poets of the burden of duplicating the exact effect of quantitative classical meters, hit on the reasonable solution of substituting trochees for the spondees. His epic love poem "Evangeline" (with its famous opening line "this is the forest primeval, the murmuring pines and the hemlocks") was so widely loved that its dactylic hexameters were memorized and recited by thousands of schoolchildren.

With the advent of free verse, dactylic passages became, rather ironically, more common in poetry. Their magnetic and insistent rhythm is one source of Whitman's power, and contemporary free verse continues to use the dactyl as a counterpoint to the iamb. It is my theory that the urge toward dactyls was one of the deepest roots of the twentieth-century free verse movement, which, after all, focused initially on "breaking," in Pound's term, not so much meter in general as the iambic foot.

Dactyls do not yet have any system of accepted rules for substitution like those that have evolved over the centuries for iambic meter. Most contemporary prosodists claim that the dactylic meter has an essentially different nature than the iambic and is simply incapable of any subtle modulation. I find this claim unconvincing, from personal experience and especially since no prosodist has given the dactyl serious attention as a potentially flexible medium. The earliest English prosodists believed that iambic pentameter was an inflexible pattern that could bear no substitutions. Why should not history also prove theorists wrong about the dactyl's limitations?

The most common length for dactylic lines is tetrameter, though poems have been written in lengths from dimeter (notably Tennyson's

"Charge of the Light Brigade" and Thomas Hood's "Bridge of Sighs": "Take her up tenderly, / Lift her with care: / Fashion'd so slenderly, / Young, and so fair!") to hexameter. Some poets also intersperse lines of anapestic or other meter among the dactylic lines, or alternate them, as in E. E. Cummings's lines,

> what if a much of a which of a wind
> gives the truth to summer's lie;
> bloodies with dizzying leaves the sun
> and yanks immortal stars awry?

Prosodists who privilege rising meters may categorize lines 1 and 3 above as headless anapestic lines, but I scan the poem as alternating dactylic and iambic lines (James McAuley's *Versification* contains a useful explanation of such alternating scansions).

When I began to write in dactyls, they were so unfamiliar to my ear that it took a while before they stopped turning into iambs every time my back was turned. Those initial dactylic efforts tended to stick with dactyls and trochees. Now, I am comfortable with more extensive variations. Looking through my dactylic poems, I see that I substitute numerous variations, including trochees, feet of one stress followed by a rest, and occasionally the *antibacchic* (' ' ˘), *cretic* (' ˘ '), *first paean* (' ˘ ˘ ˘), *molossus* (' ' ') and anapest in place of dactylic feet.

Typical variations in dactylic meter reverse variations in iambic meter. In iambic meter it is common to end lines with a "feminine" or *extra-syllable ending* (as in "to be or not to be, that is the question"). Dactylic lines may begin with the inverse, an *extra-syllable beginning (anacrusis)* as in A. E. Stallings's line, "The moon once pulled blood from me. Now I pull silver." On the other hand, where a *headless (acephalous)* iambic line begins by skipping an unstressed syllable ("Whan that April with his showres soote"), a frequent type of dactylic line, called *footless* in my own terminology (*truncated* or *catalectic*) skips either one or both final unstressed syllables. This is the case, for instance, in every other line of "The Bridge of Sighs" quoted above, and in this line from Robinson's "Pasa Thalassa Thalassa": " 'Where is he lying?' I ask, and the lights in the valley are nearer."

Dactylic lines of any length frequently include trochees and often one-stress feet, which can appear in the middle or at the end of the line. Browning uses both types in this line from "Abt Vogler": "bidding my organ obey, calling its keys to their work." Other feet including the cretic (' ˘ ') (the third foot of E .E. Cummings's line "anyone lived in a

pretty how town") and the antibacchic (' ' ˘), (the second foot of the re-
frain of Elizabeth Akers Allen's popular ballad "Rock Me to Sleep,
Mother": "Rock me to sleep, mother, —rock me to sleep!") are not un-
common in subtly wrought dactylic poetry. The dactylic lines in the
poems that follow this essay are flexible enough to encompass a line of
trochees ("playing ugly Yahoo tricks" in Lindsay's "Factory Win-
dows"); a series of antibacchics (' ' ˘) ("song-singing," "snowberry,"
"soft-mosses" in Rosetti's "Sing-Song"); fourth paeans (' ˘ ˘ ˘) ("even to
the" and "travelling a" in Hardy's "The Voice"), and even a true
spondee ("all things" in "Evangeline").

As the following selections illustrate, dactyls can create dreamy,
magical spells potent enough to weave the mystery of A. E. Stallings's
"Arachne Gives Thanks to Athena," yet they are flexible enough to sus-
tain the narrative of "Evangeline" and sturdy enough to stand up to
satire and irony, as in Vachel Lindsay's "Factory Windows" and A. D.
Hope's "Coup de Grace." As these poems illustrate, dactylic meter is a
barely tapped medium that can be modulated as subtly and fruitfully as
any other meter in English.

THOMAS HARDY

The Voice

Woman much missed, how you call to me, call to me,
Saying that now you are not as you were
When you had changed from the one who was all to me,
But as at first, when our day was fair.

Can it be you that I hear? Let me view you, then,
Standing as when I drew near to the town
Where you would wait for me: yes, as I knew you then,
Even to the original air-blue gown!

Or is it only the breeze, in its listlessness
Travelling across the wet mead to me here,
You being ever dissolved to wan wistlessness,
Heard no more again far or near?

Thus I: faltering forward,
Leaves around me falling,
Wind oozing thin through the thorn from norward,
And the woman calling.

1912

HENRY WADSWORTH LONGFELLOW

From Evangeline

Far asunder, on separate coasts, the Acadians landed;
Scattered were they, like flakes of snow, when the wind from
  the northeast
Strikes aslant through the fogs that darken the Banks
  of Newfoundland.
Friendless, homeless, hopeless, they wandered from city
  to city,
From the cold lakes of the North to the sultry Southern
  savannas,—
From the bleak shores of the sea to the lands where the
  Father of Waters
Seizes the hills in his hands, and drags them down to
  the ocean,
Deep in their sands to bury the scattered bones of
  the mammoth.
Friends they sought and homes; and many, despairing,
  heart-broken,
Asked of the earth but a grave, and no longer a friend nor
  a fireside.
Written their history stands on tablets of stone in
  the churchyards.
Long among them was seen a maiden who waited
  and wandered,
Lowly and meek in spirit, and patiently suffering all things. . . .
Sometimes she spake with those who had seen her beloved
  and known him,
But it was long ago, in some far-off place or forgotten.
"Gabriel Lajeunesse!" they said; "Oh yes! we have seen him.
He was with Basil the blacksmith, and both have gone to
  the prairies;
Couveurs-des-Bois are they, and famous hunters and trappers."
"Gabriel Lajeunesse!" said others; "Oh yes! we have seen him.
He is a Voyageur in the lowlands of Louisiana."
Then they would say, "Dear child! why dream and wait for
  him longer?" . . .
Thus did that poor soul wander in want and cheerless
  discomfort,
Bleeding, barefooted, over the shards and thorns of existence.
Let me essay, O Muse! to follow the wanderer's footsteps.

1804

VACHEL LINDSAY

Factory Windows

Factory windows are always broken.
Somebody's always throwing bricks,
Somebody's always heaving cinders,
Playing ugly Yahoo tricks.

Factory windows are always broken.
Other windows are let alone.
No one throws through the chapel window
The bitter, snarling derisive stone.

Factory windows are always broken.
Something or other is going wrong.
Something is rotten—I think, in Denmark.
End of the factory-window song.

                                    1914

CHRISTINA ROSSETTI

From Sing-Song

Dead in the cold, a song-singing thrush,
Dead at the foot of a snowberry bush,—
Weave him a coffin of rush,
Dig him a grave where the soft mosses grow,
Raise him a tombstone of snow.

                                    1872

A. E. STALLINGS

Arachne Gives Thanks to Athena

It is no punishment. They are mistaken—
The brothers, the father. My prayers were answered.
I was all fingertips. Nothing was perfect:
What I have woven, the moths will have eaten;
At the end of my rope was a noose's knot.

Now it's no longer the thing, but the pattern,
And that will endure, even though webs be broken.

I, if not beautiful, am beauty's maker.
Old age cannot rob me, nor cowardly lovers.
The moon once pulled blood from me. Now I pull silver.
Here are the lines I pulled from my own belly—
Hang them with rainbows, ice, dewdrops, darkness.

1996

A. D. HOPE

Coup de Grace

Just at that moment the Wolf,
Sharp jaws and slavering grin,
Steps from the property wood.
O, what a gage, what a gulf
Opens to gobble her in.
Little Red Riding Hood.

O, what a face full of things.
Eyes like saucers at least
Roll to seduce and beguile.
Miss, with her dimples and bangs,
Thinks him a handsome beast,
Flashes the Riding Hood smile;

Stands her ground like a queen,
Velvet red of the rose
Framing each little milk-tooth,
Pink tongue peeping between
Them, wider than anyone knows,
Opens her mimikin mouth,

Swallows up the wolf in a trice,
Tail going down gives a flick,
Caught as she closes her jaws,
Bows, all sugar and spice,
O, what a lady-like trick!
O, what a round of applause!

1968

Free Verse

MICHELLE BOISSEAU

To begin with the routine disclaimer: *free verse* is *not* the poetic equivalent of "free parking" or "free beer." Though it uses meter and rhyme nonsystematically (and often relies on thematic closural devices), free verse is still organized, like all poems, around technical constraints. As Paul Fussell notes of free verse, "every technical gesture in a poem must justify itself in meaning." These technical gestures most overtly occur in the poet's handling of lineation.

As the basic unit of metrical verse is the foot, one might say the basic unit of free verse is the line, more precisely, the interrelationship between lines and sentences. Within the poem each line must have its own integrity: its length, rhythm, and ending must be justified by what they contribute to the poem's meaning. A poem that deploys compound-complex sentences over many long lines must earn the grandeur these lines suggest. A line suddenly shorter than its neighbors must decisively earn the created emphasis through the line's context within the poem.

Although *free verse* is a twentieth-century term, its roots are ancient. We can trace its heritage, particularly in long lines, to Hebrew poetry, the King James Bible, Blake's prophetic books, and popular writers like Frances Wright and Martin Farquhar Tupper. From these strains (and features like parallelism, juxtaposition, repetition) and Emerson's dictum that poets compose not in meters but in "metre-making argument," Walt Whitman developed a verse of surprising scope and delicacy. By spooling out and reeling in his long lines, Whitman registered prophetic truth, psychic energy, physical exertion, and great visionary power. These qualities Allen Ginsberg drew on in his influential "Howl" (1950), reawakening many poets to the possibilities of the long line. Adrienne Rich's "Yom Kippur 1984," as these lines show, exploits the sweeping tone of the long-line tradition.

> What is a Jew in solitude?
> What is a woman in solitude, a queer woman or man?
> When the winter flood-tides wrench the tower from the rock,
>   crumble the prophet's headland, and the farms slide into
>   the sea . . .

By exerting strong control of the lines' internal syntactic tension—for instance, by shifting and stretching, as Rich does, the placement of caesuras within the longer line—poets can express the ebb and flow of emotion and thought. Without such attentive and meaningful tension within the line, however, poets risk forming a line that sounds flaccid or ponderous, that sinks like a kite on a slackened string.

In the early twentieth century, as they sought to "make it new"—as Ezra Pound urged—poets developed a shorter-lined free verse from eclectic models: the *vers libre* of French Symbolism; Asian syllabic poetry with its emphasis on close observation; prose fiction with its emphasis on realism, directness, and imagery; and the visual arts with their new emphasis on art as a thing. The typewriter, in wide use, encouraged poets to experiment directly with how their words might look on the page and how the negative space, the white space, framed those words.

Early on many free verse poets arranged their lines by phrases. Wallace Stevens's "Metaphors of a Magnifico," for example, takes phrasal lines to create an exacting semantic and visual equation. Short lines can intensify the weight of images, words, and their implications, can celebrate minute observation, and set a halo around the ordinary object. A poem lineated according to the phrase can seem direct, complete, and genuine. When a poem's argument is knotty (like Stevens's "The Idea of Order at Key West"), phrasal lines can help the reader sort out the steps. Slow phrasal lines can also be psychologically expressive, as in Donald Justice's "Men at Forty," where they suggest diffidence and reluctance.

But the poet must beware. Without compensating qualities—like incisiveness, resonance, sharp observation, or rich diction—phrasal lines, particularly when short, can resemble chopped-up prose, and the poet's bright epiphanies quickly appear banal and flat. However, by deftly handling enjambment—continuing the sentence past the line ending—the poet can deepen a poem's textural undercurrents. Elizabeth Bishop's work is a model; in "Song for the Rainy Season," for instance, she modulates the syntax so the sentences flow through the short lines, like water falling rock to rock, with each line delivering a small surprise.

> the brook sings loud
> from a rib cage
> of giant fern

More radical enjambment can indicate fragmentation or violence. In Gwendolyn Brooks's "We Real Cool" each line closes with "We," stressing how the pool players' self-indulgence leads to ruin: "We / Die

Soon." Consider this other famous example of enjambment from James
Wright's "A Blessing":

> Suddenly I realize
> That if I stepped out of my body I would break
> Into blossom.

The greatest emphasis within a line normally falls at its end—particu-
larly when end-stopped (next most emphasis falls at the beginning, and
least in the middle). Wright's center line acts both as part of the larger
sentence and independent from it. The enjambment of "break"—at the
line *break*—superimposes destruction onto notions of redemption,
transformation, blossoming. Coming before a shorter line, the longer
center line further suggests that the speaker requires more room for his
realization. And the final short line intensifies his discovery.

Besides the emphasis created through right-margin enjambment,
many poets—E. E. Cummings most notably—have explored the expres-
sive potential in the fluid left margin. We see this device in Pound's *Can-
tos* and W. C. Williams's longer poems, and in many poems that marked
the era of radical experimentation from the late 1950s into the 1970s. In
his "Kenyatta Listening to Mozart," for instance, Amiri Baraka wields
many lineation strategies to demonstrate the clash and conversion of
multiple cultural forces. Throughout her "Antique Father" Carolyn
Kizer uses a three-step left margin to mimic the pendulum of thought:

>   where all folly
>   become wisdom
> becomes folly again

At best radical enjambment and left-margin indentation create bold
statements, rumbling undertones, and subtle wit; overused, however, the
technique can seem coy and trite. Indeed, when any lineation strategy
comes to seem the signature of a particular era, that strategy becomes
weakened as it loses its ability to intrigue us. And any strategy in a
poem—whether rhyme or enjambment—not grounded in the poem's
greater sense will seem trivial and superfluous.

First and last, free verse is tied to the greater poetic tradition from
which it comes. A glance at an anthology of twentieth-century poetry
shows that free verse poems often look like more systematically formal
poems, arranged evenly—in couplets, quatrains, and so forth—or in
long blocks of lines, like the blank verse of Milton or Wordsworth, who,
we should remember, practiced enjambment with great sensitivity.

Throughout its development, free verse has shifted between incorporating traditional strategies and seizing radical ones. As each generation has tried some approaches and discarded others as worn out (approaches that a later generation will likely rediscover and reinvent), free verse has become so diverse and flexible that one can claim that most poets in the last one hundred years have at some point drawn from the deep well of its possibilities.

WALT WHITMAN

A Noiseless Patient Spider

A noiseless patient spider,
I marked where on a little promontory it stood isolated,
Marked how to explore the vacant vast surrounding,
It launched forth filament, filament, filament, out of itself,
Ever unreeling them, ever tirelessly speeding them.

And you O my soul where you stand,
Surrounded, detached, in measureless oceans of space,
Ceaselessly musing, venturing, throwing, seeking the spheres
    to connect them,
Till the bridge you will need be formed, till the ductile
    anchor hold,
Till the gossamer thread you fling catch somewhere, O
    my soul.

1871

WALLACE STEVENS

Metaphors of a Magnifico

Twenty men crossing a bridge,
Into a village,
Are twenty men crossing twenty bridges,
Into twenty villages,
Or one man
Crossing a single bridge into a village.

This is old song
That will not declare itself . . .

Twenty men crossing a bridge,
Into a village,
Are
Twenty men crossing a bridge
Into a village.

That will not declare itself
Yet is certain as meaning . . .

The boots of the men clump
On the boards of the bridge.
The first white wall of the village
Rises through fruit-trees.
Of what was it I was thinking?
So the meaning escapes.

The first white wall of the village . . .
The fruit-trees. . . .

                                              1918

MARIANNE MOORE

A Grave

Man looking into the sea,
taking the view from those who have as much right to it as
    you have to it yourself,
it is human nature to stand in the middle of a thing,
but you cannot stand in the middle of this;
the sea has nothing to give but a well excavated grave.
The firs stand in a procession, each with an emerald turkey-
    foot at the top,
reserved as their contours, saying nothing;
repression, however, is not the most obvious characteristic of
    the sea;
the sea is a collector, quick to return a rapacious look.
There are others besides you who have worn that look—
whose expression is no longer a protest, the fish no longer
    investigate them
for their bones have not lasted:
men lower nets, unconscious of the fact that they are
    desecrating a grave,
and row quickly away—the blades of the oars

moving together like the feet of water-spiders as if there were
    no such thing as death.
The wrinkles progress among themselves in a phalanx—
    beautiful under networks of foam,
and fade breathlessly while the sea rustles in and out of
    the seaweed;
the birds swim through the air at top speed, emitting cat-calls
    as heretofore—
the tortoise-shell scourges about the feet of the cliffs, in
    motion beneath them
and the ocean, under the pulsation of lighthouses and noise
    of bell-buoys,
advances as usual, looking as if it were not that ocean in
    which dropped things are bound to sink—
in which they turn and twist, it is neither with volition
    nor consciousness.

1924

WILLIAM CARLOS WILLIAMS

Spring and All

By the road to the contagious hospital
under the surge of the blue
mottled clouds driven from the
northeast—a cold wind. Beyond, the
waste of broad, muddy fields
brown with dried weeds, standing and fallen

patches of standing water
the scattering of tall trees

All along the road the reddish
purplish, forked, upstanding, twiggy
stuff of bushes and small trees
with dead, brown leaves under them
leafless vines—

Lifeless in appearance, sluggish
dazed spring approaches—

They enter the new world naked,
cold, uncertain of all
save that they enter. All about them
the cold, familiar wind—

Now the grass, tomorrow
the stiff curl of wildcarrot leaf

One by one objects are defined—
It quickens: clarity, outline of leaf

But now the stark dignity of
entrance—Still, the profound change
has come upon them: rooted, they
grip down and begin to awaken

1923

ELLEN BRYANT VOIGT

Ravenous

High winds flare up and old house shudders.

The dead should just shut up. Already
they've ruined the new-plowed field:
it looks like a grave. Adjacent pine-woods,
another set of walls: in that dark room
a birch, too young to have a waist,
practices sway and bend, slope and give.
And the bee at vertical rest on the outside pane,
belly facing in, one jointed limb crooked
to its mouth, the mouth at work—
my lost friend, of course, who lifelong
chewed his cuticles to the quick. Likewise
Jane who calls from her closet of walnut and silk
for her widower to stroke her breasts, her feet,
although she has no breasts, she has no feet,
exacting pity in their big white bed.
The dead themselves are pitiless—
they keen and thrash, or they lodge
in your throat like a stone, or they descend
as spring snow, as late night, as light-struck dust
rises and descends—frantic for more, more of this earth,
more of its flesh, more death, oh yes, and a few more
thousand last vast blue cloud-blemished skies.

1998

RITA DOVE

Soprano

When you hit
the center

of a note, spin
through and off

the bell lip
into heaven,

the soul dies
for an instant—

but you don't need
its thin

resistance
nor the room

(piano shawl,
mirror, hyacinth)

dissolving
as one note

pours into
the next, pebbles

clean as moonspill
seeding a path . . .

and which is it,
body or mind,

which rises, which
gives up at last

and goes home?

1998

All Composed in a Meter of Catullus: Hendecasyllabics

RACHEL HADAS

"Eleven-syllable," which translates the Greek name of this meter, describes it precisely. An opening pair of syllables (can be ˘ ˘ , ˘ ′ , ′ ˘ , or ′ ′ , but usually starts with a strong stress) is followed by a dactyl and then three trochees; the effect is a rapid, light yet emphatic, skipping rhythm with a suggestion not so much of falling as of stumbling and righting oneself. This meter turns up sparsely in Sophocles and Aristophanes, and more frequently in such Alexandrian poets as Theocritus. But hendecasyllables are more familiar, as well as more frequent, in the work of the great Roman lyric poet Catullus (84–54 B.C.E.), who used the meter for 40 of his extant 113 poems. Catullus put his personal stamp on the form to the extent that Tennyson, in his hendecasyllabic poem, refers to it as a "a metre of Catullus." Catullus's hendecasyllables make use of the lightheartedness of the meter, but like any skillful poet Catullus isn't restricted by his choice of meter to a single tone; he can be thoughtful, passionate, funny, or mordant in hendecasyllables. Many of Catullus's most familiar poems are in this meter—for example, "Vivamus, mea Lesbia, atque amemus."

With the usual postclassical substitution of accentual stress for quantity (though Tennyson proudly claims to have adhered to quantity in his version), hendecasyllables were quite popular in Italian, Spanish, and German, starting in the fifteenth century. In English, hendecasyllables have tended to be written by poets with a classical education who made more frequent use of other forms; it's as if a little of the complicated syllabic dance of this meter goes a long way. Nor is it easy to imagine a successful long poem in hendecasyllabics; Swinburne's "In the month of the long decline of roses" (not included here) feels drawn-out at thirty-eight lines, and my own "On That Mountain" at twenty-nine lines may be risking the same problem.

Is this meter then best adapted for pure lyric brevity? Just as it's hard to imagine an epic poem written in sapphics, so hendecasyllables do not lend themselves to narrative. But there's something meditative, as well as lyrical, about the meter; as the example from Frost shows, hendecasyllabics, for the English-speaking poet, can be a good form to *think* in. Why Tennyson and Frost, splendid practitioners of blank verse, and Auden, the restless technician, occasionally chose hendeca-syllabics for particular kinds of poems is an intriguing question, but part of the answer surely has to do with the kind of thoughtful, some-times mildly combative, dialectical quality (what Hollander calls the "old, upbraiding cadence") of the poems they cast in hendecasyllables.

For the aspiring writer of hendecasyllabic verse, the challenge is not so much in counting the syllables as in making all those tripping trochees fall right, *sound* right. The hendecasyllabist will also be forced to pay close attention to diction—always a salutary exercise. Will she or he prefer fairly short, familiar words, as Robert Frost and Annie Finch tend to do in the examples below? Or, as in the Tennyson and Hadas ex-amples, will she lean toward long Latinate words (irresponsible, metri-fication, indolent, presumptuous, accumulation, opalescence)? Frost sounds triumphantly like himself, whatever the meter, but to my ear, the Tennyson of "O you chorus" is an altogether sprightlier, more flirtatious personality than the somber singer of "Idylls of the King."

Hendecasyllabics are a remarkably versatile form, not only in their apparent ability to fit into many different languages, but in what might be called their transparency. That is, demanding though the meter is of its practitioner, at the same time it doesn't call much attention to itself. It might not be claiming too much to suggest that as a result of this transparency, the poet's metrical choice is, at least in our day, a kind of secret between the poet and the reader who recognizes the meter—while for readers who don't get it, nothing is lost except the delicious feeling of being in the know.

Tennyson, while managing to praise his own metrical prowess and maintain his modesty, calls attention to the athletic precision the form demands. Frost, on the other hand, never refers to the meter he is using; and accordingly countless readers have enjoyed "For Once, Then, Something" without knowing its meter. Of course for many poetry lovers rhyme is a more conspicuous marker than meter, as are the dis-tinctive stanza forms of, say, sapphics, or the fourteen lines of a sonnet. Whereas hendecasyllables simply begin and end at the poet's discretion; a poem in this meter need not be any particular length. But what Paul Fussell and others have called the metrical contract is operative imme-diately; we are in a special kind of poem, one with its own metrical laws, which are the more intriguing for being applicable to any kind of mate-rial at all.

The following examples are presented in chronological order. As far as I have been able to determine, the Tennyson poem is untitled, as is the Hollander.

ALFRED, LORD TENNYSON

O you chorus of indolent reviewers,
Irresponsible, indolent reviewers,
Look, I come to the test, a tiny poem
All composed in a metre of Catullus,
All in quantity, careful of my motion,
Like the skater on ice that hardly bears him,
Lest I fall unawares before the people,
Waking laughter in indolent reviewers.
Should I flounder a while without a tumble
Thro' this metrification of Catullus,
They should speak to me not without a welcome,
All that chorus of indolent reviewers.
Hard, hard, hard is it, only not to tumble,
So fantastical is the dainty metre.
Wherefore slight me not wholly, nor believe me
Too presumptuous, indolent reviewers.
O blatant Magazines, regard me rather—
Since I blush to beloud myself a moment—
As some rare little rose, a piece of inmost
Horticultural art, or half-coquette-like
Maiden, not to be greeted unbenignly.

1863

ROBERT FROST

For Once, Then, Something

Others taunt me with having knelt at well-curbs
Always wrong to the light, so never seeing
Deeper down in the well than where the water
Gives me back in a shining surface picture
Me myself in the summer heaven godlike
Looking out of a wreath of fern and cloud puffs.
Once, when trying with chin against a well-curb,
I discerned, as I thought, beyond the picture,

Through the picture, a something, white, uncertain,
Something more of the depths—and then I lost it.
Water came to rebuke the too clear water.
One drop fell from a fern, and lo, a ripple
Shook whatever it was lay there at bottom,
Blurred it, blotted it out. What was that whiteness?
Truth? A pebble of quartz? For once, then, something.

1923

JOHN HOLLANDER

[Self-Descriptive Hendecasyllabics]

One more version of "classical" stressed meter
Called *hendecasyllabics* (which is Greek for
Having syllables numbering eleven)
Starts right out with a downbeat, always ending
Feminine, with a kind of hesitation
Heard just after the pair of syllables (the
fourth and fifth ones) which give the line its pattern.
Three stressed syllables sometimes open up this
Line, which, used in Latin by carping Martial
(Even more by fantastical Catullus)
Still holds onto its old, upbraiding cadence.

1981

RACHEL HADAS

On That Mountain

Evidence everywhere: accumulation.
Leaves atremble and narratives of branches
ramifying, so ever more connections
stay unfinished nor ever to be finished.
Do we not all have separate destinations?
Not that it matters. Aching opalescence
held us all spellbound, motionless, atingle,
balanced like sun and rain before a rainbow,
thunder purring and lightning white as daylight.
After the storm passed, all the world was gleaming,
glossy, almost lubricious with potential,

each blade of grass a dagger in the morning,
each leaf a goblet, brimming, winking,
ready to repay some small measure of night's thunder.
Couples stood tiptoe, trembling at departure,
kissing, breathing *Oh, let me touch your wisdom;
let me then taste reciprocally your beauty.*
More than mere iridescence—transformation.
Recall the dark face, thunder cowled at midnight.
Recall the bright face, rinsed clean for separation
as we're making our several preparations,
so many roads diverging in the greenwood,
putting on the inevitable blinders—
I must keep to my path and my path only—
closing our ears to thunder and cicadas,
closing our eyes to all those trembling branches,
meekly turning our backs on opalescence,

1996

ANNIE FINCH

Lucid Waking

Once I wanted the whole dawn not to let me
sleep. One morning, then, I began to see things.
Waking woke me, came slipping up through half-light,
crying softly, a cat leaving her corner,
stretching, tall in the new gray air of morning,
raising paws much too high. She came slow-stepping
down the hallway to crouch, to call, to whisper
through the door, making still and slow the dawning
once so bird-ridden—and the sun, the curtains.

1997

Pronouncing "Carpenter": Quantitative Meter in English

ROSANNA WARREN

"Who hath taught thee so subtle a measure?" Pound had his Sextus Propertius ask in 1919—Propertius, who in his third elegy claimed to be the first to present Italian celebration *(orgia)* in Greek meter: specifically, the elegiac couplet. The impressing of Greek quantitative measures (a prosody based on varying musical *lengths* of syllables) upon the stressed system of early Latin poetry to a large extent succeeded; upon English, the classical meters have left a far more elusive mark. It is an enduring trace, however, of an important source of our versification, and still helps to define our practice, even when we hardly notice it. It is from classical meter that we have adapted the vocabulary of feet: iambs, trochees, and so forth. Classical meters remain a delicate possibility in the inner ear, to be played against accentual syllabic meters and speech rhythms, and against the vagueness of much contemporary free verse.

Modern accentual-syllabic prosody, the dominant mode in English from the sixteenth to the early twentieth century, emerged with renewed sophistication from the intense discussions about the reform of poetry in the reign of Elizabeth I. Ironically, the insistent classicizing of Roger Ascham, Gabriel Harvey, and Thomas Campion did not establish classical meters in English, but revealed to poets greater subtleties in their own vernacular forms; Spenser, Sidney, the Countess of Pembroke, and Campion himself all trained their ears on classical prosody, and turned that training to accentual-syllabic poems. Later poets in English—Milton, Tennyson, Swinburne, Hardy, Hopkins, Housman, and Pound, for instance—have consistently renewed their cadences by listening to the Greek and Latin poets.

The alcaic may serve as a model for that complex transmission, though other forms, like the sapphic, the elegiac couplet, and the hendecasyllabic, have been carried forward as well (see Schulman, Steele, and Hadas). Like the sapphic, the alcaic is suffused with the personality of its supposed creator, from the island of Lesbos at the close of the seventh century B.C.E. Alcaeus himself, with his shifting moods, his visual

86

intelligence, his exile's lament, and his denunciations of tyranny, provides a fund of feeling and allusion from which later poets draw in using his stanza. One of a family of Aeolic meters based on the *choriamb* (– ˘ ˘ –), the quatrain that bears Alcaeus's name is a marvel of metrical disruptions delicately resolved. Modulating from two hendecasyllables with iambic and choriambic base, to a nine-syllable iambic line, to a ten-syllable dactylic/choriambic line, the stanza loses its balance twice to recover it only in the final breath: it is a form that celebrates the marriage of order and disorder as the figurative soul of art. Note, in the scansion, that the *anceps* (x), a slot free to be supplied with a long or short syllable, allows the poet great freedom to speed up or retard the line in the first unit; this is a freedom Horace will restrict, insisting on strategic pause, length, and stability in the fifth syllable of the flat two lines.

The alcaic is scanned:

$$x - \breve{} - x \mid - \breve{}\,\breve{} - |\breve{} -$$
$$x - \breve{} - x \mid - \breve{}\,\breve{} - |\breve{} -$$
$$x - \breve{} - x \mid - \breve{} - -$$
$$- \breve{}\,\breve{} \mid - \breve{}\,\breve{} - |\breve{} - -$$

Alcaeus's Fragment Q, a scene of profanation and divine wrath, shows how rapidly he can pour a narrative through the dissolutions and resolutions of his form, and how he points up the drama by the centering or the enjambment of key words : "ubriss" (assaulted) at the beginning of line 8; "o Lokros," the aggressor, in the middle of line 8; "gorgopin" (grim-eyed) at the beginning of line 10; "d'aixe" (darted) at the beginning of line 12; "'aipse" (suddenly) at the beginning of line 13. This is a poetry of action and of large psychic forces, some of which take over whole stanzas:

$$\breve{} \ -$$
. . . exon
(having)

$$- \ \breve{} \ \breve{} \ - \ \ \breve{} \ -$$
. . . Pallados, a theon
(of Pallas, she of the gods)

$$- \ - \ \breve{} \ \ \ - \ \breve{} \ - \ \breve{} \ \ - \ -$$
thnatoisi theosulaisi panton
(to mortals sacrilegious of all)

$$- \ \breve{} \ \breve{} - \ \ \breve{} \ \breve{} \ - \ \ \ \breve{} \ \ - \ -$$
pikrotata makaron pephuke
(harshest   of the blessed is)

*

— — ˘ — — — — ˘ — ˘ —
kherressi d'amphoin parthenikan elon
(with hands both the maiden seizing)

— — ˘ — ˘ — ˘ — — ˘—
semnoi   parestakoisan   agalmati
(holy   standing beside   image)

— — ˘ — ˘ — ˘ — —
ubriss' o Lokros oud' edeise
(assaulted he the Lokrian nor did he fear)

— ˘ ˘— — ˘ ˘ — ˘ — —
paida   Dios polemo doterran
(the child of Zeus of war the giver)

*

— — ˘ — ˘ — ˘ ˘ — — ˘ —
gorgopin. a de deinon up' ophrusin
(grim-eyed. She then terribly under brows)

— — ˘— — — ˘ ˘ — ˘ —
eiden pelidnotheisa, kat oinopa
(looked being livid,   over the wine-dark)

— ˘ — ˘ — ˘ — —
d'aixe ponton, ek d' aphantois
(darted   sea,   dark)

— ˘ ˘ — ˘ ˘ — ˘— —
aips' anemon ekuka thuellais . . .
(suddenly of winds stirred hurricanes)

[. . . of Pallas, who of all the blessed gods is harshest to sacrilegious mortals.// With both hands seizing the maiden as she stood beside the holy image, the Locrian [Ajax] did her violence, and feared not the Daughter of Zeus, the Giver of War, // grim-eyed: but she, with dreadful frown, with anger livid, darted over the wine-dark sea and stirred black hurricanes of wind. Translation, Denys Page, 1955.]

Six centuries after Alcaeus, in 23 B.C.E., Horace published his first three books of odes, and staked his immortality (in Ode III, 30) on having introduced Aeolic song, the sapphic and alcaic stanzas, to Latin. Alcaeus in particular seems woven into his psyche. Not only does Horace use the stanza in two-thirds of his odes, but in poem after poem he celebrates Alcaeus as master musician, lover, and patriot. For a poem whose transitions in scene, scale, and feeling rival Alcaeus, we could look at 1, 9, especially in James Michie's English alcaics, which substitute English stress accent for Latin vowel length to keep the choriambic,

iambic, dactylic progression. The poem sweeps the viewer from vast, in-
human, mountainous snow-fields to a dark, erotic corner where a ring
is coaxed from a finger:

> And fields, and soft, low laughter that gives away
> The girl who plays love's games in a hiding-place—
>   Off comes a ring coaxed down an arm or
>   Pulled from a faintly resisting finger.
>
>   James Michie, 1964

The English Renaissance could be defined, in miniature, by its battles
over the imposition of classical quantitative meters upon the native ac-
centual-syllabic system, and by the increasing awareness of poets like
Sidney, the Countess of Pembroke, Spenser, and Daniel, and of theorists
like Puttenham, of what could be wrought *within* the native system.
Temperatures ran high on both sides (the classicists versus the nativists,
we could call them), and matters were not improved by the confusing but
common use in English of *accent* to mean both stress and vowel length,
and by the use of *Ryme* to mean both homophonous sound and accen-
tual rhythm (*rhyme* and *rhythm* both deriving from the Greek *ruthmos*).
Roger Ascham was not alone in lamenting the "barbarous and rude
Ryming" of English verse that clanged along with no respect for quan-
tity: "But now, when men know the difference, and have the example,
both of the best and of the worst, surelie to follow rather the *Gothes* in
Ryming than the *Greekes* in trew versifying were even to eate ackornes
with swyne, when we may freely eate wheate bread emonges men."[1]

Poets were experimenting with both acorns and wheat. In 1580,
Gabriel Harvey published his correspondence with Spenser on the sub-
ject of "our new famous enterprise for the Exchanging of Barbarous and
Balductum Rymes with Artificial Verse."[2] In the letters, Spenser wonders
how the Latin rules for syllable length (a vowel can be "naturally" long
or "long by position" when followed by two consonants) can be made
to assort with the audible reality of English stress (a phenomenon for
which there existed, as yet, no vocabulary). He complained, "For the
onely, or chiefest hardnesse, whych seemeth, is in the Accente [syllable
length]: whyche sometime gapeth, and as it were yawneth illfavouredly,
comming short of that it should, and sometime exceeding the measure of
the Number, as in *Carpenter,* the middle sillable being used short in
speache, when it shall be read long in Verse, seemeth like a lame Gosling,
that draweth one legge after hir."[3] Harvey, in spite of his classical zeal,
will not admit the deformation of stress in the pronunciation of "cár-
penter" by emphasis on classical quantity ("carpēnter"), though as in
Latin they could have coexisted ("cárpēnter"): "In good sooth . . . you

shall never have my subscription or consent . . . to make your *Carpēnter* our *Carpĕnter,* an inche longer, or bigger, than God and his Englishe people have made him."[4]

And so the affair went, stress in practice holding sway over merely theoretical quantity. In the quantitative experiments in Sidney's *Old Arcadia* and in the psalms he and his sister, the Countess of Pembroke, translated, "Latin" syllable length can be worked out abstractly by marking dipthongs, "naturally" long vowels, and vowels lengthened by double consonants; but the real rhythm of the poems, as in Campion's quantitative verse, derives from stress patterns laid over the pattern of quantity. The drama of faith in the Countess of Pembroke's Psalm 120, which may be the first alcaic poem in English, finds expression in her accentual alcaics, in which each quatrain must struggle anew through its instability to a dactylic conclusion:

> As to th'Eternall often in anguishes
> Erst have I called, never unanswered,
> Againe I call, againe I calling
> Doubt not againe to receave an answer.

After the Countess of Pembroke, not many English poets have been seduced by the alcaic. No English poet in the nineteenth century took it up with the authority of Hölderlin, who reinvigorated the form he had inherited from Klopstock. The few English exhibits stand out more as oddities than as achieved poems; Tennyson's address to Milton ("Alcaics") and Arthur Hugh Clough's "Alcaics" betray more strain than grace, and Blake's youthfully uneven pentameters in "To the Evening Star" and "To Morning" don a more erudite unevenness in their "translation" by Robert Bridges into the alcaic "Evening" and "Song" (from the chorus in *Demeter).*

It is not until Auden that the alcaic finds a real home in English after leaving the shelter of the Countess of Pembroke. Oddly enough— and the oddness bears the stamp of modernity—Auden used this lyric measure to *contradict* song. For this poet who composed songs and libretti, the problem was "not how to write in iambics but how not to write in them from automatic habit."[5] His taking up of the alcaic coincided with the period of his coming to terms with Marianne Moore's unmelodic syllabics. If the alcaic formalized the Horatian stance of a poet who appeared central to his age, it also gave him a shape for what we might call the "talking ode," a form invoking song but performing as speech and argument.[6]

In Auden's first alcaic poem, "Crisis" (called "They" in the *Collected Poems*) from April 1939, the sinister dream material sits rather inertly within the stanzas, syntactic units for the most part boxed in by line, and the alcaic's potential for expressive disturbance still unrealized. He brought the form to fulfillment only a few months later in "In Memory of Sigmund Freud." The prose rhythms twine down through the uneven quatrains, registering key shifts in thought, and resisting, while acknowledging, the lyric's undersong: subtle iambic/trochaic/anapestic lines, through which the Greek measure is, at moments, dimly audible (as in the dactylic "Puzzled and jealous about our dying"). As Freud's contribution was to disenchant and thereby to free, so Auden's elegy disenchants its alcaic predecessors through a rhetoric not easily scannable in quantitative or in accentual-syllabic feet in lines such as "a set mask of rectitude or an." But as the poem celebrates, finally, Freud's redemption of dream, it also allows a metrical spell to emerge: the play of spondee, iambs, anapests, and trochees in the last stanza establishes an authoritative order in the ear:

> One rational voice is dumb. Over his grave
> the household of Impulse mourns one dearly loved:
>   sad is Eros, builder of cities,
>   and weeping, anarchic Aphrodite.

Auden opened possibilities that later poets gratefully seized. John Hollander's "Off Marblehead" and "On the Sand Bar" relish the choriambic/iambic/dactylic progression of the original stanza, and remember Alcaeus's poems of ships in ambiguously allegorical storms. For Hollander, the allegory is textual: "Off Marblehead" begins in "a woeful silence" and ends in a "desperate stretch of unending dark," having tried to chart in its course a reading of meter from the natural world that constantly teases and eludes the imagination.

Two recent accentual-syllabic alcaics in English, Alfred Corn's "Somerset Alcaics" and Marilyn Hacker's "Going Back to the River," not only enjoy fairly strict versions of Alcaeus's cola (except for Corn's first line with its two extra syllables), but seem knowingly, if obliquely, to invoke Alcaeus as ancestral exile. Both poems concern distance from home and a troubled, imaginary return. Modernity itself is a state of exile from literary origins, and a stanza may be the only tent a poet can pitch in a shiftless world. Marilyn Hacker might be addressing Alcaeus as she concludes her poem of multiply exposed estrangements:

Life's not forever, love is precarious.
Wherever I live, let me come home to you
    as you are, I as I am, where you
        meet me and walk with me to the river.

MARY SIDNEY, COUNTESS OF PEMBROKE

Psalm 120

As to th'Eternall often in anguishes
Erst have I called, never unanswered,
Againe I call, againe I calling
Doubt not againe to receave an answer.

Lord ridd my soule from treasonous eloquence
Of filthy forgers craftily fraudulent;
And from the tongue where lodg'd resideth
Poison'd abuse, ruine of beleevers.

Thou that reposest vainly thy confidence
In wily wronging; say by thy forgery
What good to thee? what game redoundeth?
What benefitt from a tongue deceitfull?

Though like an arrow strongly delivered
It deeply pierce, though like to a Juniper
It coales do cast which, quickly fired,
Flame very hott, very hardly quenching?

Ah God! Too long heere wander I banished,
Too long abiding barbarous injury;
With Kedar and with Mesech harbour'd,
How? in a tent, in a howsless harbour.

Too long, alas, too long have I dwelled here
With frendly peaces furious enemies:
Who when to peace I seeke to call them,
Faster I find to the warre they arme them.

        Composed early 1590s

ALFRED, LORD TENNYSON

Alcaics

O mighty-mouth'd inventor of harmonies,
O skill'd to sing of Time or Eternity,
    God-gifted organ-voice of England,
        Milton, a name to resound for ages;
Whose Titan angels, Gabriel, Abdiel,
Starr'd from Jehovah's gorgeous armouries,
    Tower, as the deep-domed empyrëan
        Rings to the roar of an angel onset—
Me rather all that bowery loneliness,
The brooks of Eden mazily murmuring,
    And bloom profuse and cedar arches
        Charm, as a wanderer out in ocean,
Where some refulgent sunset of India
Streams o'er a rich ambrosial ocean isle,
    And crimson-hued the stately palm-woods
        Whisper in odorous heights of even.

Composed 1863

ROBERT BRIDGES

Song

From Chorus in *Demeter*

Lo where the virgin veilëd in airy beams,
All-holy Morn, in splendor awakening,
    Heav'n's gate hath unbarrèd, the golden
        Aerial latices set open.

With music endeth night's prisoning terror,
With flow'ry incense: Haste to salute the sun,
    That for the day's chase, like a huntsman,
        With flashing arms cometh o'er the mountain.

1914

Evening

From William Blake

Come, rosy angel, thy coronet donning
Of starry jewels, smile upon ev'ry bed,
        And grant what each day-weary mortal
            Labourer or lover, asketh of thee.

Smile thou on our loves, enveloping the land
With dusky curtain: consider each blossom
        That timely upcloseth, that opens
            Her treasure of heavy-laden odours.

Now, while the west-wind slumbereth on the lake,
Silently dost thou with delicate shimmer
        O'erbloom the frowning front of awful
            Night to a glance of unearthly silver.

No hungry wild beast rangeth in our forest,
No tiger or wolf prowleth around the fold:
        Keep thou from our sheepcotes the tainting
            Invisible peril of darkness.

1914

NOTES

1. *The Scholemaster,* posthumously published in 1570; quoted in Derek Attridge, *Well-Weigh'd Syllables: Elizabethan Verse in Classical Metres* (London: Cambridge University Press, 1974), 93.

2. Edmund Spenser, ed. J. C. Smith and E. de Selincourt, *Poetical Works* (Oxford: Oxford University Press, 1912; rpt. 1975), 623.

3. Spenser, *Poetical Works,* 611.

4. Spenser, *Poetical Works,* 630.

5. W. H. Auden, *The Dyer's Hand* (New York: Vintage, 1968), 47.

6. Auden's remarks on the relation of speech to poetic language bear pertinently on that counterpoint as played out in his alcaics: "The English-speaking peoples have always felt that the difference between poetic speech and the conversational speech of everyday should be kept small, and, whenever English poets have felt that the gap between poetic and ordinary speech was growing too wide, there has been a stylistic revolution to bring them closer again." See *The Dyer's Hand,* 24.

Off the Main Road: Some
Maverick Meters

JOHN FREDERICK NIMS

Since we live in a universe of rhythms, ideas for the meters of poetry might turn up anywhere as they did for Stravinsky, eye and ear fascinated by a windshield wiper on a rainy day. In primitive times the heartbeat was suspected to be the basis of the rhythms of every art. Breathing, walking, rowing the boat, rocking the cradle, all and more such movements might have encouraged the urgency of rhythm in what we say and write. And there is poetry itself, centuries, millennia of it, meters now lost so long that their revival would seem a revelation.

Our own poetry, when not formless, is in part accentual, in part syllabic. Since the poetry of classical Greece and Rome is neither, we might find in it something to freshen up our prosody. That their rhythms are based on length of syllable rather than accent is no use to us. We know about length, we know "hit" from "height," and use length when expressive. But we also know that our ear is not sensitive enough to it to feel a rhythm in a sequence of syllables long and short, as we clearly hear it in a sequence of accents.

But perhaps we could take over from Greek and Latin some of the formations they gave their syllables. Since neither spondee nor pyrrhic can make a meter in itself, the basic arrangements of our heavily accented English are few: probably no more than iambic, anapestic, and their mirror images. We have no basic units (*feet* we call them, as they stamp out the music) longer than three syllables. The older languages have many.

There is, for example, the four-syllable foot called *ionic a minore*, which is basically ˘ ˘ ¯ ¯, though variations are permitted. Years ago, while reading the *Bacchae* of Euripides, in which that ionic foot is the thematic figure of the choruses, I wondered if such a unit would be viable in English. Though we don't recognize it as a "foot," it is common in spoken English: "on the next train," "in a pig's eye," etc. And common as a substitute for iambs, as in Shakespeare's

$\smile$ $\smile$ $-$ $-$
Let Rome in Tiber melt, and the wide arch
$\smile$ $\smile$ $-$
Of the ranged empire fall . . .

(I will not take up the question here of whether a slight tilt of accent to-ward one of the two words of the spondee disqualifies it as spondee.)

I could not think of any poems in English whose basic meter was *ionic a minore*. It seemed worth trying. The title of my poem alludes to the meter itself, though I imagined it would suggest something like "the young Greek girl." The poem starts with two ionics:

$-$ $-$ $-$ $-$
If you could come on the late train

and continues in that rhythm. But it is not a metrical exercise; it's a poem about love and loss, driven not by its meter but by the urgency of its emotion. Meter is not the locomotive, as Pound suggested, it's only the rails on which it runs.

The Young Ionia

If you could come on the late train for
    The same walk
Or a hushed talk by the fireplace
    When the ash flares
As a heart could (if a heart would) to
    Recall you,
To recall all in a long
    Look, to enwrap you
As it once had when the rain streamed on the
    Fall air,
And we knew, then, it was all wrong,
    It was love lost
And a year lost of the few years we
    Account most—
But the bough blew and the cloud
    Blew and the sky fell
From its rose ledge on the wood's rim to
    The wan brook,
And the clock read to the half-dead
    A profound page
As the cloud broke and the moon spoke and the
    Door shook—

If you could come, and it meant come at the
      Steep price
We regret yet as the debt swells
      In the nighttime
And the *could come, if you could* hum in
      The skull's drum
And the limbs writhe till the bed
      Cries like a hurt thing—
If you could—ah but the moon's dead and the
      Clock's dead.
For we know now: we can give all
      But it won't do,
Not the day's length nor the black strength nor
      The blood's flush.
What we took once for a sure thing,
      For delight's right,
For the clear eve with its wild star in
      The sunset,
We would have back at the old
      Cost, at the old grief
And we beg love for the same pain—for a
      Last chance!
Then the god turns with a low
      Laugh (as the leaves hush)
But the eyes ice and there's no twice: the
      Benign gaze
Upon some woe but on ours no.
      And the leaves rush.

1954

Love and loss. Years later, browsing through a book on Greek meter, I read that *ionic a minore* was "the measure of passionate lamentation, of tearful sighs and groans." George Thomson, who wrote those words in his *Greek Lyric Metre*, gives half a dozen examples of its use, one a fragment of a poem by Sappho herself, 140 (a), in which worshippers of Aphrodite ask what they should do now that Adonis is dying. We might wonder whether this metrical unit, its second half heavily weighted, has indeed a synesthetic relationship with grief.

    Some affinities between meter and mood seem more than subjective. Many years after writing "The Young Ionia," I worked with what I took to be a meter keyed to the theme it dealt with. The meter itself had been in my head for years, as if waiting for the right theme to come along.

Called *galliambic,* after the Galli, or frenzied priests of Cybele, it felt like nothing in our more sober English prosody; one can see why it was thought to express the orgiastic dance of those priests:

$$\smile\ \smile\ -\ \smile\ \mid\ -\ \smile\ -\ \breve{-}\ \parallel\ \smile\ \smile\ -\ \smile\ \smile\ \mid\ \smile\ \smile\ \breve{-}$$

This wild meter is best known for the use Catullus made of it in his ninety-three-line "Attis," the story of the Phrygian counterpart of Adonis who, in a fit of religious mania, castrates himself—and lives to regret it. Almost unknown in English, the meter had been taken on by Tennyson in his "Boädicea," which he called a "far-off echo" of the Latin poem. Published with his "Experiments," it begins

   While about the shore of Mona those Neronian legionaries . . .

I long thought this was the only poem in English galliambics, until William Harmon reminded me that George Meredith had "attempted" it in his "Phaethon," which begins

   At the coming up of Phoebus, the all-luminous charioteer . . .

In both of these versions we feel the swing of the Catullan original:

      Super alta uectus Attis celeri rate maria . . .

To make sure I had some control over the maverick meter, I first translated the Latin poem:

   Over oceans sped he, Attis, in the speediest of the ships . . .

   The poem I had in mind was about Niagara; I had stood on the verge of it more than once, fascinated by its powerful sweep toward the brink and its abrupt collapse in mist and foam. Obviously this stood for a good many things I had vaguely in mind. The meter seemed appropriate because of the schizophrenia of the line itself: its first half so resolute, with twice as many strong syllables as the second; its second half so flaccid, with nearly twice as many weak syllables as the first. The rhythm dramatized, I thought, irresistible power and its abrupt collapse. To increase that impression, I added an additional weak syllable at the end. The third of the four sections of "Niagara," an evocation of the exuberant multiplicity of earth as suggested by the profusion on the onrushing river, begins:

Eyes can't leave the livid seething, its reiterative *Memento!*
Reading, in this bubble chamber, stuff of the world as
    effervescence,
Reading every life as half-life, reading in foam the one
    prognosis . . .

Mac the trucker—checkered mackinaw, sort of a baseball cap
    with earflaps,
Fists to crinkle up his beer cans—here at the falls is
    philosophical:
"Down the tube. That's life"—he's waggish, nudging his cozy
    blonde—"You know, hon?"
And she knows. We all know: Nature, making a splendor of
    our banalities,
Lavishes Niagara on us, nudging our knack for the
    anagogical.

1988

Another herky-jerky line it might be fun to test in English is the choriambus, which is rather like iambs turned inside-out: $-\,\smile\,\smile\,-$. Few of us who burst out with "Son of a bitch!" realize they have just given utterance to a classic choriamb. The usual line (the x's indicating syllables that are "common," either long or short) is: x x | $-\,\smile\,\smile\,-$ | $-\,\smile\,\smile\,-$ | $-\,\smile\,\smile\,-$ | $\smile\,-$, as in my translation of a poem of Sappho's (55) about a woman of little culture.

    You though! Die and you'll lie dumb in the dirt; nobody
        care, and none
    Miss you ever again, knowing there's no rapture can stir
        your soul;
    You've no love for the Muse, none for her flowers. Even in
        hell you'll be
    Not worth anyone's glance, lost in the vague colorless
        drifting dead.

1987

(Translators of Sappho rarely show any interest in the elaborate rhythms she was devoted to.) Her choriambics proved durable: five hundred years later Horace used them in deriding superstitions that are still with us (I, xi):

    Don't ask—knowing's taboo—what's in the cards, darling,
        for you, for me,

what end heaven intends. Meddle with palm, planet, séance,
  tea leaves?
—rubbish! Shun the occult. Better by far take in your stride
  what comes.
Long life?—possible. Or—? Maybe the gods mean it your
  last, this grim
winter shaking the shore, booming the surf, wearying wave
  and rock.
Well then! Learn to be wise; out with the wine. Knowing the
  time so short,
no grand hopes, do you hear? Now, as we talk, huffishly
  time goes by.
So take hold of the day. Hugging it close. Nothing beyond
  is yours.

1987

Like sapphics and alcaics and what James Wright called "the diffi-cult, the dazzling hendecasyllabic," the elegiac couplet has become so familiar, partly through Auden's use of it in his later work, that it hardly need be mentioned here, except as an example of how one ancient meter can be revamped so as to be half hidden and yet of service. In Co-leridge's famous lines it is "described and exemplified":

> In the hexameter rises the fountain's silvery column;
>   In the pentameter aye falling in melody back.

Though called a "pentameter," the second line has always sounded to me like another hexameter with its third and sixth foot truncated to one syl-lable: "aye" and "back." One of the most popular meters of antiquity, this couplet came to be more and more associated with "elegy" itself. When, years and years ago, I was thinking about a poem on the death of a child, I wondered if I could evoke the rich associations of that ancient meter, which Goethe had revived in modern times. I didn't want the hexameter itself to show, perhaps because of its echoes of the forest primeval. I thought there was something academic in the classic look of that couplet, too like a granite slab for the dead child. Since both of its lines have a strong caesura, I broke each in two there and made an eight-line stanza out of a pair of them. The first two of the eleven stanzas of "The Evergreen" read:

> *Under this stone, what lies?*
>   A little boy's thistledown body.
> *How, on so light a child*
>   *Gravel hefted and hurled?*

Light? As a flower entwined
    In our shining arms. Heavy
Laid in this scale—it set
    Wailing the chains of the world.

What did you say? We said:
    Bedtime, dear, forever.
Time to put out the light.
    Time for the eyes to close.
What did he do? He lay
    In a crazyquilt of fever.
His hands were already like grasses.
    His cheek already a rose.

1959

That looked lighter than a four-line block of elegiac couplets. What had been the two hexameters are now connected by off-rhyme: "body . . . heavy." What had been the "pentameters" are more conclusively linked by full rhyme: "hurled . . . world." Rhyme was a way, I thought, of drawing the stanza together. For those who remember poems from *The Greek Anthology*, the opening query may recall the centuries of sorrow recorded there, and perhaps even evoke the memory of its rhythm; quite a few of the old poems open with someone asking the circumstances of an entombment. So in a way a new form has been born out of an ancient one; it is just possible the relationship may resonate throughout the poem.

I've mentioned three ways in which an ancient meter, in my experience, has proved adaptable to modern use, two of them so old they have long been out of mind and seemed a new impulse when revived in English verse. We also find, in poetry of long ago, combinations of syllables, which we might use as musical themes or figures in our work. Two such, prominent in the older poetry, are called *glyconic* and *pherecratic* after the obscure poets who used them. Arcane as these combinations sound, not a day goes by that we do not use them hundreds of times in our native English. The glyconic figure is

$$x \; x \; \overline{} \cup \cup \overline{} \cup \overset{\cup}{\overline{}}$$

as in "When's the party about to start?" or "Where the heck has Amanda gone?" Subtract the last short (unaccented) syllable from that and you have the pherecratic figure,

$$x \; x \; \overline{} \cup \cup \overline{} \overset{\cup}{\overline{}}$$

as in "We can study in Pat's room" or "Wish you'd gimme the car keys." Neither of these gives us a word order alien to everyday English, as we can see in those examples, or in my translation of a well-known poem (I, 5) of Horace, in which the third line of each strophe is pherecratic and the fourth glyconic:

> Who's that slip of a boy, lotioned and soaped, who'll urge
> Love on you in the cool grot by the rambling rose?
>   Who've you tied back your golden
>   Curls for, Pyrrha, in just your own
>
> Simple elegant way? Oh what a shock's in store
> For him! "Count on the gods? Never again!" he'll groan,
>   Gaping, out of his depth in
>   Pitch-black hurricane-swirling seas,
>
> Who now glories in you, thinking you purest gold,
> Trusts you, "Always my own! Always my one true love!"
>   Trusts you, never suspecting
>   How deceptive your summer air.
>
> Those your glitter allures, put to no proof—lost souls!
> I? Just made it to shore, hung up my storm-drenched clothes,
>   Votive gifts for the shrine of
>   Neptune, lord of the turning tide.

1994

For the curious, the first two lines are in a meter called *Fourth* (or Greater) *Asclepiadean,* also named after an obscure poet. Note the familiar choriambs we have seen in the poems by Sappho and Horace. In spite of its cumbersome name, it also can be used without strain in natural English.

Horace uses glyconic and pherecratic rhythms in separate lines; Catullus combines them in one long line in a poem (XVII) in which he expresses his outrage at a careless husband who lets his attractive young wife wander as she will. In my translation excerpted here the long line is broken, for typographical reasons, at the caesura that divides the two meters.

> O Colonia, mad to dance
>   all the length of your bridge, and
> More than ready to do so now,
>   only fearful the trembly
> Piers supporting the poor old thing's
>   salvaged rickety timbers
> Might turn turtle and, wrong side up,
>   founder deep in the marshes—
> Heaven grant you a better bridge,
>   true to specifications,

Where your Lords of the Dance, unharmed
        can cavort in their orgies,
On condition you do one thing:
        leave me doubled up, laughing,
When you collar this village fool,
        plunge him—*plunk*—in the thickest
Scummy muck underneath your bridge,
        burbling, head over heels there.
But it's got to be where the bog's
        grimmest guckiest gumbo
Stinks to heaven as nowhere else,
        livid, color of corpses.

1995

Probably the last of my riflings of classical poetry for rhythms that might seem virginal in English is in "Water Music." With Haydn's music in the background, I researched water, thought about its glorious chemical avatars, remembered how Pindar, praising what is excellent on earth, had put water first in his first of the *Olympian* Odes. Its sixteen-line first strophe did not move like any stanza I knew in English. It seemed more like the rhythm of musical prose spaced on the page as if it were poetry. When I tried to replicate its rich pattern of longs and shorts in our accented and unaccented ones, what I came up with was,

"Nothing noble as water, no,
    and there's gold with its glamor . . ."
Pindar on trumpet—First
    feisty Olympian Ode to the horseman,
Daring us, across the years:
Look to excellence only.
Water, you're pure wonder! here's
February, and on the pane your
    frost in grisaille show how you flowered
    all last summer; it
Stencils clover, witchgrass, mullein
    meadow; between boskage gleam
Shores of Lake Michigan, her snow pagoda, junks of ice.
Farther off, spray and breaker, and your clouds
That hush color to a shadow as they pass,
While snowflakes—just a few—go moseying

Around . . . over . . .

1988

In it were some of the figures illustrated above: glyconics, mixed dactyls and trochees, but also runs of as many as seven short syllables together (impossible to duplicate in English). My poem was constructed on what I called a "Pindaric grid"—perhaps more likely to appeal to architects or puzzle-solvers than to poets today. There were six such long strophes to be written, each pair of them followed by an antistrophe that had a different but similar metrical pattern. The concluding antistrophe, after much airy and watery imagery, came back to earth with a mention of the time when, seeing the lawn white with hail, we had scooped up handfuls for a celestial highball, scotch and hail.

> that rickety pier
> Once! your shoulders bubbling moonlight as you swam
> And then—spirit of water, lithe—gleamed bare
>
> > As moon on the pier, hair swirled back,
> >   laughing at me, "Last one in. . . !" Prismatic girl
> > (Like those glorified trans-
> >   lunar dancers that Dante saw)
> > Sprinkling me with chill lake's
> >   mischievous fire. Now the tears
> > Are like fire to think . . . think . . . what I've thought and
> >   thought.
> >   But safer to think small:
> > Summer thunder, hail on the lawn;
> >   cuddling scotch-and-hail,
> > We blessed it as "heaven-sent!"
> >   Mostly water is.
> > Pray that it keep us. Our blue globe in space.
> > Our grand loves. Our least ones—like this spindly rose
> >   rambling on Pindar's lattice.

Most of the poems I have cited here, particularly this last one, are the kind one wants to do only once in a lifetime. But that once may be enough. With centuries of literature and the world around us abounding in forms, why confine ourselves to the few in fashion?

II

Stanzas

"The Bravest Sort of Verses":
The Heroic Couplet
TIMOTHY STEELE

Poets in English have employed the heroic couplet, which consists of a pair of rhyming iambic pentameters, more frequently and variously than any other traditional rhymed form. Poets have used the couplet for lyrical, epigrammatic, elegiac, dramatic, epistolary, satirical, narrative, and even, on occasion, heroic (i.e., epic) verse. They have written couplet poems in which each two-line unit is balanced and self-contained; they have composed poems in which the couplets run on in long periods over line endings in the manner of Miltonic blank verse. And we can best appreciate the versatility of the heroic couplet, and the resources it offers to poets today, by examining its history.

Though its lineage can be traced back to the ancient elegiac distich, the heroic couplet is an invention of Anglo-Norman literature and debuts in English in Geoffrey Chaucer's *Legend of Good Women.* Intermittently in this poem, and consistently in *The Canterbury Tales,* Chaucer's couplets move swiftly back and forth between action and meditation, dialogue and narrative. Chaucer fluidly modulates his pentameters, letting the caesuras float to different positions in the line and allowing the rhymes to guide the verse without disrupting its flow, as in the following description of hunters on horseback:

The herde of hertës* founden is anon,	*deer
With "Hay! Go bet! Pryke thow! Lat gon,	*Hurry, use
lat gon!*	your spurs,
Why nyl the leoun comen, or the berë,	release the dogs
That I myghte onës* mete hym with this	
sperë?"	*once
Thus seyn these yongë folk and up they	
kyllë	
These bestës wilde, and han hem at here	*have them at
willë.*	their mercy

The Legend of Good Women, F "Dido," ll. 1212–17

While there are fine passages in such fifteenth-century heroic-couplet poems as John Lydgate's *Troy Book,* the form suffers, as does the decasyllabic line in general, from the linguistic and metrical confusions that mark the transition from Middle to modern English; and only in the second half of the sixteenth century does the couplet recover its bearings. Christopher Marlowe's *Hero and Leander* is the earliest masterpiece in heroic couplets in modern English, though the poet died before finishing this work and though George Chapman's completion of it is weak. In addition to displaying a Chaucerian gift for narrative, Marlowe sometimes points his couplets aphoristically, in a manner that looks forward to the work of John Dryden, Katherine Philips, and Alexander Pope:

> It lies not in our power to love or hate,
> For will in us is over-ruled by fate. . . .
> Where both deliberate, the love is slight;
> Who ever loved, that loved not at first sight?
> *Hero and Leander,* ll 167–68, 175–76

In the verse of John Donne and Ben Jonson, the modern heroic couplet comes of age, and Jonson not only practices the form dexterously but also provides it with an acute theoretical defense. During his visit to William Drummond in Scotland, Jonson discusses his (now lost) treatise on prosody, in which, according to Drummond, "he proves couplets to be the bravest sort of verses, especially when they are broken, like hexameters; and that cross-rhymes and stanzas—because the purpose would lead him beyond eight lines to conclude—were all forced."[1] Though one-sided, this observation summarizes the key advantage of the heroic couplet vis-à-vis other rhymed forms. Even skillfully deployed, stanzas may force poets either to curtail their argument or pad it out to fill the strophic arrangement. In contrast, the couplet can flow more freely—the rhyme shaping the phrasing without obliging it to continue for, or cease after, a fixed number of lines.

This fusion of mobility and structure is evident in Jonson's three beautiful middle-length poems in heroic couplets, "To draw no envy, Shakespeare, on thy name," "Inviting a Friend to Supper," and "To Penshurst." A passage from the last named of these appears below. Penshurst was the country house of the Sidney family, and Jonson admired it not only for the modest utility of its design and the fruitfulness of its gardens and grounds, but also for the hospitality of its inhabitants, who kept their doors open to all people regardless of social class and who maintained the house so that it served rather than burdened the community around it. (Here "clown" means "a rustic." That Jonson indents the second lines of his couplets indicates that he here associates the form with the ancient elegiac distich, whose second line, a dactylic pentameter, was customarily written or printed a little ways inward from its first line, a dactylic hexameter.)

> And though thy walls be of the country stone
>> They're rear'd with no man's ruin, no man's groan,
> There's none, that dwell about them, wish them down;
>> But all come in, the farmer, and the clown:
> And no one empty-handed, to salute
>> Thy lord, and lady, though they have no suit.
>
> (ll. 45–50)

An appealing feature of Jonson's couplets is that they engage their subject sincerely, but without flourishes. Though the lines are firmly managed—with a careful and varied placement of pauses and with frequent but controlled enjambments—nothing is sacrificed to merely melodic or rhetorical effect. Each detail is given due attention and, if need be, due qualification.

The Augustan Age, with its concern for symmetry and decorum, favors the closed couplet with which many readers today identify the form. Because of its concentration, the closed couplet is capable of both epigrammatic brilliance,

> True wit is nature to advantage dressed,
> What oft was thought, but ne'er so well expressed.
>> Alexander Pope, *An Essay on Criticism*, ll. 297–98

> The danger chiefly lies in acting well;
> No crime's so great as daring to excel.
>> Charles Churchill, *Epistle to William Hogarth*, ll. 51–52

and forceful moral analysis:

> Ill fares the land, to hastening ills a prey,
> Where wealth accumulates, and men decay;
> Princes and lords may flourish, or may fade;
> A breath can make them, as a breath has made;
> But a bold peasantry, their country's pride,
> When once destroyed, can never be supplied.
>> Oliver Goldsmith, *The Deserted Village*, ll. 51–56

However, the limitations of the closed couplet are nearly as great as its strengths. Its modulatory range is fairly narrow, and in it the part sometimes undermines the whole. So far as each couplet stands on its own, argument slows, and logical or narrative progression flags.

With Dryden's translation of Virgil's *Aeneid* and Pope's translation of Homer's *Iliad*, the pentameter couplet becomes "heroic," though *heroic couplet* is actually a relatively recent coinage. To be sure, from the sixteenth century onward, the pentameter is often characterized as "heroic"; yet the *Oxford English Dictionary* has no entry for "heroic couplet," and the unabridged second edition of *The Random House Dictionary of the English Language* reports that the phrase gained currency only in 1900–1905. (This date, however, evidently errs on the side of lateness, since Walter William Skeat, in his 1894 edition of *The Legend of Good Women*, says of the meter of Chaucer's poem: "he introduces a new metre, previously unknown to English writers, but now famous as 'the heroic couplet.'") Further, the adjective *heroic* has really never suited the couplet specifically, any more than it has suited the iambic pentameter generally. Modern-language verse forms do not imply a particular *ethos*—a particular character or disposition—in the way that ancient ones did. The pentameter has proved useful for epics for the same reason that it has been useful for other genres. It is long enough to accommodate a virtually limitless range of modulation, yet not so long that it lumbers or regularly breaks down into shorter rhythmical segments, as the English hexameter and heptameter tend to do. And Dryden's *Aeneid* and Pope's *Iliad* notwithstanding, English epic is no way tied to the pentameter couplet, but finds expression as well in more elaborately rhymed stanzas (e.g., Spenser's *Faerie Queene*) and in blank verse (e.g., Milton's *Paradise Lost*). For that matter, even with respect to Dryden and Pope, we are more likely to associate the heroic couplet with their satiric or mock-epic poems like *MacFlecknoe* and *The Rape of the Lock* than with their translations of epic.

Contrary to what is sometimes said, the Romantics and Victorians produced a substantial body work in heroic couplets, though nineteenth-century poets largely preferred such forms as the sonnet, the ballad, and blank verse. Interesting Romantic heroic-couplet poems include Wordsworth's "Evening Walk," Byron's *English Bards and Scotch Reviewers,* Keats's *Endymion* and *Lamia,* and John Clare's wonderful couplet poems about birds and birdnests. Of the great Victorians, the most notable practitioner of the heroic couplet is Robert Browning, who often runs the pentameters over the line and couplet endings. The opening lines of "My Last Duchess" illustrate his technique.

That's my last Duchess painted on the wall,
Looking as if she were alive. I call
That piece a wonder, now: Frà Pandolf's hands
Worked busily a day, and there she stands.
Will 't please you sit and look at her? I said
"Frà Pandolf" by design, for never read
Strangers like you that pictured countenance,
The depth and passion of its earnest glance,
But to myself they turned (since none puts by
The curtain I have drawn for you, but I)
And seemed as they would ask me, if they durst,
How such a glance came there; so, not the first
Are you to turn and ask thus.

Though Browning's enjambments may initially appear haphazard, he carefully correlates them with meaning. "Frà Pandolf's hands / Worked busily a day," gives the sense of the activity of the artist. The runover of "since none puts by / The curtain I have drawn" communicates the way the count has pulled open the drape to reveal his wife's picture (and is now gradually uncovering the picture of his tyrannical treatment of her). Similarly, the enjambment, "not the first / Are you to turn and ask thus," reinforces the image of the duke's companion, who has just shifted his eyes, in uneasy query, from the picture to the duke.

Though the heroic couplet is not nearly as widespread in the twentieth century as it was in earlier centuries, the later period features as many masterpieces in the form as any other age. Outstanding poems in the frequently enjambed couplet include Robert Bridges's "Elegy: The Summer House on the Mound" and Yvor Winters's "The Slow Pacific Swell." Equally fine, but more regularly observant of the couplet unit, are William Butler Yeats's "Adam's Curse" and "The Folly of Being Comforted." Robert Frost's excellent poems in heroic couplets are too numerous to list, but we should mention his "Tuft of Flowers," "Our Singing Strength," "A Winter Eden," "The Egg and the Machine," "The Armful," "The Figure in the Doorway," and "A Young Birch," as well as such heroic-couplet sonnets as "Into My Own" and "Once by the Pacific." J. V. Cunningham frequently uses the heroic couplet for his memorable epigrams. Frances Cornford employs it in her fine descriptive verse about Cambridgeshire, as does Helen Pinkerton in some of her best devotional poems, including "The Gift" and "The Romantic Eros." Thom Gunn has composed powerful poems about the AIDS epidemic—"To a Friend in Time of Trouble," "Lament," and "Courtesies of the

Interregnum"—in heroic couplets. Edgar Bowers in "Wandering" and Robert Lowell in "Between the Porch and the Altar" have written remarkable poem-sequences in the form. The poems by X. J. Kennedy and Dick Davis cited in the selection section of this entry illustrate additional and superb examples of contemporary heroic couplets. And in addition to writing such exceptional heroic-couplet poems as "Transit," Richard Wilbur, in his translations of Molière's major comedies, has provided the English stage with wonderfully fresh and actable dramatic heroic-couplet verse.

So far as my feelings are concerned, I like the heroic couplet because it is so elegant and unfussy. Since rhyme calls attention to the line ending, I prefer not to enjamb unless it enhances meaning. However, I am no devotee of the closed couplet; and if I generally conclude lines at phrase and clause endings, I like to extend sentence structure from one couplet to another, in the manner of poets like Chaucer and Frost. This procedure, I believe, allows the poet liberty of syntax, without sacrificing the focusing power of the couplet unit. On the one occasion when I wrote a longish poem in heroic couplets, I tried to establish a context to allow running on the line with some frequency: because of the length of the poem, I felt it was imperative to maintain a forward-moving energy and avoid clunkiness. And in this poem, which was entitled "Near Olympic" and which described the neighborhood in Los Angeles in which my wife and I were living, I was attempting to do the sort of thing that Jonson did in "To Penshurst." By means of the couplet, I wished to render the sense of a place in all its vivid multiplicity, yet at the same time to give that multiplicity the stability and preservative power of the couplet.

Loving stanzaic verse, the sonnet, and blank verse, I do not wish to suggest that the couplet is better than other forms. But it is a great pleasure to write in it and a great pleasure to read fine poems written in it. The heroic couplet has been delightfully and vitally with us for six hundred years. May it be with our descendants for another six hundred![2]

ANNE BRADSTREET (C. 1612–72)

Before the Birth of One of Her Children

All things within this fading world hath end,
Adversity doth still* our joys attend;   *always
No ties so strong, no friends so dear and sweet,
But with death's parting blow is sure to meet.
The sentence past is most irrevocable,

A common thing, yet oh, inevitable.
How soon, my Dear,* death may my steps   *the poet's
   attend,   husband
How soon't may be thy lot to lose thy friend,
We both are ignorant, yet love bids me
These farewell lines to recommend to thee,
That when that knot's untied that made us one,
I may seem thine, who in effect am none.
And if I see not half my days that's due,
What nature would, God grant to yours
   and you;
The many faults that well you know I have
Let be interred in my oblivious grave;
If any worth or virtue were in me,
Let that live freshly in thy memory.
And when thou feel'st no grief, as I no harms,
Yet love thy dead, who long lay in thine arms.
And when thy loss shall be repaid with gains
Look to my little babes, my dear remains.
And if thou love thyself, or loved'st me,
These O protect from step-dame's injury.
And if chance to thine eyes shall bring this
   verse,
With some sad sighs honour my absent hearse;
And kiss this paper for thy love's dear sake,
Who with salt tears this last farewell did take.

MARY WORTLEY MONTAGU (1689–1762)

Summary of Lord Lyttelton's *Advice to a Lady*

Be plain in dress and sober in your diet;
In short, my deary, kiss me, and be quiet.

JOHN CLARE (1793–1864)

Field Path

The beans in blossom with their spots of jet
Smelt sweet as gardens wheresoever met;
The level meadow grass was in the swath;
The hedge briar rose hung right across the path,
White over with its flowers—the grass that lay
Bleaching beneath the twittering heat to hay
Smelt so deliciously, the puzzled bee
Went wondering where the honeyed sweets could be;
And passer-by along the level rows
Stooped down and whipt a bit beneath his nose.

X. J. KENNEDY (1929–)

Old Men Pitching Horseshoes

Back in a yard where ringers groove a ditch,
These four in shirtsleeves congregate to pitch
Dirt-burnished iron. With appraising eye,
One sizes up a peg, hoists and lets fly—
A clang resounds as though a smith had struck
Fire from a forge. His first blow, out of luck,
Rattles in circles. Hitching up his face,
He swings, and weight once more inhabits space,
Tumbles as gently as a new-laid egg.
Extended iron arms surround their peg
Like one come home to greet a long-lost brother.
Shouts from one outpost. Mutters from the other.

Now changing sides, each withered pitcher moves
As his considered dignity behooves
Down the worn path of earth where August flies
And sheaves of air in warm distortions rise,
To stand ground, fling, kick dust with all the force
Of shoes still hammered to a living horse.

DICK DAVIS (1945–)

Into Care

Here is a scene from forty years ago:
A skinny, snivelling child of three or so

Sits on a table, naked and shamefaced.
A woman dabs his body to the waist

With yellow pungent ointment and he feels
Her shock as she remarks, "Look at the weals

On this boy's back." Her colleague steps across:
Gently she touches him. He's at a loss

To think what kind of "wheels" she sees, but knows
That here at least there will be no more blows.

NOTES

1. Notes of Ben Jonson's *Conversations with William Drummond of Hawthornden, January M.DC.XIX* (London: Printed for the Shakespeare Society, 1842), 5–8.
2. The best way to learn about the heroic couplet is to read good poems that embody the form. But there are as well a number of helpful critical studies, the most comprehensive of which is William Bowman Piper, *The Heroic Couplet* (Cleveland: Press of Case Western Reserve University, 1969).

The Self-Engendering Muse:
Terza Rima

FELIX STEFANILE

In Italian *terza rima* means third rhyme. This term specifies the completion of a rhyme scheme based upon the number three. You will note, in the opening six lines of Dante's *Divine Comedy,* the masterwork of terza rima, that rhyme *b,* the middle rhyme of the first tercet, becomes the third rhyme of the second tercet, and closes the thought unit.

At the mid-point of our life's passage I	a
Came to myself inside a gloomy wood	b
With not a trail in sight to reckon by.	a
What happened is hard telling, if I could,	b
Trees thick and snag-and-tangle, height and breadth,	c
The thought brings back the fear I had withstood.[1]	b

The same ratcheting device occurs in the next six lines of the poem. Note how middle rhyme *d* of the first tercet here becomes the concluding rhyme of the following tercet.

To say still more about it would be death;	c
Yet, for the benefit that I found there,	d
I'll tell of other things I came back with.	c
The way I got there I cannot make clear,	d
So dazed I was, but at a certain turn	e
I gave up all my bearing to the air.	d

With the exception of rhyme *a,* which is the "On" switch of a poem in terza rima, and rhyme *z,* the "Off" switch of a paradigm poem in this form, the third rhyme is the gear that drives a composition using this scheme: *aba bcb cdc ded efe . . . yzy z.* Dante's *Divine Comedy* is made up of over 13,500 lines in this order, and each canto of his epic is closed off with rhyme *z.*

Of course, all of the rhymes of terza rima, excluding rhymes *a* and *z,* are third rhymes. It is this combinatorial medley of effects, rhymes surging forward and overlapping at the same time, and the cognitive re-arrangement of the six-line frame in which a set of rhymes do their work, that gives to terza rima its unique continuity. The continuity is accompanied, however, by a sense of expectancy, for the rhyme that intrudes as a middle rhyme in one tercet is then foregrounded in the tercet that follows, and *then* disappears. Echo becomes semantic freight in a poem of this kind. Dante seems to have been aware of this added quality of echo, for from time to time he would pick up a previous rhyme, from a few lines before, and repeat the same rhyme sound, and also—challenge of challenges for any serious poet—the same rhyme word. To borrow a term from acoustical technology, the technique of third rhyme offers surround sound.

The origin of terza rima in the twelfth or thirteenth century in Italy remains a matter of conjecture. All we know for certain is that Dante was the grand disseminator of the device. I like the theory that relates it to the influence of the sonnet, invented in Sicily in the early part of the thirteenth century. The sestet of the sonnet bears striking affinity for terza rima, especially in its most frequently used rhyme scheme of *cde cde.* Dante was steeped in classical rhetoric. This served his voracious imagination well in his poetry. He shared the medieval fascination for the symbolical potency of number. Part of this cultural thinking included the concept of the number three as signifying the Holy Trinity, six the creation of Adam, and so on. Such number clues abound in *The Divine Comedy.* It would have been a simple matter for him to devise a terza rima pattern out of the sestet of the Italian sonnet. Within a generation or so of his epic, both Boccaccio and Petrarch were writing in terza rima; and Chaucer had brought the form to England after a voyage to Italy.

We usually compose terza rima poems in iambic pentameter, our answer to the Italian eleven-syllable line. This is not a rule set in stone; in fact many poets have varied from Dante's norm, as even the brief anthology following this essay shows. In the case of Archibald MacLeish's saga, *Conquistador,* which was awarded the Pulitzer Prize in 1932, the classical rhyme scheme undergoes sequences of off-rhyme, syncopated rhyme of masculine and feminine endings, alliterative stress meter, and other tricks of the poet's trade: yet the groundbass to his music remains the terza rima score. In English, as in Italian, poets have also made use of the form as a stanza. In the selection of poems, I have offered as rich a range of adaptations of the form as space allows. In some instances I can only show excerpts of a poem, but I hope such excerpts instill aspiration, as well as inspiration.

For persons new to terza rima my advice is to be patient, in the sense that all serious poets are patient about revision. Changing the end words of such a poem, especially at the beginning or the end of the poem, will prove exasperating, and challenging. You will also find yourself having to think in six-line units, because of the importance of that third rhyme. This will be tough at times, but fun as well. When I first began working with terza rima, the structural constraints taught me things about grammar and syntax that I didn't think could be known. Because terza rima tends to be end-stopped with every tercet, it demands that we rediscover the beauties of the lowly comma, the semicolon, even the dash. Terza rima also trains poets away from writing three-line sentences, by no means a bad accomplishment. Reading the poem aloud, of course, as with all fixed forms, is the best way to discover where you have been fudging, or padding to fill out the line until the rhyme. For sustained illustrations, I suggest looking up those versions of *The Divine Comedy* that have been rendered into English in the terza rima form, especially those by Laurence Binyon, Dorothy L. Sayers, and Peter Dale, poets whose devotion to the form is instructive indeed.

Robert Frost's "Acquainted with the Night" is, in my opinion, the most impressive English-language terza rima poem of the twentieth century. (I would give the palm to Shelley's "Ode to the West Wind" for the nineteenth century.) Originally published in 1924 in the *Virginia Quarterly Review*, Frost's poem has been an acknowledged classic for decades, and the line in which its title occurs is now embedded in our idiom. Have another look at the poem—you have surely encountered it before—as it appears at the end of this essay. Check out the rhyme scheme: night-rain-light, lane-beat-explain, feet-cry-street, by-height-sky, right-night. Frost has given us surround sound with a vengeance. Not only has he returned to rhyme *a* of the first tercet in his fourth tercet, where rhyme *e* should be, but like Dante he repeats the same rhyme word of the first line as the rhyme word of the concluding line of his couplet. But Frost's cunning does not stop here. It may be argued that rhyme *c*, initiated by "beat," is an off-rhyme of rhyme *a*. Furthermore, the word "cry," which initiates rhyme *d* in the terza rima pattern, is in assonance with rhyme *a*. There is more to be said about the semantic, as well as the prosodic, architectonics of this poem, but perhaps enough has been said. On the possibilities of meter and matter, that is to say the coupling of sound and sense, Frost has gone as far as a great poet can: he has not only delivered a poem on the dark night of the soul, as Dante did, but he has written a poem about poetry, about form, about, you might say, the ecstasy of structure. "Acquainted with the Night" is an etude. In a deep, deep way, Frost's music is about music.

In English the critical material on terza rima is sparse, but the paucity of such scholarship has never deterred our poets. Since Wyatt's day the form has attracted and intrigued our best writers: a list, offered only at random, would include stellar work achieved by poets like Byron, Shelley, Thomas Hardy, W. H. Auden, Seamus Heaney, Elizabeth Jennings, and more recent poets like Suzanne Noguere and Greg Williamson. When you compose a poem in terza rima, you join a noble company.

ROBERT FROST

Acquainted with the Night

I have been one acquainted with the night.
I have walked out in rain—and back in rain.
I have outwalked the furthest city light.

I have looked down the saddest city lane.
I have passed by the watchman on his beat
And dropped my eyes, unwilling to explain.

I have stood still and stopped the sound of feet
When far away an interrupted cry
Came over houses from another street,

But not to call me back or say good-by;
And further still at an unearthly height,
One luminary clock against the sky

Proclaimed the time was neither wrong nor right.
I have been one acquainted with the night.

1924

ELIZABETH JENNINGS

Answers

I kept my answers small and kept them near;
Big questions bruised my mind but still I let
Small answers be a bulwark to my fear.

The huge abstractions I kept from the light;
Small things I handled and caressed and loved.
I let the stars assume the whole of night.

But the big answers clamoured to be moved
Into my life. Their great audacity
Shouted to be acknowledged and believed.

Even when all small answers build up to
Protection of my spirit, still I hear
Big answers striving for their overthrow

And all the great conclusions coming near.

1970

JACQUELINE OSHEROW

London, before and after, the Middle Way

Where shall I begin, the Metropolitan Line
Or on the South Bank, aimless, all those years ago?
So many cities in my poems, but never London

Though I spent years spying on it from a window
At the top front of a smoky two-tiered bus
In traffic so torturously slow

I'd exchange the daylight for the swifter darkness.
But first, my cortege of houses scaled its hill,
Ladies in waiting to the dowager St. Pancras,

Where I'd picture a Victorian giant's doll,
From amidst a life both dutiful and sumptuous,
Peering out a turret at our perfect standstill.

Some days, I'd just linger on the bus,
Vaguely on the watch for random poetry,
Biding my time, postponing hopelessness—

In love with a Londoner who didn't love me—
I'd stay on for the view from Blackfriars Bridge,
The one part of the route the bus took swiftly,

The towers of Parliament a fleet mirage
Of majesty in that expanse of gray,
Squat, terraced houses in their dotage.

London had used up its store of poetry
And etched it on bronze plaques, paved in the ground.
I found them as I drifted down a walkway,

Aimless, on the South Bank, in the wind,
Unnerved every time Big Ben's dull gong
Bellowed out a quarter hour's end.

Sweet Themmes runne softly, till I end my Song.
Even then, I knew I'd never write like that—
But I was young; I could imagine I was wrong,

Pleased to have at least a bronze plaque intimate
That I might sing away my wasted yearning,
Real life might not matter to a poet . . .

1996

NOTE

1. The translation from Dante is my own.

The Quatrain

JOHN HOLLANDER

Quatrains, or rhymed staves of four lines, are usually thought of as hav-
ing lines of equal length and, often (though by no means always) as being
cross-rhymed (*abab*, or even *abba*). But there are several sorts of quatrain,
and these should be distinguished at the outset. They can function as in-
dependent epigrammatic poems of their own, whether in a witty or more
plangent mode, or as stanzaic units in a poem of eight lines or more. Their
structure can vary considerably. In English—which I shall be primarily
considering—their line length can range from a possible (although ex-
ceedingly rare) monosyllable, up to lines of fourteen syllables or more. As
was previously noted, they can rhyme *abab*, *abba*, *aabb*, *aaba*, *abxb* or
even, exceedingly rarely, *aaaa*. They can serve as stanzas, or even function
as a clearly marked part or section of a strophic scheme, for example as
in a Shakespearean sonnet (cross-rhymed) or in an Italian one *(abba)*.

Two strands of tradition lead to the quatrain in English verse. One is
neoclassical: Greek and Latin elegiac verse is written in couplets of a
hexameter followed by a shorter pentameter; many of the epigrams of the
Greek Anthology were comprised of two couplets, and the disposition of
the syntax and the argument through these, whether flowing through the
four lines, or using a disjuncture between the first and last two for com-
parison or contrast, framed early versions of the four-line poem. A qua-
train provides a good deal of structural potential for its length, and al-
lows for more density and subtlety than the hit-and-run witty power of
a couplet. In fact, a classical couplet often expands in translation into a
quatrain, as in the case of Shelley's adaptation (in alternate pentameter
and trimeter, *abab*) of an elegiac couplet, ascribed to Plato, to a boy
named Aster ("star"):

> Thou wert the morning star among the living,
> Ere thy fair light had fled;
> Now, having died, thou art as Hesperus, giving
> New splendour to the dead.   c. 1821

Or similarly, in a satiric mode, Ben Jonson's epigrammatic quatrain,
pentameter *aabb*, "To the Ghost of Martial,"

Martial, thou gav'st far nobler epigrams
To thy Domitian, than I can my James;
But in my royal subject I pass thee:
Thou flattered'st thine, mine cannot flattered be.   1616

It is in this style of satiric epigram that we find those extremely rare in-
stances of the *aaaa* rhyming pattern, for example the revised but re-
ceived version of Tom Brown's celebrated off-the-cuff translation of a
couplet of Martial's:

> I do not like thee Dr. Fell,
> And why it is I cannot tell;
> But this I know and know full well,
> I do not like thee Dr. Fell

(although the redundancy here is intentionally marked, as matching an
analogous one in the Latin original). Similarly, in Blake's powerful epi-
gram, the single rhyme seems less designed than necessitated by the
powerful, startling and sentiment-smashing reiteration:

> What is it men in women do require?
> The lineaments of gratified desire.
> What is it women do in men require?
> The lineaments of gratified desire.

The other tradition we associate with the development of the ballad
stanza in the early sixteenth century, with its *abxb* rhyme and alternat-
ing four- and three-beat lines. The most celebrated quatrain from this
period is the haunting, anonymous

> Westron winde, when will thou blow,
> The smalle raine down can raine?
> Christ if my love were in my armes,
> And I in my bed againe.   c. 1520?

The rhyme links the two superficially disjunct pairs of lines, causing one
to consider the deeper but oblique connection. It may be, of course, that
this quatrain is a fragment from the beginning of a ballad (the next
stanza perhaps beginning, "That night he roamed the barren heath, /
The moonlit heath and dry").

The ballad stanza's counterpart was in hymnody, the so-called
common metre of the metrical psalter (as in Sternhold and Hopkins's
1562 version of Ps. 137, "by the waters of Babylon . . ."):

Whenas we sat in Babylon,
    the rivers round about,
And in remembrance of Ziòn
    the tears for grief burst out.

From the lowercase letters starting lines 2 and 4 can be discerned the couplet from which this form of quatrain-as-stanza emerged, the four-teeners used in Chapman's *Iliad,* and Arthur Golding's wonderful 1567 Ovid: "Of shapes transformde to bodies straunge, I purpose to en-treate, / Ye gods vouchsafe (for you are they yroughte this wondrous feate) . . ."

By the early seventeenth century, these two strands have interwo-ven, and quatrains can either be stanzaic, or independent epigrammatic poems of their own. In the following examples, the reader may observe a variety of functions to which the linear structure of the quatrain may be put, entailing conjunctions, disjunctions, oppositions, parallels, buildups to a punch line or to a more gentle closure.

INDEPENDENT QUATRAINS

Cross-Rhymed, Iambic Pentameter
(Almost Invariably Epigrammatic)
I strove with none, for none was worth my strife,
    Nature I loved, and next to Nature, Art:
I warmed both hands before the fire of Life;
    It sinks; and I am ready to depart.   1853
    Walter Savage Landor, "On His Seventy-fifth Birthday"

Good Fortune, when I hailed her recently,
Passed by me with the intimacy of shame
As one that in the dark had handled me
And could no longer recollect my name.   1969
            J.V. Cunningham, "Epigram #76"

Her name, cut clear upon this marble cross,
Shines, as it shone when she was still on earth;
While tenderly, the mild, agreeable moss
Obscures the figures of her date of birth.   1931
                Dorothy Parker, "The Actress"
                ("Tombstones in the Starlight")

The present author used this pattern to translate the Malay *pantun*, an epigrammatic form in which the first two and last two lines form seem referentially disjunct until some deeper trope connecting them becomes clear:

> Pantuns in the original Malay
> Are quatrains of two thoughts, but of one mind.
> Athwart these two pontoons I sail away
> While touching neither. Land lies far behind.   1988
> > John Hollander "Catamaran"

Pentameter, Rhymed *aabb*
> O Shadow, in thy fleeting form I see
> The friend of fortune that once clung to me.
> In flattering light thy constancy is shown;
> In darkness, thou wilt leave me all alone.   1894
> > John Bannister Tabb, "The Shadow"

Cross-Rhymed, Tetrameter
> Stand close around, ye Stygian set,
> > With Dirce in one boat conveyed!
> Lest Charon, seeing, may forget
> > That he is old and she a shade.   1831
> > > Landor, "On Dirce"

"Ballad Stanza" Quatrain
> All dripping in tangles green,
> Cast up by a lone sea,
> If purer for that, O Weed,
> Bitterer, too, are ye?   1888
> > Herman Melville, "The Tuft of Kelp"

As with the old "Westron winde," this could either be an independent epigram or a fragment of an abandoned poem.

> Declaiming Waters none may dread—
> But Waters that are still
> Are so for that most fatal cause
> In Nature—they are full   c. 1884
> > Emily Dickinson, no. 1595 in Johnson's text

Rhymed *aabb*, Tetrameter
In contact, lo! the flint and steel,
By spark and flame, the thought reveal
That he, the metal, she the stone
Had cherished secretly alone.   1906
                              Ambrose Bierce, "Alone"

STANZAIC QUATRAINS

***In Memoriam* stanza, Rhymed *abba*, Tetrameter**
Earliest occurrence, Sidney's 1585 metrical translation of Psalm 37, here
also stipulating, as Sidney frequently does, alternate masculine and fem-
inine endings.

> Frett not thy self, if thou do see
> That wicked men do seeme to flourish:
> No envy in thy bozome nourish
> Though ill deedes well succeeding be.

Sidney is followed by Shakespeare, "The Phoenix and the Turtle," Ben
Jonson "An Elegy," Lord Herbert of Cherbury, Carew, Marvell, D. G.
Rossetti, and, of course, Tennyson, whose *In Memoriam* gives the
stanza its commonly used name.

> Now rings the woodland loud and long,
>   The distance takes a lovelier hue,
>   And drown'd in yonder living blue
> The lark becomes a sightless song.   1850
>   Alfred, Lord Tennyson, *In Memoriam*, CXV

(For a poetic consideration of this stanza, see my "Others Who Have
Lived in This Room" from *In Time and Place*.)

Unrhymed, Iambic Trimeter, Feminine Ending
The multitude of infantes
A good man holdes, resembleth
The multitude of arrowes,
A mighty Archer holdeth   c. 1595?
           Mary Herbert, Countess of Pembroke,
                metrical version of Psalm 127

Cross-Rhymed, Pentameter, aside from
Sonnet Sections

These examples show a development in its use from narrative to com-
memoration, to meditation.

> This dismal Gall'ry, lofty, long and wide;
>   Was hung with Skelitons of ev'ry kinde;
> Humane, and all that learnèd humane pride
>   Think made t'obey Man's high immortal Minde. 1650
>   Sir William Davenant, *Gondibert*, III

> His Ashes in a Peaceful Urn shall rest,
>   His name a great Example stands to show,
> How strangely high Endeavours may be blest,
>   Where Piety and Valor jointly go.   1659
>   John Dryden, "Heroick Stanzas, etc."

> Far from the madding crowd's ignoble strife
> Their sober wishes never learn'd to stray;
> Along the cool sequester'd vale of life
> They kept the noiseless tenor of their way.   1751
>   Thomas Gray, "Elegy Written in a
>   Country Church-yard"

> I'll walk where my own nature would be leading—
>   It vexes me to choose another guide—
> Where the grey flocks in ferny glens are feeding,
>   Where the wild wind blows on the mountainside. 1850
>   Emily Brontë, "Stanzas"

"RUBAIYAT" QUATRAINS

The celebrated quatrain form adapted by Edward Fitzgerald from the
Persian *rubaiyat* (literally, "quatrains," an independent, epigrammatic
mode) of Omar Khayyam is pentameter rhymed *aaxa*:

> Awake, for morning in the bowl of night
> Has flung the stone which puts the stars to flight
> And Lo! the hunter of the East has caught
> The Sultàn's turrets in a noose of light.   1859

James Merrill remarked in conversation once that Fitzgerald's lines characteristically sagged with a sequence of monosyllables in the third and fourth feet (as they do in ll. 1, 2, and 4 above). Like Swinburne before him (in "Laus Veneris" and "Relics"), Merrill himself used this quatrain form stanzaically, in one section of his remarkable "Lost in Translation," and in his very late poem "Home Fires," partially in response to my own *Rubaiyat*-like sequence, *Tesserae*. The one precursor in English poetry I can think of for the singular movement of Fitzgerald's *aaxa* stanza is one invented by Tennyson for "The Daisy," published two years before Fitzgerald first saw the Persian manuscript of Omar Khayyam. Tennyson, incidentally, claimed that his invented stanza was an adaptation of a classical alcaic: the feminine ending of the unrhyming line is consistent throughout the poem:

> How richly down the rocky dell
> The torrent vineyard streaming fell
> To meet the sun and sunny waters,
> That only heaved with summer swell.   1855

(If Tennyson's subsequent stanza had daughters/quarters/porters as its rhymes, the interlocking effect, analogous to that of terza rima, would be identical to that used by Robert Frost in the interlocking tetrameter quatrains of his "Stopping by Woods on a Snowy Evening.")

Cross-Rhymed, Accentual 6, 5, 6, 5

> If I pass during some nocturnal blackness, mothy and warm,
>   When the hedgehog travels furtively over the lawn,
> One may say, "He strove that such innocent creatures should
>   come to no harm,
>   But he could do little for them; and now he is gone."
>   Thomas Hardy, "Afterwards," 1917

Rhymed *abxb,* Three Beats

> It was down in old Joe's bar-room
> In a corner by the Square,
> They were serving drinks as usual,
> And the usual crowd was there   c. 1910?
>   Anonymous, "St. James Infirmary"

Rhymed *aabb*, Anapestic Tetrameter

The blackbird has fled to another retreat,
Where the hazels afford him a screen from the heat,
And the scene where his melody charm'd me before
Resounds with his sweet flowing ditty no more.   1782
                    William Cowper, "The Poplar Field"

Flow gently, sweet Afton, among thy green braes,
Flow gently, I'll sing thee a song in thy praise
My Mary's asleep by thy murmuring stream
Flow gently, sweet Afton, disturb not her dream.   1792
                    Robert Burns, "Afton Water"

Or, used less elegiacally and more bouncily,

The Assyrian came down like the wolf on the fold
And his cohorts were gleaming in purple and gold;
And the sheen of their spears was like stars on the sea,
When the blue wave rolls nightly on deep Galilee.   1815
                    Lord Byron, "The Destruction of Sennacherib"

**Cross-Rhymed Tetrameter (Also Known in Hymnody
as "Long Metre")**

Therefore the love which us do bind,
But Fate so enviously disbars
Is the conjunction of the mind
And opposition of the stars.   1681
                    Andrew Marvell, "The Definition of Love"

Between the sunlight and the shade
A man may learn till he forgets
The roaring of a world remade,
And all his ruins and regrets;   1916
                    Edwin Arlington Robinson, "Hillcrest"

**Sapphic Stanza, Three Long Lines Unvarying
Rhythmically, one short one, unrhymed**

As Sion standeth very firmly stedfast,
Never once shaking: soe, on high, Jehova
Who his hope buildeth, very firmly stedfast,
            Ever abideth.   c. 1595?
Mary Herbert, Countess of Pembroke, metrical version of Psalm 125

So the goddess fled from her place, with awful
Sound of feet and thunder of wings around her
While behind a clamour of winging women
      Severed the twilight.   1866
             A. C. Swinburne, "Sapphics"

Rhymed, Adapted Sapphic

As here, for example, where the comic effect is enhanced by the feminine ending always emerging in the stanza's short, final line.

Miniver scorned the gold he sought,
    But sore annoyed was he without it;
Miniver thought, and thought, and thought,
    And thought about it.   1910
       Edwin Arlington Robinson, "Miniver Cheevy"

Alcaic Stanzas of Various Sorts, with Two Identical Long Lines Followed by Two Identical or Varied Shorter Ones

These may be rhymed, as

He nothing common did or mean
Upon that memorable scene:
    But with his keener eye
    The axe's edge did try.   1650
       Andrew Marvell, "Horatian Ode"

The rising moon has hid the stars;
Her level rays, like golden bars,
    Lie on the landscape green,
    With shadows in between.   1841
     Henry Wadsworth Longfellow, "Endymion"

Or unrhymed:

Now air is hush'd, save where the weak-eye'd bat,
With short shrill shriek flits by on leathern wing,
Or where the beetle winds
His small but sullen horn   1748
       William Collins, "Ode to Evening"

(It may be noted that in both Marvell's and Collins's poems, the stanzas are run together without break.) A host of other adaptations of Greek or Latin four-line strophes are possible, such as Auden's in "In Memory of Sigmund Freud," where the verse's system is purely syllabic, and the lines are arranged eleven, eleven, nine, ten.

There are obviously a considerable number of ways in which line length and rhyme scheme can be varied, and they cannot be explored here. One particularly beautiful device may be noted, in a pattern of cross-rhymed trimeter, two pentameters and trimeter.

> Wither, midst falling dew,
> While glow the heavens with the last steps of day
> Far, through their rosy depths, dost thou pursue
> Thy solitary way?   1822
> William Cullen Bryant, "To a Waterfowl"

Here there is a constant pull against the tendency of the stanza to re-combine into an un- or internally rhymed tetrameter quatrain, depending upon the syntactic arrangement in each case.

Limited space forbids a more detailed exploration of some of these other possibilities, for example among Hardy's broad array of stanza forms. But it might be noted that, among major twentieth-century poets, Hart Crane deployed a wide range of stanzaic quatrain types, for example cross-rhymed with three pentameters and a final dimeter—a trace of the sapphic stanza again ("Indiana" from *The Bridge*); pentameter quatrains, with random rhyme and assonance ("To Brooklyn Bridge," ditto); unrhymed tetrameter ("Praise for an Urn," etc.) Crane's use of these is, rhetorically and generically, most instructive.

Sapphics

GRACE SCHULMAN

The sapphic stanza is a form that urges intensity. Since its Greek origins, it has had a lively history in Western poetry. The form is named after Sappho, a sixth-century Greek poet from Lesbos, but it may have been invented by Alcaeus, her male contemporary and fellow practitioner. Although Catullus, who lived centuries later, introduced the stanza into Latin, it was Horace who provided the sapphic model for Roman poets and for their followers. He created a four-line sapphic stanza by breaking in two the third line of an earlier three-line stanza.

English sapphics imitate the classical form. The poem may have any number of stanzas, but it is usually brief. In each sapphic stanza, the first three lines are hendecasyllabic, comprising eleven syllables of four trochees and a dactyl, and arranged as trochee trochee dactyl trochee trochee ($\bar{} \breve{} \mid \bar{} \breve{} \mid \bar{} \breve{} \breve{} \mid \bar{} \breve{} \mid \bar{} \breve{}$).

Spondaic substitutions are possible in the second and last feet; where x indicates that metrical option.

$$\bar{} \breve{} \bar{} \quad \bar{} \breve{} \breve{} \bar{} \breve{} \bar{}$$
$$\quad x \qquad\qquad x$$

The fourth line is called an *adonic,* after the cry to Adonis:

$$\bar{} \quad \breve{} \quad \breve{} \ \bar{} \ x$$
O Ton Adonin, it whispers, in a

$$\prime \ \breve{} \ \breve{} \ \prime \ \breve{}$$
passionate outcry

that promises

$$\prime \ \breve{} \ \breve{} \ \prime \quad \breve{}$$
never to leave you.

Writing the adonic is the release, the reward, at the end of the three hendecasyllabic lines of tenderly falling rhythm. Attempting sapphics is alluring because of the varied examples of others who have.

To be sure, sapphics in English can only approximate quantitative meter, the system using syllable length rather than stress as the metrical

base. (See the sections by Warren and Hadas.) The "long syllable" has
a long vowel or diphthong, or any vowel followed by more than one
consonant. Because that pattern of vowel lengths cannot be heard in
English, poets have usually imitated the classical form by substituting
stress measures for the inaudible quantities. On the other hand, some of
the most interesting examples imitate length as well as stress.

And there are more domesticated versions. Sapphics became popu-
lar in the English medieval period, many of the poems acquiring metri-
cal variations and rhyme. In the Renaissance, there were attempts to ap-
proximate syllable length rather than stress, notably by Richard
Stanyhurst and Mary Herbert, Countess of Pembroke. Others are really
accentual-syllabic, as, for example, Thomas Campion's "Rose-Cheekt
Lawra," the poem "offered as an example of the English Sappick."

> Rose-cheekt Lawra, come,
> Sing thou smoothly with thy beawties
> silent musick, either other
>   Sweetely gracing.
>
> Lovely formes do flowe
> From concent devinely framed;
> Heav'n is musick, and thy beawties
>   Birth is heavenly.
>
> These dull notes we sing
> Discords neede for helps to grace them;
> only beawty purely loving
>   Knowes no discord:
>
> But still mooves delight,
> Like cleare springs renu'd by flowing,
> Ever perfect, ever in them-
>   selves eternall.

Still others of this period more closely reproduce classical sapphics.
The difference can be seen in two powerful poems by Sir Philip Sidney.
One, "Get Hence Foule Griefe," is only loosely sapphic-derived, with
an iambic pentameter base and metrical variation.

> Get hence foule Griefe, the canker of the minde:
> Farewell Complaint, the miser's only pleasure:
> Away vayne Cares, by which fewe men do finde
>   Their sought-for treasure,

The other, "Cleophila," more closely conforms to sapphic meter.

> If mine eyes can speake to doo harty errande,
> Or mine eyes' language she doo hap to judge of,
> So that eyes' message be of her receaved,
>   Hope we do live yet.

Nearer to the classical meter, too, is Fulke Greville's *Caelica* VI, which is reprinted here.

On the other hand, Isaac Watts uses hendecasyllabic lines in his mighty poem "The Day of Judgement":

> When the fierce north wind with his airy forces
> Rears up the Baltic to a foaming fury,
> And the red lightning with a storm or hail comes
>   Rushing amain down . . .

William Cowper imitates the sapphic meter in "Lines Written under the Influence of Insanity," exchanging the trochee in the first foot for the dactyl in the third.

Some milestones in English sapphics allude to the form's namesake, the poet whom classical writers called "the tenth muse." Sappho and her young companions celebrated art and worshipped Aphrodite, and in their aesthetic endeavors sought to call into the present an ideal beauty. In "Sapphics," Swinburne's use of the form augments the subject, a vision of Sappho and her songs. He closely re-creates the classical pattern by using stress measures and also by attempting to make syllable length coincide with stress:

> Ah the singing, ah the delight, the passion!
> All the Loves wept, listening; sick with anguish,
> Stood the crowned nine Muses about Apollo;
>   Fear was upon them,
>
> While the tenth sang wonderful things they knew not
> Ah the tenth, the Lesbian! the nine were silent,
> None endured the sound of her song for weeping;
>   Laurel by laurel . . .

Thomas Hardy's "The Temporary the All," included here, is a resolute reproduction of the sapphic pattern. So, too, is James Merrill's "Arabian Night," among contemporary examples. Other recent efforts include

William Meredith's "Effort at Speech," which exhibits hendecasyllabic lines in the manner of Cowper's poem, with exchanges of trochee and dactyl in the first and third feet:

> Climbing the stairway grey with urban midnight,
> Cheerful, venial, ruminating pleasure,
> Darkness takes me, an arm around my throat and
> *Give me your wallet.*

In "Erinna to Sappho," James Wright anglicizes the form in a way that resembles Herbert's "Vertue," using iambic tetrameter with a final trimeter end line. Here, Erinna describes her lover's vision of a fleeting human figure, perhaps a ghost.

> If ghost it was, or melon rind,
> Or stag's skeleton hung to dry,
> Lover, or song, or only wind
> Sighing your sigh.

As for prime modern Catullus translations, I think of Jane Wilson Joyce's "Catullus 51" and W. S. Merwin's "Catullus XI," with its glorious last stanza:

> But as for my love, let her not count on it
> As once she could: by her own fault it died
> As a flower at the edge of a field, which the plow
> Roots out in passing.

John Hollander has composed upwards of eight fine poems in English sapphics. "A Find" begins:

> Early middle-late: it was still a time of
> Night when seen and unseen embraced in corners;
> Borrowed light lent out yet again had slipped from
> Shoulders of surface;
>
> Light lay spilled below, as if brightness had been
> Poured, and all the hollows of evening filled with
> Variously substantive shadow. It was
> then that I saw her . . .

Recently Rachel Hadas, adding to her "Mars and Venus," has written an elegant twenty-three-stanza poem in sapphics. In "Greek Gold," she captures the essence of an exhibit of Greek objects for its immediate impact and in terms of a transcendent ideal.

> Penises erect if you stoop to squinny,
> two rams nose to nose on a golden bracelet
> face off. That their bodies have been distilled to
>   heads, genitalia
>
> gives the leaps fresh urgency. A demotic
> tarnished silver version I bought in Delphi
> used to catch my delicate wrist-skin in be-
>   tween the two muzzles.

In a note to "Sapphics at a Trot," quoted in full here, Alfred Corn writes that he attempted to make syllable length and stress coincide—and they do. In "Greek Gold" the two bases of meter coincide as well, but Hadas, a poet and classics scholar, says she is unaware of the attempt. Some of the best formal efforts are instinctive, however; poets trained or untrained in quantitative meter can so read and so love the form as to bear a touch of it in their emotions.

In Marilyn Hacker's poetry, sapphic stanzas contain contemporary, even demotic, language. Appropriately, she writes of her daughter, Iva, in "Cleis," a poem in sapphic stanzas named for Sappho's daughter. "Chiliastic Sapphics" is set in her apartment in Paris, where she plans to

> Flip in a cassette while I read the papers;
> drought and famine, massacres. Cloistered sisters'
> voices raise the Kyrie. A gay pastor
>   who was abducted
>
> last week rated photographs and a headline.

Because of space restrictions, I can but tally other models, all of them sapphics-inspired: Robert Southey, "The Widow"; Samuel Taylor Coleridge, "Love"; Thomas Hardy, "The Seven Times," "After the Last Breath"; Ezra Pound, "Apparuit"; John Frederick Nims, "Sappho to Valéry"; Louis MacNeice, "June Thunder"; Richmond Lattimore, "Legend for a Shield"; Hyam Plutzik, "I Am Disquieted When I See Many Hills"; Lewis Turco, "Visitor"; John Hollander, "Heart of Snow," "Erinna to Sappho," "The Lady of the Castle," "A Thing So Small"; Marilyn Hacker, "Elevens," "Year's End," "A Note Downriver"; Timothy Steele, "Sapphics against Anger." The list is far from complete. As a

Gothic cathedral points to heaven, those versions form a structure that aspire toward the original ideal. Like a Gothic cathedral, the structure they form may never be finished.

SIR PHILIP SIDNEY

Cleophila

If mine eyes can speake to doo harty errande
Or mine eyes' language she doo hap to judge of,
So that eyes' message be of her receaved,
    Hope, we do live yet.

But if eyes faile then, when I most doo need them,
Or if eyes' language be not unto her knowne,
So that eyes' message doo returne rejected,
    Hope, we doo both dye.

Yet dying, and dead, doo we sing her honour;
So become our tombes monuments of her praise;
So becomes our losse the triumph of her gayne;
    Hers be the glory.

If the senceless spheares doo yet hold a musique,
If the Swanne's sweet voice be not heard, but at death,
If the mute timber when it hath the life lost,
    Yeldeth a lute's tune,

Are then humane mindes priviledg'd so meanly,
As that hatefull death can abridge them of powre,
With the voyce of truth to recorde to all worldes,
    That we be her spoiles?

Thus not ending, endes the due praise of her praise
Fleshly vaile consumes; but a soule hath his life,
Which is helde in love, love it is, that hath joynde
    Life to this our soule.

But if eyes can speake to doo harty errande,
Or mine eyes' language she doo hap to judge of,
So that eyes' message be of her receaved,
    Hope, we doo live yet.

1602

FULKE GREVILLE

From Caelica, VI

Eyes, why did you bring unto me those graces,
Grac'd to yield wonder out of her true measure,
Measure of all joys, stay to fancy traces,
    Model of pleasure?

Reason is now grown a disease in reason,
Thoughts knit upon thoughts free alone to wonder,
Sense is a spy, made to do fancy treason,
    Love I go under.

Since then eyes' pleasure to my thoughts betray me,
And my thoughts reason's level have defaced,
So that all my powers to be hers, obey me,
    Love be thou graced.

Grac'd by me, Love? No, by her that owes me,
She that an angel's spirit hath retained
In Cupid's fair sky, which her beauty shows me,
    Thus I have gained.

1633

WILLIAM COWPER

Lines Written during a Period of Insanity

Hatred and vengeance, my eternal portion,
scarce can endure delay of execution,
Wait with impatient readiness to seize my
    Soul in a moment.

Damned below Judas: more abhorred than he was.
Who for a few pense sold his holy Master
Twice betrayed Jesus me, the last delinquent,
    Deems the profanest.

Man disavows, and deity disowns me:
Hell might afford my miseries a shelter;
Therefore hell keeps her ever hungry mouths all
    Bolted against me.

Hard lot! emcompassed with a thousand dangers;
Weary fait, trembling with a thousand terrors;
I'm called, if vanquished, to receive a sentence
        Worse than Abiram's.

Him the vindictive rod of angry justice
Sent quick and howling to the center headlong.
I, fed with judgement, in a fleshly tomb, am
        Buried above ground.

                                        1774

THOMAS HARDY

The Temporary the All

Change and Chancefulness in my flowering youthtime,
Set me sun by sun near to one unchosen;
Wrought us fellowlike, and despite divergence,
        Fused us in friendship.

"Cherish him can I while the true one forthcome—
Come the rich fulfiller of my prevision;
Life is roomy yet, and the odds unbounded."
        So self-communed I.

'Thwart my wistful way did a damsel saunter,
Fair, albeit unformed to be all-eclipsing;
"Maiden meet," held I, "till arise my forefelt
        Wonder of women."

Long a visioned hermitage deep desiring,
Tenements uncouth I was fain to house in:
"Let such lodging be for a breath-while," thought I,
        "Soon a more seemly.

"Theft high handiwork will I make my life-deed,
Truth and Light outshow; but the ripe time pending,
Intermissive aim at the thing sufficeth."
        Thus I. . . . But lo, me!

Mistress, friend, place, aims to be bettered straightway,
Bettered not has Fate or my hand's achievement;
Sole the showance those of my onward earth-track —
        Never transcended!

                                        1898

ALFRED CORN

Sapphics at a Trot

Horses aren't always averse to bridles,
Yet the best is seldom a lowly numbskull.
Take it out today for a canter and you'll
Feel the resistance.

Sappho cinched strong lines to her icy darlings,
Who, alas, seemed not to appreciate them.
No, the fact remains that a cozy lave life's
Not very likely—

When, that is, you choose to become a poet.
Eager, are you, ready to jump? Terrif, but
Tunes to hoof it by are a nightmare if your
Meter is awkward.

Music, is that you with a score to guide us?
Tender overtures can appease resentment.
Beauty owes a ride to the groom allaying
Stress with a rhythm.

1997

Ottava Rima

JACQUELINE OSHEROW

Ottava rima, an eight-line rhyming stanza with an *abababcc* rhyme scheme, originated in Italian as ideally suited to poetic narration, with its strong propulsion mechanism—another *a,* yet another *b*—punctuated, and, at times, counteracted, by built-in caesuras—the surprising finality of the immediately and differently rhymed couplet, after the (by now seemingly endlessly repeating) *a*'s and *b*'s. And, indeed, in Ariosto's *Orlando Furioso,* the form provides space for infinite entertainment: a long and complicated narrative, complete with a trip to the moon on a hippogryph, and a host of witticisms and poetic flourishes occasioned by the form's restrictions and demands. In an ottava rima stanza, the three insistent alternating rhymes simultaneously move the narrative forward, hold diverse—often digressive—material together and call attention to themselves, creating endless opportunities for charm and amusement in acknowledging the complications of their proper execution. They can also encourage commentary and meditation, and intense lyricism, with those same rhymes functioning as a kind of scaffolding. The couplet, on the other hand, provides a stopping point, a summation, a turn, or perhaps even a punch line—humorous or poetic. Often, in an ottava rima poem, the narrator upstages the narrative with his own bravura performance—either through rhyme-generated witticisms or highly lyrical elaboration—always justified by those echoing rhymes. Tasso made his *Gerusalemme liberata,* an ottava rima masterpiece of the later Italian Renaissance, lyric and contemplative, as well as narrative—and rarely funny.

The flexibility of the form—its potential for narrative, meditative, lyric, and humorous movement—and sonority—is vividly exploited in its great English manifestations. Wyatt, who appears to be the first practitioner of the form in English, used it for epigram, apparently to showcase his ingenuity at the French court. His Epigram XLI tells a story, displays his ample wit, and makes a bawdy pun all at once. Keats, on the other hand, in *Isabella, or The Pot of Basil,* tells his tale with an emphasis on its lyric potential; he uses the repetitive form not only to move the story forward, but to highlight its pathos and his own ability to wring it for all that it's worth. Many of Yeats's greatest meditative lyrics are written in ottava rima. There are entire poems like "Sailing to Byzantium," "Coole Park and Ballylee, 1931," "The Circus Animals' Desertion" and "Among School Children" as well as sections of many others ("Nineteen Hundred and Nineteen" and "Meditations in Time of Civil War"). In "Among School Children," we see how the form enables Yeats to explore a vast amount of material—including a minihistory of ancient Greek philosophical thought—in what is after all only sixty-four lines of poetry. In Yeats, ottava rima becomes a dignified form, beautiful, and slow-moving—in some ways reminiscent of the ottava rima of *Gerusalemme liberata;* to use Yeats's own terminology, it holds a poem's center, while sending its various shoots off, almost simultaneously, in any number of directions. Yeats often exploits the form's potential to set something up, using his first six lines to ensure a profound resonance at the final couplet.

But it is surely in Byron's *Don Juan* that the form, as form, has its most exhilarating impact on English poetry. The relationship between form and content in this poem is not merely inextricable; it's an extravagant and all-consuming love affair. The form is the poem's propelling power, its raison d'être, its launching pad, and its bridle. *Don Juan* represents the most satisfying match of form and content in English since Shakespeare devised his particular variant on the sonnet. Ottava rima perfectly accommodates the single most important element of *Don Juan:* the speaker's own seemingly inexhaustible personality. His endless supply of wit, his vast knowledge and intelligence, his self-importance and self-deflation, his political and social outrage, his enormous appetites and his genuine poetic humility and ambition are all embraced by this roomy eight-line stanza, which, in Byron's hands, can hold together the most incongruous subject matter with the crazy glue of its repeating pattern. Even when he's addressing painful issues, Byron seems always to be having a blast. And it is, finally, that blast, that pleasure, that is the great legacy of ottava rima. Whether the poet meets its significant demands with lyricism or with humor, he makes available to himself an all-encompassing capaciousness, the giddy idea that he and his poems can take on—and take in—anything and everything they desire.

SIR THOMAS WYATT

Epigram XLI

She sat and sewed that hath done me the wrong
Whereof I plain and have done many a day,
And whilst she heard my plaint in piteous song
Wished my heart the sampler as it lay.
The blind master whom I have served so long,
Grudging to hear that he did hear her say,
Made her own weapon do her finger bleed
To feel if pricking were so good indeed.

c. 1542

JOHN KEATS

From Isabella, or The Pot of Basil

53

And she forgot the stars, the moon, and sun,
    And she forgot the blue above the trees,
And she forgot the dells where waters run,
    And she forgot the chilly autumn breeze;
She had no knowledge when the day was done,
    And the new morn she saw not: but in peace
Hung over her sweet basil evermore,
And moisten'd it with tears unto the core.

54

And so she ever fed it with thin tears,
    Whence thick, and green, and beautiful it grew,
So that it smelt more balmy than its peers
    Of basil-tufts in Florence; for it drew
Nurture besides, and life, from human fears,
    From the fast mouldering head there shut from view:
So that the jewel, safely casketed,
Came forth, and in perfumed leafits spread.

55

O Melancholy, linger here a while!
    O Music, Music, breathe despondingly!
O Echo, Echo, from some sombre isle,
    Unknown, Lethean, sigh to us—O sigh!

Spirits in grief, lift up your heads, and smile;
    Lift up your heads, sweet Spirits, heavily,
And make a pale light in your cypress glooms,
Tinting with silver wan your marble tombs.

1818

LORD BYRON

From Don Juan, Canto I

22

'Tis pity learnèd virgins ever wed
    With persons of no sort of education,
Or gentlemen, who, though well-born and bred,
    Grow tired of scientific conversation.
I don't choose to say much upon this head,
    I'm a plain man and in a single station,
But—oh ye lords and ladies intellectual!
Inform us truly, have they not henpecked you all?

62

Wedded she was some years and to a man
    Of fifty, and such husbands are in plenty;
And yet I think instead of such a one
    'Twere better to have two of five and twenty,
Especially in countries near the sun.
    And now I think on't, *mi vien in mente,*
Ladies even of the most uneasy virtue
Prefer a spouse whose age is short of thirty.

1819

From Don Juan, Canto XIV

4

A sleep without dreams, after a rough day
    Of toil, is what we covet most; and yet
How clay shrinks back from more quiescent clay!
    The very suicide that pays his debt
At once without installments (an old way
    Of paying debts, which creditors regret)
Lets out impatiently his rushing breath,
Less from disgust of life than dread of death.

5

'Tis round him, near him, here, there, everywhere;
   And there's a courage which grows out of fear,
Perhaps of all most desperate, which will dare
   The worst to *know* it. When the mountains rear
Their peaks beneath your human foot, and there
   You look down o'er the precipice, and drear
The gulf of rock yawns, you can't gaze a minute
Without an awful wish to plunge within it.

6

'Tis true, you don't, but pale and struck with terror,
   Retire. But look into your past impression
And you will find, though shuddering at the mirror
   Of your own thoughts in all their self-confession,
The lurking bias, be it truth or error,
   To the *unknown*, a secret prepossession
To plunge with all your fears—but where? You know not
And that's the reason why you do—or do not.

7

But what's this to the purpose, you will say.
   Gent. reader, nothing, a mere speculation,
For which my sole excuse is, 'tis my way.
   Sometimes *with* and sometimes without occasion
I write what's uppermost without delay.
   This narrative is not meant for narration,
But a mere airy and fantastic basis
To build up common things with commonplaces.

                                        1823

WILLIAM BUTLER YEATS

Among School Children

I

I walk through the long schoolroom questioning;
A kind old nun in a white hood replies;
The children learn to cipher and to sing,
To study reading-books and history,
To cut and sew, be neat in everything
In the best modern way—the children's eyes
In momentary wonder stare upon
A sixty-year-old smiling public man.

II

I dream of a Ledaean body, bent
Above a sinking fire, a tale that she
Told of a harsh reproof, or trivial event
That changed some childish day to tragedy—
Told, and it seemed that our two natures blent
Into a sphere from youthful sympathy,
Or else, to alter Plato's parable,
Into the yolk and white of the one shell.

III

And thinking of that fit of grief or rage
I look upon one child or t'other there
And wonder if she stood so at that age—
For even daughters of the swan can share
Something of every paddler's heritage—
And had that colour upon cheek or hair,
And thereupon my heart is driven wild:
She stands before me as a living child.

IV

Her present image floats into the mind—
Did Quattrocento finger fashion it
Hollow of cheek as though it drank the wind
And took a mess of shadows for its meat?
And I though never of Ledaean kind
Had pretty plumage once—enough of that,
Better to smile on all that smile, and show
There is a comfortable kind of old scarecrow.

V

What youthful mother, a shape upon her lap
Honey of generation had betrayed,
And that must sleep, shriek, struggle to escape
As recollection or the drug decide,
Would think her son, did she but see that shape
With sixty or more winters on its head,
A compensation for the pang of his birth,
Or the uncertainty of his setting forth?

VI

Plato thought nature but a spume that plays
Upon a ghostly paradigm of things;
Solider Aristotle played the taws

Upon the bottom of a king of kings;
World-famous golden-thighed Pythagoras
Fingered upon a fiddle-stick or strings
What a star sang and careless Muses heard:
Old clothes upon old sticks to scare a bird.

VII

Both nuns and mothers worship images,
But those the candles light are not as those
That animate a mother's reveries,
But keep a marble or a bronze repose.
And yet they too break hearts—O Presences
That passion, piety or affection knows,
And that all heavenly glory symbolise—
O self-born mockers of man's enterprise;

VIII

Labour is blossoming or dancing where
The body is not bruised to pleasure soul,
Nor beauty born out of its own despair,
Nor blear-eyed wisdom out of midnight oil.
O chestnut-tree, great-rooted blossomer,
Are you the leaf, the blossom or the bole?
O body swayed to music, O brightening glance,
How can we know the dancer from the dance?

1927

Spenser's Eponymous

R. S. GWYNN

The Spenserian stanza consists of eight lines of iambic pentameter and a ninth of hexameter, with a rhyme scheme of *ababbcbcc;* I have always considered it a marvelous ugly duckling among the English fixed forms. In skilled hands it is capable of soaring to great heights, but its inherent difficulties seem sufficiently daunting to deter novices from attempting it; ineptly handled, it waddles along awkwardly with its forty-nine webbed iambic feet mired in mud. It has a long and estimable tradition behind it, but its appearance in the English canon is not, as is, say, the case with blank verse or the sonnet, one that displays a continuous history and development. Instead, it has appeared at widely spaced intervals as the form of choice for several individual great examples, but it has never had an extended vogue. Nor has the triumph of one poet seemed to have had much influence on his contemporaries and followers. It is presently undergoing one of its fallow periods; no poet has really made much use of it in the present century.

Other than the fact that the Spenserian (if we discount the nonce stanzas of odes) is the longest of the conventional fixed stanza forms, what are its particular difficulties? The foremost of these, it seems to me, is the same problem that arises in the octave of the related Spenserian sonnet (and in the Petrarchan as well); that is, the *b* rhyme, which must be used four times. Since the Spenserian has most often been employed in long narratives, the poet is quickly going to run up against the limits of our notoriously rhyme-poor language. The results are easy enough to foresee: syntax that is badly wrenched to accommodate the pattern, the use of unfamiliar words or even archaisms and neologisms to expand the list of possible rhymes (especially as the poet lands on the fourth *b*), resort to the most banal (and thus easiest) rhyming sounds like the long *e*, the weak *-ing*, or *-ite*, and a discursiveness that naturally occurs when the poet finds that he or she cannot accommodate all of the intended thought or incident to the formal demands and thus must write a second stanza to accommodate the excess baggage, then a third, a fourth, and so on ad infinitum.

Additionally, two further difficulties reside in the form's terminal alexandrine. One lies in the received wisdom that the alexandrine has little tradition in English poetry and even less success. The rare great poem written in alexandrines (I think of Sidney's "Loving in Truth and Fain in Verse My Love to Show") always seems suspiciously lax, so accustomed are we to the pentameter. Even in Sidney's great sonnet, the workshop-trained pruner of excess might carp that "in verse" in the first line and "dear she" in the second are little more than verbal cellulite. Also, the symmetry of the even-footed line generally causes the medial caesura, strong enough in four-foot lines, to become even more pronounced, leading, if the poet is not careful, to a jingling closure that doesn't fit well with the preceding eight pentameters. And finally there is the question of closure itself. The alexandrine (reinforced by the final couplet rhyme) tends to bring the stanza to a jarring stop that is, to my ear, even more pronounced than that of the *ottava rima*. In a form primarily used for narratives, this results in a strong break in continuity every nine lines, a quality that many critics have noted when praising the curious virtues of Spenser, whose narrative technique has often been found comparable to the pages in an illuminated Medieval manuscript.

We do not know much about the antecedents of the Spenserian. Its first eight lines have the same rhyme scheme employed by François Villon in his verse testaments and ballades, though Villon's meter is octosyllabic. Chaucer uses the same rhyme scheme with pentameters in "The Monk's Tale," and this would seem to be the most likely source of Spenser's stanza, though both rime royal and *ottava rima* share some similarities to it. After Spenser, the stanza virtually disappeared until the late 1700s, when poets like Shenstone and Thomson used it; in the Romantic era it had a surprising resurgence, first with Wordsworth (and the nonce stanzas Wordsworth employs in "Resolution and Independence" and "Ode to Duty" seem to be derived from it), then later with Byron ("Childe Harold's Pilgrimage"), Shelley ("Adonais"), and Keats ("The Eve of St. Agnes"), who for my money brought the stanza to a level of perfection that has not been approached since. After the Romantics, it makes a fleeting appearance in Tennyson (the first five stanzas of "The Lotos-Eaters") and Arnold before vanishing. I know of three contemporary poets—Michael McFee, Wayne Koestenbaum, and Annie Finch—who have attempted it, albeit in rather irregular manner, and I have written a couple of poems in the form myself. Mary Kinzie and Rachel Hadas also have poems in *A Formal Feeling Comes* that are written in stanzas derived from the Spenserian. Doubtless there are other practitioners, but I am not aware of them.

The Spenserian seem to me most appropriate for a stately, solemn movement. Unlike *ottava rima*, which has largely (following Byron) been put to comic purposes, the Spenserian does not lend itself to humor; indeed, some of Byron's most thoughtful moments appear in sections of "Childe Harold's Pilgrimage" where Harold speculates on his daughter's life in England or meditates on the career of Napoleon. Given the present distrust against the more ornate poetic forms, it seems unlikely that it will experience a renaissance soon. Still, no one could have predicted seventy-five years ago that the sestina would become one of the most common verse forms in English (as Dana Gioia notes in a witty poem, it has become a ubiquitous assignment in beginning creative writing classes) or that another complicated import, the villanelle, should become so popular. Michael Lind's recent epic poem, *The Alamo,* was written in creditable rime royal, and it may be that some future poet will find a subject that will lift the Spenserian to its potential glory.

I have written three poems in this form. One, an attempt at a mock-romance called "How the Black Knight Got That Way," was abandoned almost as quickly as it was begun. A draft of it exists on a computer disk stored in my safe-deposit box. The other two were published. Oddly, both were, in different senses of the term, occasional poems. I wrote the first for my mother at Christmas, and it was published in the *Plains Poetry Journal,* a little magazine, now defunct, that was hospitable to poems written in traditional forms. Here is the final stanza of "The Dream Again":

> So let the light grow dim, allow this dream
> Its one still moment, where none may intrude
> To hang the stockings which can only seem
> Empty reminders of the magnitude
> Of love we neither compass nor conclude.
> Let the deep twilight gather to the chime
> Of three brass angels circling in the nude,
> Tinkling above their candles as they climb
> The wall in shadows, marking nothing more than time.

The second was written for a more public occasion, the rededication ceremony for the restored "Old Main" building at my graduate alma mater, the University of Arkansas, in 1991. I had the pleasure of sitting on the dais with a former Miss America and of reading it to the largest crowd I have ever faced, which included the venerable ex-senator J. William Fulbright. Governor Clinton was even supposed to attend but had to send his regrets, as he was apparently busy with more pressing affairs elsewhere.

Two Views from a High Window

Fayetteville, 1971–1991

Above a Midas-trove of golden leaves
And, by *his* reckoning, on a higher plane
Than other men; shaded by peeling eaves
In a drab third-floor office in Old Main,
The teaching fellow shuts his Blake again,
Turns to the window and the splendid day,
And scrapes his nails against a dusty pane,
Etching a mandala. Not far away,
Cheers echo when a marching band begins to play.

Below him, late already for the game,
A crimson-clad alumnus tries to show
His family where the sidewalk bears his name.
His wife and two teenagers urge his slow
Progress along with tugs, then finally throw
Their hands up in despair and hurry on,
Leaving him to his reverie, bent low
Over the concrete. When he finds his own,
He waves and calls, stumbles, and finds himself alone.

Almost alone, that is; as he regains
His wind and balance, he is made aware
Of movement high above his head. He trains
His eyes on a high window and a pair
Of steel-rimmed glasses with a cloud of hair
And tangled beard framing a pale, pinched face.
For one long moment they exchange a stare—
Two beings crossing paths in outer space,
Each wondering at the strangeness of an alien race.

But leave them there, fast-forwarding the scene
Two decades. Now the furniture is new;
The Chairman's office sparkles and, with clean
Windows, commands an even finer view.
Do the two men here look familiar, too?
The host draws mandalas upon his neat
Desk blotter while the older, well-to-do
Visitor carefully inspects a sheet
Of paper, signs, waits patiently for his receipt;

Then rises, tugs his carmine tie and vest,
And, helped to get his matching jacket on,
Receives a final thanks for his bequest.
The door clicks shut. The Chairman, now alone,
Looks out on a horizon that has grown
Daily a little nearer for the sake
Of futures that no longer are his own.
Stroking his beard, he reaches down to take
A book out of the bottom drawer: *Visions of Blake.*

Below him, coming up the concrete walk,
Striding across the closed ranks of the dead,
His daughter and her best friend—freshmen—talk
About the game and weekend just ahead.
Approaching them, an old man in a red
Blazer looks down, searching. Each window, lit
With an autumn morning's gold, an aura spread
Across the bricks—each pane reflecting it—
Holds an abundance that could well be infinite.

EDMUND SPENSER

From The Faerie Queene, Book I, Canto 4

21

And by his side rode loathsome Gluttony,
    Deformèd creature, on a filthie swine,
    His belly was up-blowne with luxury.
    And eke with fatnesse swollen were his eyne,
    And like a Crane his necke was long and fyne,
    With which he swallowd up excessive feast,
    For want whereof poore people oft did pyne;
    And all the way, most like a brutish beast,
He spuèd up his gorge, that all did him deteast.

22

In greene vine leaves he was right fitly clad;
    For other clothes he could not weare for heat,
    And on his head an yvie girland had,
    From under which fast trickled down the sweat:
    Still as he rode, he somewhat still did eat,
    And in his hand did bearre a bouzing can,

Of which he supt so oft, that on his seat
His dronken corse he scarse upholden can,
In shape and life more like a monster, then a man.

23

Unfit he was for any worldly thing,
    And eke unhable once to stirre or go,
    Not meet to be of counsell to a king,
    Whose mind in meat and drink was drownèd so,
    That from his friend he seldome knew his fo:
    Full of diseases was his carcass blew,
    And a dry dropsie through his flesh did flow:
    Which by misdiet daily greater grew:
Such one was Gluttony, the second of that crew.

1596

LORD BYRON

From Childe Harold's Pilgrimage, Canto 3

42

    But quiet to quick bosoms is a hell,
    And *there* hath been thy bane; there is a fire
    And motion of the soul which will not dwell
    In its own narrow being, but aspire
    Beyond the fitting medium of desire;
    And, but once kindled, quenchless evermore,
    Preys upon high adventure, nor can tire
    Of aught but rest; a fever at the core,
Fatal to him who bears, to all who ever bore.

43

    This makes the madmen who have made men mad
    By their contagion; Conquerors and Kings,
    Founders of sects and systems, to whom add
    Sophists, Bards, Statesmen, all unquiet things
    Which stir too strongly the soul's secret springs,
    And are themselves the fools to those they fool;
    Envied, yet how unenviable! what stings
    Are theirs! One breast laid open were a school
Which would unteach mankind the lust to shine or rule:

44

Their breath is agitation, and their life
A storm whereon they ride, to sink at last,
And yet so nurs'd and bigotted to strife,
That should their days, surviving perils past,
Melt to calm twilight, they feel overcast
With sorrow and supineness, and so die;
Even as a flame unfed, which runs to waste
With its own flickering, or a sword laid by
Which eats into itself, and rusts ingloriously.

1816

JOHN KEATS

From The Eve of St. Agnes

27

Soon, trembling in her soft and chilly nest,
In a sort of wakeful swoon, perplex'd she lay,
Until the poppied warmth of sleep oppress'd
Her soothed limbs, and soul fatigued away;
Flown, like a thought, until the morrow-day;
Blissfully haven'd both from joy and pain;
Clasp'd like a missal where swart Paynims pray;
Blinded alike from sunshine and from rain,
As though a rose should shut, and be a bud again.

30

And still she slept an azure-lidded sleep,
In blanched linen, smooth, and lavender'd,
While he from forth the closet brought a heap
Of candied apple, quince, and plum, and gourd;
With jellies smoother than the creamy curd,
And lucent syrops, tinct with cinnamon;
Manna and dates, in argosy transferr'd
From Fez, and spiced dainties, every one,
From silken Samarcand to cedar'd Lebanon.

31

These delicates he heap'd with glowing hand
On golden dishes and in baskets bright
Of wreathed silver: sumptuous they stand

In the retired quiet of the night,
Filling the chilly room with perfume light.—
"And now, my love, my seraph fair, awake!
Thou art my heaven, and I thine eremite:
Open thy eyes, for meek St. Agnes' sake,
Or I shall drowse beside thee, so my soul doth ache."

32

Thus whispering, his warm, unnerved arm
Sank in her pillow. Shaded was her dream
By the dusk curtains: —'twas a midnight charm
Impossible to melt as iced stream:
The lustrous salvers in the moonlight gleam;
Broad golden fringe upon the carpet lies:
It seem'd he never, never could redeem
From such a stedfast spell his lady's eyes;
So mus'd awhile, entoil'd in woofed phantasies.

33

Awakening up, he took her hollow lute,—
Tumultuous,—and, in chords that tenderest be,
He play'd an ancient ditty, long since mute,
In Provence call'd, "La belle dame sans mercy":
Close to her ear touching the melody;—
Wherewith disturb'd, she utter'd a soft moan:
He ceased—she panted quick—and suddenly
Her blue affrayed eyes wide open shone:
Upon his knees he sank, pale as smooth sculpted stone.

1818

The *Décima:* A Poetic Journey from Spain to New Mexico

PAT MORA

One of the many benefits of being bilingual is the opportunity to explore poetic forms in more than one language, from more than one tradition. Of course, we all can and do borrow, and we burrow into forms from other cultures and lands, but there's a particular burst of pleasure, I think, in discovering a form in a familiar language, particularly for those of us whose languages in complex ways and for complex reasons have been suppressed in this country.

When beginning my last poetry collection, *Aunt Carmen's Book of Practical Saints,* I decided to explore a variety of forms in my two home languages, English and Spanish. I had taken only the required Spanish classes in college years ago, and although no expert on traditional prosody in English, knew more about sonnets and sestinas than about *romances,* ballads; *coplas,* short lyrical stanzas; and *décimas.* The word *décima* means "tenth" and also refers to the traditional poetic form that originated in Spain, rhyming ten-line stanzas in octosyllabic meter with four rhymes in various patterns, including *abaabcdcdc.*

Because my book was to be written in the voice of an older woman in New Mexico, I had a particular interest in the form as it might have been heard here in the United States. I vaguely knew that the Mexican poet Sor Juana Inés de la Cruz, referred to as *la décima musa,* the tenth muse, a phrase with reverberations, had written décimas. Translator Alan Trueblood in his introduction to *A Sor Juana Anthology* comments on the skill of her verbal portraits in the single décimas 126 and 127 included here as examples of the form.

Poets such as Juan de Mena and Fray Iñigo de Mendoza at the time of John II wrote in this pattern found in the writings of Spanish poets since the fifteenth century. The form is also sometimes referred to in Spain as an *espinela* for the writer credited with first using it with some consistency, Vicente Martínez Espinel (1551–1624), more remembered as the author of the picaresque novel *Marcos de Obregón* (1618) than for his poetry. Espinel used what is often considered the traditional pattern of *abbaaccddc* later used on this continent. The décima's early popularity increased when incorporated by Félix Lope de Vega (1562–1635), the most prolific playwright of the Siglo de Oro, Spain's Golden Age of drama, a popularity that continued into the eighteenth and nineteenth centuries in, for example, the work of Juan Meléndez-Váldes (1754–1817).

As Octavio Paz states, "Poetry is made out of the very substance of history and society—language," and the form traveled on Spanish sailing vessels with the Conquest to Latin America and from Mexico and to *la frontera*, the border. A collection of décimas written primarily in central Mexico, *La décima en México*, was published in Buenos Aires in 1947, but the form also flourished as an oral tradition, and in song it seems to have traveled north to what is now the U.S.-Mexico border.

To discover how the décima had fared in this country, I opened two books, *With His Pistol in His Hand*, by the father of Chicano folklore, Américo Paredes, and *The Folklore of Spain in the American Southwest*, by Aurelio M. Espinosa. The book by Paredes had aided me some years back in understanding the *corrido*, the popular border ballad, when I'd attempted one after my father's death, and the volume by Espinosa was extremely helpful when I searched for forms popular in early New Mexico.

Paredes states that the décima's influence in Mexico in the 1800s was also evident in the 1860s and 1870s along the border. Men of Mexican descent learned the oral form from the early settlers, their grandfathers, "and their fathers preferred the *décima* to the *corrido*." Though the corrido is now the more popular sung form, the décima, was, according to Paredes, once heard from Panama to the plains.

That this complex form written by poets in seventeenth-century Spain is also an oral tradition in New Mexico is proof, according to Espinosa, of "the extraordinary vigor and persistence of Spanish tradition" in that state. Espinosa attributes décimas to what he calls "educated people." An interesting example probably written in the late 1800s is "El idioma español" ("The Spanish Language") by New Mexican lawyer, politician, and poet, Jesús María H. Alarid, a defense of his native language that begins, "Hermoso idioma español / Qué te quieren proscribir?" ("Oh beautiful Spanish language / Why do they wish to banish you?")

My spirits soar when I hear or read of a poetic tradition doing its rhythmic work in the mouths of those far from universities. It is, then, with interest that I've read the proceedings of a recent conference in the Canary Islands. *La Décima Popular en la Tradicion Hispánica* helped me to understand that the décima traveled not only geographically but also across the borders of class as evident in the words of the participants who refer to the form as mirroring the soul of the people, as emerging from small communities. Held at the Universidad de Las Palmas de Gran Canaria in 1992, that year of celebrating and snarling about *el encuentro,* the "encounter" of Europe and this continent, the conference united *decimistas,* also known as *decimeros,* practitioners of the improvised oral form, with professors who study oral traditions. Included in all the gracious formality that is part of any official symposium in Spanish are references to the sustained presence of this form, *la musa popular.* And décimas themselves, rich with wordplay, flavored the event and the subsequent volume from beginning to end. Poets and scholars eloquently stated a dedication to the form, praising *la cenicienta,* "the Cinderella" of traditional oral forms in Spanish. Even the official greeting from the local city council is in the form of a *décima con planta.* I can imagine the dramatic stating of the words, the democratic claiming, so to speak, of the form for all, that though the tradition begins with Espinel, it is no longer his alone, now the domain of any singer: "Aunque el poeta inventor / fuera Vicente Espinal, / la décima ya no es de él, / sino de cualquier cantor."

In Spain the ballad form, the *romance* with its octosyllabic, assonant rhyme is now more popular perhaps because of its flexibility, but at the conference, today's troubadours from various countries in the Americas spoke and sang with pride of the form they have obviously internalized, their rhyming and rhythmic response. They stressed the need to have memorized many examples, to know the range of the form both as a mark of respect to their predecessors, but also to be able to create new versions, the combining of tradition and invention. The occasions for the recitations can be verbal duels at which decimistas' ability to respond with verbal grace garners the respect of the audience, their own community members.

When I began to explore the décima myself, I knew little of even the brief history I've mentioned. I sat at my desk in Santa Fe trying to discover a traditional poetic structure that would seem appropriate for Aunt Carmen, a sacristan and natural poet, if you will, in addressing a particular saint in prayer. I would read about the life of a saint, one popular in the Mexican and Southwest pantheon; study an image if possible, and then turn to the books on form. Throughout the writing process, I hoped—one of the more important ingredients in the writing endeavor. In this instance, I hoped that I would discover a form in English or Spanish that would enhance our understanding of that saint's unique spirit. For some saints, a lullaby or lilting rhyme seemed the appropriate choice, but for the mystic and intellectual Saint Teresa of Ávila, I wanted a more elegant form, and yet one that would not seem artificial to the speaker since prayer at its purest is the union of mind and heart. Knowing that Sor Juana had written décimas and that they had also been sung in the pine-covered hills of New Mexico helped my decision.

In sixteenth- and seventeenth-century Spain, a popular form of the décima evolved that ultimately most interested me. The poem opens with a *cuarteta* also called a *redondilla* or a *planta*, quatrain; or with a five-line *quintilla*. Lines from this opening stanza are then repeated in the succeeding décimas; the first line of the opening quatrain becomes the last line of the first single décima, the second line in the quatrain, the last line of the second single décima; producing, then, a *décima con planta*, a poem of forty-four lines. The word *décima* is used both for the single ten-line poem or stanza and for an entire poem that uses a series of single décimas. It was the structure, the challenge of verbal weaving and the possibilities for resonance that intrigued me rather than the rhyme scheme. The example I've included that begins "A esta aldea bien venida" is from the Nativity play *Los pastores de Belén (The Shepherds of Bethlehem)* by Lope de Vega. Since the translation does not rhyme, as so often happens when the translator of a historical selection is not a poet, I encourage you to attempt to read the Spanish version aloud even if you do not speak the language.

I wonder now why I chose to avoid the traditional rhyme schemes. *Saints* was written as a whole piece rather than as a collection, and perhaps at that point in the manuscript I wanted to tone the rhyme down a bit, to balance formal structures and yet create the natural, informal voice of a devout woman struggling with faith. Intrigued by the process of creating an overture that then echoes in the piece, I will attempt the *décima con planta* again, incorporating rhyme.

I am a beginner in experimenting with traditional poetic forms and am still exploring when they release or impede my work; but like the décima I was, and am, on a journey in language—whoops, in languages!

Sor Juana

126
En un anillo retrató a la señora
condesa de Paredes; dice por qué

Este retrato que ha hecho
copiar me cariño ufano,
es sobrescribir la mano
lo que tiene dentro el pecho:

que, como éste viene estrecho
a tan alta perfección,
brota fuera la afición;
y en el índice la emplea,
para que con verdad sea
índice de corazón.

127
Al mismo intento

Éste, que a la luz más pura
quiso imitar la beldad,
representa su deidad,
mas no copia su hermosura.
En él, me culto asegura
su veneración mayor;
mas no muerstres el error
de pincel tan poco sabio,
que para Lysi es agravio
el que para mí es favor.

1988

English translations by Alan Trueblood

9 (126)
*Having had a portrait of Her Ladyship,
the Countess de Paredes, painted on a
ring, she tells why*

This portrait, which love's dedication
caused to be copied here,
is the hand's indication
of all the breast holds dear.
For such extreme perfection
the breast offered little space,
hence the overflow of affection
on the index has found a place,
which finger by grace of art
is index of the heart.

10 (127)
On the same subject

The portrait was hoping to catch
a beauty divinely bright;
divinity caught it aright
but beauty it could not match.
In it my worship has secured
the goal of its veneration,
but the faulty brush's creation
has left Lysis' beauty obscured.
Thus piety places its trust
in a portrait to beauty unjust.

1988

LOPE DE VEGA

Los pastores de Belén

A esta aldea bien venida
seáis, niña tierna y fuerte,
porque habéis de dar la muerta
al que nos quitó la vida.
　Eva, primera pastora,
la vida al mundo quitó
mas ya, hermosa labradora,
si por ella se perdió,
por vos se restaura agora;
la vida entonces perdida
venís, naciendo, a traer;
pues se nos traéis la vida,
¿quién, como vos, puede ser
a esta aldea bien venida?
　Mató, un león animoso,
yendo a Tamnata Sansón,
y volviendo cuidadoso,
halló en el muerto león
un panal dulce y sabroso.
¿Qué mucho que el hombre acierte
este enigma celestial,
y que, si a vos se convierte,
como león y panal,
seáis, niña tierna y fuerte?

Pero como del león
salió a Sansón el panal,
ya que tan distintios son,
de vos, panal celestial,
saldrá el cordera a Sion.
Éste dará muerte al fuerte
enemigo, y vos daréis
vida al mundo de tal suerte,
que tierna y fuerte seréis,
pues habís de dar la muerte.
    Apenas pudo tener
de que a una mujer burló
la sierpe antigua placer,
cuando Dios la amenazó
con el pie de otra mujer.
Si vos, reina esclarecida,
la luna habéis de pisar
vos seréis del sol vestida,
la planta que ha de matar
a quien nos quitó la vida.

1985

English translation by Aurelio M. Espinosa

Welcome be to this village
gentle and virtuous maiden,
since you come to destroy him
who deprived us of our life.
    Eve, our very first shepherdess,
deprived the world of all life,
but now, most beautiful maiden,
if through her this came to pass,
through you life is now restored;
our life lost to us through her
you now have come to restore.
Therefore if you bring us life,
whom else can be welcome more,
welcome be to this village?
    Samson, going to Tamnata,
did kill a ferocious lion,
and approaching with great care

he found inside the dead lion
a honeycomb sweet and savory.
What wonder can there be then
that the enigma is solved,
and that we consider you
as both honeycomb and lion,
gentle and virtuous maiden?
    And just as from the lion
the sweet honeycomb came forth,
both being entirely different,
from you, celestial honeycomb,
the lamb will come forth to Zion.
For the lamb will then destroy
the common enemy, and you
will restore life to the world,
by being gentle and strong,
since you come to destroy him.
    Hardly any satisfaction
did the old serpent receive
when it did deceive a woman,
for God straightway threatened it
with another woman's heel.
If you, most illustrious queen,
shall rest your feet on the moon,
the rays of the sun will clothe you
for you are to destroy the one
who deprived us of our life.

                                        1985

PAT MORA

Santa Teresa de Ávila

"If I had not been so wicked . . ."
Your words reveal your character,
Stern, aware of hell's punishments,
Forever, ever and ever.

A child, you raced hand in hand
with your brother, shortcut to heaven,
a beheading by Moors, savored
the honey taste of martyrdom,

your soul zipping to joy. Wicked?
No. Though stern, I hear your humor,
"I can be had for a sardine,"
life like "a night in a bad inn."
Sly, forever peering inside,
"If I had not been so wicked . . ."

Restless. What to do with so much of you?
Come walk around this church, compose
letters, books. Your charms will make
priests dizzy, woman at forty who
finds herself again, as we do
if blessed. Take me to His Majesty's
whispers, white light enters, lifts
us from this wood. You urge yourself,
"Cold simpleton, not think much, love much."
Your words reveal your character.

Years you vomited. Was it passion
you spewed, an excess of spirit
your body, like a rigid rose,
unable to hold such longings?
The mind can't save us forever.
Even one ever blinding as yours
burrowed to lose consciousness
from pain of self-entanglement,
in terror sought blessed safety,
stern, aware of hell's punishments.

Head aching, you demanded prayer,
poverty, purity, but savored
"holy madness," cleaned out cozy
convents like you purged your body,
yet opened your lips to His, sweet face
transporting you. Your body,
no pastel lover, knew fire, burned
gloriously. Kindle my spirit,
Doctora, set me burning to light
forever, ever and ever.

1997

III

Received Forms

The Folk Ballad

W. D. SNODGRASS

The word *ballad* has meant such various things in different times and places that it's nearly impossible to give a definition—indeed to make *any* statement about ballads—that won't be challenged by some scholar or specialist. As with many general terms or abstractions, we all agree that such a thing exists but squabble fiercely about its specifics. Yet, since experts—folklorists, musicologists, literary scholars, critics—not only agree that the folk ballad does exist but that it has great significance as an art form, I will try to give a general description that will apply to most examples.

Nearly everyone agrees that the Folk Ballad tells a story—one which, whether its tone is serious or comic, deals with matters deeply important to its community. Earlier, heroic or epic songs had told of the exploits of kings or warrior heroes on whom the fate of a nation or racial group might depend. Such songs might include many events and could be very long—two thousand lines would not be unusual. The ballads, instead, tend to focus on a single action involving the problems of some individual, whether king or commoner, and are correspondingly much shorter. In the epic song, it might be important whether the king found a wife—begetting an heir who could prevent revolt or invasion affected the whole community—but whether he *liked* that wife mattered only if it led to events that affected the larger group. The newer concerns of the ballad reflected more settled times, when men could give more thought to personal emotions: love, domestic strife, individual triumphs or griefs, the supernatural, the meaning of human life. Yet, in spite of this concern with personal matters, the narrator tends to be detached and to make little comment, though attitudes and opinions may be strongly present in the choice of details and figures of speech. This detachment is reflected in most early styles of performance; the singing may have many musical ornaments but is seldom dramatic or performer-oriented.

Despite important exceptions, most ballads were composed and sung by common people rather than professional musicians or entertainers. However composed, they became part of the common heritage and were passed on orally from person to person, often across national and language borders. Though texts can cross such barriers more easily than melodies, stories often take on new characteristics in a new language or among a different people. The earliest examples seem to have appeared in France in the late thirteenth century, then were disseminated through most of Europe and parts of Asia by conquest, migration, or the spread of commerce, especially by workers and merchants of textiles. At a much later date, they were collected and written down (sadly, often without their melodies) by folklorists, poets, or other enthusiasts; thus, they may exist in many different versions. Indeed, in some areas each singer may have his or her own version of a particular ballad. Since collectors or editors were usually more learned or literary than the "folk" who sang the ballads, many songs come to us in revised or "improved" versions. This, of course, scandalizes folklorists and ethnomusicologists, for whom authenticity is paramount. Among the examples given here, "Frankie and Johnny" has been suspected of such contamination. Yet, since such revisions sometimes brought improvements, indeed sometimes turned quite ordinary texts into masterpieces, I find it hard to regret the process. I am glad to know of the song's history, but if this be impurity, I vote for impurity.

Unlike heroic or epic songs, usually composed line by line, folk ballads are composed in stanzas, so having a more obviously patterned form. Even the single event on which they focus will tend to be symmetrically shaped—the final stanza or scene will tend to look back to, and finish out, the action started in the beginning. In the beginning of "Sir Patrick Spence" we see the king seated with the Scottish lords at his knee; at the end we see Sir Patrick with the lords "at his feet"—his courage and sense of duty make him king among the dead. Often (as in "Edward" or "Lord Randal," not included here for reasons of space) the first half of each stanza is a question answered in the second half. Phrases can be repeated in the same position (especially in a first line), stanza after stanza. Likewise, most of a stanza can be repeated as an answer by a second speaker. Together with this patterning, ballads tend to have a more compressed and meaningful style of language and structure. Formulaic expressions ("her lily-white hand," "he turned him right and round about") are also frequent.

Most Scottish and English ballads, on which I will concentrate, have their origins in the late fifteenth and early sixteenth centuries, though some include much earlier materials. Again, most ballads were not collected or printed until much later, often till the eighteenth century, and changes may have occurred during this long period of oral transmission. The most authoritative collection was made by James Francis Child of Harvard University and published between 1882 and 1898; nearly all ballads are identified by their number in his collection. The melodies, seldom given by Child, have been collected and published by Bertrand H. Bronson of the University of California, Berkeley, during the present century.

The meter of most English or Scottish ballads is best described as a loose iambic verse with freedom to add or omit light syllables between stresses. If, however, this happens frequently or if many secondary stresses are added, the meter is more easily described as accentual or stress verse (see lines below from "Hind Horn"). The most common stanza form—called a four-by-four, or ballad stanza—has four accents in the first and third lines; often, these lines will break into half lines. In the second and fourth lines the last stress is replaced by a pause. (See "Sir Patrick Spence" or "Little Mattie Groves.") All the units (half lines, lines, and two-line segments) will tend to coincide with syntactic groups. The largest break will end the second line, where the melody will replace the missing stress with a rest or extended cadence note. In some ballads, the second line may also have four accents; in still others (e.g., "The Great Sealchie of Sule Skerry") all lines may have four full accents.

A number of ballads use rhyming couplets as a stanza:

> Hynde Horn's bound, love, and Hynde Horn's free;
> Whare was ye born? or frae what cuntree?
> > "Hind Horn," Child no.17G, not included here

Again, a couplet of this sort can be extended into a quatrain or an even longer stanza by a second couplet, by repeating lines, adding refrains, or short lines that fill out material already introduced. The narrative, in itself, may still be told largely in what boils down to a couplet.

Refrains appear fairly often, though more frequently in regions where the ballad (as its name implies) was still closely involved with dancing and with group singing. These refrains may relate closely to the ballad's story (as in "Edward"), may consist of "nonsense" syllables or seem unrelated in tone (as in "The Three Ravens"), or may relate to the dancers' movements ("Bow down, bow down" in "The Twa Sisters," Child no.10, not given here). When ballads were sung by a communal group, the leader usually sang the narrative lines while the chorus sang the refrains; elsewhere (e.g., in France), the leader would sing a line to the first half of the melody, and the chorus repeated that line to the second half. In "The Three Ravens" a narrative in couplets has been extended into a seven-line stanza by using repeated lines as well as refrains. When such ballads are printed, it is common to save space by printing in full the first (and perhaps the last) stanza, giving only the narrative couplets for the rest. If the ballad is to have full effect, however, the unprinted lines should be spoken or read since the refrain, appearing in succeeding stanzas, may have differing or cumulative meanings (e.g., the various meanings of the word "downe" in "The Three Ravens").

In "Little Mattie Groves," the rhyme form runs *xaxa,* in other ballads *abab;* still other variants and more complicated stanzas (as noted above) may also appear. The rhymes themselves need not always be exact, and in many cases the passage of time and dialect will have weakened previously full rhymes.

Of the examples we can give here, "Sir Patrick Spence" is certainly one of the most famous and widely admired. The contrast of the live king with the dead Sir Patrick, the opposition of stanzas 5 and 6 showing Sir Patrick's despair then determination, the ominous moon balanced against the image of the ladies' faces, the singer's admiration for Sir Patrick and his mockery of the Scottish lords with their "bluid-red wine," their featherbeds and "cork-heild" shoes (fancy French pumps that can't keep them afloat)—all create an unforgettable effect. At first reading, "The Three Ravens" seems grim, but its final attitude is actually hopeful: though we die, perhaps slain under our shield (i.e., by treachery?) and certain ravens will try to live by devouring our defeated bodies, there are also faithful creatures who will protect us and so carry on our values in the world.

Many songs and folktales are haunted by myths about seals. "The Great Sealchie of Sule Skerry" is a supernatural being, able to swim the seas as a seal or to come upon land as a human. In this ballad, he is not only able to give a baby to a human woman in ways she doesn't understand, but also can appear and disappear at will, and can predict his own death. This echoes a mythic archetype: the monstrous beast-lover who will be killed by, or will turn into, the true and benign love. "Little Mattie Groves" is typical of many ballads of jealousy and revenge. Here, a cowardly peasant is trapped between the dangerously neurotic Lady Gay and her blustering, violent husband. The husband, alone, survives to learn something—his power is useless in the face of human passions. If we cannot echo his view of them as "the fairest folk / In all of Engeland," we share his regret that none *could* stay his hand.

Some scholars or experts may object to the inclusion of "Frankie and Johnny" among our examples. Not given in Child's collection, it is American in source, and of later provenance than the other examples. Yet, the American poet Randall Jarrell often referred to it as one of the five or six best poems made in the United States and it does, indeed, have many of the qualities of the ballads we've considered. Though one of the few ballads better spoken than sung, it was composed by popular musicians (black singers and pianists) in a small, tight-knit community. It is based on an actual event—Frances Baker did actually shoot Albert Johnson—but has been much transformed in repeated tellings. The brilliant use of imagery is very similar to that of "Little Mattie Groves." Jarrell remarked that to show Johnny in bed with Alice Fry but wearing a horseman's costly hat—probably a gift from Frankie—tells more about his character than most writers could reveal in three volumes. Frankie's embodiment in a red kimono returning to the hotel is a sign of how she earns her living and also a symbol of, on the one hand, her salable parts and, on the other, of her passionate rage. Similarly, in "Little Mattie Groves" Lady Gay's claim that the horn blast is her father's reveals both that she is a shepherd's daughter who has married out of her station and that she now longs for the warmth of the sheepfold and the peasant community. Though Mattie later says that she "lies," she may not know whose horn she hears; still, having lured Mattie there, it is her business to keep sharp senses about her. Her refusal to save her life, which Arling offers, suggests that this was her intention from the first. The powerful Arling, meantime, is first brought so low that he begs her to lie about loving him, then is reduced to brute, senseless violence. His transformation parallels Frankie's conscience wakening to see that although "he done her wrong," she had no right to commit a deeper wrong against him. This involves seeing that one person cannot really own and control another; that she must turn away from Johnny, now a source of bitter recrimination, to the Lord she feels certain will accept her.

SIR PATRICK SPENCE

The king sits in Dumferling toune,
    Drinking the blude-reid wine: *[blood-red]*
"O whar will I get me a skeely sailor,   *[skillful]*
    To sail this schip of mine?"

Up and spak an eldern knicht,   *[elderly*
    Sat at the kings richt knee: *knight]*
"Sir Patrick Spence is the best sailor,
    That sails upon the se."

The king has written a braid letter,   *[broad,*
    And signd it wi his ain hand,   *important]*
And sent it to Sir Patrick Spence,
    Was walking on the sand.

The first line that Sir Patrick red,
    A loud lauch lauched he;   *[laugh]*
The next line that Sir Patrick red,
    The teir blinded his ee.   *[tear . . . eye]*

"O wha is this has done this deid,   *[who]*
    This ill deid don to me,
To send me out this time o' the year,
    To sail upon the se!"

"Mak hast, mak hast, my mirry men all   *[haste]*
    Our guid schip sails the morne":
"O say na sae, my master deir,
    For I feir a deadlie storme.

"Late, late yestreen I saw the new moone,   *[last night]*
    Wi' the auld moone in hir arme,
And I feir, I feir, my master deir,
    That we will cum to harme."

O our Scots nobles wer richt laith   *[right loath]*
    To weet their cork-heild schoone;   *[shoes]*
Bot lang owre a' the play wer playd,   *[long before]*
    Their hats they swam aboone.   *[around]*

O it's mony and mony a featherbed
    Went flutterin' to the fame;   *[foam]*
And it's mony and mony a Scot's lord's son
    Will never mair come hame.

O lang, lang may their ladies sit,
    Wi' their fans into their hand,
Or eir they see Sir Patrick Spence
    Cum sailing to the land.

O lang, lang may their ladies stand,
    Wi' their gold kems in their hair   *[combs]*
Waiting for thar ain deir lords,
    For they'll se thame na mair.

Haf owre, haf owre to Aberdour   *[Halfway*
    It's fiftie fadom deip,   *over]*
And thair lies guid Sir Patrick Spence,
    Wi' the Scots lords at his feit.

The Three Ravens

There were three ravens sat on a tree,
    Downe a downe, hay downe, hay downe
There were three ravens sat on a tree,
    With a downe.
There were three ravens sat on a tree,
They were black as they might be
    With a downe derrie, derrie, derrie,
        down, down.

The one of them said to his make,   *[mate]*
"Where shall we our breakfast take?"

"Downe in yonder greene field,
There lies a knight slain under his shield.

"His hounds they lie down at his feete,
So well they can their master keepe.

"His haukes they flie so eagerly,
There's no fowle dare him come nie."   *[nigh, near]*

Downe their comes a fallow doe,
As great with yong as she might goe.

She lift up his bloudy hede,
And kist his wounds that were so red.

She got him up upon her backe,
And carried him to earthen lake.

She buried him before the prime,
She was dead herselfe ere even-song time.

God send every gentleman,
    Downe a downe, hay downe, hay downe
God send every gentleman,
    With a downe.
God send every gentleman,
Such haukes such hounds, and such a leman   *[lover]*
    With a downe derrie, derrie, derrie,
        down, down.

The Great Sealchie of Sule Skerry

An earthly nourrice sits and sings   [nurse]
And still she sings, "Baa, lilly ween;   [little baby]
It's little ken I my bairn's fadir,   [know . . .
Nor less the land that he staps in."   baby's father]
                                                  [stops, dwells]

Then up rose one at her bed-fit   [bed feet]
And a grumly guest I'm sure was he,   [frightening]
Saying, "Here am I, thy bairn's fadir
Although I be not comely."

"I am a man upon the land;
I am a sealchie in the sea,
And when I'm far and far frae land
My dwelling is in Sule Skerry."

"It was na weel," quo the maiden fair,   [not good]
"And a goodly thing it never could be
For the Great Sealchie of Sule Skerry
To cam and aught a bairn to me."   [give]

And he has ta'en a purse of gold
And he has pat it on her knee
Saying, "Give thu me my little young son
And take thu up thy nourrice fee.

"It shall com to pass on a summer's day
When the sun shines haet on every stane   [hot . . . .
That I shall take my little young son   stone]
And teach him how to swim the faem.   [foam]

"And thu shalt marry a gunner proud
And right good gunner I'm sure he'll be
And the very first shot they ever he shoots
Wil kill both my young son and me."

Little Mattie Groves

O holy day, high holy day,
  The best day of the year;
Little Mattie Groves to church did go
  Some holy words to hear.
  (Repeat line as refrain.)

He spied some ladies wearing black
  As they come into view,
But Arling's wife was gaily clad,
  The flower of the few.

She trippèd up to Mattie Groves,
  Her eyes so low cast down;
Said, "Pray do stop the night with me
  As you pass through the town.

"Oh pray, oh pray, with me come stay;
  I'll hide thee out of sight,
And serve you there beyond compare
  And sleep with you the night."

"I cain't not go, I dare not go;
  I fear 'twould cost my life;
For I know you by your metal ring
  To be Lord Arling's wife."
  The great Lord Arling's wife.

"This may be false; this may be true;
  I cain't deny hit all.
But Arling's gone to consecrate
  Lord Henry of Whitehall."

Her purty page did listen well
  To all that they did say,
And ere the sun did set again
  He quickly sped away.

O, he did run the King's highway;
  O he did swim the tide.
He ne'er did stop untwill he come
  To great Lord Arling's side.

"What news, what news, my boldy boy;
  What news bring you to me?—
My castle burned, my tenants robbed,
  My lady with baby?"

"No wrong hath 'fell your farms and lands
    While ye have been away;
But Mattie Groves is bedded up
    With your fair Lady Gay."

"If this be false," Lord Arling said,
    "As I take hit to be,
I'll raise a scaffil tower up
    And hangèd you shall be."

"Lord Arling, if what I have said
    Is false as false can be,
You needn't raise a scaffil up
    But hang me to a tree."

Lord Arling called his merry men
    And bad them with him go
But bound them ne'er a word to say
    And ne'er a horn to blow.

Among Lord Arling's merry men
    Be those who wish no ill
And the bravest of all blew a blast on his horn.
    A blast so loud, so shrill.

"What's this? What's this?" cried Mattie Groves,
    "A horn so loud, so clear?
'Tis nothing more than Arling's men,
    The ones that I do fear."

"Lie down, lie down," cried Arling's wife,
    "And keep my back from cold;
'Tis nothing but my father's horn
    That calls the sheep to fold."

Now Mattie Groves he did lie down;
    He tuck a nap of sleep;
And when he woke Lord Arling was
    A-standing at his feet.

"How now? How now?" Lord Arling cried,
    "How do you like my sheets?
How do you like my new-wedded wife
    What lies in your arms asleep?"

"Oh, hit's very well I like your bed;
    Hit's well I like your sheets;
But hit's best I like your Lady Gay
    What lies but hain't asleep."

"Put on, put on, put on man's clothes
    As quick as e'er you can:
In England it shall ne'er be said
    I slewed a naked man."

"I cain't not rise, I dare not rise,
    I fear 'twould cost my life
For you have got two bitter swords
    And I hain't got a knife."

"I know I've got two bitter swords;
    They cost me deep in purse;
But you shall have the bestest one
    And I shall take the worst."

The firstest stroke little Mattie struck
    He hurt Lord Arling sore.
The nextest stroke Lord Arling struck;
    Little Mattie struck no more.

"Rise up, rise up, my gay young wife;
    Draw on your purty clothes,
And tell me do you like me best
    Or like you Mattie Groves?"

Oh, she lifted Mattie's dying face,
    She kissed from cheek to chin,
"Oh, hit's Mattie Groves I'd rather have
    Than Arling and all his kin."

Oh, he's took his wife by the lily-white hand
    And led her to the hall
And cut off her head with his bitter sword
    And stove it agin the wall.

"Ah, woe is me, my merry men;
    Why stayed you not my hand?
For here I've slewed the fairest folk
    In all of Engeland."
    In all of Engeland.

Frankie and Johnny

Frankie and Johnny were lovers, O, how that couple
   could love,
Swore to be true to each other, true as the stars above.
[*Refrain*]: *He was her man, but he done her wrong.*

Frankie she was his woman, everybody knows,
She spent one hundred dollars for a suit of Johnny's clothes.
[*Refrain*]

Frankie and Johnny went walking, Johnny in his bran'
   new suit,
"O good Lawd," says Frankie, "but don't my Johnny
   look cute?"
[*Refrain*]

Frankie went down to Memphis; she went on the
   evening train.
She paid one hundred dollars for Johnny a watch and chain.
[*Refrain*]

Frankie went down to the corner, to buy a glass of beer;
She said to the fat bartender, "Has my loving man been here?
He was my man, but he done me wrong."

"Ain't going to tell you no story, ain't going to tell you
   no lie,
I seen your man 'bout an hour ago with a girl named
   Alice Fry.
If he's your man, he's doing you wrong."

Frankie went back to the hotel, she didn't go there for fun,
Under her long red kimono she toted a forty-four gun.
[*Refrain*]: *He was her man, but he done her wrong.*

Frankie went down to the hotel, looked through the window
   so high,
There was her lovin' Johnny a-lovin' up Alice Fry;
[*Refrain*]

Frankie threw back her kimono, took out the old forty-four;
Roota-toot-toot, three time she shoot, right through that
   hotel door.
She shot her man, 'cause he done her wrong.

Johnny grabbed off his Stetson, "O good Lawd, Frankie,
    don't shoot,"
But Frankie put her finger on the trigger, and the gun went
    roota-toot-toot,
He was her man, but she shot him down.

"Roll me over easy, roll me over slow,
Roll me over on my left side, 'cause my wounds are hurting
    me so,
I was her man, but I done her wrong."

With the first shot Johnny staggered; with the second shot
    he fell;
When the third bullet hit him, there was a new man's face
    in hell.
[*Refrain*]

Frankie heard a rumbling away down under the ground,
Maybe it was Johnny where she had shot him down.
He was her man, and she done him wrong.

Oh, bring on your rubber-tired hearses, bring on your
    rubber-tired hacks,
"They're taking my Johnny to the buryin' groun' but they'll
    never bring him back.
He was my man, but he done me wrong."

Then Judge he said to the jury, "It's plain as plain can be.
The woman shot her man, so it's murder in the
    second degree."
[*Refrain*]

Now it wasn't murder in the second degree, it wasn't murder
    in the third.
Frankie simply dropped her man, like a hunter drops a bird.
[*Refrain*]

"Oh, put me in that dungeon. Oh, put me in that cell.
Put me where the northeast wind blows from the southeast
    corner of hell.
I shot my man 'cause he done me wrong."

Frankie walked up to the scaffold, as calm as a girl could be,
She turned her eyes to heaven and said, "Good Lord, I'm
    coming to thee.
He was my man, and I done him wrong."

The Ballade:
Exquisite Intricacy

JUDITH BARRINGTON

Oscar Wilde once wrote about his days at Oxford that they were "days of lyrical ardours and of studious sonnet-writing; days when one loved the exquisite intricacy and musical repetitions of the ballade, and the villanelle with its linked long-drawn echoes and its curious completeness . . . days, in which I am glad to say, there was far more rhyme than reason."[1] Many poets have shared Wilde's delight at the ballade's intricacy, but many must have found it frustrating too, since the French forms have been generally considered much more demanding of the English-speaking poet than forms such as sonnets and ballads.

The masters of the form are Charles d'Orléans (1394–1465) and François Villon (1431–c. 1463), with the work of Villon, in particular, remaining influential into modern times. Before Villon and d'Orléans, Guillaume de Machaut, Eustache Deschamps, and Christine de Pizan all contributed to the establishment of the ballade as a popular form. Like other French poetry, the ballade (from the Latin, *ballare:* "to dance") grew out of the songs of the troubadors, rising to prominence relatively soon after lyric poems separated from the music that had previously accompanied them. The last poet to combine musical and poetic talent was the fourteenth-century Machaut, who played a major role in establishing the fixed genres that dominated French poetry for a hundred years after his death: the lai, virelay, *chanson royale, complainte,* rondeau, and ballade, with the last two being the most popular.[2]

Many of the ballades of d'Orléans were written during the twenty-five years he was captive in England after the French defeat at the Battle of Agincourt. Surprisingly, he wrote little about war, but used his poetry instead to reflect on his confinement and his inner life, particularly his homesickness for France. According to David Fein, he "refused to sacrifice depth of thought or sharpness of imagery to the demands of his chosen medium."[3] He wrote love ballades, which are presumed to be addressed to his wife, and laments after her death. He also used the form in forty letter-poems to the duke of Burgundy, requesting help in securing his release. After his return to France, he turned increasingly to the rondeau and wrote sad poems about sickness and old age, though they were still marked by his cynical tone and occasional wit and humor.

Villon, by contrast, was not a member of the aristocracy: far from it. He was born in 1431, the same year that Joan of Arc was burned at the stake. Poor but educated, he fended for himself and became involved in the fringes of criminal society, which caused him to flee Paris at least twice and spend some time in jail, which strongly influenced his subject matter and view of society.[4] According to Louis Untermeyer, "No English craftsman has ever put a very considerable fraction of the force and passion which Villon burned into his ballades. Villon's compositions, strict in pattern, are bitter and bawdy and brilliantly spontaneous."[5]

In France, the ballade remained popular through the fourteenth and fifteenth centuries before being neglected for more than two hundred years and then revived by Théodore de Banville (1802–1891). In England, it enjoyed a much shorter popularity, when Chaucer and a few of his followers toyed with it, but never felt as bound to the fixed form as the French poets did. According to Edmund Gosse, the ballade was reintroduced to English poets in 1876, when their interest was sparked by the circulation in London of de Banville's *Trente-Six Ballades Joyeux*.[6] In that same year, Robert Louis Stevenson published an essay on d'Orléans, and the following year one on Villon.[7] From then on poets such as Austin Dobson, Algernon Charles Swinburne, G. K. Chesterton, and Wilde kept it in circulation. Of this group, it was Dobson who reintroduced the form to the English literary scene, but Swinburne who surpassed all his contemporaries in mastering it.

Although Dobson considered the ballade unsuitable for "the treatment of grave and elevated themes," Villon had already used it effectively as a tool for social commentary, and later poets writing in English, such as Richard Wilbur and Louis MacNeice, certainly transcended the light-verse label put on it by Dobson. In the late twentieth- and early twenty-first-century, poets like Marilyn Hacker, Dudley Randall, Mary Kinzie, and Judith Johnson have continued to grapple with its complexity.

The *ballade* has twenty-eight lines divided into three octaves and one quatrain (the envoi). The rhyme scheme, which holds firm throughout the poem, not merely within stanzas, is as follows: stanzas 1, 2 and 3: *ababbcbC* (the capital letter designating a refrain). Envoi: *bcbC*. No rhyme can be repeated, even if spelled differently: the rhyming syllable must be different in sound (thus "see" and "sea" are not allowed). Variations include the *ballade supreme*, with three ten-line stanzas and four rhymes, and the *double ballade* or *double ballade supreme*, with six stanzas of eight or ten lines respectively. There is also the *double refrain ballade,* which is structured like the regular ballade, but in which the fourth line of each stanza is also given over to a refrain. Chant royal is also a member of the ballade family. It has five eleven-line stanzas and one five-line envoi with the last line of each stanza being a refrain. The rhyme scheme here is *ababccddedE;* and the envoi *ddedE.* The ballade is a syllabic form, whose lines have eight syllables (though the ballade supreme more often has ten syllables per line).

Having tried to write chant royal myself, I can attest to the fact that the major difficulty in all these forms stems from the relatively few rhymes available in English as opposed to French. It is particularly hard to maintain the freshness of rhyming words since the same rhymes occur throughout the poem. The refrains, too, can be difficult, since they must recur in a natural way that does not seem tacked on.

In choosing the examples below, I have tried to trace the form through its various historical manifestations, as well as to demonstrate the variety of subjects explored within its boundaries. Villon's "Ballade (of the ladies of bygone times)," in particular, spawned many translations, adaptations, and responses, both from his contemporaries and from ours. Its refrain, "Mais où sont les neiges d'antan?" continues to strike a chord; as William Carlos Williams said, Villon expressed "with a mere question, deftly phrased, the profundity of the ages."[8] I have given here the translation by Gabriel Dante Rossetti, which, apart from a variant rhyme in the envoi, adheres closely to the form. There are also adaptations and parodies of this ballade by Andrew Lang, de Banville, Gosse, Galway Kinnell, and Hacker, among many others.

The tribute to Villon by Swinburne, included below, is an example of the ballade supreme.

FRANÇOIS VILLON

Translated by Dante Gabriel Rossetti (1828–1882)

The Ballad of Dead Ladies

Tell me now in what hidden way is
　　Lady Flora the lovely Roman?
Where's Hipparchia, and where is Thais,
　　Neither of them the fairer woman?
　　Where is Echo, beheld of no man,
Only heard on river and mere,—
　　She whose beauty was more than human? . . .
But where are the snows of yester-year?

Where's Heloise, the learned nun,
    For whose sake Abeillard, I ween,
Lost manhood and put priesthood on?
    (From Love he won such dule and teen!)
    And where, I pray you, is the Queen
Who willed that Buridan should steer
    Sewed in a sack's mouth down the Seine? . . .
But where are the snows of yester-year?

White Queen Blanche, like a queen of lilies,
    With a voice like any mermaiden,—
Bertha Broadfoot, Beatrice, Alice,
    And Ermengarde the lady of Maine,—
    And that good Joan whom Englishmen
At Rouen doomed and burned her there,—
    Mother of God, where are they then? . . .
But where are the snows of yester-year?

Nay, never ask this week, fair lord,
    Where they are gone, nor yet this year,
Except with this for an overword,—
    But where are the snows of yester-year?

ALGERNON CHARLES SWINBURNE (1837–1909)

A Ballad of François Villon

Prince of all Ballad-Makers

Bird of the bitter bright grey golden morn
    Scarce risen upon the dusk of dolorous years,
First of us all and sweetest singer born
    Whose far shrill note the world of new men hears
    Cleave the cold shuddering shade as twilight clears;
When song new-born put off the old world's attire
And felt its tune on her changed lips expire,
    Writ foremost on the roll of them that came
Fresh girt for service of the latter lyre,
    Villon, our sad bad glad mad brother's name!

Alas the joy, the sorrow, and the scorn,
    That clothed thy life with hopes and sins and fears,
And gave thee stones for bread and tares for corn

And plume-plucked jail-birds for thy starveling peers
    Till death clipt close their flight with shameful shears;
Till shifts came short and loves were hard to hire,
When lilt of song nore twitch of twangling wire
    Could buy thee bread or kisses; when light fame
Spurned like a ball and haled through brake and briar,
    Villon, our sad bad glad mad brother's name!

Poor splendid wings so frayed and soiled and torn!
    Poor kind wild eyes so dashed with light quick tears!
Poor perfect voice, most blithe when most forlorn,
    That rings athwart the sea whence no man steers
    Like joy-bells crossed with death-bells in our ears!
What far delight has cooled the fierce desire
That like some ravenous bird was strong to tire
    On that rail flesh and soul consumed with flame,
But left more sweet than roses to respire,
    Villon, our sad bad glad mad brother's name?

Envoi

Prince of sweet songs made out of tears and fire,
A harlot was thy nurse, a God thy sire;
    Shame soiled thy song, and song assoiled thy shame,
But from thy feet now death has washed the mire,
Love reads out first at head of all our quire,
    Villon, our sad bad glad mad brother's name.

ROSE E. MACAULAY (1881–1958)

Ballade of Dreams

"Captain, for what brave hire
        Sail'st thou upon this sea?"
"I have dreamt a dream of desire,
        And I seek no other fee.
Shores sweet with rosemary
        Down to blue waters grew—
. . . I dreamt: yet I say to thee
        Only our dreams are true.

"I see the gleam of a spire,
  The hint of a shadowed tree,
The glint of the sun, like fire,
  Where haply that land may be."
"In dreaming your youth may flee,
  Captain and vagrant crew."
"Good luck to our vagrancy!
  Only our dreams are true."

"The sea has a deadly ire,
  Her sorrows are ill to dree;
Does not thy sailing tire?
  What of thy Arcady?"
"I bear with adversity,
  Bear with the sea's great rue.
I have dreamt of a port . . . ay me!
  Only our dreams are true."

Envoi

Sailors of all degree,
  This I do say to you—
Voyage on hopefully,
  Only our dreams are true.

G. K. CHESTERTON (1874–1936)

A Ballade of Suicide

The gallows in my garden, people say,
Is new and neat and adequately tall.
I tie the noose on in a knowing way
As one that knots his necktie for a ball;
But just as all the neighbors—on the wall—
Are drawing a long breath to shout "Hurray!"
The strangest whim has seized me . . . After all
I think I will not hang myself today.

To-morrow is the time I get my pay—
My uncle's sword is hanging in the hall—
I see a little cloud all pink and grey—
Perhaps the rector's mother will *not* call—
I fancy that I heard from Mr. Gall

That mushrooms could be cooked another way—
I never read the books of Juvenal—
I think I will not hang myself today.

The world will have another washing day;
The decadents decay; the pedants fall;
And H. G. Wells has found that children play,
And Bernard Shaw discovered that they squall;
Rationalists are growing rational—
And through thick woods one finds a stream astray,
So secret that the very sky seems small—
I think I will not hang myself today.

Envoi

Prince, I can hear the trumpet of Germinal,
The tumbrils toiling up the terrible way;
Even today your royal head may fall—
I think I will not hang myself today.

DUDLEY RANDALL (1914–)

The Southern Road

There the black river, boundary to hell,
And here the iron bridge, the ancient car,
And grim conductor, who with surly yell
Forbids white soldiers where the black ones are.
And I re-live the enforced avatar
Of desperate journey to a dark abode
Made by my sires before another war;
And I set forth upon the southern road.

To a land where shadowed songs like flowers swell
And where the earth is scarlet as a scar
Friezed by the bleeding lash that fell (O fell!)
Upon my father's flesh. O far, far, far
And deep my blood has drenched it. None can bar
My birthright to the loveliness bestowed
Upon this country haughty as a star.
And I set forth upon the southern road.

This darkness and these mountains loom a spell
Of peak-roofed town where yearning steeples soar
And the holy holy chanting of a bell
Shakes human incense on the throbbing air
Where bonfires blaze and quivering bodies char.
Whose is the hair that crisped, and fiercely glowed?
I know it; and my entrails melt like tar
And I set forth upon the southern road.

O fertile hillsides where my fathers are,
And whence my woes like troubled streams have flowed,
Love you I must, though they may sweep me far.
And I set forth upon the southern road.

NOTES

1. Oscar Wilde, review of Pater's *Appreciations,* in *Walter Pater: The Critical Heritage,* ed. R. M. Seiler (New York: Routledge and Kegan Paul, 1980).

2. David Fein, *Charles d'Orléans* (Boston: Twayne, 1983).

3. See Fein, *Charles d'Orléans.*

4. Anthony Bonner, trans. and ed., *The Complete Works of François Villon* (New York: David McKay, 1960).

5. Louis Untermeyer and Carter Davidson, *Poetry: Its Appreciation and Enjoyment* (New York: Harcourt Brace, 1934).

6. Letter from Edmund Gosse, Andrew Lang, and Austin Dobson to Helen Louise Cohen, 1911, quoted in Helen Louise Cohen, *Lyric Forms from France: Their History and Their Use* (New York: Harcourt, Brace, 1922).

7. Robert Louis Stevenson, "Charles d'Orléans" (*Cornhill,* 1876) and "François Villon, Student, Poet and House Breaker" (*Cornhill,* 1877).

8. William Carlos Williams, introduction to Villon, *Complete Works.*

The Blues

RAYMOND R. PATTERSON

Like Tennyson's flower in the crannied wall—"I pluck you out of the crannies,"—the blues, rightly understood, rewards attention. It is a uniquely American poetic form with roots in oral performance and musical improvisation. It evolved from late-nineteenth-century southern rural field hollers (periodic shouts from a laborer) and work songs structured on African musical, verbal, and communal patterns, later influenced by European and Hawaiian instrumental techniques. Wandering blues performers carried the music from plantation crossroads to juke joints and county fairs, eventually to town and city street corners and vaudeville theaters across the South.

By 1900 distinct blues performance styles such as Mississippi Blues, Memphis Blues, Texas Blues, and Chicago Blues had emerged. "The Father of the Blues," W. C. Handy (1875–1958), and other composers adapted the music and lyrics for popular audiences. Phonograph recordings carried the blues north to New York and abroad. By 1912, according to the *OED, blues* (plural in form but also used with a singular verb) was established in the English language to identify "a music of mournful and haunting character, originating among Negroes of the Southern U.S., freq. in a twelve-bar sequence using many 'blue' notes [flatted thirds and sevenths that produce valuable intonations]."

Compositions like Handy's "Saint Louis Blues" popularized the "classic" blues lyric stanza: three lines of iambic pentameter, rhymed *AAa,* each with a caesura. The first line makes a statement that is repeated in the second line (sometimes with modification). The third line provides a rhymed response to the statement:

> I hate to see de evenin' sun go down
> I hate to see de evenin' sun go down
> Cause mah baby, he don lef' dis town.

Handy's lyric, its language simple, direct, and resonant, is instructive and deserves examination. Its opening line states an opposition to viewing the setting sun. The line is repeated, without modification; its single image, the sun going down, lends the statement a plangency and poignance. The third line concludes the statement and reveals the cause of the emotion. It also discloses its irony: an episode of transient earthly love counterposed to a recurring, cosmic event.

Blues repetition as a means of gaining time to improvise a response to a life situation, when used as a poetic device, can have many subtle effects. Repetition in Handy's "I hate to see de evenin' sun go down" emphasizes the speaker's state of mind and enacts the painful and re-peated viewing of the sunset. In blues stanzas where a repeated line is altered by a few words or their arrangement, repetition can be a rhyth-mic or sound device. When the second line is not altered, as in Handy's stanza, repetition can suggest conviction, a sincerity and concern for clarity, or a willingness to repeatedly confront and accurately state a painful circumstance.

Skillfully posed (through hyperbole, understatement, etc.), a re-peated blues statement, like a "field holler," simultaneously calls for and delays (coming from a distance) a blues response. This dynamic lies at the heart of the three-line blues and gives it its form. Guided by rhyme, slant rhyme, or any signal locating a condition of distress, the response line arrives from a place distant enough to reveal the statement in its larger context. The result is an expanded perception of the circum-stance, a recognition of its humor or irony, leading to a blues transcen-dence. This process is described by Ralph Ellison in *Shadow and Act:*

> The blues is an impulse to keep the painful details and episodes of a brutal experience alive in one's aching consciousness, to fin-ger its jagged grain, and to transcend it, not by the consolation philosophy but by squeezing from it a near-tragic, near-comic lyricism. As a form, the blues is an autobiographical chronicle of personal catastrophe expressed lyrically.

Perennial blues subjects like unhappy love, difficult times, hard luck, fruitless labor (work gang and prison farm), natural disaster, root-lessness find expression through the concrete particulars of reported cir-cumstance. A stanza from Clara Smith's "Freight Train Blues" illustrates another approach to the subject of travel and unhappy love.

> I'm goin' away just to wear you off my mind.
> I'm goin' away just to wear you off my mind.
> An I may be gone for a doggone long long time.

Woody Payne's "Hellhound on my Trail," sung by the legendary Robert Johnson, is an existential view of rootlessness.

> I got to keep movin', I got to keep movin',
> Blues fallin' down like hail, blues fallin' down like hail,
> Hmmm—blues fallin' down like hail, blues fallin' down
>   like hail,
> And the day keep on worryin' me, there's a hellhound on
>   my trail.

Leadbelly's "Good Morning Blues" mocks and challenges life's difficulties:

> Good mornin' blues, blues, how do you do?
> Good mornin' blues, blues, how do you do?
> I'm doin' all right, good mornin', how are you?

Whatever the theme, the blues intends to give human emotions (traditionally those of a marginalized folk) "a local habitation and a name."

Blues poems have no fixed number of stanzas, and several variations of the *AAa* rhyme pattern may occur in the same lyric. (Handy's "Saint Louis Blues" uses a variety of rhyme schemes in three-line and four-line stanzas.) Eric Sackheim's *The Blues Line: A Collection of Blues Lyrics from Leadbelly to Muddy Waters* suggests the range of possibilities. John and Alan Lomax's 1935 *American Ballads and Folk Songs* illustrates an *AAA* stanza in "Dink's Blues":

> When my heart struck sorrow de tears come rollin' down
> When my heart struck sorrow de tears come rollin' down
> When my heart struck sorrow de tears come rollin' down

Other variations dispense with rhyme and use the third line of the opening stanza as a refrain for succeeding stanzas, or rhyme each of the three lines with a different word. Some stanzas use four lines, as in Elvie Thomas's "Motherless Child Blues":

> Oh daughter daughter please don't be like me
> Oh daughter oh daughter please don't be like me
> Oh daughter oh daughter please don't be like me
> To fall in love with every man you see

As in other lyric expression, coherence in blues poems depends on imagery and tone, as much as on developing idea or narrative. Some traditional blues lyrics simply assemble stanzas of discrete engagements with the bitter facts of life, expressing them in vivid, concrete images.

Blues diction is eclectic. Blues dialect is traditionally nonstandard, its syntax not restricted to "normal" patterns. Blues language is heavily influenced by the kind of African-inflected English Walt Whitman reported hearing when he walked the streets of mid-nineteenth-century New York City. Speculating on its potential for poetry, he wrote in his *American Primer* that it "gave hints of the future modifications of all words of the English language for musical purposes, for a native grand opera in America." The language of the blues is "language for musical purposes."

Following the rhythms of ordinary speech, the usual blues line is iambic pentameter. James Merrill in his 1988 "Education of the Poet" lecture for the Academy of American Poets addressed the aptness of the blues pentameter this way:

> Very much in the air as I was growing up—thanks to Pound and Dr. Williams and some of my own contemporaries, like John Ashbery and Allen Ginsberg—was the injunction to forge a "new measure." The pentameter—so went the argument— wasn't a truly American line. I had to wonder if these patriots had ever heard of the blues. "I hate to see the evening sun go down"—wasn't that an effortless and purely native music?

Although the blues accommodates fragmentation, discontinuity, and "otherness," qualities that modernists Eliot, Williams, Pound, Stein, H.D., and others would have recognized as materials for a "new" poetry, a strictly observed cultural hegemony (and the sometimes indecent language and subject matter of the blues) kept the form from receiving serious literary consideration. It was not until Langston Hughes (1902–1967) and Sterling A. Brown (1901–1989) published their first blues poems that poets began to consider the literary possibilities of the form. Both Hughes and Brown used the blues form to celebrate the language and experience of a marginalized people. "Midwinter Blues," published in 1926, captures the blues attitude of stoicism and shows Hughes's innovatively breaking the three-line stanza to indicate for the reader the blues caesura:

> I'm gonna buy me a rose bud
> An' plant it at my back door.
> Buy me a rose bud,
> Plant it at my back door
> So when I'm dead they won't need
> No flowers from the store.

Sterling A. Brown's "New St. Louis Blues," published in 1931, is an obvious comment on W. C. Handy's lyric. Its three sections address bad luck, natural disaster, and despair in traditional stanzas. The opening section begins:

> Market Street woman is known fuh to have dark days,
> Market Street woman noted fuh to have dark days,
> Life do her dirty in a hundred onery ways.

Hughes changed several dialect spellings ("my" for "ma," for example) that appeared in an earlier publication of "Midwinter Blues," relying on the poem's diction and syntax to suggest its blues voice.

Among blues poems written in the third decade of the twentieth century, Richard Wright's "Red Clay Blues" deserves notice. It begins:

> I miss that red clay, Lawd, I
> Need to feel it on my shoes.
> Says miss that red clay, Lawd, I
> Need to feel it on my shoes.
> I want to see Georgia, cause I
> Got them red clay blues.

W. H. Auden's "Funeral Blues" is a more imaginative handling of the form. Its four-line stanzas of rhymed couplets substitute the traditionally colloquial language of the blues for the traditionally formal language of elegy. The result is an ironic counterstatement to grief. It begins:

> Stop all the clocks, cut off the telephone,
> Prevent the dog from barking with a juicy bone,
> Silence the pianos and with muffled drum
> Bring on the coffin, let the mourners come.

Auden's "Refuge Blues" uses three-line stanzas of rhymed couplets and an ironic refrain:

> Say this city has ten million souls,
> Some are living in mansions, some are living in holes:
> Yet there's no place for us, my dear, yet there's no place for us.

Poets writing blues poems use many strategies. Purists insist on the "classic" three-line form and its dynamic of perception and transcendence. They are inspired to attempt with language what the authentic blues performance accomplishes with word, music, spectacle, and occasion. Poets who find the three-line form limiting write blues in free verse or use other traditional forms. More often, the term *blues* is no more than a convenient label to signal the mood of the poem.

Since midcentury, African-American poets of widely different styles and orientations (Jayne Cortez, Mari Evans, Sterling Plumpp, Eugene B. Redmond, Sonia Sanchez, for example) have employed elements of the blues in their work. Beat poets of the 1950s, notably Allen Ginsberg, explored jazz and blue models, and Robert Creeley recalls Jack Kerouac saying that he wanted "to be considered as a jazz poet blowing a long blues in an afternoon jazz session on Sunday." The opening stanza of "4 AM Blues," written with music by Ginsberg, suggests a traditional use of the form:

> Oh when you gonna
> > lie down by my side
> When the spirit hits you
> > please lie down by my side
> Three nights you didnt come home
> > I slept by myself & sighed

The following poems are samples of how poets today are using the blues.

ISHMAEL REED

Oakland Blues

> Well it's six o'clock in Oakland
> and the sun is full of wine
> I say, it's six o'clock in Oakland
> and the sun is red with wine
> We buried you this morning, baby
> in the shadow of a vine
>
> Well, they told you of the sickness
> almost eighteen months ago
> Yes, they told you of the sickness
> almost eighteen months ago
> You went down fighting, daddy. Yes
> You fought Death toe to toe

O, the egrets fly over Lake Merritt
and the blackbirds roost in trees
O, the egrets fly over Lake Merritt
and the blackbirds roost in trees
Without you little papa
what O, what will become of me

O, it's hard to come home, baby
To a house that's still and stark
O, it's hard to come home, baby
To a house that's still and stark
All I hear is myself
thinking
and footsteps in the dark

1989

SHERLEY ANNE WILLIAMS

Any Woman's Blues

every woman is a victim of the feel blues, too.

Soft lamp shinin
            and me alone in the night.
Soft lamp is shinin
            and me alone in the night.
Can't take no one beside me
            need mo'n jest some man to set me right.

I left many peoples and places
            tryin not to be alone.
Left many a person and places
            I lived my life alone.
I need to get myself together.
            Yes, I need to make myself to home.

What's gone can be a window
            a circle in the eye of the sun.
What's gone can be a window
            a circle, well, in the eye of the sun.
Take the circle from the world, girl,
            you find the light have gone.

These is old blues
            and I sing em like any woman do.

These the old blues
> and I sing em, sing em, sing em. Just like any
> woman do.

My life ain't done yet.
> Naw. My song ain't through.

1975

JANE COOPER

Wanda's Blues

Ortega Public School, 1932

Wanda's daddy was a railroadman, she was his little wife.
Ernest's sister had a baby, she was nobody's wife.
Wanda was the name and wandering, wandering was their
   way of life.

Ernest's sister was thirteen, too old for school anyway.
When Ernest couldn't pass third grade, they kept him
   there anyway,
hunched up tight in a littler kid's desk with his hair sticking
   out like hay.

But Wanda was small and clean as a cat, she gave
   nothing away.

At school the plate lunch cost ten cents, milk was a
   nickel more.
Shrimps were selling for a nickel a pound—those shrimpers'
   kids were real poor,
they lived in an abandoned army camp, the bus dropped
   them off at the door.

Gossip in the schoolyard had it that Wanda swept and sewed
and cooked the supper for her daddy when he wasn't on
   the road.
She never told where she ate or she slept, how she did her
   lessons, if she had an ol' lamp. . . .
That wasn't the traveling man's code.

Wanda was smart and watchful, we let her into our games.
Wanda always caught on quick whether it was long division
   or games.
She never gave a thing way except for her lingering name.

I would say it over: *Wanda Wanda*

April, and school closed early. We never saw her again.
Her daddy loved an empty freight, he must have lit out
   again.
Wanda-a-a-a the steam whistle hollered. O my
   American refrain!

1996

ESTELLA CONWILL MAJOZO

The Malcolm Calling Blues

(for James Turner and Ken McIntyre)

a note low and guttural
from the hollow of the horn—
a note low and guttural
from the hollow of the horn—
breath over brass
changes how we mourn.

you know
markings in the sand
bid the spirit come in—
markings in the sand
bid the spirit come in
but for calling Brother Malcolm
make his sign on the wind

yeah
a note low and guttural
let it change on the horn—
let it wail—let it wake—
let it range on the horn
till the note low and guttural
makes a way on the horn.

hum of the earth
knows truth don't lie—
hum of the earth gon'
make the devil cry
saying martyred flesh
can multiply—

saying all those notes
can holler from the horn
hundreds hallelujah
up and holler from the horn
'cause breath over brass
changes how we mourn—

breath over brass
changes how we mourn.

1991

RAYMOND R. PATTERSON

Computer Blues

I put my troubles in the computer
To find out what's troubling me.
I say I put my troubles in the computer
To see what's the matter with me.
My card had so many holes,
Holes was all that I could see.

But that old computer moaned,
That old computer groaned and cried.
That old computer moaned,
It just groaned and cried.
It shook so hard, my, my,
It broke right down and died.

Computer man come running
And said I had blowed the fuse.
Computer man came running.
He said, Hey, you blowed the fuse,
Ain't no computer built
That can stand the blues.

Well, if I had just stopped and thought,
I might have knowed,
Ain't no machine
Can handle that load.

1989

Taking Shape: The Art of
Carmina Figurata

JAN D. HODGE

Pattern or shaped poetry is almost as old as poetry itself, and examples can be found in virtually all cultures. Poems written in various shapes— an egg, a panpipe, a pair of wings—have survived from classical Greek times. Renaissance England produced many shaped poems—altars, columns, stars, circles—the best known and best of them being George Herbert's "Easter Wings." Though "Easter Wings" is a fine poem by any standard, the poetry of such exercises is usually undistinguished, and later critics like Addison considered them "false wit," especially when there was little integration of subject and shape. That seems a fair assessment too of such exercises as this recasting of Proverbs 23:29–32, in which the passage is arbitrarily broken into lines and poured into a shape:

Who hath woe? Who hath sorrow? Who
hath contentions? Who hath wounds
without cause? Who hath redness
of eyes? They that tarry long at
the wine! They that go to
seek mixed wine! Look
not thou upon the wine
when it is red, when
it giveth its color
in the
cup,
when it
moveth itself
aright.
At
the last it
biteth like a serpent
and stingeth like an adder!

At least Herrick's pillar and Panard's eighteenth-century French verse celebrating drink have the integrity of line and rhyme to recommend them, but with rare exceptions, shaped verse has not earned high regard as a literary form.

There are, of course, other types of visual poetry than purely imitative shapes. Early this century the French poet Guillaume Apollinaire published a series of what he called *calligrammes,* characterized by unconventional calligraphy or typography to suggest the dislocation and simultaneity of cubist art, and a few of them, like "La Cravate," do resemble more traditional carmina. In the 1950s a movement began in Europe and Brazil known as "concrete poetry"—perhaps more ideogram or visual pun than poetry. Examples include Reinhard Döhl's "Pattern Poem with an Elusive Intruder," in which the word *apfel,* repeated over and over in the shape of an apple, is interrupted by one "wurm." At least one student has parodied this in a poem called "Oops": "ovum ovum ovum ovum sperm ovum. . . ." Mary Ellen Solt's "Forsythia" uses that word acrostically as the bush's base and repeats its letters strung along telegraph code to form its branches. Dorthi Charles's "Concrete Cat" is drawn with the names of its parts—"whiskers" forming its whiskers, "stripestripe . . ." defining its body, and so on; beside it lies an upside-down "mouse."

My focus, however, is not on visual effects such as these, but on those that supplement more conventional poetic elements to help create or reinforce meaning. The stanza shape in William Carlos Williams's "The Red Wheelbarrow," for instance, might suggest wheelbarrows; clearly the poem's meaning does not depend on that shape, but the totality of the poem is consistent with and may be enhanced by that visual effect. Typographical eccentricities in the work of E. E. Cummings, often disguising highly traditional forms, sometimes create miniature "concrete poems" within a larger context (as when he writes "mOOn"), and there is an essential correlation between shape, statement, and image(s), verbal and visual, in his poem about loneliness and a falling leaf, which trails narrowly down the page, the deliberate placement also creating a visual pun on "loneliness."

In the poem "A Vertical Reflection" by Paul McCallum, obviously the words ascend as the released balloon ascends, but the poem has meaning beyond that trick. Elementary school children love discovering how to read the poem, but go on to discuss perceptively the character of the girl and the implications of the figurative language; other readers can appreciate as well the speaker's envy and that suggestive qualification that becomes finally the foundation of the poem: "Sometimes."

In the true *carmen figuratum* ("shaped song"), however, form imitates subject much more directly, as in Herbert's "Easter Wings" or Panard's bottle. Though most shaped poems remain curiosities, several

<pre>
                    sky
                    the
                    to
                    it
                      fed
                    hand
                  an open
                    with
                    and
                  laughter
                  with her
                  balloon
                    a
                    filled
                    who
                    girl
                  the little
                  I envy
                  Sometimes
</pre>

A Vertical Reflection

modern poets have given them more serious attention. May Swenson used such visual design in several of her poems, such as her butterfly-shaped "Unconscious Came a Beauty," "Out of the Sea, Early" (describing an ocean sunrise), or the mountain-shaped "Night Practice," and Alfred Corn has written correspondingly shaped poems about a conch and a classical column. Yet even these examples, except for Corn's conch, are less strict than the *carmen figuratum* as practiced, for example, by John Hollander, whose *Types of Shape* contains poems about and in the shape of (among other things) a lightbulb, an ice cream bar, a cup, a cat, the state of New York, and the particularly striking "Swan and Shadow."

Using a typewriter (or typewriter font on a computer) invites exactness of letter count and spacing as an element in design, which increases the challenge considerably. (With computer graphics, of course, one can stretch or squeeze virtually any words to any shape, but that seems to me to violate the spirit of the form.) Hollander's "lineation principle" allows him no breaks within lines, which severely limits possible subjects and visual effects; only "Swan and Shadow" departs from that principle, and then only "for the interrogative monosyllables put by the question mark–like neck to the body."[1]

My own serious interest in shaped poetry began when I read Paul Fussell's *Poetic Meter and Poetic Form*. Fussell argues that shaped poems don't work very well because the visual effect so overwhelms the poetic that "we feel the two dimensions are not married: one is simply

in command of the other." Arguing further that perhaps their greatest
limitation is the scarcity of visual objects which can be imitated—as he
put it, "wings, bottles, hourglasses, and altars, but where do we go from
there?"—he suggests that the art of the *carmen figuratum* belongs more
to the typographer than to the poet. The formal challenge was obviously
different from that of the sonnet or the villanelle, but I wanted to make
shaped poems that work as poems, accepting integrity of the shape
rather than of the line as the formal principle. (I've always liked the pre-
Romantic notion of poet as maker, and while I always welcome inspi-
ration, I find it rather unreliable.)

An example will illustrate some of the problems encountered in
writing *carmina figurata*, such as crafting syntax so that small words fall
where they must. "Pandanggo sa Ilaw" is a Filipino folk dance in which
the dancers hold lighted oil lamps in their hands. Wood carvings of such
dancers provided the models for a pair of poems. In a relatively late
worksheet, I had worked out the design for her:

```
                    the
                 grace of
                the dancer
                the rays of
                the flame
                 realize
                  beauty
          as         pure         as
         the   tutubi rising    over
         the water and catching the
         moon with its gossamer wings
         precious as fruit on the palm
         trees of evening humble as shy
         makahiya noli tangere   touch       her
            not in her modesty   see         how
            she  glances aside   as she weaves of
            two  shining stars    a cincture
            of  firelight and
     fay    a  magical premise
     see  how  the goldenwhite
     traces    of light hang in
                the air a garland
                 of sweet sampagita
                  adorning her beauty
                   this bright gumamela
                    liveliest bloom
                     in a piging
                     of rarest
                    delights
                    treasure
                 that   best
                 art    love
                 can    give
                 if     art
                 is     but
                        the
                        joy
                        of
                         it
```

The first half wasn't too bad except for the rhythmically awful "noli tangere" (a clumsy allusion to José Rizal's novel *Noli Me Tangere*), but the end of the poem (her legs, with that tricky succession of short words), was downright ghastly in both sound and sense. The lines preceding them weren't much better. "This bright gumamela [a big red flower], / liveliest bloom / in a piging / of rarest / delights" was clumsy and trite as a metaphor, and there was no reason for using "piging" (banquet) instead of "garden." It took many more frustrating trials before the language, simile, and music of those lines were right, but it is surprising how many possibilities for revision there are even in such an uncompromising form. Here is the final version of the poem; note that the design has been slightly modified. "Tutubi" is Tagalog for dragonfly; "makahiya," the "shy plant," has leaves that close instantly when touched; "sampagita," the Philippine national flower, is often woven into garlands; "magandang babae" (mah-gahn-dahng bah-bah-ee) means "beautiful woman."

```
                              the
                           hands of
                          the dancer
                          the rays of
                           the flame
                            realize
                            beauty
                 as         pure        as
                 the   tutubi rising  over
              the water and catching the
              moon on its cellophane wings
              stainless as rain on the palm
              trees of evening modest as shy
              makahiya fine as a tourmaline      sky
                how she enchants us see        how
                she   glances aside   as she weaves of
                two   shining stars      a cincture
                of   firelight and
          fay    a   magical purlieu
        see how     the goldenwhite
        ribbons     of light hang in
                     the air a garland
                      of sweet sampagita
                       to accent her grace
                        magandang babae your
                         dancing is like
                           the play of
                           the angel
                          of light
                         bless us
                      with   what
                      you    know
                      the    soul
                      of      joy
                              and
                              the
                              art
                               of
                                it
```

Certainly finding shapes that are both pleasing in themselves and accommodating of intelligible English syntax is a major challenge; one soon learns, for instance, to avoid thin vertical elements. The greater challenge, of course, is finding the right words to form the right shape, especially if one also chooses to write metrically. It is good to keep in mind John Ciardi's definition of a game, "making things difficult for the fun of it." The triumph comes, as with any form, when the form itself discovers the right language, and the nonvisual elements (rhythm, sound patterns, syntax, diction, metaphor) seem married to the form rather than forced into submission to it.

GEORGE HERBERT (1593–1633)

Easter Wings

Lord, who createdst man in wealth and store,
Though foolishly he lost the same,
Decaying more and more,
Till he became
Most poor:
With thee
O let me rise
As larks, harmoniously,
And sing this day thy victories:
Then shall the fall further the flight in me.

My tender age in sorrow did begin:
And still with sicknesses and shame
Thou didst so punish sin,
That I became
Most thin.
With thee
Let me combine,
And feel thy victory;[2]
For, if I imp my wing on thine,
Affliction shall advance the flight in me.

1633

ROBERT HERRICK[3]

The Pillar of Fame

Fame's pillar here, at last, we set,
Out-during marble, brass, or jet,
Charm'd and enchanted so
As to withstand the blow
Of overthrow:
Nor shall the seas,
Or OUTRAGES
Of storms orebear
What we up-rear,
Tho Kingdoms fall,
This pillar never shall
Decline or waste at all;
But stand for ever by his owne
Firme and well fixt foundation.

1648

GUILLAUME APOLLINAIRE

LA CRAVATE
DOU
LOU
REUSE
QUE TU
PORTES
ET QUI T'
ORNE O CI
VISILÉ
OTE-   TU VEUX
LA   BIEN
SI   RESPI
           RER

JOHN HOLLANDER

Swan and Shadow

```
                    Dusk
                 Above the
           water hang the
                     loud
                    flies
                    Here
                    O so
                    gray
                    then
            What                A pale signal will appear
            When            Soon before its shadow fades
            Where          Here in this pool of opened eye
            In us     No Upon us As at the very edges
            of where we take shape in the dark air
              this object bears its image awakening
                ripples of recognition that will
                    brush darkness up into light
even after this bird this hour both drift by atop the perfect sad instant now
                  already passing out of sight
              toward yet-untroubled reflection
            this image bears its object darkening
            into memorial shades Scattered bits of
            light     No of water Or something across
            water        Breaking up No Being regathered
            soon          Yet by then a swan will have
            gone             Yes out of mind into what
                    vast
                    pale
                    hush
                    of a
                   place
                    past
            sudden dark as
             if a swan
                 sang
```

NOTES

1. John Hollander, *Types of Shape* (New Haven: Yale University Press, 1991), xxiii.

2. Most editions insert the words "this day" in this line, which violates the metrical structure of the poem. The lines have, respectively, five, four, three, two, one, one, two, three, four, and five feet, which like the rhyme scheme coincides with the visual structure. That structure also underscores the poem's thematic, metaphorical, and dramatic movement, with the shortest lines—"Most poor" and "Most thin"—also marking the transition from sinner to one redeemed through God ("With thee"). Early editions printed the poem vertically.

3. This is the final verse in Herrick's volume *Hesperides* (1648).

Gists, Piths, and Poison-Pills:
The Art of the Epigram

X. J. KENNEDY

The epigram is brief, closely packed, and single-minded in making its point. Often it is a versified sneer. From that definition, you might think it a mere nasty little bug, deserving only to be stepped on. In fact, some poetry editors hold that view. They are the kind who prefer godawfully serious poems, and mistake length in poetry for importance. Yet when it clicks, an epigram in verse can be memorable, funny—even beautiful, to anyone who can relish the deft placing of words inside tight space.

The history of the epigram stretches back at least twenty-five hundred years. The name comes from the Greek *epigraphein,* "to inscribe," suggesting a few words carved on a monument. A *very* few: people who chisel their words into stone, toiling over every syllable, aren't inclined to blather. Indeed, some ancient Greek epigrams read like epitaphs, or terse tombstone inscriptions:

> I, Dion of Tarsus, lived sixty years and died.
> I never married. Too bad my father did.

This anonymous epigram is from the *Greek Anthology,* that amazing scrap-heap of poems by various hands written over a time span of fifteen centuries. Contemporary epigrammatists still write epitaphs:

> Here lies Sir Tact, a diplomatic fellow
> Whose silence was not golden, but just yellow.
> Timothy Steele

Epitaph on a Minor Poet

> The idol of the smaller press
> receives no mail at this address,
> but clutches in an iron grip
> life's ultimate rejection slip.
>
> Gail White

Not restricted to the graveyard, epigrams can touch on all kinds of matters. The most celebrated epigrammatist who ever lived was a Roman, Martial, who used the epigram to write social commentary, observations about love, literary criticism, and more. In the first century A.D. he prefaced a collection of his epigrams,

> Here he is whom you read and clamor for,
> tasteful reader, the very Martial world-
> renowned for pithy books of epigrams
> and not even dead yet. So seize your chance:
> better to praise him when he can hear
> than later, when he'll be literature.
> Translated by William Matthews

In Elizabethan times, when classical learning had made its way belatedly into England, whole books of epigrams were popular among the gentry. They boasted items such as this one by Sir John Harington, sometimes called the best epigram in English:

> Treason doth never prosper; what's the reason?
> For if it prosper, none dare call it treason.

Many later epigrammatists, too, have been lovers of Greek or Latin, among them Alexander Pope in the eighteenth century. His most famous contribution to the form is his "Epigram, Engraved on the Collar of a Dog which I gave to His Royal Highness":

> I am his Highness' dog at Kew;
> Pray tell me, sir, whose dog are you?

We read that, feel kicked, and go on chewing it as though it were a bone. Another neoclassicist fond of epigrammatic precision was Walter Savage Landor. He couldn't abide the poems of his contemporary William Wordsworth, who had turned away from the classics to write, in Landor's view,

> Dank, limber verses stuffed with lakeside sedges,
> And propped with rotten stakes from broken hedges.

In writing epigrams, most poets gain control over their natural tendency to blab. Besides, an epigram permits them to get a gripe off their chests.

Once, after concocting a little poison-pill called "On Someone Who Insisted I Look Up Someone," I had that sense of relief. You may have met pests like the one who inspired me. You're about to go on a trip, and he saddles you with an obligation to look up somebody who happens to live where you're going—his Aunt Essie, or somebody he met at a party.

> I rang them up while touring Timbuctoo,
> Those bosom chums to whom you're known as *Who?*

I felt grateful to the pest—and to the Muse, that so many *m*-sounds occurred there. When you tool things over twenty or thirty times, effects like that can happen. Of course, there's always the danger that a poem will turn into a clogged mishmash of excessive thoughtiness, and need to be scrapped after all.

It helps an epigram mightily if you can get some surprise or funny twist into the last line. Give it a stinger in its tail. As William Blake said, an epigram can have "a sliding noose at the end." In English, the neatness of rhyme lends bite to an epigram, but to be sure, it is possible to write epigrams in free verse. For scathing examples, see Ezra Pound's series of epigrams, too long to quote here, "Moeurs Contemporaines," in his *Personae*.

Writing epigrams appeals to poets who like to toil over miniatures, poets who tend to be harshly self-critical. For them, writing an epigram keeps the agony of writing a poem nice and brief. As yet, I don't have a bad case of that problem, but have to admit that it's a relief to finish a poem, any poem, and feel my brain suddenly freed from an invisible hook. I suspect that that great master of concision J. V. Cunningham (1911–1985) became more and more self-critical as he aged. Over the course of his career his poems shrank down from as many as thirty-six lines to nothing but epigrams at the end—but ah, what epigrams!

> There is a ghost town of abandoned love
> With tailings of used hope, leavings of risk,
> Deserted cherishings masked with new life,
> Where the once ugly is now picturesque.

If you want to write epigrams, you need to be tough on yourself. You have to be willing to churn out dozens of the damned things, and throw away all but the luckiest. To end with, let me offer four more samples of recent American epigrams, just to prove that the form is still alive and stinging.

FRED CHAPPELL

Conservative

He trudges Main Street into a murky rut,
And thinks such normal thoughts that he's a nut.

JOHN FREDERICK NIMS

Critic: Coterie Review of Books

Of writers he likes four, and thunders rage,
Eyes shut, at other venturers on the stage.
Suppose one sacred cow, though, loose a *moo*—
He's at the udder slurping, eyes goo-goo.

RICHARD MOORE

Overheard at a Feminist Conference

Sisters, this may sound ominous,
But we all have a touch of the mom in us.

BRUCE BENNETT

Mack the Epigram

So deft his thrust, so lightning-swift and true,
his victim stammered "Thanks!" before he knew.

Ghazal: To Be Teased into DisUnity

AGHA SHAHID ALI

The ghazal goes back to seventh-century Arabia, and its descendants are found not only in Arabic but in various other languages, including Farsi, Urdu, Turkish, Pashto, Hindi, and Spanish. The model most in use is the Persian, of which Hafiz (1325–1389)—that makes him a contemporary of Chaucer's—is the acknowledged master, his tomb in Shiraz a place of pilgrimage. Ghalib (1797–1869) is the acknowledged master of that model in Urdu—the only language I know whose mere mention evokes poetry. Lorca also wrote ghazals—*gacelas*—taking his cues from the Arabic form and thus citing in his Catholic way the history of Muslim Andalusia. As *The Princeton Encyclopedia of Poetry and Poetics* informs us, the ghazal was introduced to Western poetry "by the romanticists, mainly Fr. Schlegel, Ruckert, and von Platen (*Ghaselen*, 1821) in Germany, and was made more widely known by Goethe who in his *West-ostlicher Divan* (1819) deliberately imitated Persian models."

The ghazal has a stringently formal disunity. The ghazal is made up of thematically independent couplets held (as well as not held) together in a stunning fashion. Each couplet is autonomous, thematically and emotionally complete in itself: one couplet may be comic, another tragic, another romantic, another religious, another political. (There is, underlying a ghazal, a profound and complex cultural unity, built on association and memory and expectation, but that need not detain me here.) A couplet may be quoted by itself without in any way violating a context—there is no context, as such.

Then what saves the ghazal from what might be considered arbitrariness? A technical context, a formal unity based on rhyme and refrain and prosody. All the lines in a ghazal can appear to have—because of the quantitative meters of Persian and Urdu—the same number of syllables; to establish this metrical consistency, the poets follow an inner ear rather than any clearly established rules, as in English. To quote the Marxist historian Victor Kiernan—a translator of Iqbal and Faiz, two of Urdu's most important poets:

> Urdu metres, mainly derived from Persian, are varied and effec-
> tive. They are based on a quantitative system which divides the

foot into sound-units composed of long vowels and vowelized or unvowelized consonants. Urdu has, properly, no accent; on the other hand, Urdu verse, evolved for public declamation, can be recited with a very strong accentual rhythm, the stresses falling on almost any syllable in accordance with the quantitative pattern. This pattern cannot be reproduced with much fidelity in English, where quantity plays a considerable but an undefined and unsystematic part, and where two long (or strong) syllables cannot be made to stand side by side in a fixed order, as they do habitually in Urdu verse.[1]

However, some rules of the ghazal are clear and classically stringent. The opening couplet (called *matla*) sets up a scheme rhyme *(qafia)* and refrain *(radif)* by having it occur in both lines. Then this scheme occurs only in the second line of each succeeding couplet. That is, once a poet establishes the scheme—with total freedom, I might add—s/he becomes its slave. What results in the rest of the poem is the alluring tension of a slave trying to master the master. A ghazal has five couplets at least; there is no maximum limit. A ghazal, as such, could go on forever.

To strike a pose of third-world snobbery: a free-verse ghazal is a contradiction in terms. Imagine a sestina without those six words. What would be the point? Because, as I've noted elsewhere, its "charms often evade the Western penchant for unity—rather, the unities—the ghazal can be a truly liberating experience. When students ask about a poem such as *The Waste Land* —How does it hold together?—I suggest a more compelling approach, a tease: *How* does it *not* hold together? I underscore *How* to emphasize craft."[2] The first real ghazal in English— the first authentic approximation of the form—is John Hollander's:

> For couplets the ghazal is prime; at the end
> Of each one's a refrain like a chime: "at the end."

Having seen or heard this opening couplet, one would know that the *radif* is "at the end" and the *qafia* a word or syllable that would rhyme with "ime." Thus the second line of every following couplet will end with "at the end" immediately preceded by a rhyme for "ime." Hollander continues:

> But in subsequent couplets throughout the whole poem,
> It's this second line only will rhyme at the end.

He goes on with thematically autonomous couplets:

On a string of such strange, unpronounceable fruits,
How fine the familiar old lime at the end!

All our writing is silent, the dance of the hand,
So that what it comes down to's all mime, at the end.

Dust and ashes? How dainty and dry! we decay
To our messy primordial slime at the end.

Two frail arms of your delicate form I pursue,
Inaccessible, vibrant, sublime at the end.

You gathered all manner of flowers all day,
But your hands were most fragrant of thyme, at the end.

There are so many sounds! A poem having one rhyme?
A good life with a sad, minor crime at the end.

Each new couplet's a different ascent: no great peak
But a low hill quite easy to climb at the end.

Two-armed bandits: start out with a great wad of green
Thoughts, but you're left with a dime at the end.

Each assertion's a knot which must shorten, alas,
This long-worded rope of which I'm at the end.

To mark the end of the ghazal, often a poet has a signature couplet *(makhta)* in which s/he can invoke her/his name pseudonymously or otherwise. Hollander, charmingly, pseudonymizes:

> Now Qafia Radif has grown weary, like life,
> At the game he's been wasting his time at. THE END.

Notice that with the exception of the first and last couplets, the poem would not in any way suffer by a rearrangement of the couplets. Nor would the ghazal suffer if one would simply delete some of its couplets. Do such freedoms frighten some of us?

Hollander has done something quite remarkable here, for by having "at the end" as his *radif* he has caught the particular spirit of the form. For, as Kiernan notes, "within the ghazal, the poet almost always adopts the stance of a romantic hero of one kind or another: a desperate lover intoxicated with passion, a rapt visionary absorbed in mystic illumination, an iconoclastic drunkard celebrating the omnipotence of wine." In this century, especially among left-wing poets, the poet is often the committed revolutionary intoxicated with the struggle for freedom. "He presents himself as a solitary sufferer, sustained by brief flashes of ecstasy, defined by his desperate longing for some transcendant object of desire," which may be "human (female or male), divine, abstract, or ambiguous; its defining trait is its inaccessibility." Hollander's "at the end" is masterly, for it contains the possibility of being imbued with such longing and loss!

What is missing in unrhymed ghazals is the breathless excitement the original form can generate. The audience (the ghazal is recited a lot) waits to see what the poet will do with the scheme established in the opening couplet. At a *mushaira*—the traditional poetry gathering to which sometimes thousands of people come to hear the most cherished poets of the country—when the poet recites the first line of a couplet, the audience recites it back to him, and then the poet repeats it, and the audience again follows suit. This back and forth creates an immensely seductive tension because everyone is waiting to see how the suspense will be resolved in terms of the scheme established in the opening couplet. For example, if Hollander were to recite,

You gathered all manner of flowers all day,

the audience would repeat it and so on, and then when he'd come to

But your hands were most fragrant of thyme . . .

the audience would be so primed and roused by this time that it would break in with "at the end" even before Hollander would have a chance to utter the phrase. And then, in raptures, it would keep on *Vaah-Vaah*-ing and *Subhan-Allah*-ing. If the resolution is an anticlimax, the audience may well respond with boos. I should mention that ghazals are often sung. Some of the great singers of India have taken ghazals and placed them gently within the framework of a *raga* and then set the melodic phrase (which contains the individual lines of the ghazal) to a *tala* (cycle of beats). The greatest of them all was Begum Akhtar. This seemingly "light" form can lead to a lot of facile poetry (haiku-ishly, one could say), but in the hands of a master? Ghalib's ghazals reveal a great tragic poet, Faiz's a great political one.

Below I offer a selection of what some contemporary poets have been doing with the form. In writing this particular ghazal, I stole some phrases from Laurence Hope's utterly sentimental "Kashmiri Love Lyric," which begins "Pale hands I loved beside the Shalimar":

Where are you now? Who lies beneath your spell tonight
before you agonize him in farewell tonight?

Pale hands that once loved me beside the Shalimar:
Whom else from rapture's road will you expel tonight?

Those "Fabrics of Cashmere—" "to make Me beautiful—"
"Trinket"—to gem—"Me to adorn—How—tell"—tonight?

I beg for haven: Prisons, let open your gates—
A refugee from pity seeks a cell tonight.

Lord, cried out the idols, *Don't let us be broken;*
Only we can convert the infidel tonight.

In the heart's veined temple all statues have been smashed.
No priest in saffron's left to toll its knell tonight.

And I, Shahid, only am escaped to tell thee—
God sobs in my arms. Call me Ishmael tonight.

                                                    1987

RAFIQUE KATHWARI

Jewel House Ghazal

In Kashmir, half asleep, Mother listens to the rain.
In another country, I feel her presence in the rain.

A rooster precedes the Call To Prayer At Dawn:
God is a name dropper: all names at once in the rain.

Forsythia shrivel in a glass on her nightstand;
at my window sill, wilted petals, a petulance in the rain.

She must wonder who will put on the kettle,
butter the crumpets, offer compliments to the rain.

God yawns, performs ablutions, across oceans
water in my hands becomes a reverence in the rain.

At Jewel House in Srinagar, Mother reshapes my ghazal.
"No enjambments!" she says. "Wah, wah," my chants in
    the rain.

"Rafique," I hear her call my name over the city din.
The kettle exhales: my mother's scents in the rain.

                                                    1997

DANIEL HALL

Souvenir

He gazed into the air, searching for a word in my language.
I blinked. Across the pool a zephyr stirred, in my language.

Where was I? Where was he? Where he looked, remembering?
The air was his release; his burden, my language.

Our silence was the air itself, and the moment timeless
 (though a timeless moment is absurd, in my language).

So it would always be with us, back and forth:
what he implied in his, I inferred in my language.

Plain speech? There's no such thing! I can't tell you
How much the overwrought can undergird in my language

Did he clear his throat? Did rain fall? Can there really be
a ringing bell or a singing bird in my language?

He blurted out the word in his own tongue, like a bell rung,
a distant bell, whose very speech was slurred, in my language.

Who am I now, gone crystalline with waiting, listening
for what I still have never heard in my language?

                                                    1997

JONATHAN MUSGROVE

Sara's Ghazal

Your holy arms open, bid me, *Take this body.*
To taste your sweet blood must I forsake this body?

The rain mimics worm-simple movements of a kiss.
Lonely eyes ask, *How much love to make to this body?*

Fear and dream make a lovely pact: fuel and the fire.
Still, only your clumsy hands can wake this body.

Do you belong among incense, silver goblets?
Wind rattling stained glass will not shake this body.

Take me from dark confessional to beginning
Time before sharp talons of guilt rake this body.

My soft prayer is swirling-tongue invitation.
Feel passion, Sara, fucking can't break this body.

                                                    1997

NOTES

1. See *Poems from Iqbal*, trans. Victor Kiernan (London: John Murray, 1955).

2. I borrow this from my not altogether correct essay "Ghazal: The Charms of a Considered Disunity," from *The Practice of Poetry*, ed. Robin Behn and Chase Twitchell (New York: HarperPerennial, 1992).

Haiku

JEAN HYUNG YUL CHU

Haiku, like all good verse, is a way of seeing, a sort of frame or threshold. What marks the form, in particular, is its sheer sense of economy. Matsuo Bashō (1644–1694), the founder of haiku, transformed the verse into the forceful lyric we recognize today during the last decade of his life while traveling through Japan, infusing the haiku form with the spareness required by his itinerant life. This sort of frugality may be difficult to conceptualize in our complex modern world. Current images of travel bring to mind planes, cars, the tourist with luggage on wheels. Bashō's quest for divinity in the mundane is more likely to see its counterpart in the cook who fashions odds and ends into a meal, a child who swaps king for hobo with a flick of her bedsheet, the writer who makes art from words. This lean and uncluttered form seems to lend itself to the body's dailiness, its endurance and brevity. Richard Wright's daughter has said that her father's haiku, written in the last eighteen months of his life, "were self-developed antidotes against illness, and that breaking down words into syllables matched the shortness of his breath." The compressed form together with haiku's injunction for plain language weeds out abstractions to unearth images that are fresh and clear. By doing so, as Yosa Buson (1716–1783) noted, haiku "use[s] the commonplace to escape the commonplace."

In addition to the spare form, a seasonal reference that grounds the poem in time and place is crucial for haiku writers. There's a historical reason and a philosophical reason. Haiku began as a kind of collaborative game of call and response called *renga* in sixteenth-century Japan (see Higginson and Harter, "Japanese-Style Linked Forms"). *Hokku* (the earlier term for haiku), meaning "starting verse" after its role in the renga, functioned as a kind of shorthand that marked the time and place of the renga's composition by referring to traditional seasonal themes such as deep autumn or plum blossoms. Focusing on the seasons also allowed the poets to convey the experience of being embedded in the earth's rituals and cycles; in Zen Buddhism the term for this experience is "spontaneity." Haiku poets conveyed this attentiveness to one's place in the cosmos by capturing the simultaneous nature of apparently disparate things. For example, Masaoka Shiki's (1867–1902) "A temple

in the hills: / the snoring from a noon siesta— / and a cuckoo's trills"
(trans. Harold G. Henderson), and Ito Shou's (1859–1943) "under this,
/ heroes' bones . . . / left-over snow" (trans. William J. Higginson) ex-
press humanness, not as distinct from nature, but simply as another phe-
nomenal thing.

An important aspect to keep in mind as a Western reader or writer
of haiku is the difference between Christian and Buddhist conceptions
of nature. American verse written in the New England Protestant tradi-
tion evinces a sense of nature that is fallen, a text in which we can read
the hand of God. In the Buddhist cosmology that informs haiku, nature
is not fallen, and there is no creator-being that refers us to a higher plane
of existence. Compare, for example, Robert Frost's "Nothing Gold Can
Stay" with Yosa Buson's haiku.

Nothing Gold Can Stay

Nature's first green is gold,
Her hardest hue to hold.
Her early leaf's a flower;
But only so an hour.
Then leaf subsides to leaf.
So Eden sank to grief,
So dawn goes down to day.
Nothing gold can stay.

and Yosa Buson's haiku (translated by Robert Hass):

The petals fall
and the river takes them—
plum tree on the bank.

In Frost's poem, the first buds of spring recall a lost Edenic condition.
In Buson's haiku, the tree, by virtue of being stripped to its origin and
essence, seems to impart a sense of peacefulness.

The rules for haiku are easy. Richard Wright told his young daugh-
ter: "Julia, you can write them, too. It's always five, and seven and
five—like math. So you can't go wrong." Many English-speaking trans-
lators and writers, however, have adapted the original form to address
the twin needs of remaining faithful to their idea of haiku and the de-
mands of English poetic language. For example, Wright incorporated
into his haiku the translator R. H. Blyth's suggested rhythmic scheme of

two beats in the first line, three beats in the second, and two beats in the last line to give the poem a sense of coherence.

No. 31

In the falling snow
A laughing boy holds out his palms
Until they are white.

Paul Muldoon's "Hopewell Haiku" in his book *Hay* (1998) maintains the five-seven-five syllabic count, and throws in end rhymes (in the following example, slant rhymes) in the first and third lines to underscore the haiku's discrete, compact form:

LXXXVIII

That wavering flame
is the burn-off from a mill.
Star of Bethlehem.

In Lawson Fusao Inada's "Just as I Thought," Inada invokes the one-line vertical form of traditional haiku to reflect the feeling of being in midfall:

Just as I thought:
Acorns
Fall
What
Did
They
Call

Other versions, however, convey only the feel of haiku. For example, although we can hear echoes of Bashō in the Imagists' injunction for "direct treatment of the thing," neither Ezra Pound's famous imagist poem, "In a Station of the Metro," nor Amy Lowell's variation on Yosa Buson's haiku, "Perched upon the muzzle of a cannon / A yellow butterfly is slowly opening and shutting its wings," maintains the three-line seventeen-syllable count. However, the rapid shifts and dissolves, together with the intimate feeling generated between the poet and the object, invoke the spirit of haiku. Writers of haiku have also explored the relationship between autobiographical prose and haiku, the most famous example being

Bashō's *Narrow Road to the Interior* (Oku-no-Hosomichi, 1694). Though the hokku in the following excerpt could stand alone, it works to complete the prose through discordance and attention to sound:

> In the demesne of Yamagata, the mountain temple called Ryu-shakuji. Founded by Jikaku Daishi, an unusually well-kept quiet place. "You must go and see it," people urged; from here, off back toward Obanazawa, about seven li. Sun not yet down. Reserved space at dormitory at bottom, then climbed to the temple on the ridge. This mountain one of rocky steeps, ancient pines and cypresses, old earth and stone and smooth moss, and on the rocks temple doors locked, no sound. Climbed along the edges of and crept over boulders, worshipped at temples, penetrating scene, profound quietness, heart/mind open clear.

> Stillness—
> the cicada's cry
> drills into the rocks.

Translated by Robert Hass

In tandem with the strong tradition of haiku translations in the English language (beginning with Lafcadio Hearn's *Exotics and Retrospectives* [1898], W. G. Aston's *A History of Japanese Literature* [1899], and Basil Hall Chamberlain's "Bashō and the Japanese Poetical Epigram" [1902]), American poets have been reimagining haiku in exciting ways: from Gerald Vizenor's blending of haiku and Ojibway forms; to the use of haiku by Beat poets such as Gary Snyder as an alternative to the values of American mass culture; to the crossing of haiku and jazz/blues traditions in Sonia Sanchez's *Like the Singing Coming off the Drums* (1998), and Lawson Fusao Inada's "Listening Images" in *Legends from Camp* (1993) and "Just as I Thought" in *Drawing the Line* (1997); to the fusion of haiku and language poetry aesthetics in John Yau's "Genghis Chan: Private Eye XXIII (Haiku Logbook)" in *Forbidden Entries* (1996); to the "free-style" haiku of Japanese American internees in *May Sky: An Anthology of Japanese American Concentration Camp Kaiko Haiku* (1997) as an expression of their desire for freedom in a new country. As seen in this very limited synopsis, the evolution of haiku has been rich and complex, infecting and informing our understanding of images and poetic language, calling readers and writers of haiku to the pleasures of tradition without abandoning the possibilities of modern reinvention.

MATSUO BASHŌ (1644–1694)

Translated by Robert Hass

Deep autumn—
my neighbor,
how does he live, I wonder?

Even in Kyoto—
hearing the cuckoo's cry—
I long for Kyoto.

KAGA NO CHIYO (1703–1775)

Translated by Jane Hirshfield

The morning glory!
It has taken the well bucket,
I must seek elsewhere for water.

KOBAYASHI ISSA (1763–1827)

Translated by Cid Corman

only one guy and
only one fly trying to
make the guest room do

YOSA BUSON (1716–1783)

Translated by R. H. Blyth

The horse's tail
Caught in the bramble
On the withered moor.

MASAOKA SHIKI (1867–1902)

Translated by Harold G. Henderson

A lightening flash:
    between the forest trees
    I have seen water.

GARY SNYDER (b. 1930)

A great freight truck
    lit like a town
through the dark stony desert.

SONIA SANCHEZ (b. 1935)

my bones hang to
gether like pinched dragonflies
shake loose my skin

Hip-Hop Rhyme Formations:
Open Your Ears

TRACIE MORRIS

In the African diaspora of North America during and after the age of disco, dense, intense manipulations of language have defined a generation globally. This essay is an introduction to one important poetic tool being utilized by hip-hop artists. I was spurred to write this article as a poet who has been influenced by and utilizes these techniques in my own work (even those poems without "traditional" hip-hop themes). I have also been dismayed by the lack of academic respect for this genre's poetic form. The poetic techniques rapidly refined between the midseventies and now, while affected by previous movements, have their own distinctive sound, development, and offshoots. Some folks don't understand hip-hop because they don't know how to listen. The two main principles to keep in mind when listening to hip-hop are the patterns and intricacies of rhyme and what is called the *flow,* the way the words fit with the music or beat. Like rhyme and flow, the effects of the genre push one's ears forward.

The early underground patterns of most "raps" or "rhymes" were usually of the classic *abab* or *abcb* pattern of blues and other types of popular song. (Slant rhymes were occasionally added to the *a* lines, but refrains were not always considered essential.) What made them new was the disco music and the generational difference. The Sugar Hill Gang's "Rappers' Delight," as the first recorded rap record to get major distribution, easily exemplifies this:

> What you hear is not a test,
> I'm rapping to the beat
> and me, the groove and my friends
> are gonna try to move your feet

Rappers, while speaking in a voice relevant for their generation, were part of a long line of poets using conventional poetic forms to explore unconventional themes or unconventional forums. The independent distribution network (word-of-mouth, trunk-of-car to hand or Black record store to Black consumer) among its supporters helped distinguish the music at that time more than the organization of the words.

That changed substantially in 1986 with the introduction of MC Rakim, of the duo Eric B. and Rakim. His rapid delivery as well as his quantum leap in rhyme techniques—using internal rhyme, slant rhyme, assonance, and consonance extensively within one song—as well as classic end rhyme patterns, completely changed the environment and single-handedly sophisticated the listening abilities of the audience:

> Stop buggin', a brutha said
> Dig 'em/ I neva dug 'em
> he couldn't follow the leader long enough
> so I drug 'em

> Rap is rhythm and poetry
> cuts create sound effects
> you might catch up if
> you follow the records he wrecks

Significantly, Rakim used rhyme to generate a soundscape with the DJ. The recording also demonstrates how Rakim used the internal rhyme to counterpoint the sounds (conventional music, cutting and scatching) created by DJ Eric B.

Since Rakim's debut as an MC, playing assonance, consonance, and internal rhyme off against the music (or a capella) has become standard for many hip-hop artists. And even though the well-known LL Cool J still employs a classic end rhyme pattern and refrains exploring unconventional themes (usually sexual in nature), which technically keeps him more in line with the blues form, Rakim's influence on the genre is still audible in the progressive development of momentum, based on increased rhyme and repetition (particularly the assonance and consonance in the second verse).

> It's our first time together
> and I'm feeling kind of horny,
> conventional methods of
> making love kinda bore me.

> I wanna knock ya block off
> get ma rocks off
> Blow ya socks off,
> Make sure ya G-spot's soft

The next major shift in rhyme usage by rappers was presented by Biggie Smalls a.k.a. The Notorious B.I.G., who manipulated the stresses or accentuation of words, thereby changing the scansion to create consistent patterns in end rhyme or internal rhyme schema. His focus on scansion development makes him more similar to Spanish-speaking poets who emphasize this aspect of "legitimate rhyme."

One of the newer and, I feel, revolutionizing voices in hip-hop is Busta Rhymes. Although several MCs have synthesized a regional tonal style—either southern United States or Caribbean—to inform their delivery (Biggie Smalls, Snoop Doggy Dogg, KRS One, Luther Campbell, and Hammer among others), Busta Rhymes has advanced his usage of tone to develop slant rhyme and rapidity to amazing levels. Sexist recidivism and generational differences notwithstanding, his broad reach in this area is reminiscent of Linton Kwesi Johnson's use of Jamaican dialect in his poetry to make non-Jamaicans sensitized to the possibilities of these sounds. While Busta doesn't speak exclusively this way, he does use subtle Caribbean-based inflections combined with African Americanisms and his own new sounds for hip-hop. Busta also builds upon the rhyme devices developed by his hip-hop predecessors.

When a poet, rapper, MC, lyricist—or whatever a wordsmith influenced by hip-hop calls him or herself—describes others in the genre, there is invariably a critique of flow. Part rhythm, rhyme, timing, and technique, flow is almost intangible but refers to the musicality of the artist's delivery. While the artists mentioned previously have credibility as far as their content is concerned, their flow—their ability to make the words do intricate musical work through the delivery—is always looked at as a separate consideration. When critics of the genre (especially outsiders to it) complain about content, they often dismiss this other critical aspect of the wordsmiths' technique, which helps legitimize them to the community.

Flow is the crucial component in "freestyling"—improvising rhymes to vocalized, established beats. Cyphers, groups of people who get together spontaneously to rhyme on topics available only at the moment (to insure that the rapper isn't reciting a previously remembered rhyme), develop flow and test it. Although the content matters, a rapper or rap-influenced poet can get away with less-than-brilliant word choices if his or her flow is "on point." But if the flow doesn't work or falters, the person could be a genius and still "fall off." The now-defunct but legendary Freestyle Fellowship combined jazz with poetic improvisation and flow with dizzying acuity.

As in jazz, combination and influence are crucial. Collaborating with a producer and/or DJ, a rapper must modulate tone, voicing, and inflection so that they complement the other sounds. Sometimes this means becoming more minimalist, sometimes more dense. The environment developed by the DJ—through sound layering, cutting, sampling, and scratching has also developed the ear of the listener. Rakim with Eric B., and Notorious B.I.G. with Puff Daddy a.k.a. Sean "Puffy" Combs, are examples of successful collaborations.

The DJ manipulation of sound, by using familiar or strikingly foreign material, sets the context for an artist who wishes to be seen as pushing the genre somewhere new or being in good company. These snatches of the familiar (in a postmodern sense) or the unfamiliar (to convey a more experimental point of view) are in the work of both the "musician" and the "vocalist." References to popular culture—from well-known brands of expensive champagne and liquor with funk beats to underscore the "playa" aesthetic, to urban street sounds such as alarms for the "ghetto realism" aesthetic, to music from other cultures or unusual instruments such as violins in the forefront to imply that the artist is cutting edge or "the new shit"—underscore the direction of lyric content. Furthermore, *cutting,* the systematic interruption of the conventional musical pattern with another record or sound to create a new pattern; or loop and *scratching,* using the sound of a vinyl album (or digital sound equivalent) being interrupted within the groove to create the distinctive sound of the amplified needle literally scratching the recorded pattern, make new choices available to the vocal artist. These sounds can be imitated by the vocalist (e.g.: Rahzel, the Godfather of Noise—performer with The Roots who exactly duplicates many of the sounds DJs make).

Hip-hop influenced poets are in the approximate age range of the rappers, and cannot help but be influenced by them and the world they've made. There is a strong emphasis on assonance, consonance, and combinations with end rhyme. In fact, for most identifiable rap/rhyme styles, there is a poetic equivalent. But there are some significant distinctions between rappers and poets influenced by them.

When hip-hop/rap emerged, it was predominantly male. Some women (especially earlier in the genre's development) did not have as much legitimate access as men (they were the exception rather than the rule). They certainly had to address themselves, at that time, from stance presented by men (e.g., MC Lyte and Latifah). Other women influenced by the genre turned to poetry to explore that voice in a more hospitable context. Now many women are prominent in hip-hop poetry. Other key differences between hip-hop poets and rappers have to do with how they perform. Hip-hop poets generally work unaccompanied, and lyrical content can have less emphasis on the "I." In rapping (with its relation to the Caribbean "toasting" tradition) this is unusual. Conventional hip-hop posturing and other physical cues and body language are not as present in hip-hop poets, and hip-hop poets refer, in text and tone, to non-hip-hop poets much more often than MCs do. Finally, hip-hop poets are more consistently political in content than rappers likely due to less marketplace pressure on the poets.

The rhyme and flow as technique push the listeners' ears forward whether they are ready to move or not. The ear, sensitized to patterns, and searching for them, is one step ahead of conscious absorption. As the unconventional, nuanced, and increasingly dense rhyme doesn't lend itself, initially, to mnemonic facility, this "pushing ahead" becomes the focus and purpose of the rhyme. As the audiences develop more skills in hearing the different elements at play, the demands for more sophisticated word use begins to affect other genres in that generation. Consequently, more R&B artists are employing these ideas in order to remain relevant. This will inevitably affect other popular musics, too.

Hip-hop has been a major literary force for over twenty years. Not only has it made an impact as a genre in and of itself, but it has been the primary force behind the resurgence of the "spoken word" movement even for those who don't use the techniques. By developing the sophistication of the audience's ear for patterns and musical compatibility, en masse, rappers/MCs have made poetic form more relevant. The specific techniques, intricacies, and developments have not reached this level of prominence in poetry across the board in a couple of centuries. I have yet to see sufficient intergenerational respect or inquiry into the mechanics of this form and the profundity of its development. As hip-hop rhyming in both recorded music and, to a lesser degree, in performance poetry, is an overground, mass-media phenomenon at this point and part of an interdisciplinary art form, it certainly can't be an oversight. I cannot help but think that these forms are so easily dismissed because the community they emerged from is Black. A more complete examination of the poetic tools used by specific MCs and poets not included in this commentary, the use of simile and metaphor, postmodernist critique, commercialization, the reinvention of words, the renewed interest in all forms of poetry, in fact, poetry's renewed relevancy for many people under forty, are other areas to explore within the context of hip-hop poetry that could not be touched upon in the context of this essay, given space limitations. I can only hope that this is the beginning of a scholastically respected investigation of this important aesthetic movement. This academic appreciation can only hope to sufficiently underscore the well-earned admiration of the community and generation that created it.

Japanese-Style Linked Poems

WILLIAM J. HIGGINSON AND
PENNY HARTER

Japanese linked poetry originated as a kind of game. One poet would offer the challenge of a three-line opening stanza, and another would add a two-liner, then a third would add a stanza in three lines, and so on, alternating three- and two-line stanzas until a hundred-stanza poem was created. Over time various lengths were used, and the collaborative linked poem dominated Japanese poetry for several centuries. Today the best-known exponent of linked poetry is Bashō (surname Matsuo, 1644–1694), who developed the style known then as *haikai no renga*—now called *renku*—into a high art. Renku mixes elements of the earlier court tradition with the interests of common people. Bashō preferred a thirty-six-stanza length, the most common form today, though shorter forms are also used. While the popularity of renku waned in the nineteenth century, it has been making a comeback in Japan and generating interest in North America for the last several decades.

Here we discuss the Americanized version of renku that pays homage to Bashō-style composition, and that now has groups of adherents in Boston, New York, Milwaukee, Santa Fe, and San Francisco. Many others compose similar poems by letter, fax, and e-mail. Although linked poetry is sometimes called "old people's poetry" because it takes so long to learn the rules, a poet new to the genre is often welcome at a renku session.

RENKU RULES: LINK AND SHIFT

The primary objective of writing a renku is having a good time. But, as in most parlor games, renku's rules present a real challenge—while they help the players produce the most varied and interesting poem possible. The main rule is to keep moving to new material. In any three consecutive stanzas, there should be no direct connection in subject matter, style, or tone between the first and third, though each must connect with the second. In other words, any two succeeding stanzas form a poetic unit, but three in a row do not. A renku is not a narrative.

The opening stanza or "starting verse" *(hokku)* of a renku is very much like a haiku. (It will help people to write renku if they are familiar with haiku, which see.) But over the years haiku lost a requirement necessary to renku composition. Since it takes a party to write a renku, there are almost always hosts and guests. By tradition, one of the guests writes the hokku. And this hokku must, usually in some metaphorical manner, compliment the host. The host returns the compliment in the second stanza, so it stays fairly close to the first, but the third stanza breaks away from the other two, while still connecting to the second. For example, here are the opening three stanzas of a joint Japanese-American renku session held in Milwaukee:

Lake Michigan
tinted with morning fog—
sound of a bell   —Ichiyo Shimizu

autumn footprints
scattered on damp sand   —Mary Conley

sixteenth night
started to read an old novel
and quit   —Shinkū Fukuda

Visiting renku master Ichiyo Shimizu from Osaka compliments his hosts' aesthetics in placing the sound of the bell in the morning fog. Mary Conley responds with the poignant "autumn footprints" on the lakeshore. Sado Island renku master Shinkū Fukuda breaks the mood by shifting from morning to night and dropping an old romance to enjoy the bright moonlight, which starkly reveals the footprints one night after the full moon—the sixteenth night of a lunar month.

There are many techniques for linking two consecutive verses. The following examples illustrate some of the important methods:

Linking through words *(kotobazuke):* Pick up a key word or phrase in the previous verse and give it a twist; pun, capitalize on familiar phrases, relate sounds or parallel striking grammatical patterns; allude to a piece of well-known literature.

Clearing brush he finds
someone's wedding ring   —Gloria Procsal

moving awry
with the sunspot
a widow spider   —Frederick Gasser

(The direct connection here is "wedding" and "widow" relating to marriage. "Moving awry" also links slightly with the action in the previous stanza.)

up the stairs from the subway
a tangled mass of men   —T. M. Ramirez

in quiet desperation
she stitches and stitches
seam after seam   —Ursula Sandlee

(Alludes to Thoreau's famous saying from *Walden,* "The mass of men lead lives of quiet desperation." Note that there is no other apparent connection except possibly in nervous agitation.)

Linking through things *(monozuke):* Extend the preceding by continuing an action or a description; provide an action for the previous setting or a setting for the previous action; reverse an action; make a sudden shift in locale or focus, or move from pole to pole—from large to small, close to distant, darkness to light, and so on—like cutting from scene to scene in a movie.

a happy little boy
gathers up seashells   —Elizabeth Searle Lamb

the photo album
wife & six kids
& grainy Calais   —Michael McClintock

(Scene becomes picture in album.)

the neon goes out . . .
behind the motel
sunrise over the mountains —Cor van den Heuvel

when WHIZ! go the pinwheels
at the used car lot   —Anita Virgil

(Focus shifts from background to foreground, adding detail—note also the contrast between peaceful quiet and sudden action.)

Linking through "scent" *(nioizuke):* Echo the mood or tone of the previous stanza using different materials.

in the empty house
the clock strikes as usual —Paul O. Williams

transcribing
the Diamond Sutra
a bow for each letter   —Kris Kondo

(The regularity and calm of the bowing echo those of the empty house, which becomes the emptiness of Buddhism.)

the clairvoyant's cat
stares into sunrise   —Patricia Neubauer

church usher
above the boutonniere
the fixed smile   —L. A. Davidson

(The stare and the smile present similar moods; these also link by action and by parallelism.)

In all linking, one must be careful not to make the middle verse of three a pivot between two similar verses. Any *a-b-a* pattern creates a poem-stopping triptych effect. An unwanted repetition between two verses separated by only one verse is called a "throwback" *(uchikoshi).* Bashō's later disciples suggested categorizing stanzas as referring to "place" (verses without people), "self" (verses that can be understood as first person), "other" (verses in second or third person), or "mixed" (verses with a nondescript group of people). To help avoid throwbacks, poets see that the first and third stanzas in any three consecutive verses are not in the same category. For example, if the first of three verses is a "self" verse, the third verse must be in a different category, such as "place" or "other."

This guideline supports the general imperative that a renku not resemble a continuous narrative, but be rather like an oriental scroll

painting, shifting from place to place, close to distant, people to land-
scape, and season to season.

TOPICS: THE SEASONS, LOVE,
AND OTHERS

Moving through a range of seasons by including special words and
phrases called "season words" *(kigo)* is one key to renku variety. The
starting verse or hokku must reflect the season of composition. Spring
and autumn normally appear for at least three verses in a row, but not
more than five. Summer and winter, less attractive aesthetically, may ap-
pear only once or perhaps in two consecutive verses (up to three in
poems over fifty stanzas). A completed renku must have all four seasons.

Season words name phenomena that either occur only at certain
times of the year or have become associated with particular seasons
through tradition. For example, the crocus blooms in spring; geese mi-
grate south in autumn. Frogs represent spring because that is when we
first become aware of their singing; the moon suggests autumn because
it is so prominent at that time of year. However, any phenomenon that
actually occurs at other times of the year may be modified to show a dif-
ferent association: hibernating frogs represent winter; a hazy moon,
spring. Holidays and a number of other human activities indicate sea-
sons as well, such as plowing and planting in spring and harvesting in
autumn. Typically half or more of the stanzas in a renku will be sea-
sonal, and movement from season to season and within the seasons
forms an important texture. The seasons do not follow calendar order,
but occupy certain places for aesthetic reasons. For example, in a renku
that starts in a season other than autumn, the autumn moon will typi-
cally fall in the fifth stanza, thus placing this prized image near the be-
ginning of the poem and initiating a run of verses in autumn—tradi-
tionally the most attractive season. And, no matter when a renku starts,
the next to the last verse must mention blossoms—indicating the blos-
soming cherry trees of spring. (Americans frequently mention some
other spring-blossoming tree in this position, not having the profound
attachment of the Japanese to blossoming cherries.)

Depending on the length of a renku, the moon and blossoms may
appear more than once, but always at some distance, and always in
different seasons with different characteristics. A second moon may be
a "cold moon" of winter; the middle of the poem may have falling
blossoms instead of the more positive blooming preferred near the
poem's end.

Interwoven with this larger pattern of the seasons are alternating patches of verses with nonseasonal topics. Love is a favorite, usually appearing more than once, normally at about one-quarter of the way through and again near the two-thirds mark. Typically in pairs or trios, love verses deal more often with the pain of separation or loss than with joy or sexuality, though these also may appear. Like the seasons, love is often expressed indirectly.

Other popular topics in renku—which appear at least once in a poem but usually not more than once in a short poem (thirty-six or fewer stanzas)—are travel, religion, current events, and historical persons or events. Weather must show at least three or four different aspects, often tied in with the seasons. Landscapes, seascapes, and indoor settings must show great variety, as must human activities and types of people. In addition to good times, illness and often death will put in their appearances. The overall effect of a completed renku should be like a mandala, incorporating all aspects of existence.

RENKU MOVEMENTS

In addition to the seasons, a basic overall rhythm helps shape a renku and give it a unity not unlike that of a sonata or other musical form. The opening stanzas form the "introduction" *(jo)* and occupy the first page when a renku is written out formally. The number of stanzas varies according to the overall length. A fifty-stanza renku has an eight-stanza introduction; a thirty-six-stanza renku has six; a twenty-stanza renku, four. These opening stanzas avoid violence, love, vulgar language, and negative images. They are like the beginning of a party, during which people graciously introduce one another and speak politely.

Turning the page and moving into the "development" *(ha)* of a renku is like the middle of the party, when people are feeling good and having a good time, perhaps a little high, getting excited, gossiping, and so on. Think of the varied and rapidly changing conversation at the height of a good cocktail party. But writing renku is better: you find out not only what's on other people's minds but also how they make connections.

As a renku moves on to its final page, the so-called fast close *(kyū)* with the same number of verses as the first, the tone calms down but the tempo quickens. Linking becomes more direct, images and actions simpler. People at the party start getting ready to go, and language moves toward the essentials. An optimistic mood helps move things toward the end; the final verse ends the poem on a positive note.

SAMPLE RENKU

"The Kite's Feathers" was written by Bashō and his disciples Kyorai, Bonchō, and Fumikuni in 1690. It is the first of four renku included in *Monkey's Raincoat (Sarumino)*, considered the greatest of the seven anthologies published by Bashō's group during his lifetime. Perhaps because Fumikuni was new to the Bashō school, this poem is fairly orthodox in structure and is a common model for study by beginners in renku.

The first column below represents the Japanese in romanized transliteration, the second presents an English translation, and the third gives the authors' names and indicates the seasons and some other topics. (Note: The seasons are abbreviated to their first two letters, and parentheses enclose the season word; a dash indicates a seasonless verse.) In the translation (by Higginson) I have tried to maintain the two-three-two and three-three-beat rhythms that seem ideal for renku in English, though of course some Japanese verses require more words to communicate their meaning than this form allows. Trying to write renku in five-seven-five/seven-seven syllabic verse often results in wordy and awkward English, just as such translations usually include more than is justified in the original text. The excerpt below presents the first six and the latter twelve of the original thirty-six verses.

1   *tobi no ha mo*   The kite's feathers
     kaitsukuroinu   also get a preening—   Kyorai
     hatsushigure   first winter rain   wi (kite = hawk)

2   *hitofuki kaze no*   a single gust of wind   Bashō
     konoha shizumaru   and the leaves quiet down   wi (dry leaves)

3   *momohiki no*   britches wet
     asa kara nururu   since early this morning   Bonchō
     kawa koete   crossing the river   —/river

4   *tanuki o odosu*   a bamboo bow cocked   Fumikuni
     shinohari no yumi   to frighten badgers away   —/animal

5   *mairado ni*   on the lattice door
     tsuta haikakaru   ivy vines creep . . .   Bashō
     yoi no tsuki   the evening moon   au (moon)

6   *hito ni mo kurezu*   they give to no one   Kyorai
     meibutsu no nashi   the place's famous pears   au (pear)

Verses 7–24 cover a wide range of topics.

	* * *	* * *	
25	*uki hito o* *kikokugaki yori* *kugurasen*	wretched fellow let him come through the mock-orange hedge	Bashō —/courtly love
26	*ima ya wakare no* *katana sashidasu*	"now at our parting" she hands him his sword	Kyorai —/love/warrior
27	*sewashige ni* *kushi de kashira o* *kakichirashi*	restlessly a comb messes the lines of the hairdo	Bonchō —/anguish/fashion
28	*omoikittaru* *shinigurui mi yo*	with determination looks ready for death!	Fumikuni —/mettle/death
29	*seiten ni* *ariakezuki no* *asaborake*	in a pale sky the morning moon at daybreak	Kyorai au (moon)/calm
30	*kosui no aki no* *hira no hatsushimo*	in autumn lake-waters Mt. Hira's first frost	Bashō au/lake/frost/ named place
31	*Shiba no to ya* *soba nusumarete* *uta o yomu*	a rustic gate . . . buckwheat stolen and still he composes poems	Fumikuni au (buckwheat)
32	*nunoko kinarau* *kaze no yūgure*	acclimating to padded clothes in the wind of evening	Bonchō wi (padded clothes)
33	*oshiōte* *nete wa mata tatsu* *karimakura*	crowding together sleeping only to get up again— a brief lodging	Bashō —/travel
34	*tatara no kumo no* *mada akaki sora*	the bellows-cloud still reddens the sky	Kyorai —/industry (a forge)
35	*hitokamae* *shirigai tsukuru* *mado no hana*	an isolated building where they make cruppers: blossoms by the window	Bonchō sp (cherry blossoms)
36	*biwa no furuha ni* *konome moetatsu*	among the loquat's old leaves the new growth flares	Fumikuni sp (new growth)

For a complete translation and commentary on "The Kite's Feathers" see one of the editions *of Monkey's Raincoat* mentioned in the bibliography.

The following twelve-stanza renku demonstrates a shorter form, less constrained by rules than the longer forms and a good place for beginners to start. In this example, written in March 1998 in Santa Fe, New Mexico, Connie Meester, who was new to renku, worked with the two of us. We started this renku one afternoon and completed it by passing it back and forth over the next two days. Comments at the right indicate the seasons, some other topics, and types of verses: place, self, other, or mixed.

Twelve-Stanza Renku: Triangle of Snow

1	Triangle of snow	
	on the face of the Jemez—	CM
	call of a raven	sp (local phenomenon)/
		mountain/bird//place
2	deep in the spring garden	WJH
	finding . . . herself	sp/garden//other
3	two bay leaves	
	into the soup pot	PH
	steam on the window	wi (soup)/food/[love?]//self
4	a pair of pines, one limb	CM
	broken from each	—/love//place
5	who is he?	
	this lame dog	PH
	crossing traffic	—/animal/traffic//place
6	ah, my pure white horse	WJH
	over the full moon	au (moon)/animal/drugs//self
7	fire in the sumac	
	she turns her back	CM
	to an empty hearth	au (sumac "fire")//other
8	nailed in the apple tree	PH
	a few weathered boards	—/tree//place
9	mourning dove	
	huddled against the rail—	CM
	my sister's grave	—/bird/building detail/death//self

10 a black swallowtail   WJH
    flickers over the crowd   su (swallowtail)/insect//mixed

11 the baby giggles
    as cherry petals land   PH
    on her nose   sp (cherry petals)/baby//other

12 clear stream salmon   CM
    tracing the sunrise   sp (salmon run)/fish//place

These few examples can only give one the beginnings of an idea of what it is like to write renku. Those interested in pursuing the forms and the fun will want to take a look at the best online resource for further information on the rapidly expanding range of linked forms based at least loosely on the Japanese tradition; log on to the Open Directory's page on the topic: http://dmoz.org/Arts/Literature/Poetry/Forms/Haiku_and_Related_Forms/Linked_Poems/.

Writing linked poems, Japanese-style, goes back several hundred years. Yoshimoto (1320–88), one of the first to write guidebooks for others who wanted to play, said "Ultimately, the purpose of a linked poem is to delight those composing it." So, lonely poets, have a party, and write a poem together with some friends.

Form Lite:
Limericks and Clerihews

GAIL WHITE

No one knows who wrote the first villanelle; the origins of the ballade and sestina are likewise lost in the mists of time. But we know exactly who wrote the first clerihew, because it's named for him. (Had the limerick been christened in the same fashion, it would now be called "the eddie.")

> Edmund Clerihew Bentley
> mostly wrote incompetently,
> but managed to save his face
> by writing *Trent's Last Case*.

The classic Trent mystery, however, is not Bentley's only claim to fame. As a young schoolboy, Bentley amused his friend Gilbert Keith Chesterton by inventing the verse form to which he gave his middle name. One of his most famous original verses is this:

> Sir Christopher Wren
> Said, "I am going to dine with some men.
> If anyone calls,
> Say I'm designing St. Paul's."

From which it can be seen that the basic rules of the clerihew are very simple:

1. The first line invariably is a famous person's name.
2. The lines are of uneven length and scansion, and there are usually just four lines that rhyme *aabb*.
3. The intent is humorous.

Of course, rules are no sooner made than they begin to be broken. Sometimes the clerihew's first line contains more than a name. Here is one of Bentley's variations:

238

The people of Spain think Cervantes
Equal to half a dozen Dantes,
An opinion resented bitterly
By the people of Italy.

The following contemporary examples of the form are from Henry
Taylor's *Brief Candles.*

Judas Iscariot
missed the sweet chariot
but swung pretty low
in his wasteland of woe.

Hélène Cixous,
she who
speaks of discourse as clitoral,
is not being literal.

John Berryman
hailed the grim ferryman
at a point from which his descent could be reckoned
at thirty-two feet per second per second.

And one more of mine:

Thomas Hardy
Could really kill a party.
In an effort to effervesce,
He would read selections from *Tess.*

Edward Lear (d. 1888), that amiable watercolorist and gifted non-
sense poet, is generally credited with inventing the limerick. Lear's orig-
inal version is not likely to induce convulsive laughter in the modern
reader. It lacked surprise, the last line generally being only a variation of
the first line. For example:

There was a Young Lady of Welling
Whose praise all the world was a-telling.
She played on the harp, and caught several carp,
This accomplished Young Lady of Welling.

Lear turned this stuff out by the pound, but its charm palls rather
quickly. Practitioners of the art soon dropped the repeated rhyme and

broke the third line into two. The basic line is an iambus followed by two anapests (There *was* a young *man* from Hong *Kong*). The length of the middle lines is slightly variable, and both masculine and feminine endings are used.

It also did not take the world's poets long to discover the limerick's possibilities as a vehicle for creative obscenity. This one has been attributed to Swinburne:

> There was a young girl from Aberystwith
> Who took grain to the mill to get grist with,
> Where the miller's lad Jack
> Threw her flat on her back
> And united the organs they pissed with.

Close readers will observe an affinity between the limerick and the Anglican clergy. Can anyone imagine that the bishops of Birmingham and Buckingham are anything other than Church of England? Here is one of my more printable favorites:

> The vicar of Dunstan St. Just,
> Consumed by insatiable lust,
> Raped the bishop's prize owls,
> His hens and pea-fowls,
> And a little green lizard, which bust.

W. S. Gilbert wrote many of his lyrics in a rapid limerick form that must have kept Sullivan busy thinking up new melodies for them. From *The Yeoman of the Guard* comes this advice on making love:

> It is purely a matter of skill,
> Which all may attain if they will,
> But every Jack,
> He must study the knack,
> If he wants to make sure of his Jill!

The following recent examples of the form are gathered from the pages of the admirable Chicago magazine, *Light Quarterly*:

> Jill Williams, "The Subject of a Limerick"
>
> There once was a gerund named Angling
> Whose bed action needed untangling.
> Far worse than the predicate
> Surrounding his etiquette
> Was the sight of his participle dangling.

C. W. Christian warns the young:

> Observe now the plump anaconda
> Who stretches from hither to yonda.
> > The lump in his belly
> > Is not toast and jelly,
> A thought that small children should ponda.

Max Gutmann, "More Travels of Alice":

> When she stood at the Great Wall of China,
> Alice said, "I would hate to malign a
> > Famous site, but it's cracked
> > And so old! It, in fact,
> Makes think of my first husband, kin'a."

The limerick is so much a part of our consciousness that it seems to have been around forever. It's easy to imagine the company at Plato's Symposium raising their voices in a chorus of "There once was a Persian named Xerxes / whose soldiers were castrated turkeys." But the million limericks in existence are mostly products of the twentieth century, and with them the moderns can look the ancients in the face and claim to have made a major contribution to civilization.

A Wand Made of Words:
The Litany Poem

NANCY WILLARD

Let me start by explaining what the litany, as a poetic form, is not. It is not a liturgical prayer in which phrases are sung or chanted by a leader alternating with phrases sung or chanted in response by the congregation. As a poetic form, the litany can be described as an incantatory recitation built on a simple pattern: every line, or nearly every line, starts with the same word.

The simplest litany I know appears in the picture book *Good Night Moon,* though many other picture book texts make use of this form because it is so versatile.

> Goodnight comb
> Goodnight brush
> Goodnight nobody
> Goodnight mush
> And goodnight to the old lady whispering "hush"
>
> 1975

When I teach the litany form to my students, I begin with two traditional poems that are still tied to their magical and liturgical origins. The first is Psalm 150. Joyful and impersonal, it opens with the following lines:

> Hallelujah!
> Praise God in his holy temple;
>   praise him in the firmament of his power.
> Praise him for his mighty acts;
>   praise him for his excellent greatness.
> Praise him with the blast of a horn;
>   praise him with lyre and harp.

The poet who uses the litany form to praise more secular pleasures finds that it allows for great expansiveness within the elegance of its formulaic opening. In *Song of Myself,* Whitman's long lines give momentum to a catalog of people seen both as individuals and studies for a genre painting:

> The pilot seizes the king-pin, he heaves down with a
>   strong arm,
> The mate stands braced in the whale-boat, lance and
>   harpoon are ready,
> The duck-shooter walks by silent and cautious stretches,
>   The deacons are ordain'd with cross'd hands at the altar,
> The spinning-girl retreats and advances to the hum of the
>   big wheel.

1855–71

A poem written as a single sentence can break out of the catalog structure. In Linda Pastan's "Because," nearly every line is a dependent clause and the poem moves with the speed and suspense of a well-wrought narrative.

Because

> Because the night you asked me,
> the small scar of the quarter moon
> had healed—the moon was whole again;
> because life seemed so short;
> because life stretched before me
> like the darkened halls of nightmare;
> because I knew exactly what I wanted;
> because I knew exactly nothing;
> because I shed my childhood with my clothes—
> they both had years of wear left in them;
> because your eyes were darker than my father's;
> because my father said I could do better;
> because I wanted badly to say no;
> because Stanley Kowalski shouted "Stella . . . ;"
> because you were a door I could slam shut;
> because endings are written before beginnings;
> because I knew that after twenty years
> you'd bring the plants inside for winter
> and make a jungle we'd sleep in naked;
> because I had free will;
> because everything is ordained;
> I said yes.

1998

Remove the formulaic opening from these lines, and the poem transforms itself into a narrative about a young woman's indecision. The litany form puts distance between the reader and the speaker and turns the story into a meditation on a larger theme: the paradox of our ability to want what we do not want and to desire opposites.

Why are poems in this form so seductive? Why do readers who loathe cats read Christopher Smart's meditation on his cat Jeoffrey with grudging admiration and genuine delight? Isn't it because the litany can amuse and astonish us without baffling us, a quality it shares with dreams? Like dreams it explains nothing, even while it buries the connections between images whose significance is so private as to be unfathomable on a first reading. An excerpt from Mark Strand's "From a Litany" demonstrates this tension between the personal statements and the public voice:

> I praise the secrecy of doors, the openness of windows.
> I praise the depth of closets.
> I praise the wind, the rising generations of air.
> I praise the trees on whose branches shall sit the Cock of
>   Portugal and the Polish Cock.
> I praise the palm trees of Rio and those that shall grow in
>   London.
> I praise the gardeners, the worms and the small plants that
>   praise each other.
> I praise the sweet berries of Georgetown, Maine and the song
>   of the white-throated sparrow.

1970

The second example of a traditional litany poem that I give my students is "The Killer," a Cherokee curse that is still rooted in its shamanistic origins. Since this poem will probably be less familiar to the readers of this book, I give the entire text below as it appears in Jerome Rothenberg's *Technicians of the Sacred*:

> The Killer
> after A'yu^{n}ini
>
> Careful: my knife drills your soul
>   listen, whatever-your-name-is
>   One of the wolf people
> listen   I'll grind your saliva into the earth
> listen   I'll cover your bones with black flint
> listen   "   "   "   "   "   " feathers

```
listen        "    "    "    "    "    "   rocks
Because you're going out where it's empty
              Black coffin out on the hill
listen        the black earth will hide you, will
              find you a black hut
              Out where it's dark, in that country
listen        I'm bringing a box for your bones
              A black box
              A grave with black pebbles
listen        your soul's spilling out
listen        it's blue
```

                                                    1969

The reason for the imperative in traditional litanies is obvious: the speaker is singing or chanting to a particular audience, whether a whole congregation or a single malevolent spirit. But when Whitman uses it near the end of "Starting from Paumanok," he is addressing a more general audience of readers known and unknown, present and future, and his repetition of "See" at the beginning of each line gives the poem an urgency it would not otherwise have:

> See, steamers steaming through my poems,
> See, in my poems immigrants continually coming and landing

When the formulaic verb is *let,* the imperative is directed at fate, which may or may not be listening, and therefore to mortal ears sounds like a wish, or even a blessing. Denise Levertov's "Psalm Concerning the Castle" began with the contemplation of a painting so intense that it became an image of harmony in the soul.

> Let me be at the place of the castle.
> Let the castle be within me.
> Let it rise foursquare from the moat's ring.
> Let the moat's waters reflect green plumage of ducks, let
>   the shells of swimming turtles break the surface or be
>   seen through the rippling depths.
> Let horsemen be stationed at the rim of it, and a dog,
>   always alert on the brink of sleep.

                                                    1983

The images are ordered as the eye would see them, starting at the bottom of the painting and slowly raising one's gaze to the roof and to the young queen who has the broad view that her high station gives her. As the poem progresses, Levertov shifts more and more of her formulaic beginnings to the interior sections of the poem. In the last ten lines, the viewer steps back and surveys the whole scene.

> Let the young queen sit above, in the cool air, her child in
>   her arms; let her look with joy at the great circle, the
>   pilgrim shadows, the work of the sun and the play of
>   the wind. Let her walk to and fro. Let the columns
>   uphold the roof, let the storeys uphold the columns,
>   let there be dark space below the lowest floor, let the
>   castle rise foursquare out of the moat, let the moat be
>   a ring and the water deep, let the guardians guard it,
>   let there be wide lands around it, let that country
>   where it stands be within me, let me be where it is.

This arrangement echoes those Mother Goose rhymes that start small and open up like a telescope because of the accumulated details and their word-for-word repetition. "The House That Jack Built" is probably the best-known example, but a lesser-known rhyme, "This Is the key of the Kingdom," in *The Oxford Nursery Rhyme Book,* is closer to the spirit of Levertov's poem.

Why do so many litanies leave us spellbound? Is it because they leap over our powers of reason and let us hear the voice of our ancestral muse, whom some call prayer, some call play, and some call magic?

Musical Form and Formalist Poetry

ROB HARDIN

Consider the history of the following idea: of a sympathetic relationship between music and poetry. It is an idea that literary purists have resisted. Since the end of the Victorian period, the aesthetic union of music and verse has been derided by many critics as a too-venerable wedding. Frequently, the attempt to transpose musical forms into poetry, prosody into musical notation, has been viewed by critics as artificial. Poets have been ostracized critically for taking the idea of music too literally. Most of all, musician-poets have been rebuked in the twentieth century, in the wake of modernism's anti-Romantic aesthetic. Yet critical dismissals ring hollow in the impurity of this moment. At a point in history when the notion of aesthetic purity is suspect, complaints of artificiality sound equally suspicious.

Certain twentieth-century critics have argued that the relationship between music and poetry is as commonplace as the Romantic image of the Aeolian harp. To the degree to which this argument is not captious, it is true. Distinctions between music and poetry were not always *de rigeur;* the synthesis of the two arts was once a vital tradition. That is why the first English master of aesthetic synthesis is nearly as old as tradition itself: a sixteenth-century eclectic named Thomas Campion.

Campion was a poet as well as a musician. His celebrity rests on a handful of perfect lyrics for which he composed definitive musical settings. A quintessential artist of the Renaissance, he was both learned and versatile. A gifted practitioner and an ingenious theorist, he wrote important treatises on both music and prosody. In languages ancient and modern, he proved a gifted polyglot. Much of his poetry appropriates the technique of Latin poetry, and many of his finest lyrics are translations of Latin poems. As a poet and theorist, Campion's objective was to introduce Latin quantitative meter into English. In his view, the weight of an accent lay in the length of the vowel. His appropriation of Latin prosody proved useless to most English poets, but his own use of the technique yielded beautifully modulated verse.

It may be said that every great poet has written a treatise on prosody, a treatise that consists of the poetry itself. In Campion's case, his musical compositions play an integral part. It is fascinating to note how his musical settings reflect his theory of quantity and stress. For example, in his ayre, "Mistress, since You So Much Desire," an unusual setting of the word *shadowe* lends a felicitous twist to the rhythm of the line. Yet the overall effect is of chiseled simplicity, of variety and balance. In his greatest work, the severity of his methods seems only to enliven his art. His genius achieved measured grace through an escape artist's pyrotechnics.

After Campion, the most famous transposer of English verse into music was Sidney Lanier. For Lanier, a classically trained flautist, perfect prosody consisted of an incantatory rhythm, with accentual stresses underlined by alliteration and assonance. Rhythmic interest was created not by modulation but by the contrast between regular meter and irregular stanza structure.

This idea of "perfect" accentual prosody emerged not from Lanier's musical background but from the practice of Victorian poets like Tennyson and Swinburne. While Campion endeavored to create effects previously unattainable in English, Lanier strove to write the smoothest line possible. That one is arresting and the other occasionally soporific has to do with Lanier's literary aesthetic, not his limitations as a musician.

Some critics, like John Hollander, have argued that Campion is a greater poet than Lanier partly because Campion was not "a professional musician in the modern sense." This is not quite true. Campion was no musical amateur but rather a composer of subtle and rarefied taste. On the other hand, Lanier shows a distinct lapse of taste in his music compositions, while his poetry has lasted due to its originality and craftsmanship. Lanier's most ambitious musical transcriptions of poetry are to be found in his brazen edifice *The Science of English Verse*. This study of prosody makes an attempt to synthesize and categorize the musical implications of prosody according to Lanier's personal methods. His knowledge of music theory, combined with an equal knowledge of versification, lead to an architectonic vision of prosody, which he illustrates with several musical "arrangements." Furthermore, his attention to the gradations of tone, color, and rhythm predates the exactitudes of modern linguistics. For example, in his "arrangement" of twenty-five lines from the Saxon epic *The Battle of Malden*, Lanier finds—and this must have enraged musically illiterate critics—patterns for which "there *is* no name in prosody."

The technical problem of prosodic transcription was solved by both Campion and Lanier, but in ways that led to idiosyncratic work rather than useful solutions. On the one hand, Campion imposed Latin quantity on English prosody, resulting in a felicitous sense of rhythm. Rhythmic verve was increased by his mastery of the Renaissance lute song. Yet Campion's example is singular and rarely imitated.

On the other hand, Lanier's exhaustive study of prosodic transposition allowed him to fine-tune the musical effects of his verse. But his late Victorian aesthetic often led to a deadening regularity no matter how varied the meter and rhyme scheme of his stanza.

Certainly, mid-twentieth-century poet Louis Zukofsky was attentive to the music of words. But his concept of music stressed the autonomy of poetic language. In his view, the relationship between music and poetry implied mutual independence. This interdisciplinary theory entered directly into the compositions of his wife, musician Celia Zukofsky. According to her notes, Celia Zukofsky's *L.Z. Masque* is a "five-part score." It is written for five "Voices" that do not convey a single stratified narrative, as in a conventional opera, but rather interweave distinct narratives contrapuntally, as in a multilingual medieval motet. While her notation is specific, she leaves the intricacies of synchronization to the performers. Unlike the other musician-poets I have mentioned, she manages to avoid musical problems that stem from attempting to transpose poetic rhythm. Within the modernist margin in which she worked, she found the key to the marriage of metrics: a perfect balance between correspondence and independence.

Both limiting and liberating, her method pointed the way to later collaborations between musicians and poets in which the microstructure was dictated neither by music nor words but by a third notation that allowed the arts to remain independent in quadrants of structured time.

Celia Zukofsky's solution to prosodic transcription is one that works in terms of her own idiosyncratic notation but not, unfortunately, in conventional music notation. Therefore in order to arrive at a practical solution that could be applied to conventional notation systems, one that was not limited to avant-garde technique, I returned to the work of Campion and Lanier.

Like Campion, I wanted to introduce arbitrary techniques and technical non sequiturs for their aesthetic effect. Unlike Campion, I wanted to avoid prosodic dogma. I felt no need to replace previous concepts of poetic rhythm with a compendium of perishable tenets. Like Lanier, I hoped to transcribe poetic rhythm accurately, but without compromising the sound of the poetry prior to the imposition of the barline.

In writing both the poem "The Justine Variations" and its musical setting, I considered the problem of transposition from a dual perspective.

Prosodically, I wanted to write a poem that used variation form as it is truly practiced in music: a theme, usually simple, that is developed structurally and motivically in a series of variations, each with its own miniature form and characteristic tone.

Compositionally, I decided to set the poem by notating the rhythmic hesitations and fluctuations I encountered when reading the poem aloud. It was my decision to view the barline not as a fixed correlate to poetic meter but as a rough or arbitrary correlate, so that barline and meter did not necessarily correspond.

Stylistically, the piece was to appropriate the music of several centuries, but with an impurity that tropes Campion's eclectic dissonance. If I were to view the history of music and prosody as corresponding to the modernist notion of aesthetic boldness, then I would place my "Justine Variations" before *L.Z. Masque* because my technique is less radical than Celia Zukofsky's. However, I question the idea that unconventionality is progress. Aesthetically, an *a capella* mass from the sixteenth century is not necessarily less advanced than an improvisation for morphed grenade and nail file. That a breakdown of conventional musical/poetic structure should mark any piece as inherently modern seems rather a dated notion of aesthetic progress. Thus I have placed my piece after Celia Zukofsky's because it follows hers chronologically (historically in the mechanical sense).

Though prosody and music theory are taught separately, and though few students will ever master one art, let alone two, the compositional processes of music and poetry can no longer be dismissed as merely divergent. Technological breakthroughs have led to what is now a familiar figure, the computer virtuoso of graphics, text, and sound. Technology has also led to greater exactitude in measuring musical and prosodic time. Furthermore, our contemporary view of history may well lead to a skeptical view of aesthetic progress and allow the practicing poet-composer to employ techniques once derided as anachronistic. One can truthfully say again, as Campion said, in his introduction to the *Fourth Booke of Ayres:*

> Some words are in these Bookes which have beene cloathed in Musicke by others, and I am content they then served their turne: yet give mee now leave to make use of mine owne. . . .

Here Ends the Essay.

THOMAS CAMPION

From "Followe Thy Fair Sun"

Fol - lowe thy faire sunne, un - hap - py shad-dowe:

Though thou, though thou be blacke as night, And she made all of

light, Yet fol - low thy faire sunne, un - hap - pie shad - - dowe.

SIDNEY LANIER

From The Battle of Malden

Byrht - noth math-el - o - de, bord haf-en - o - de

wand wac - ne æsc, word - um mæl - de,

yr - re and an - ræd a - geaf him and-swar-e: "ge-

- hyrst thu, sæ - li - da, hwæt this folc seg - eth? hi

wil - lath eow to ga - fo - le gar - as syl - lan,

CELIA ZUKOFSKY

Fugues

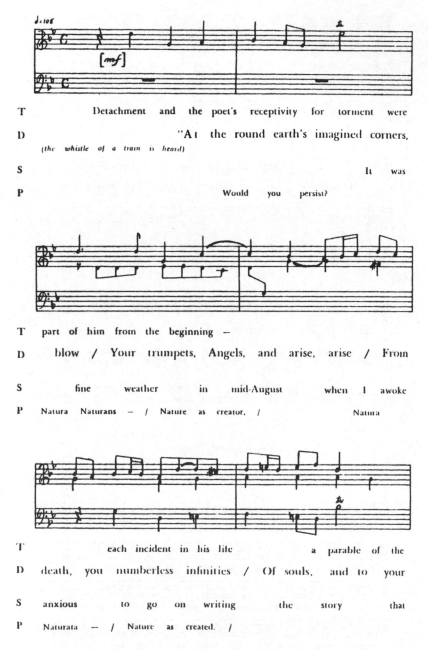

T   Detachment and the poet's receptivity for torment were

D   "At the round earth's imagined corners,

(the whistle of a train is heard)

S   It was

P   Would you persist?

T   part of him from the beginning —

D   blow / Your trumpets, Angels, and arise, arise / From

S   fine weather in mid-August when I awoke

P   Natura Naturans — / Nature as creator, /   Natura

T   each incident in his life   a parable of the

D   death, you numberless infinities / Of souls, and to your

S   anxious to go on writing the story that

P   Naturata — / Nature as created. /

ROB HARDIN

Justine Variations

The Pantoum's Postcolonial Pedigree

VINCE GOTERA

In his prosody primer *Rhyme's Reason,* John Hollander writes, "The *pantoum* comes, through French . . . from Malay *(pantun)* and is rather like a combination of *villanelle* with the unfolding motion of *terza rima*." If not for the momentary nod to Malay ancestry, Hollander's description would suggest a wholly European flavor and flesh. Nothing could be further from the truth. Before we can understand the pantoum as it has filtered from France in the 1800s into Anglo-American verse, we must first acknowledge its Malay origin. The pantoum, like all things appropriated by colonizers, has a fascinating postcolonial pedigree.

Muhammad Haji Salleh, in his critical study *Tradition and Change in Contemporary Malay-Indonesian Poetry,* lays out the traditional ground rules: "A *pantun* is a quatrain with an abab rhyme. Each line contains between 8 and 12 syllables. The first two lines prepare us in image, sound and suggestion for the meaning proper in the last two." Here is his example of a well-known pantun, "intense and compact":

> *Tinggi, tinggi simatahari,*
> > *Anak kerbau mati tertambat,*
> *Dari dahulu sasya mencari*
> > *Baru ini saya mendapat.*

> Higher and higher climbs the sun,
> > The young buffalo dies at its peg,
> So long have I waited my only one,
> > Only now are you found.

The prefatory couplet, called the *pembayang,* typically depicts common imagery drawn from Malay life. The closing couplet, or *maksud,* clarifies meaning. Both halves mirror one another: image and statement, scene and comment. Pembayang and maksud are indispensable complements, sometimes linked more by sonic device than conventional sense. Together pembayang and maksud portray ineffable cultural and universal truths. Even in translation, we can sense this in the pantun above. The speaker is so obsessed with his beloved that he neglects routine, to the point of financial (and personal) ruin, the loss of his water buffalo. At the same time, there is a fascinating parallel between the day's progress to its noontime apotheosis and the love affair, imaged ironically through the truncated life cycle of the domesticated buffalo.

The pantun has an intricate prosody—internal rhyming at caesurae, syllabic patterning, a bardic rhythm and intonation—that is tied directly to linguistic features in the Malay language. François-René Daillie in *Alam Pantun Melayu: Studies on the Malay Pantun* describes, for example, how five-syllable word clusters are created by reduplicating words and adding an affix, as in *jentu-berjentu;* these clusters provide a familiar pantun texture. In the pantun quoted above, we can see this reduplication in *Tinggi, tinngi* without the affix. Beyond such linguistic wordplay, the pantun encapsulates Malay civilization; according to Daillie,

> A pantun is a universe in a nutshell. . . . Each separate pantun can be compared to one of the many islets of an archipelago: although it looks like an isolated dot on the surface of the sea, it is part, together with other islets, of one submerged continent whose higher summits only peek out. Similarly, though each of them exists as an independent entity, pantuns communicate in an underlying context which is the traditional world of Malays.

More importantly, the pantun is a popular form, used by common folk for a variety of purposes, to express love, lyricism, and other verities.

As we know it in contemporary Anglo-American verse, the pantoum (note the French spelling), is comprised of quatrains wherein the second and fourth lines of any stanza return as the first and third lines of the subsequent stanza. When the pantoum is rhymed, this interlocking refrain results in an *abab bcbc cdcd* scheme. The final stanza resurrects the first and third lines of the first stanza (the only lines not yet repeated) in reverse order. Sometimes these lines return as a couplet envoi, also reversed. The pantoum thus achieves full circle, with identical opening and closing lines. No set number of stanzas is typical, though to interlock, one needs at least two quatrains. The pantoum's circling, however, requires substantially more than two stanzas; quite often, the reader can apprehend a kind of spiraling away from the opening gambit with a "sense of an ending" discernible when one feels the pantoum starting to slide back to its initial topic.

To illustrate in verse, here are the opening lines from "Monologue d'Outre Tomb" (an anonymous nineteenth-century British example).

Morn and noon and night
Here I lie in the ground;
No faintest glimmer of light,
No lightest whisper of sound.

Here I lie in the ground;
The worms glide out and in;
No lightest whisper of sound,
After a lifelong din.

And so on. Here is the closing quatrain.

Blind as a mole or bat,
No faintest glimmer of light,
And wearing a shovel hat,
Morn and noon and night.

One can certainly note here how the pantoum as first practiced in English could be seen as a predominantly humorous form, especially in end-stopped lines, rhymed closely.

The pantoum, as inherited from the French, is only an imperfect imitation of a subset of the pantun universe, the interlocking pantun berkait that some Malay readers find less interesting, less culturally relevant than the pure pantun. The pantoum mimics the form of pantun berkait without retaining the crucial content: the metaphysical interplay between pembayang and maksud. There have nevertheless been attempts to incorporate this interplay into the pantoum. According to the *New Princeton Encyclopedia of Poetry and Poetics,* "different themes [are] developed concurrently, one in the first couplet and the other in the second of each quatrain"; John Hollander, in *Rhyme's Reason,* puts it this way: "a touch of riddle is preserved in that the first half of each quatrain is about something wholly different from the second half." This development echoes the traditional interaction between pembayang and maksud, but very few pantoums in English actually follow this rule.

In the last couple of decades, American poets have elevated the pantoum into a rare art, dealing with weighty political and personal issues while complicating its lineal strategies. Peter Meinke's "Atomic Pantoum," reprinted here, deals with fears of the Cold War, commenting on technology and its potential complicity with the dangerous side of humanity; note also that Meinke's lines are more enjambed than those above, thus cranking up the tension and unease in the poem. Philip Dacey's "Libyan Pantoum" deals with a smaller "cold" war:

America and Libya in the mid-80s; at the same time, Dacey experiments with syntax so that a line containing a phrase returns with that phrase split into two separate sentences: "For all the good air / There's more that's bad" transmutes into "There's more. That's bad, / "That's bad, the people say." Other experimentation includes altering the lines as they cycle so that the repetition is only of key words, as Pamela Stewart does in "Punk Pantoum." In addition, where Dacey uses full rhyme, Stewart uses an occasional slant rhyme (such as "bruise" with "horse") then ends with a richly rhymed couplet, and Meinke dispenses with rhyme altogether. Unfortunately, lack of space prohibits me from reprinting Marilyn Hacker's fine though longish examples, such as "Pantoum" in her collection *Taking Notice* and "Market Day" in *Going Back to the River*. As with many other poetic forms, Hacker is a leading practitioner of the contemporary pantoum.

When I teach the writing of pantoums, I often advise students to seek a subject matter that is obsessive, naturalizing the mannered repetitions to make them seem motivated and sensible given the speaker's disposition. My own "Chain-Letter Pantoum" may illustrate: chain letters often dramatize obsession, gyrating around the letter's projected procreation ad infinitum. I wanted to replicate how such letters sometimes unravel, incrementally crazier with each example of misfortunes awaiting those who break the chain. The poem begins with a reasonably close rhyme—"consequence" and "friends"—but this quickly devolves into *very* distant slant rhyme—"possible" with "family." At the same time, diction increasingly flickers and fluctuates as lines recycle, and sometimes only obscure soundplay parallels lines: "Iceland" becomes "island"; "Haraldsdottir" mutates into "holiday" in a consonantal dance of *h, l,* and *d.* At the end, a sensible tone recurs (suggested by a closer rhyme in "leave" and "love"), but the injunction "Don't throw this letter away!" has now been made shrill by derangement in midpoem.

My final example, Shirley Geok-lin Lim's "Pantoun for Chinese Women," is significant for artistic as well as political reasons. Born and raised in Malaysia, Lim is precisely positioned to retake the form, divest it of postcolonial baggage. As an influential American writer, Lim is politically situated to comment on human rights in China from a feminist viewpoint. In terms of form, Lim does not employ the opposition of pembayang and maksud, so that her poem partakes more of Western flavor, but in her title the spelling of "pantoun," with its declamatory ending on the letter *n,* clearly leans toward Malay usage. In terms of content, Lim concentrates on a characteristically Asian American topic, confronting the rule/role of tradition. Lim's noteworthy achievement is her decolonization of the so-called French form, bringing pantun and pantoum—both in Malaysia and in the United States—finally home.

PETER MEINKE

Atomic Pantoum

In a chain reaction
the neutrons released
split other nuclei
which release more neutrons

The neutrons released
blow open some others
which release more neutrons
and start this all over

Blow open some others
and choirs will crumble
and start this all over
with eyes burned to ashes

And choirs will crumble
the fish catch on fire
with eyes burned to ashes
in a chain reaction

The fish catch on fire
because the sun's force
in a chain reaction
has blazed in our minds

Because the sun's force
with plutonium trigger
has blazed in our minds
we are dying to use it

With plutonium trigger
curled and tightened
we are dying to use it
torching our enemies

Curled and tightened
blind to the end
torching our enemies
we sing to Jesus

Blind to the end
split up like nuclei
we sing to Jesus
in a chain reaction

1983

PAMELA STEWART

Punk Pantoum

Tonight I'll walk the razor along your throat
You'll wear blood jewels and last week's ochre bruise
There's a new song out just for you and me
There's sawdust on the floor, and one dismembered horse

You'll wear blood jewels and last week's final bruise
I got three shirts from the hokey-man at dawn
There's sawdust on the floor, and, ha, his dismembered horse:
Rust-stained fetlock, gristle, bone and hoof . . .

They'll look good hanging from the shirt I took at dawn.
Bitch, let's be proud to live at Eutaw Place
With rats, a severed fetlock, muscle, bone and hooves,
George will bring his snake and the skirt Divine threw out.

For now, I'm glad we live at Eutaw Place
Remember how we met at the Flower Mart last Spring?
George wore his snake and the hose Divine threw out—
Eating Sandoz oranges, we watched the ladies in their spats.

Remember how you burned your hair at the Flower Mart
    last May?
I put it out with Wes Jones' checkered pants,
The pulp of oranges and that old lady's hat—
I knew I loved you then, with your blistered face and tracks

That I disinfected with Wes Jones' filthy pants.
There's a new song out just for you and me
That says I'll always love you and your face. Let's make
    new tracks
Tonight, dragging the white hot razor across our throats,
    and back . . .

1979

VINCE GOTERA

Chain-Letter Pantoum

Don't throw this letter away! Horrible consequences!
Jeff Slaymaker of Cleveland, Ohio laughed when he got this.
Mail a copy today to five of your closest friends.
He lost both his legs in a terrible car crash.

Jeff Slaymaker of Cleveland, Ohio laughed when he got this.
Wonderful rewards will follow! Love makes it all possible.
He lost both his legs in a terrible car crash.
Don't let godawful events happen in your family.

Wonderful rewards will follow! Love makes it all possible.
Jesus Matamoros of Bogota, Colombia paid no attention
and let godawful events happen in his family!
That day, his wife and five children left him.

Jesus Matamoros of Bogota, Colombia paid no attention,
but he won three thousand in a lottery. Still,
that day, his wife and five children left him.
In Iceland, Eva Haraldsdottir wrote out only two copies
      to mail.

She won five thousand in a lottery, but they stole
it all from her at the Reykjavik airport before she left
for an island holiday. Eva wrote out only two copies to mail,
and see what happened. So don't fail. Love

reveals it all, makes it all possible. Before you leave
for work today, mail five copies to your closest friends.
See what can happen? Don't fail love!
Don't throw this letter away! Horrible consequences!

1990

SHIRLEY GEOK-LIN LIM

Pantoun for Chinese Women

"At present, the phenomena of butchering, drowning and
leaving to die female infants have been very serious."
(*The People's Daily*, Peking, March 3rd, 1983)

They say a child with two mouths is no good.
In the slippery wet, a hollow space,
Smooth, gumming, echoing wide for food.
No wonder my man is not here at his place.

In the slippery wet, a hollow space,
A slit narrowly sheathed within its hood.
No wonder my man is not here at his place:
He is digging for the dragon jar of soot.

That slit narrowly sheathed within its hood!
His mother, squatting, coughs by the fire's blaze
While he digs for the dragon jar of soot.
We had saved ashes for a hundred days.

His mother, squatting, coughs by the fire's blaze.
The child kicks against me mewing like a flute.
We had saved ashes for a hundred days.
Knowing, if the time came, that we would.

The child kicks against me crying like a flute
Through its two weak mouths. His mother prays
Knowing when the time comes that we would,
For broken clay is never set in glaze.

Through her two weak mouths, his mother prays.
She will not pluck the rooster nor serve its blood,
For broken clay is never set in glaze:
Women are made of river sand and wood.

She will not pluck the rooster nor serve its blood.
My husband frowns, pretending in his haste
Women are made of river sand and wood.
Milk soaks the bedding. I cannot bear the waste.

My husband frowns, pretending in his haste.
Oh, clean the girl, dress her in ashy soot!
Milk soaks our bedding, I cannot bear the waste.
They say a child with two mouths is no good.

1989

Strange Tales and Bitter Emergencies: A Few Notes on the Prose Poem

ESSAY BY MICHEL DELVILLE
SELECTIONS BY
MAXINE CHERNOFF

While some critics have traced the origins of the American prose poem to such reputed precursors as Hawthorne's *American Notebooks,* Poe's *Eureka,* Emerson's essays, or Thoreau's *Walden,* most consider Gertrude Stein's *Tender Buttons* (1914) as the first instance of a consciously cultivated tradition of the genre. Despite the achievements of Stein and a number of other prominent modernist writers such as William Carlos Williams (*Kora in Hell,* 1918) and Sherwood Anderson (*Mid-American Chants,* 1918), the genre inexplicably vanished almost completely from the American literary scene in the 1920s, only to reemerge in the late 1960s and early 1970s with the appearance of several full-length collection of prose poems by writers such as Russell Edson, Michael Benedikt, Robert Bly, W. S. Merwin, David Ignatow, and other representatives of what was later to be called the American "prose poem revival." Michael Benedikt's introduction to *The Prose Poem: An International Anthology* (1976) was the first significant attempt by an American poet to describe the genre's formal features. Benedikt defines the prose poem as "a genre of poetry, self-consciously written in prose, and characterized by the intense use of virtually all the devices of poetry, which includes the intense use of devices of verse. The sole exception to access to the possibilities, rather than the set priorities of verse is, we would say, the line break." On a formal level, this conception of the prose poem as a form transposing the rhythmic effects and metrical "parallelism" of verse onto the medium of prose is reminiscent of Amy Lowell's "polyphonic prose," whose outward attributes of poeticity relied precisely on "the recurrence of a dominant thought or image, coming in irregularly and in varying words, but still giving the spherical effect . . . imperative in all poetry."

Lowell's insistence on "the absolute adequacy of the manner of a passage [of polyphonic prose] to the thought it embodies" also echoes Baudelaire's oft-quoted definition of the genre as "the miracle of a poetic prose, musical though rhythmless and rhymeless, flexible yet strong enough to identify with the lyrical impulses of the soul, the ebbs and flows of revery, the pangs of consciousness."

In recent years, formal definitions have tended to emphasize not so much the genre's affinities with the technical devices of verse, which are conspicuously absent from most prose poems published in the second half of this century, as its capacity to reclaim and subvert a number of modes and subject matters that have come to be associated more or less exclusively with prose genres. According to Stephen Fredman, the prose poem evidences "a fascination with language (through puns, rhyme, repetition, elision, disjunction, excessive troping, and subtle foregrounding of diction) that interferes with the progression of story or idea, while at the same time inviting and examining the prose realms of fact and reclaiming for poetry the domain of truth." Other critics, like Jonathan Monroe and Margueritte Murphy, rely on Mikhail Bakhtin's theories on the novel in highlighting the prose poem's inherently "dialogical" or "heteroglot" nature and see it as a self-consciously subversive genre existing mainly by reference to other genres, which it tends to include or exclude, subscribe to or subvert.

It seems to me that the great majority of prose poems published in the United States in the last twenty-five years can be roughly divided into two main categories: a "narrative" and a "language-oriented" trend. The first kind bears affinities with short narrative prose forms, whether literary or nonliterary, such as the fable, the parable, the dream narrative, the journal entry, or even the stand-up comedy joke. The publication, in 1964, of Russell Edson's *The Very Thing That Happens* inaugurated what has since then become the most popular subgenre of the American prose poem: the neosurrealist, absurdist fable. As exemplified by Edson's "The Optical Prodigal," the "fabulist" prose poem often sets out to turn the didactic function of the fable against itself and thereby favor a logic of indeterminacy whose purpose is to defeat the reader's aesthetic and moral expectations. Such prose poems, Edson has explained, "[reach] beyond the lesson to tell a strange tale for its own sake."

This conception of the prose poem as a short piece of narrative (one might add unornamented and unlyrical) prose "disguised" as a poem is not an altogether unprecedented phenomenon. One is here reminded of the work of Max Jacob, whose playful fantasies collected in *Dice Cup* (1916) are akin to many contemporary American prose poems. In the United States, Kenneth Patchen's generic medleys collected in *The Famous*

Boating-Party (1954) also prefigure the "narratives of consciousness" made famous by Edson and Benedikt. On a superficial level, what Jacob, Patchen, and other American "fabulist" prose poets have in common is an ability to tell a strange, snowballing tall tale for its own sake and twist it into a self-contained poem. Other recurrent features include an interest in burlesque situations and oddities of rhetoric, as well as a renewed emphasis on the comic struggle between the rational mind and the associational dynamics of the poetic imagination, a tendency most apparent in the works of Henri Michaux and Julio Cortzár, to whom the works of many American prose poets are directly or indirectly indebted. Lastly, these works frequently gesture toward their own artificiality and constructedness, an effect many have since identified as a "postmodern" feature. In "Peggy in the Twilight" a characteristic example of James Tate's use of "the deceptively simple packaging [of the prose poem]: the paragraph," the "speaker's" account of his first encounter with a rather mysterious and elusive woman builds up to a last, mock-epiphanical twist. Paul Hoover's "How Did You Get the Elephants Here?" is the story of a story that does not want to be itself and eventually loses its way in the meanders of the narrator's consciousness. In this particular kind of prose poem, the plot is, in many ways, a "pseudoplot," one in which, in Maxine Chernoff's words, "the idea of character remains a linguistic fact" and is therefore liable to present "a fuller and more realized linguistic reality." Summarizing the poetics of paradox, invention, and possibility that informs the genre, Chernoff offers the following advice to the fledgling writer of absurdist prose poems:

1. Narrate step by step something that is impossible to do.
2. Create and describe an invention that doesn't or can't exist.
3. Speak in the voice of someone with an outrageous or never before conceived of occupation.

The other main "camp" on the American prose poem scene is largely represented by prose poets whose work is associated with language poetry. Many of them were directly or indirectly influenced by Gertrude Stein's *Tender Buttons,* from which the following "still life" is taken:

A Box

Out of kindness comes redness and out of rudeness comes rapid same question, out of an eye comes research, out of selection comes painful cattle. So then the order is that a

white way of being round is something suggesting a pin and
it is disappointing, it is not, it is so rudimentary to be
analysed and see a fine substance strangely, it is so earnest to
have a green point not to red but to point again.

By disrupting and parodying the conventions ruling realistic representa-
tion, "A Box" seeks to question nothing less than language's capacity to
make sense. More generally, Stein's "cubist" descriptions defy interpre-
tation precisely because they subvert the social consensus according to
which most people call a spade a spade (or a poem a poem) and use lan-
guage to mean "what it says." By blurring the distinction between the
abstract and the concrete, the psychological and the physical world,
they draw our attention to the arbitrary nature of mimetic and analyti-
cal discourses, including their claims to descriptive and argumentative
coherence.

Lyn Hejinian's "poetic autobiography," *My Life,* is an example of
how some language (prose) poets, despite and, in a sense, because of
their dedication to open and indeterminate forms and structures, occa-
sionally resort to regularly repeating forms and patterns. The second,
expanded edition of *My Life* (an excerpt from which follows) consists
of forty-five sections of forty-five sentences—each section standing for a
year of the author's life—resulting in a poetic investigation of the rela-
tionship between writing and memory. Other examples of the use of
procedural poetics in language-oriented prose poems include Ron Silli-
man's *Tjanting* (1981), which is written according to the Fibonacci
number series.

As the pieces included in this short anthology suggest, the various
directions represented by the prose poem as it has been practiced and
reinvented by American poets in the last thirty years cannot possibly be
confined to the two main competing camps I have identified as the fab-
ulist and the language-oriented trends. Moreover a full-length analysis
of each of these strands would reveal an extreme diversity of styles and
approaches. Whereas, for a brief instance, Maxine Chernoff's early
prose poems collected in *A Vegetable Emergency* (1976) seem influ-
enced by the verbal and imagistic extravagance of Henri Michaux, her
more recent works (such as "How Lies Grow") move back and forth be-
tween the deep and the trivial in a way that somehow privileges the lyri-
cal potential of the genre and preserves a connection with the intimacy
of subjective experience. Lydia Davis's "The Fish" also differs from her
more habitual microtales (many of which are firmly rooted in the ab-
surdist strand made famous by Edson) and sketches a tale of loneliness
and psychological confinement. The title poem of Amy Gerstler's *Bitter*

Angel, which superficially appears as a typical surrealist dreamscape, reads in fact like the paradoxical memory of an as yet unattainable vision, one that leads to several alternative resolutions at the same time as it seeks to qualify its own apocalyptic excesses. For Gerstler, as for Chernoff and Davis, verbal play, irony, and pastiche are not incompatible with the expression of personal and public anxieties.

Edson, Chernoff, Hejinian, Gerstler, and several other leading prose poets have created new formal and ideological possibilities for what remains a relatively young genre still in the process of self-definition. Moving back and forth between lyrical, narrative, philosophical, and critical material, the prose poem can be seen as part of a more general movement in contemporary literature toward the dissolution of generic boundaries. In this respect, one could argue that one of the reasons for the growing popularity of the genre in the United States and elsewhere is precisely its self-proclaimed hybridity, a feature the prose poem shares with a number of other centaurial neologisms, such as the "lyric short story," the "poetic novel," or, more recently, the paraliterary works of Barthes, Baudrillard, and Derrida. In the course of its repeated and often brittle attempts to define and re-create itself, the prose poem has transformed the concerns of contemporary poetics by focusing attention on considerations of form, mode, genre, and representational strategies all too often ignored by poets and critics. Starting from the assumption that poetry can gain from a renewed interaction with other forms of writing, it has so far succeeded in expanding the possibilities of contemporary poetry in a significant way, notably by reclaiming a number of methods and functions that lie outside the traditional ambit of poetry in verse.

RUSSELL EDSON

The Optical Prodigal

A man sees a tiny couple in the distance, and thinks they might be his mother and father.

But when he gets to them they're still little.

You're still little, he says, don't you remember?

Who said you were supposed to be here? says the little husband. You're supposed to be in your own distance; you're still in your own foreground, you spendthrift.

No no, says the man, you're to blame.

No no, says the little man, you're out of proportion. When you go into the distance you're supposed to get smaller. You mustn't think that we can shrink and swell all the time to suit everybody coming out of the distance.

But you have it wrong, cries the man, we're the same size, it's you who are refusing to be optically correct.

It's you, says the little husband, you just can't go blundering into the distance without some prior warning.

This has never happened before, says the man, and I've been in the distance many times.

You ought to go back to where you started and try it again, says the man, you might even have disappeared by then.

We never change our size, we concentrate at all times; it's you who is the absentminded one. You are the one out of proportion, and it's you throwing everything out of scale; so get going, cries the little husband.

Out of proportion. . . ? says the man.

Totally, without any optical intelligence, no consideration for scale, says the little husband.

Don't you recognize me? says the man.

No no, our son lives in the distance, says the little husband.

1977

LYDIA DAVIS

The Fish

She stands over a fish, thinking about certain irrevocable mistakes she has made today. Now the fish has been cooked, and she is alone with it. The fish is for her—there is no one else in the house. But she has had a troubling day. How can she eat this fish, cooling on a slab of marble? And yet the fish, too, motionless as it is, and dismantled from its bones, and fleeced of its silver skin, has never been so completely alone as it is now: violated in a final manner and regarded with a weary eye by this woman who has made the latest mistake of her day and done this to it.

1986

MAXINE CHERNOFF

How Lies Grow

The first time I lied to my baby, I told him that it was his
face on the baby food jar. The second time I lied to my baby,
I told him that he was the best baby in the world, that I
hoped he'd never leave me. Of course I want him to leave me
someday. I don't want him to become of those fat shadows
who live in their mothers' houses watching game shows all
day. The third time I lied to my baby I said, "Isn't she nice?"
of the woman who'd carressed him in his carriage. She was
old and ugly and had a disease. The fourth time I lied to my
baby, I told him the truth, I thought. I told him how he'd
have to leave me someday or risk becoming a man in a bow
tie who eats macaroni on Fridays. I told him it was for the
best, but then I thought, I want him to live with me forever.
Someday he'll leave me: then what will I do?

1990

JAMES TATE

Peggy in the Twilight

Peggy spent half of each day trying to wake up, and the
other half preparing for sleep. Around five, she would mix
herself something preposterous and '40s-ish like a
Grasshopper or a Brass Monkey, adding a note of gaiety to
her defeat. This shadowlife became her. She always had a
glow on; that is, she carried an aura of innocence as well as
death with her.

I first met her at a party almost thirty years ago. Even then
it was too late for tragic women, tragic anything. Still, when
she was curled up and fell asleep in the corner, I was
overwhelmed with feelings of love. Petite black and gold
angels sat on her slumped shoulders and sang lullabies to her.

I walked into another room and asked our host for a
blanket for Peggy.

"Peggy?" he said. "There's no one here by that name."

And so my lovelife began.

1995

PAUL HOOVER

How Did You Get the Elephants Here?

They were sent by ship from Africa to Texas then suspended
from helicopters and flown to Chicago over patchwork fields
and towns. Since they were small at the time, they were
curious rather than frightened. Along the way, people looked
up in amazement, glad they had a story to tell. But after a
while they sank into a depression from which they never
recovered. Nobody knows quite why. One of the pilots was
Mongomery Schuyler. He was from a wealthy family that
despised what he did for a living. He used to visit the zoo
now and then to stick his head in their mouths. Then he
disappeared. Here's a picture of the guy. I thought I saw him
on TV once, waving goodbye from the door of a plane, but
actually it was Gertrude Stein. The thing about TV is, the
closer you look at a thing, the more it falls apart—into a
thousand dots—but when you look even closer you see trees
and things.

1987

LYN HEJINIAN

from *My Life*

Yet we insist　　The windows were open and the
that life is full　　morning air was, by the smell of the
of happy chance　　lilac and some darker flowering scrub,
　　　　　　　　filled with the brown and chirping trills
　　　　　　　　of birds. As they are if you could have
　　　　　　　　nothing but quiet and shouting. Arts,
　　　　　　　　also, are links. I picture an idea at the
moment I come to it, our collision. Once, for a time, anyone
might have been luck's child. Even rain didn't spoil the
barbecue, in the backyard behind a polished traffic, through
a landscape, along a shore. Freedom then, liberation later.
She came to babysit for us in those troubled years directly
from the riots, and she said that she dreamed of the day
when she would gun down everyone in the financial district.
That single telephone is only one hair on the brontosaurus.

The coffee drinkers answered ecstatically. If your dog stays out of the room, you get the fleas. In the lull, activity drops. I'm seldom in my dreams without my children. My daughter told me that at some time in school she had learned to think of a poet as a person seated on an iceberg and melting through it. It is a poetry of certainty. In the distance, down the street, the practicing soprano belts the breeze. As for we who "love to be astonished," money makes money, luck makes luck. Moves forward, drives on. Class background is not landscape—still here and there in 1969 I could feel the scope of collectivity. It was the present time for a little while, and not so new as we thought then, the present always after war. Ever since it has been hard for me to share my time. The yellow of that sad room was again the yellow of naps, where she waited, restless, faithless, for more days. They say that the alternative for the bourgeoisie was gullibility. Call it water and dogs. Reason looks for two, then arranges it from there. But can one imagine a madman in love. Goodbye; enough that was good. There was a pause, a rose, something on paper. I may balk but I won't recede. Because desire is always embarrassing. At the beach, with a fresh flush. The child looks out. The berries are kept in the brambles, on wires on reserve for the birds. At a distance, the sun *is* small. There was no proper Christmas after he died. That triumphant blizzard had brought the city to its knees. I am a stranger to the little girl I was, and more—more strange. But many facts about a life should be left out, they are easily replaced. One sits in a cloven space. Patterns promote an outward likeness, between little white silences. The big trees catch all the moisture from what seems like a dry night. Reflections don't make shade, but shadows are, and do. In order to understand the nature of the collision, one must know something of the nature of the motions involved—that is, a history. He looked at me and smiled and did not look away, and thus a friendship became erotic. Luck was rid of its clover.

1987

AMY GERSTLER

Bitter Angel

You appear in a tinny, nickel-and-dime light. The light of
turned milk and gloved insults. It could be a gray light you're
bathed in; at any rate, it isn't quite white. It's possible you
show up coated with a finite layer of the dust that rubs off
moths' wings onto kids' grubby fingers. Or you arrive
cloaked in a toothache's smoldering glow. Or you stand
wrapped like a maypole in rumpled streamers of light torn
from threadbare bedsheets. Your gaze flickers like a silent
film. You make me lose track. Which dim, deluded light did I
last see you in? The light of extinction, most likely, where
there are no more primitive tribesmen who worship clumps
of human hair. No more roads that turn into snakes, or
ribbons. There's no nightlife or lion's share, none of the
black-and-red roulette wheels of methedrine that would-be
seers like me dream of. You alone exist: eyes like
locomotives. A terrible succession of images buffets you:
human faces pile up in your sight, like heaps of some flunky's
smudged, undone paperwork.

1990

The Metrics of Rap

DJ RENEGADE

Unbeknownst to most rappers, critics, and lovers of rap music, rap lyrics are written according to highly structured rules that come from two systems. This is illustrated by examining the word *rap*. In Standard English it means "to hit or strike with a sharp blow," that is, "to percuss." In the Black Vernacular it means "to talk, esp. skillfully." If we combine these two meanings we arrive at "percussive speaking." Because all rappers are simultaneously poets and musicians (verbal percussionists), and raps are written to be performed over drum tracks, some of these rules come from poetry and some from music.

The strongest poetic influences on rap are popular poems with four beats per line (**Ee**nie **mee**nie, **my**nie **moe/ Catch** a **ti**ger **by** the **toe**) and the "toast," an African-American oral narrative poem, which usually extols the adventures of an antihero (often a pimp or hustler). Early raps usually employed couplets *(aabbccdd)*. But now, regular rhyme schemes have given way to complex syncopated patterns that include a great deal of serial, internal, and cross-rhyming and sometimes avoid end rhyme altogether. Although metaphor and symbolism abound in the better raps, simile is by far the preferred literary device.

Most rap lyrics utilize one of two forms; one we'll call a *rhyme*, the other a *rap song*. The primary difference is that a rhyme is a single long stanza, often a narrative with as many lines as the writer wants, while a rap song borrows its structure from the popular song, and usually has sixteen lines to a stanza, and three or four stanzas, with a *hook* or repeating chorus in between.

Raps are written against a four-beat line. I say against because, although there are four beats in each line, the beats are syncopated. Exactly where they fall depends on the rhythm of the drum track. This is why one must hear a rap performed in order to know how the beats are to be rapped. The amount of syllables in each line varies from four to sixteen. Rappers don't utilize a set number of syllables per line any more than a musician would utilize a set number of notes per bar.

Most popular black American music has four beats of music to each bar, and ranges from 80 to 130 beats per minute (bpm). If a rapper wanted to rap in 3/4 or 6/8 time, then they would need to write a line with three or six beats of verse respectively. Bpm are very important because as they go higher, there is less actual time between beats of music to rap the words. Thus at 90 bpm you could easily rap a line with sixteen syllables, but at 112 bpm that same line would be more difficult, and above 120 bpm it would be impossible to remain intelligible. Rappers compensate for this by having fewer unstressed syllables between beats as the bpm increase. Beyond a certain point however (around 120 bpm) some rappers simply rap one line over two bars of music. They then either rap slower or add more unstressed syllables between the beats to fill up the space.

Here are two basic types of line that are used depending on the bpm of the drum track.

In the most common form (95 to 120 bpm), one line has four to sixteen syllables, and four beats (that is, one bar's worth).

From Follow the Leader

RAKIM

Follow me into a solo
Get in the flow—and you can picture like a photo
Music mixed mellow maintains to make
Melodies for MC's motivates the breaks
I'm everlastin, I can go on for days and days
With rhyme displays that engrave deep as X-rays
I can take a phrase that's rarely heard,
FLIP IT, Now it's a daily word.

Under 95 bpm you find the second prosody, where there are eight stressed syllables, but still only four beats of verse to four beats of music, and sixteen to twenty-four syllables to a line.

From Tha Crossroads

BONE THUGS-N-HARMONY

God bless you workin on a plan to Heaven follow the Lord
   all twenty-four seven
days. God is who we praise even though the devil's all up in
   my face.

But He's **keepin** me safe and in my **place**, say **grace** to
   engage the race without a **chance** to face
the **judge**. Say again, my soul won't **budge**. **Grudge**, because
   there's no mercy for **thugs**.
Ooh, what can I **do**? It's all about a **fam**ily and how we **roll**.
Can I get a **witness**? Let it un**fold**. We living our **lives** til
   eternal our **souls**.

One might wonder if rappers consciously understand all that is
going on with the prosody of their genre. This quotation from Derek At-
tridge on the use of language is instructive: "In order to employ lan-
guage, we do not need to understand how it works, any more than we
need to understand the musculature of the leg to be able to walk."[1] Al-
though it's not necessary for the writer of a rap to have a conscious
knowledge of poetic prosody or music theory to construct their rhymes,
he or she must have knowledge of other raps, a finely honed sense of
rhythm, and feel for what will and will not fit in his or her style of rap-
ping. For the critic, however, an understanding of the underlying rules
is essential to appreciating the true merits of rap as a form of poetry.

TERENCE NICHOLSON (A.K.A. SUB-Z)

Don't Run

I **drop** the hot phos**phor**ous **chor**us, semi-**porous**
brains can't re**tain**, **left** indelible **ink** stains
in the driveway, after **slaught**ering **alph**abets.
Nicked my **fing**er with the **pen**, made a **tor**niquet.
Gave Hertz a **ring** to **rent** a Bronco with **five** gears,
they **heard** a black **voice** and **said**, "They only
   had **Wag**oneers."
But that's irrelevant, **be**ing that **now** I'm on **trial**,
I **guess** next, they'll **say** the **jury** had Vitiligo.
If you **throw** a stone, when I **throw** it back it'll **crack**
your whole **glass men**agerie, like fine haber**dash**erie.
I **flaunt po**ems like Bau**de**laire,
a rare **craft** these days, **claims** an 8th street **sooth**sayer.
Groove child, this **style causes** spine **curv**age,
stashing my **bills**, cause now I'm only **spend**ing
   loose **verb**iage.
(cough) **Don't run**, I'm **feeling** my **oats**,
hit you with the **truth** serum, and **hide** the **ant**idote.

Darkcide

Comin' from the other side of the tracks,
the reverse angle attack, niggas fall like the Nasdaq
Index. Infected by the noxious fumes,
funk be consumin' em, like a verbal vacuum.
The Nemesis, no limit to this, elevational
bottomless pit, you're hit like a Mack with no brake fluid.
The Dark One, Gorgon Hortical Don
me not, but play the low key like a ninja from the Octagon.
In a smokescreen of a rhyme, I lost ya,
but you steady plottin on me like Boris and Natasha.
Voodoo child since a juvenile, travel the night
landscape while, I swing it Nosferatu
style. There's a bad moon on the rise, I synchronize
my power moves with celestial hip hop grooves.
Doctors ain't have the antidote, so I'm pumpin
a hundred volts, to make a speaker throb from my steel
pulse. Jeeps levitate on the block, what they're hearin'
is the frosty mic delivery, better known as Sub- Z.
I've arisen, givin' syllabic hypnotism
to MC's knots leaving bloodclots and aneurysms.
For you and yours, I'ma bump it, a funk
revelation, just when you thought you heard the last trumpet.
More maneuvers than the city of Baltimore
got gold crowns. You on the darkcide of town.

Chorus: Come on everybody, let's all get down.
  Come on everybody to the dark side of town(x 4)

I be the midnight mixer, verb trickster, decongest
clogged brain channels like Triaminic Elixir.
The black hole in rap history, Nostra-
damus couldn't predict the onset of my wizardry.
My euphemisms refract like prism lights
on dimwits, leaving the full spectrum of insight.
I crystallize the conceptual mind frame
in rap context, then disappear like Racer X.
My antics are characteristic of a cut-throat's
tactics, without the ruffneck theatrics.
Liquified linguistics, be elevating
the art of MC'ing to that of a Sufi mystic.
So I, heat it up like a thermonuclear reactor,

but remain frigid, due to the Zero factor.
Mercury rules my astrological sign,
but Galileo couldn't chart my course, when I'm gettin
mine. I'm way out, like the Nebula of Andromeda,
Leonard Nimoy couldn't explain the phenomena,
crushing Eddie Bauer Gore-Tex, when I flex
the Cold Rock Stuff, givin them Eskimoes a complex.
Like that, EQ's detect my spirit on the ADAT,
like AWAC jet satellites, so honey, stay back.
How could commentators speak on my dialect,
when they spellbound, they on the dark side of town.

My Cipher Go Way Back

As night falls, my mood changes, street lights
hover, above the hot asphalt I walk.
Life accelerates, I'm consumed gazin' to the Northwest
sky, I see another full moon.
It be callin' me, I feel the anxiety setting in.
Like Sitting Bull, I be wanting to dance with the Wolves.
I compose my posture, having no focus gets you late,
I got the thrust to make a cipher elevate.
I travel like Ulysses with these poetries,
mockeries I make of Plato, niggas think I'm Socrates,
(see what I'm sayin'), but I go back millenniums
from the oral tradition, I get open like Venetians.
Breathe, to relieve the tense mind, hence I
meditate, on gettin' to 9th and O Street by nine.
Freestyle U., the phat venue,
some call it a circle of spirits, when I bless instrumentals.
I enter the ritual ceremony of holy
mindstates, suspects disintegrate.
Take the square root of a thought, to the power of the tenth,
word strength, I bear the key to the Labyrinth,
to unlock the mind-blocked souls. Verbal detox-
ification, I rock the public relations
abilities, correctional facilities,
recruit mindslaves, but I got runaway brainwaves.
Frauds be reciting their writing,
but their tablets crumble to rubble in the clash of the Titans.
Metaphilosophical maestro, I knife throw

verbs, like a carnival magician, they call me Micro.
A-SAP, I give dap to my crew,
throw on my knapsack and push back to the H.Q.
My Ebony shade masquerades my light,
but on stage I be makin em' lose sight.

Chorus

Spiritual rhyme theory,
live and direct, microphone checks be like communes,
with gods and deities predating the Aztecs.
Towers of babbling MC's collapse,
hear their horn blowing taps, it's Armageddon, their time's
elapsed, rap scripture reveals, their fate's sealed,
two entities can't occupy the same mic, and both be real.
Cold killers ain't got time to rhyme, street crime
took em all, so it's last call for who the bell chimes.
Professin' with the mentality of adolescents,
I can't see none of that garbage niggas be stressin.
I'll probably never get a record deal, cause I ain't gotta
prove my hardness, but I'ma set it off regardless.
I cock the hammer back, intellectual slugs bust,
enlightened souls emerge from the dust.
My formula's designed to rock your nucleus, a rhyme
paradox, blast from the past, give you future shock.

Chorus

My cipher takes me
from my physical plane, to pyramid heiroglyphs,
I return, passin' words down like old Yoruba myths.
Out of body experience, captive listeners
became my prisoners, Hunafi rebel type business.
Clever like Aeon Flux, I conduct schemes
of mental espionage, I'm camouflaged as you daydream.
Demolition of your third optical vision,
turn a Rapper's Delight into a cataclysm.
It's like that, Jack, keep on,
from my chromosomes, my verbal embryos are born.
But let time tell it, in 3009, when archaeologists
find broken mics among my ancient relics.
Lame brain game plans, to shallow man be deep,
while they thinking hopscotch, my mind takes quantum leaps.
My theology be rhythm, hip hop's my religion.

MC'S carry my gospel like homing pigeons.
I bring it to em from the tabernacle of soul,
my whole flock blows spots,
since the days of banging on the mailbox.
The Rhyme Stoppers Committee, we respond
to the call, like Bat Signals above Gotham City.
In my temple reciting chants, entranced envisioning
myself immortalized, in a B-Boy stance.
Snatching them jokers with no trace, alias Big Ace,
destroy their whole data base, and still keep a poker face.

© 1999 Terence Nicholson

NOTE

1. See Derek Attridge, *The Rhythms of English Poetry* (New York: Longman, 1982), 59.

Rondeaux and Roundels

THOMAS M. DISCH

Of the various French forms that have been transplanted to English by contemporary poets the rondeau has been one of the least cultivated and, when the attempt is made, least likely of success. While sestinas and villanelles have become almost as common as brie and camembert, the rondeau is rare to the point of extinction. The reason for this lies not in some greater inherent difficulty. Sonnets are harder to write; likewise the ballade, pantoum, and villanelle. But all those forms are likely to produce work worth the price of a picture frame, while most rondeaux in English are apt to come across as greeting cards.

There are two basic constraints: (1) the first word or words of line 1 must reappear twice as a refrain, in the ninth line and again in the final (fifteenth) line; (2) there are but two rhymes in the thirteen nonrefrain lines of the three stanzas, and they are ordered so: *aabba//aab* + refrain//*aabba* + refrain. Identical rhymes are frowned on (though many poets sneak them in). The thirteen lines must be in the same meter; iambic lines of four or five feet are commonest. A stanza break after the first five lines is usual but not required. The lines rhyming in *b* may or may not be indented. The author of the unsigned commentary in the eleventh edition of the Britannica maintains that "the one great fault of the rondeau as a vehicle for deep emotion" springs from "the too frequent recurrence of the rhymes," which results in "the suggestion of extreme artificiality—of 'difficulty overcome.'" He does concede that "the rondeau is, however, an inimitable instrument of gaiety and grace in the hands of a skilled poet."

Damned with such qualified praise, and with a standard repertory of examples drawn from the work of Beaux Artes versifiers of the late Victorian and Edwardian eras, the English roundeau has come to be thought the effetist fop of formalist poetry—not quite so inconsequential as the triolet (a form all but incapable of expressing a thought more complex than "Isn't that lovely!"), but doomed in the same way to mere prettiness, a corset so tight as to make dancing impossible.

The rules of the French rondeau were codified by the Parnassian, Théodore de Banville, in his *Petit traité de poesie française* of 1872. De Banville cites the rondeaux of Vincent Voiture (1598–1648) as the perfected examples of the form, which Voiture had revived after a century's dormancy, taking the work of Clement Marot (1496–1544) as his model. Marot in turn had inherited the form from the troubadour era. As to the strictness of the rules governing the rondeau, Gleeson White, the editor of *Ballades and Rondeaux* (Appleton, 1884), the first collection of English verse in French form, offered advice that may rankle but that still represents received wisdom:

> A study of rondeaus will show, both in ancient and modern examples, some little alteration of the rhyme-order, and a few trivial differences in other respects. But . . . the rondeau of Voiture may be taken as the typical form to be imitated—the one that has, by process of selection, been proved to be the best to display the subject of the poem, and to work in the refrains to the best advantage. Like the sonnet, the perfected form is jealously guarded. The genius which consists in breaking rules is looked upon with suspicion in all these [French] forms, but especially in this one. . . . [T]he trifling evasion of the rhyme-order, a want of exactitude on the repetition of the refrain, is apt to be taken as evidence of lack of power to conform gracefully to the bonds, and not as an outburst of genius that is too strong to be confined in such puny fetters.

Though theory forebears to dictate what the rondeau shall be about, there has been a tacit understanding that, like the sonnet, the roundeau is best suited to courtly compliments, to professions of love, and to complainings on the same score. While the sonnet evolved to treat of broader matters, the discursive scope of the rondeau tended to shrink over time. Rondeaux were valued precisely for their daintiness—poetic teacups exquisitely wrought that held but a thimbleful of thought.

The history of the English rondeau is brief as its repertory is meager. Barring such early sports as Wyatt's "Help me to seek," most English rondeaux were written within the lifetime of the English poet who did most to cultivate the form in our language, Austin Dobson (1840–1921). Indeed, Dobson himself wrote a significant percentage of the entire supply, including a small sheaf that Voiture himself might not have sniffed at. He was also, at times, a rondeau machine, inscribing one giftbook after another with innocuous little nothings. Dobson was in his seventies during the Great War, at which time he published a sequence of flag-waving poems that represented the nadir of his own reputation and that of the rondeau, from which neither has ever quite recovered— *Rondeax of the Great War and Other Poems,* to be found in *The Complete Poetical Works of Austin Dobson.*

A little time before Dobson's misguided effort to turn the rondeau into a *marche militaire,* another gray eminence, Algernon Swinburne (1837–1909), had tried to make the rondeau do service across the entire discursive spectrum of the lyric. It was not Voiture's classic form that Swinburne used, but an abbreviated version of his own invention, which he termed the *roundel.* It is four lines shorter than the roundeau, and the refrain first appears after the third line. Swinburne dashed off a hundred of these minirondeaux and published them in 1909 as *A Century of Roundels,* which must be one of the lamest creations for which any poet of the first rank has ever admitted responsibility. Swinburne notoriously favored sound over sense, and in the echo chamber of his roundels he manages to say virtually nothing at all about (to cite only a few titles): "Birth and Death," "Death and Birth," "Autumn and Winter," "Babyhood," "Sorrow," and "Sleep."

I say that as one who has succumbed and who believes, despite all the caveats above, that the rondeau has a much wider expressive and discursive range than it has generally been credited with. Two years ago, having agreed to teach a workshop on French forms, it was urged upon me by a friend that I ought to practice more of what I meant to preach. I'd written only sestinas and villanelles till then. I made a quick study of the rondeau, conning the rules and tracking down any specimens I could find. The result was my first rondeau, "Smashing China," which represented my instant gut reaction to the twaddle I'd been reading as well as an admission to having caught the bug myself (my overlong refrain was "I like the sound of it").

In the course of the next two or three weeks I went on a bender of writing rondeaux, spurred in part by being told (by the friend noted above) that my firstlings were not properly rondeaux. They might observe the form, but they lacked the requisite spirit of courtly love and graceful compliment. The form was a spur in itself: the challenge of finding new ways to make the refrain pay off, so that its first appearance works as a hinge and its next return offers surprise and not just closure; the challenge of knitting together the two sets of rhymes so that one's fancy does not seem in thrall to a rhyming dictionary. Not counting miscarriages, I ended up with a set of eleven rondeaux of uncommon distinction. Alas, that distinction was not their quality but the fact that they were uniformly defective, lacking in each case the fifth line of the third stanza. There are eleven of them, so perhaps they constitute a new form all their own—the rondolino? the roundette? But no, I'm afraid what they constitute is a mistake.

It is as though I'd spent a month in Lyons, believing myself all the time to be in Paris. Yet, if I dined well, enjoyed the sights, and learned a little of the language, surely it was not time misspent? Even so, let me counsel you, reader: if you intend to try your own hand at the rondeau, be attentive and be precise. Take your pattern from Voiture and Dobson, or begin by using the training wheels of the roundel. Finally, bear in mind the words of Gleeson White: "The genius which consists in breaking rules is looked upon with suspicion in all these forms, but especially in this one."

SIR THOMAS WYATT (1503–1542)[1]

What No, Perdy

What no, perdy, ye may be sure!
Think not to make me to your lure,
　　With wordes and chere so contrarieng,
　　Swete and sowre contrewaing;
To much it were still to endure.
Trough is trayed where wraft is in ure;
But though ye have had my hertes cure,
　　Troiw ye I dote without ending?
　　　　What no, perdy!

Though that with pain I do procure
For to forett that ons was pure,
　　Within my hert shall still that thing,
　　Unstable, unsure, and wavering,
Be in my mynde without recure?
　　　　What no, perdy!

VINCENT VOITURE (1598–1648)[2]

Rondeau

Ma foi, c'est fait de moi, car Isabeau
M'a conjuré de lui faire un rondeau.
Cela me met en une peine extrême:
Quoi! treize vers, huit en eau, cinq en ème!
Je lui ferais aussitot un bateau.

En voila cinq pourtant en un conceau.
Faisons'en huit en invoquant Brodeau,
Et puis mettons, par quelque stratagême:
　　Ma foi, c'est fait.

Si je pouvais encor de mon cerveau
Tirer cinq vers, l'ouvrage serait beau;
Mais cependant je suis dedans l'onzième:
Et ci je crois que je fais le douzième:
En voila treize ajustes au niveau.
      Ma foi, c'est fait.

AUSTIN DOBSON (1840–1921)

The Same Imitated

You bid me try, BLUE-EYES, to write
A rondeau. What! forthwith?— To-night?
   Reflect. Some skill I have, 'tis true;
   But thirteen lines! —and rhymed on two!—
"Refrain," as well. Ah, helpless plight!

Still there are five lines—ranged aright.
These Gallic bonds, I feared, would fright
   My easy Muse. They did, till you—
      You bid me try!

That makes them eight. The port's in sight:
'Tis all because your eyes are bright!
   Now just a pair to end in 'oo'—
   When maids command, what can't we do!
Behold! the ROUNDEAU, tasteful, light,
      You bid me try!

After Watteau

"EMBARQUONS-NOUS!" I seem to go
Against my will. 'Neath alleys low
   I bend, and hear across the air—
   Across the stream—faint music rare—
Whose "cornemuse," whose "chalumeau"?

Hark! was not that a laugh I know?
Who was it, hurrying, turned to show
   The galley swinging by the stair?—
      "Embarquons-nous!"

The silk sail flaps, light breezes blow;
Frail laces flutter, satins flow;
    You, with the loveknot in your hair,
    "Allons, embarquons pour Cythère";
You will not? Press her, then, PIERROT,—
    "Embarquons-nous!"

W. E. HENLEY (1849–1903)[3]

The Gods Are Dead

The gods are dead? Perhaps they are! Who knows?
    Living at least in Lempriere undeleted,
The wise, the fair, the awful, the jocose,
    Are one and all, I like to think, retreated
In some still land of lilacs and the rose.

Once high they sat, and high o'er earthly shows
    With sacrificial dance and song were greeted.
Once . . . long ago: but now the story goes,
        The gods are dead.

It must be true. The world a world of prose,
    Full-crammed with facts, in science swathed and sheeted,
Nods in a stertorous after-dinner doze.
Plangent and sad, in every wind that blows
    Who will may hear the sorry words repeated—
        The gods are dead.

MATTHEW RUSSELL, S.J. (1834–1912)[4]

My First Rondeau

My first rondeau, this is the hour
Predestined to behold thee flower,
    Thy petals opening without flaw,
    Obedient to a hidden law,
Like spring's young leaves in sun and shower.

Whence cometh the mysterious power
Which doth sounds deftly ordered dower?
    Whose were the happy eyes that saw
        The first rondeau?

Now art thou rounded, like a tower
O'erhanging some fair garden bower;
  Yet thou, like nobler works, shalt fa'
  Into oblivion's ravening maw:
For instance, who now reads "The Giaour,"
    My first rondeau?

My Last Rondeau

My dying hour, how near art thou?
Or near or far, my head I bow
  Before God's ordinance supreme;
  But ah, how priceless then will seem
Each moment rashly squandered now!

Teach me, for thou canst teach me, how
These fleeting instants to endow
  With worth that may the past redeem,
    My dying hour!

My barque, that late with buoyant prow
The sunny waves did gaily plow,
  Now through the sunset's fading gleam
  Drifts dimly shoreward in a dream.
I feel the land-breeze on my brow,
    My dying hour!

ELINOR WYLIE (1885–1928)[5]

Rondeau: A Windy Day

O shameless day! a daring stress,
A sweet but insufficient dress
Of windy hair in billows piled—
Lock to bright lock unreconciled—
Is round your virgin nakedness,
    O shameless day!

We might expect, you must confess,
Some rosy blushes, soft distress—
Your clear regard is like a child,
    O shameless day!

Your self-possession in the press
Of sunbeams struggling with success
To kiss you by blue-eyes beguiled—
Your eyes so innocently wild!—
Is like some maiden sorceress,
        O shameless day!

                                    Summer of 1904

ALGERNON SWINBURNE (1837–1909)

How a Roundel Is Wrought

A roundel is wrought as a ring or a starbright sphere,
With craft of delight and with cunning of sound unsought,
That the heart of the hearer may smile if it pleasure his ear
    A roundel is wrought.

Its jewel of music is carven of all or of aught—
Love, laughter, or mourning—remembrance or fear—
That fancy may fashion to hang in the ear of thought.

As a bird's quick song runs round, and the hearts in us hear—
Pause answers to pause, and again the same strain caught,
So moves the device whence, round as a pearl or tear,
    A roundel is wrought

TOM DISCH

Rondeau for Emporio Armani

What is Armani? What if not money
Made visible? So too, Dior, Gianni
    Versace—even, in a sense
    Reeboks and Nikes. The pretense
That these scruffy slacks or a gunny-

Sack from Sak's or Playboy bunny
Lingerie are sartorially stunning
    Is bunk. They're nothing but Expense.
        What is Armani

Doing, though, that everyone in Cunning
101 doesn't do as well? Money
   Smells so good. We've no defense
Against our appetites. It isn't funny.
      What is? Armani.

MARILYN HACKER

Two Rondeaux *from* Love, Death, and the Changing of the Seasons [6]

"Why did Ray leave her pipe tobacco here
in the fridge?" Iva asks me while we're
rummaging for mustard and soy sauce
to mix with wine and baste the lamb. "Because
cold keeps it fresh." That isn't what she means,

we both know. I've explained, there were no scenes
or fights, really. We needed time to clear
the air, and think. What she was asking, was,
"Why did Ray leave

her stuff if she's not coming back?" She leans
to extremes, as I might well. String beans
to be sautéed with garlic, then I'll toss
the salad; then we'll eat. (Like menopause
it comes in flashes, more or less severe:
why did you leave?)

"Now that you know you *can,* the city's full
of girls—just notice them! It's not like pull-
ing teeth to flirt," she said, "or make a date."
It's quite like pulling teeth to masturbate
(I didn't say), and so I don't. My nice

dreams are worse than nightmares. As my eyes
open, I know *I* am; that instant, feel
you with me, on me, in me, and you're not.
Now that you know

you don't know, fantasies are more like lies.
They don't fit when I try them on for size.
I guess I can, but can't imagine what
I'd do, with whom, tonight. It's much too late
or soon, so what's yours stays yours. It has until
now. That, you know.

                         1986

NOTES

1. Sir Thomas Wyatt, best remembered for the first successful cultivation of the sonnet in English, did the same service for the rondeau. Wyatt's eight surviving rondeaux are complaints of love withheld or betrayed. The refrain, "What no, perdy!" could be translated, roughly, as "Well, ex-cuse me!" as delivered by Steve Martin. Wyatt's rondeaux, like his sonnets, require a fair amount of decoding before they can be savored as poems. Thus, "Trough is trayed where wraft is ure" means "Truth is betrayed (or tried) where craft is in use." Most modern editions of Wyatt provide decryption for their readers, but to read them in that form is like buying preshrunk jeans.

2. Voiture's "Rondeau" and its imitation by Austin Dobson are more often offered as exemplars of the roundeau than any other specimens of the form. The difference between the two poems is typical of the sea change the form has undergone from French to English. Voiture's, for all its cleverness, is diffident almost to plainness; Dobson's wears a periwig. "Forthwith," forsooth! Yet readers who can't develop an immune reaction to archaisms had better steer clear of the rondeau altogether. Note that both poets permit themselves the use of identical rhymes. By its deft allusions to details of Watteau's familiar painting, Dobson is able to suggest a fairly complex vignette of temptation and yielding. The cornemuse is a kind of bagpipe; the chalumeau a reed instrument of low register. "Frail laces flutter, satins flow" is self-referential to Dobson's rondeaux at their prettiest.

3. John Lempriere's *Classical Dictionary* of 1788 was for the Victorians what Robert Graves's *The Greek Myths* is for contemporary readers. Henley, an imperial jingoist and a mentor of the young Kipling, is best remembered now as the author of "Invictus": "I am the master of my fate: I am the captain of my soul."

4. Matthew Russell, S.J., is the editor of the 1898 anthology, *Sonnets on the Sonnet,* a multilingual gallery of mirrors in sonnet form. Besides 150 self-reflecting sonnets, Russell offers an appendix of rondeaux on the rondeau, and villanelles on the villanelle, etc., from which this pair is drawn. Note that Russell permits himself to vary the refrain of "My First Rondeau," by changing "my" to "the." The point he loses for that minor blemish is more than made up for by the discursive widening it permits. Russell's nicest finesse is his use of the refrain in "My Last Rondeau." He has taken the easiest kind of refrain, an apostrophe, and in its final appearance allowed it to be read as an appositive. The breeze on his brow is his dying hour.

5. "A Windy Day" is the first known poetic work of Elinor Wylie. Here the refrain-as-apostrophe is unvaried, and there is even one refrain more than the form requires. From the evidence of "by blue-eyes beguiled," one may also suspect that nineteen-year-old Elinor has just read Dobson's version of Voiture. But set against that is Wylie's air of joy in springtime—her own, the century's, and that of her sex, free at last to wear "a sweet but insufficient dress."

6. Except for these two rondeaux, and some few other poems, Marilyn Hacker's great verse diary *Love, Death, and the Changing of the Seasons* is comprised of sonnets. But these two are enough to show what a pliant and pithy form the rondeau can be, in the hands of a master craftsman. Besides

paring away such ornamental features as indentations that telegraph the rhyme scheme and capital letters at the start of each line, Hacker offers a major innovation by introducing a third rhyme. The Hacker rondeau is rhymed: *aabbc/cab* + refrain/*ccbba* + refrain. This loosening of the rondeau's corset gives it the suppleness, nearly, of a sonnet, with, still, that opportunity for a ta-da! that comes with the deft deployment of the refrain, as at the end of Hacker's second rondeau.

Sestina: The End Game

LEWIS TURCO

Although the sestina is of medieval French origin, attributed to Arnaut Daniel in the late twelfth century and used by other Gallic poets and by Italians including Petrarch and Dante (from whom it received its Italian name), its popularity in English is primarily a twentieth-century phenomenon, particularly in the United States. In English the sestina is generally written in iambic pentameter or, sometimes, in decasyllabic meters. Its thirty-nine lines are divided into six sestet stanzas and a final triplet envoy (or envoi). The six end words or *teleutons* of the lines of the first stanza are repeated *in a specific order* as end words in the five succeeding sestet stanzas. In the envoy, the six end words are also picked up, one of them being buried in, and one finishing, each line.

The order in which the end words are reused appears to have its roots in numerology, but what the significance of the pattern was originally is now unknown. The sequence of numbers is 6-1-5-2-4-3. Obviously, the series is just 1-2-3-4-5-6 with the last three numbers reversed and inserted ahead of the first three: 6-1-5-2-4-3. If the end words of stanza 1 are designated ABCDEF (the capital letters signifying repetitions) and the sequence 615243 is applied to it, the order of repetitions in the second stanza will be FAEBDC. Apply the sequence to the second stanza, and the third stanza will be CFDABE. Continuing in this process will give us ECBFAD in the fourth stanza, DEACFB in the fifth, and BDFECA in the sixth sestet. The order of repetitions in the three lines of the envoy is BE/DC/FA.

The oldest British example that I could find—a double sestina, actually—is by Sir Philip Sidney: "You Goat-Herd Gods" from his sixteenth-century *Arcadia*. The version given here has had its spelling modernized. It is not merely a double sestina (twelve sestet stanzas rather than six), but a pastoral dialogue, or eclogue, as well.

Between the early English Renaissance and the Victorian period the sestina seems to have gone underground. I have paged through the works of most of the major British and American poets and many of the minor ones from Chaucer to Longfellow without having found an example before Algernon Charles Swinburne's "The Complaint of Lisa," another double sestina, and "Sestina," which Swinburne made to rhyme *ababab* as well, thus turning its stanzas into Sicilian sestets and increasing the difficulty of the form, but some of the earliest French and Italian sestinas also rhymed, so this was not really an experiment. Sir Edmund Gosse, a contemporary, also wrote a "Sestina," and, as sometimes was the fashion, he italicized the *teleutons*. Not long after the turn of the century Ezra Pound—that great mover and shaker of modernism—returned to the dramatic mode of Sidney and wrote the monologue "Sestina: Altaforte"; this, together with his "Sestina for Isolt," seems to have set off a steady trickle, if not a flood, of traditional and experimental sestinas.

The dedicatory poem "To Hedli" from Louis MacNiece's *Collected Poems, 1925–1948* is a sestina, as are W. H. Auden's "Paysage Moralisé"; R. P. Blackmur's "Mr. Virtue and the Three Bears"; Sara DeFord's "My Grandfather Planted a Tree Orchard"; Roy Fuller's "Sestina"; Elizabeth Bishop's "A Miracle for Breakfast" and tetrameter "Sestina"; Donald Justice's spin off "Sestina: A Dream"; James Merrill's "Tomorrows," which uses the numbers one through six as the *teleutons;* William Dickey's "*Etude:* Andantino"; Jane Cooper's "Morning on the St. John's"; Miller Williams's "On the Way Home from Nowhere, New Year's Eve," and Tom Disch's clever utilization of the length of the form, "The Thirty-Nine Articles," about turning forty years of age.

T. S. Eliot—Pound's partner in so many things—in part 2 of "The Dry Salvages," the third of his *Four Quartets,* wrote an experimental sestina in which the lengths of the lines varied generally from tetrameter to hexameter and many of the ultimate words showed falling rhythms. Nor did Eliot repeat the *teleutons* in every stanza; instead, he simply rhymed the lines *abcdef* except in stanza 6, where he repeated the *teleutons* in the same order as in stanza 1. The poem has no envoy; instead, Eliot added an unbroken tail of thirty-nine lines; in effect, then, the "envoy" is exactly the same length as another whole sestina, some of the end words of which are repeated either exactly or with variations, but in no specific order. For instance, the word *meaning* ends lines 9, 11, and 13 of this "caudate sestina" in which it is also a question whether the lines continue to be written in verse or dissolve into prose, some of which rhymes.

The problem with the sestina is, generally, that the repeated end words can be obtrusive. To draw the reader's attention *away* from the repetitions, poets often enjamb their lines so that sentences and phrases are not end-stopped on the *teleutons,* or they may use, on occasion, homographs of the end words, like *wind* (as in "south wind") and *wind* (as in "wind your own clock"), or even such ploys as *can* and *toucan*— I employed both techniques in a disguised sestina titled "The Forest of My Seasons" in *Awaken, Bells Falling* (1968).

In his "Age and Indifferent Clouds," Harry Mathews deliberately used such words as "hippopotamus" and "bronchitis," thus drawing the reader's attention *to* the *teleutons* rather than away from them, and the beginnings of the lines doubled the difficulty by making puns and ringing variations of six herbs and plants, which might go unnoticed because the end words take so much of the reader's attention. Donald Justice's "Sestina: Here in Katmandu" has no envoy and its line lengths vary, generally between four stresses and one, and Alan Ansen's "A Fit of Something against Something" is a "diminishing sestina" that starts out normally but then begins to lose words until in the envoy all that's left are the *teleutons* of each line.

In 1979 my poetic alter ego "Wesli Court" took advantage of the obsessive quality of the sestina's repetitions in "The Obsession," one of the poems in a sequence titled *Letters to the Dead* that rings the changes on the rhymed iambic pentameter sestet. The first line of "The Obsession" contains *all* six of the end words, and the same basic line is repeated incrementally as the first line of succeeding stanzas. Each time the line is repeated the syntax is transposed by hypallage; nonetheless the lines always make sense. Because all six end words do appear in this line, a particular problem arises at the envoy, for it cannot be of three lines. Instead, the refrain line reappears a seventh time as a one-line envoy rather than as the normal triplet, but with the sense of the original first line reversed.

ELIZABETH BISHOP

Sestina

September rain falls on the house.
In the failing light, the old grandmother
sits in the kitchen with the child
beside the Little Marvel Stove,
reading the jokes from the almanac,
laughing and talking to hide her tears.

She thinks that her equinoctical tears
and the rain that beats on the roof of the house
were both foretold by the almanac,
but only known to a grandmother.
The iron kettle sings on the stove.
She cuts some bread and says to the child,

It's time for tea now; but the child
is watching the teakettle's small hard tears
dance like mad on the hot black stove,
the way the rain must dance on the house.
Tidying up, the old grandmother
hangs up the clever almanac

on its string. Birdlike, the almanac
hovers half open above the child,
hovers above the old grandmother
and her teacup full of dark brown tears.
She shivers and says she thinks the house
feels chilly, and puts more wood in the stove.

It was to be, says the Marvel Stove.
I know what I know, says the almanac.
With crayons the child draws a rigid house
and a winding pathway. Then the child
puts in a man with buttons like tears
and shows it proudly to the grandmother.

But secretly, while the grandmother
busies herself about the stove,
the little moons fall down like tears
from between the pages of the almanac
into the flower bed the child
has carefully placed in the front of the house.

Time to plant tears, says the almanac.
The grandmother sings to the marvelous stove
and the child draws another inscrutable house.

1946

SIR PHILIP SIDNEY

You Goat-Herd Gods

A Dialogue between Strephon and Klaius

Strephon. You goat-herd Gods who love the grassy mountains,
You nymphs that haunt the springs in pleasant valleys,
You satyrs joyed with free and quiet forests,
Vouchsafe your silent ears to plaining music
Which to my woes gives still an early morning
And draws the dolor on till weary evening.

Klaius. O Mercury, foregoer to the evening,
O heavenly huntress of the savage mountains.
O lovely star, entitled of the morning,
Which that my voice does fill these woeful valleys,
Vouchsafe your silent ears to plaining music
Which oft hath Echo tired in secret forests.

Strephon. I that was once free-burgess of the forests,
Where shade from sun and sports I sought at evening;
I that was once esteemed for pleasant music
Am banished now among the monstrous mountains
Of huge despair, and foul affliction's valleys,
Am grown a screech-owl to my self each morning.

Klaius. I that was once delighted every morning,
Hunting the wild inhabitants of forests,
I that was once the music of these valleys,
So darkened am, that all my day is evening,
Heart-broken so, that mole-hills seem high mountains
And fill the vales with cries instead of music.

Strephon. Long since, alas, my deadly, swinish music
Hath made itself a crier of the morning
And has with wailing strength climbed highest mountains:
Long since my thoughts more desert be than forests;
Long since I see my joys come to their evening
And state thrown down to over-trodden valleys.

Klaius. Long since the happy dwellers of these valleys
Have prayed me leave my strange, exclaiming music
Which troubles their day's work, and joys of evening.
Long since I hate the night, more hate the morning;
Long since my thoughts chase me like beasts in the forests,
And make me wish myself laid under mountains.

Strephon. Me seems I see the high and stately mountains
Transform themselves to low, dejected valleys;
me seems I hear in these ill-changed forests,
The nightingales do learn of owls their music;
Me seems I feel the comfort of the morning
Turned to the mortal serene of an evening.

Klaius. Me seems I see a filthy, cloudy evening
As soon as sun begins to climb the mountains;
Me seems I feel a noisome scent, the morning
When I do smell the flowers of these valleys;
Me seems I hear, when I do hear sweet music,
The dreadful cries of murdered men in forests.

Strephon. I wish to fire the trees of all these forests;
I give the sun a last farewell each evening;
I curse the fiddling finders-out of music:
With envy do I hate the lofty mountains
And with despite despise the humble valleys;
I do detest night, evening, day, and morning.

Klaius. Curse to myself my prayer is, the morning:
My fire is more than can be made with forests;
My state more base than are the basest valleys;
I wish no evenings more to see, each evening;
Shamed I have my self in sight of mountains
And stopped my ears, lest I grow mad with music.

Strephon. For she whose parts maintained a perfect music,
Whose beauty shone more than the blushing morning,
Who much surpassed in state the stately mountains,
In straightness passed the cedars of the forests,
Has cast me, wretched, into eternal evening
By taking her two suns from these dark valleys.

Klaius. For she, to whom compared the Alps are valleys,
She, whose least word brings from the spheres their music,
At whose approach the sun rose in the evening,
Who, where she bent, bore in her forehead morning,
Is gone, is gone from these our spoiled forests,
Turning to deserts our best pastured mountains.

Strephon, Klaius. These mountains witness all, so shall
    these valleys,
These forests too, made wretched by our music:
Our morning hymn is this, and song at evening.

                                        Sixteenth c.

WESLI COURT

The Obsession

Last night I dreamed my father died again,
A decade and a year after he dreamed
Of death himself, pitched forward into night.
His world of waking flickered out and died—
An imagine on a screen. He is the father
Now of fitful dreams that last and last.

I dreamed again my father died at last.
He stood before me in his flesh again.
I greeted him. I said, "How are you, father?"
But he looked frailer than last time I'd dreamed
We were together, older than when he'd died—
I saw upon his face the look of night.

I dreamed my father died again last night.
He stood before a mirror. He looked his last
Into the glass and kissed it. He saw he'd died.
I put my arms about him once again
To help support him as he fell. I dreamed
I held the final heartburst of my father.

I died again last night: I dreamed my father
Kissed himself in glass, kissed me goodnight
In doing so. But what was it I dreamed
In fact? An injury that seems to last
Without abatement, opening again
And yet again in dream? Who was it died

Again last night? I dreamed my father died,
But it was not he—it was not my father,
Only an image flickering again
Upon the screen of dream out of the night.
How long can this cold image of him last?
Whose is it, his or mine? Who dreams he dreamed?

My father died. Again last night I dreamed
I felt his struggling heart still as he died
Beneath my failing hands. And when at last
He weighed me down, then I laid down my father,
Covered him with silence and with night.
I could not bear it should he come again—

I died again last night, my father dreamed.

1979

The Sonnet

MARILYN HACKER

What does the sonnet do (for the contemporary anglophone writer) to make it so persistently attractive, yet so frequently reviled? Despite modernism and the ensuing hegemony of "free verse," an overwhelming number of twentieth-century poets have written sonnets: persistent "formalists," like Frost and Auden, but also American iconoclasts like E. E. Cummings, James Wright, June Jordan; the Irish poets Seamus Heaney and Derek Mahon, anglophone poets of other origins like Indian poet Reetika Vazirani, Iranian Mimi Khalvati, Dominican Julia Alvarez. Yet American student readers tend to come to the sonnet with prejudices entirely disproportionate to their limited experience of it. The average American college senior may have once read three of Shakespeare's sonnets, with little literary or historical background, yet "knows" that the sonnet is constricting, "difficult" (but trivial), artificial, archaic. Still, one virtue of the American institution of "creative writing" classes is that, as with other forms and freedoms, students reading canonical and contemporary sonnets in the perspective of attempting one themselves discover, along with the pitfalls, the possibilities opened in the fourteen-line labyrinth. Often, students, having composed an initial sonnet, write a sequence of linked ones, and go back to their literary anthologies to discover Donne, Yeats, Millay, and Cummings, with the special interest of connoisseurs, having learned to appreciate the process as well as the product. One such student said of his first attempt at writing a sonnet that it was like moving into a new, small-seeming room, and discovering that there was nonetheless room for all of his furniture. (Or, one decides ruthlessly what furnishings are disposable. Or one builds new furniture for the room.) Students' reactions to the sonnet seem emblematic of those of most contemporary readers: it's a form that invites close engagement, and that engagement often becomes a kind of dialogue with its past and present uses and connotations.

In a contentious and peculiarly American part of that dialogue, the sonnet remains the chosen scapegoat for every tirade against the supposed limitations/artificiality/hobbling of the free spirit imputed to "formal verse," every declaration of its irrelevance to the literary expression of feminists, African Americans, the progressive working class, the post-modern sensibility. These charges have continued from Pound and W. C. Williams to Amiri Baraka, Adrienne Rich, and Diane Wakoski (who once equated sonnet writing with fascist politics!) and are doubtless re-iterated in brand-new manifestoes. There is no equivalent emotionally charged debate in Great Britain or in Ireland: perhaps because the son-net, if an "interloper" from the Romance languages, nonetheless has five hundred years of history in their literature, whereas it is a more recent import to the United States, arriving at the end of the eighteenth century. But Pound, like every apprentice poet of his generation, wrote countless sonnets including the beautiful and much-anthologized "A Virginal," from his 1912 pamphlet *Riposte*. H.D., that modernist's modernist, for whose early work the rubric of "Imagism" was conceived, prefaced *Red Roses for Bronze* (1930) with a sonnet, dedicated to her life companion Winifred Bryher. African American poet Gwendolyn Brooks in her first book, *A Street in Bronzeville* (1944), used a sonnet sequence to elegantly and economically depict black soldiers returning from World War II to quotidian American racism and segregation.

The sonnet has perhaps the most polyglot and varied history of any European poetic form. It has at different times represented the claims of popular language over learned Latin; the aspirations of an intellec-tual or artistic meritocracy in a world of inherited power; idealized love implicitly contrasted with arranged, dynastic marriages; the ambitions of aristocrats; women's longing for autonomy; the soul's struggle with faith and fear of death. The sonnet's invention is credited to a poet called Jacopo (or Giacomo) da Lentini, in Sicily in the early thirteenth century, who developed the fourteen-line model we know from a gen-eralized lyric in "popular" language (Italian; not Latin) meant to be sung: (*sonetto* = little sound or song) by combining two Sicilian qua-trains—rhyming *abababab*—with a sestet rhymed *cdecde*. This rhyme scheme varied until the adoption and use (first by Guittone d'Arezzo; then indelibly by Petrarch in the fourteenth century) of the double en-velope quatrain on two rhymes *(abbaabba)* followed by a sestet (the last six lines) using two or three rhymes in a varied pattern: (*cdecde, cdeedc, ccddee* are three possibilities). The Italian sonnet was written in hendecasyllabic verse: lines of eleven syllables, not regularly stressed (accentual) as is English iambic pentameter (or as Latin verse was) so that the presence of rhyme was necessary to mark the form and turn-ings of the poem. Simply by looking at these rhyme schemes, the reader sees that all these versions of the sonnet almost predicate a poem whose "argument" divides into two parts, a premise set out in the octave (first eight lines), with the sestet contradicting it, modifying it, or giving a concrete proof. The form also easily incorporates the "if . . . /then" structure of a syllogism.

Some feminist critics have claimed that the sonnet, suggesting as it does, in the Petrarchan model, a male poet addressing a distant, idealized and, above all, silent woman, is the *nec plus ultra* of poetic form enacting the negation of the female subject. But women poets' use of the sonnet goes virtually back to its origins. One of the first women poets (samples of whose work we have extant) to write in a modern European language was "La Compiuta Donzella"—a pseudonym meaning "the accomplished" or "learned maiden." She lived in Florence in the second half of the thirteenth century, predating Dante and Petrarch, and wrote, among other poems, sonnets, three of which survive, only some twenty years after the form had been fixed. And the subject of her sonnets? Not a lover, unattainable or otherwise, but her desire to escape from a marriage arranged by her father and become a nun—which reminds this reader, at least, of another sometime sonneteer, Mexican poet Sor Juana Inés de la Cruz, who, four hundred years later, took the veil in order to pursue her real vocation of writing and study. (When the sonnet was introduced in France in the mid–sixteenth century, it was quickly taken up by Louise Labé.)

While we primarily think of Dante Alighieri as the author of the terza rima epic *Commedia*, his *La Vita nuova*—a more direct, personal sequence of sonnets and canzone interspersed with prose commentary, relating the poet's love for Beatrice, her unattainability, and loss to death—also marks the history of the sonnet. It was certainly one model for Francesco Petrarca, or Petrarch, in writing the sequence of 366 sonnets and canzone called the *Rime sparse* (scattered poems) composed between 1327 and 1366, which the poet continued revising and rearranging until his death in 1373. The poems chronicle the poet's amorous obsession with Laura—again a woman seen in the poet's youth, idealized, never known—through her lifetime, and after her death in 1348, of the plague. Laura herself, from accounts by Petrarch (outside the poems) and others, was a married woman, possibly the mother of eleven children—though no reference to her marriage or maternity occurs in the sequence. Petrarch's influence on the sonnet's later history was and remains vast: not only on form but on the choice and treatment of subject matter, reflected in modern sequences like Edna St.Vincent Millay's *Fatal Interview*, John Berryman's *Sonnets*, Robert Lowell's *The Dolphin*, Adrienne Rich's *XXI Love Poems*. The association of the sonnet with love, specifically with meditations on love's ideal versus its temporal possibility, on love as both a barrier to religious transcendence and a means to achieve it, love as a source of spiritual metamorphosis, love as a way to focus upon the natural and political world, mark the form's history in every language.

In the 1530s, the British poet-courtier Sir Thomas Wyatt encountered the sonnet during his travels in Italy and Spain and brought the form, and the Petrarchan model of the sonnet sequence, back to England. His own sonnets, including translations of Petrarch, showed an immediate preference for a closing couplet in the sestet, which would become characteristic of the "English sonnet" while it was rare in the Italian. Though some early English sonnets used a shorter line, iambic pentameter quickly became the sonnet's meter. Wyatt's friend Henry Howard, the earl of Surrey, also wrote sonnets on the Petrarchan model. Surrey made a significant innovation in establishing the model of four quatrains and a couplet, rhyming *abab cdcd efef gg,* a pattern he found more congenial to the comparatively rhyme-poor English language. Not poet-scholars like Petrarch, both Wyatt and Surrey were active in the court of King Henry VIII, one an ambassador, the other a soldier: both were accused of treason in the course of tumultuous careers, and Surrey died on the headsman's block before his thirtieth birthday.

In the late sixteenth century, hundreds of poets wrote thousands of sonnets: they were the rap music of the day. Two of the greatest English sonneteers, Edmund Spenser and William Shakespeare, both produced their masterpieces in the form in the 1590s. For both, the sonnet in sequence, where individual sonnets are pieced into a narrative mosaic, was the site of their achievement. The first English woman writer to publish a sonnet sequence was Lady Mary Wroth, niece of Sir Philip Sidney. In the line of her uncle's *Arcadia,* she published, in 1621, a long mixed-genre work entitled *Urania,* combining prose narrative with a sequence of eighty-three sonnets and nineteen other lyrics, *Pamphilia to Amphilanthus,* in which the speaker is a woman, her beloved a man.

It was inevitable that the sonnet, associated with idealized human love, should also enact the desire for another distant beloved, as the soul's longing for God is frequently depicted in Christian Renaissance writings. Religious sonnets became common by the end of the sixteenth century, but it was John Donne (whose early poetry, celebrating very carnal erotic love, largely avoided the sonnet form) who, in *La Corona* and the *Holy Sonnets* (c. 1610, published after his death in 1621) developed the form's potential for passionate and intellectually complex religious expression.

Wroth and Donne each wrote one sequence called a "crown of sonnets"—in which each sonnet after the first one opens with the last line of the preceding poem: the last sonnet in the sequence ends with the opening line of the first. These are usually seven to fourteen sonnets in length: the seven of Donne's "La Corona" is the most frequent number. The crown of sonnets, like the form itself, originated in Italy, but late-sixteenth-century English crowns were written by Samuel Daniel and George Chapman; Sidney had included a crown of linked ten-line stanzas in the *Arcadia*.

In spite of Milton, who further broadened the scope of subject matter to political protest and satire, fewer sonnets were being written in England by the late seventeenth century. The form was revived a hundred years later by Cowper and Gray. It flourished in the early nineteenth century when Wordsworth wrote some five hundred sonnets on themes as varied as the French Revolution, Milton, and the form itself. His contemporaries, including Keats, Shelley, Southey, and Elizabeth Barrett Browning, used sonnets to attack slavery and restrictive trade laws, to idealize love, to describe nature and address other poets, living and dead. Later in the century, Gerard Manley Hopkins took a fresh approach to meter with "sprung rhythm"—in which any number of unstressed syllables (along with the one necessary stressed one) may be used in a poetic "foot"—replacing the ten-or-eleven syllable pentameter.

The sonnet did not appear widely in American poetry until the late eighteenth century, brought to prominence in the nineteenth by Longfellow. Perhaps the most widely quoted American sonnet was written in 1883, by Emma Lazarus, a poet of Portuguese Jewish descent: "The New Colossus" is the poem inscribed on the base of the Statue of Liberty.

Twentieth-century American poets produced modernism, which included a reaction against received forms. But the century was also a rich one for the sonnet in English. W. B. Yeats, Robert Frost, Elinor Wylie, Wilfred Owen, E. E. Cummings, Edna St. Vincent Millay, Dylan Thomas, W. H. Auden, Muriel Rukeyser, all wrote memorable sonnets, each one bringing his or her own idiosyncratic vocabulary, images, obsessions. African American poets James Weldon Johnson, Paul Laurence Dunbar, Claude McKay, and Margaret Walker found the sonnet appropriate for public protest against oppression and declarations of racial dignity. But the poet who definitively inscribed the sonnet into African American literature is Gwendolyn Brooks, whose playfully elaborate sentence structure and wordplay epitomize the connection between ironically elevated Black diction and Renaissance and Miltonic syntax and wit.

More than with any other lyric form, the writer of one sonnet often goes on to a second, connected one, and then to a third or a hundredth: this was true of Petrarch, Shakespeare, Millay, and is true today of Seamus Heaney, Marie Ponsot, or Julia Alvarez. (This seems less self-evident when one thinks of the paucity of sequences of villanelles or rondeaux.) The sonnet is more direct, less "tricky" than other forms inherited by English from Romance languages: it does not require repeated words or lines. Its Italian form is very like a mixture of the two most flexible and utilitarian "blocks" of verse narrative: the quatrain and terza rima. At the same time, the separation of discrete poems in the sequence deflects one's expectation of narrative, permits cinematic shifts in time, place, point of view. There is a paradox in the sonnet sequence, in the act of starting a second sonnet on completing the first: the four-teen-line poem whose initial attraction includes the imminent necessity of closure also proves to be open-ended. Rewriting the last line of a just-completed sonnet to start a new one (and commence a crown) is a prime example of that paradox. Contemporary crowns of sonnets have been written by Marie Ponsot, Marilyn Nelson, Marilyn Hacker, Alberto Ríos, George Macbeth, J. D. McClatchy, Robyn Selman, Mimi Khalvati: the last four have written "heroic" crowns of fifteen sonnets in which the last (or first) poem is made up of the first lines of the fourteen others. But sequences prolong themselves without repeated lines. Edna St. Vincent Millay's "Sonnets from an Ungrafted Tree" is a stark New England narrative about a farm wife; Hayden Carruth's "Sonnets" limn a love affair between a man in his sixties and a much younger woman. The British poet Tony Harrison's cycle of sixteen-line Meredithian sonnets, a meditation on class and language, becomes an elegy to his working-class father. Cuban American physician-poet Rafael Campo uses the same form to write about family and ethnic culture—and about love between men, and community medicine, in sixteen-sonnet *canciones*.

The sonnet sequence also influences poems not specifically composed within its formal strictures. Robert Lowell's *History, For Lizzie and Harriet,* and *The Dolphin,* in fourteen-line blank verse sections, resonate as sonnet sequences. Adrienne Rich developed her youthful poetic strength in the exercise of traditional English prosody, which she rejected in the 1960s as incompatible with progressive and feminist political engagement. Still, the sonnet sequence shadows important poems at every stage of her career, including "Snapshots of a Daughter-in-Law" and *XXI Love Poems.* Perhaps it is precisely because of modernism's critical resistance to the sonnet that contemporary poets have reexamined it and "made it new" with heterodox content and language at once demotic and experimental. And this (paradoxically) is congruent with its origins: a poem in "popular" language that could be read or written by anyone (not only clerics and scholars) and that incited its writers to fresh examination of their evolving languages' interactions with the human world.

WILLIAM SHAKESPEARE

Sonnet 73

That time of year thou mayst in me behold
When yellow leaves, or none, or few, do hang
Upon those boughs which shake against the cold,
Bare ruin'd choirs where late the sweet birds sang.
In me thou seest the twilight of such day
As after sunset fadeth in the west,
Which by and by black night doth take away,
Death's second self, that seals up all in rest.
In me thou seest the glowing of such fire
That on the ashes of his youth doth lie,
As the death-bed whereon it must expire,
Consum'd with that which it was nourished by.
      This thou perceiv'st which makes thy love more strong,
      To love that well which thou must leave ere long.

c. 1590
English sonnet

JOHN DONNE

Holy Sonnet XIX

Oh, to vex me, contraries meet in one:
Inconstancy unnaturally hath begot
A constant habit: that when I would not
I change in vows, and in devotion.
As humorous is my contrition
As my profane love, and as soon forgot:
As riddlingly distempered, cold and hot,
As praying, as mute; as infinite, as none.
I durst not view heaven yesterday; and today
In prayers and flattering speeches I court God:
Tomorrow I quake with true fear of his rod.
So my devout fits come and go away
Like a fantastic Ague: save that here
Those are my best days, when I shake with fear.

c. 1609; published 1621
Italian sonnet (with concluding couplet in sestet)

WILLIAM WORDSWORTH

Nuns fret not at their convents' narrow rooms;
And hermits are contented with their cells;
And students with their pensive citadels;
Maids at the wheel, the weaver at his loom,
Sit blithe and happy; bees that soar for bloom
High as the highest Peak of Furness-fells,
Will murmur by the hour in foxglove bells:
In truth the prison into which we doom
Ourselves, no prison is: and hence for me,
In sundry moods, 'twas pastime to be bound
Within the Sonnet's scanty plot of ground;
Pleased if some Souls (for such there needs must be)
Who have felt the weight of too much liberty,
Should find brief solace there, as I have found.

1807
Italian sonnet

GERARD MANLEY HOPKINS

The Windhover

to Christ our Lord

I caught this morning morning's minion, king-
   dom of daylight's dauphin, dapple-dawn-drawn Falcon,
     in his riding
   Of the rolling level underneath him steady air,
     and striding
High there, how he rung upon the rein of a wimpling wing
In his ecstasy! then off, off forth on swing,
   As a skate's heel sweeps smooth on a bow-bend: the hurl
     and gliding
   Rebuffed the big wind. My heart in hiding
Stirred for a bird,—the achieve of, the mastery of the thing!

Brute beauty and valour and act, oh, air, pride, plume here
   Buckle! AND the fire that breaks from thee then,
     a billion
Times told lovelier, more dangerous, O my chevalier!

No wonder of it: shéer plód makes plough down sillion
Shine, and blue-black embers, ah my dear,
    Fall, gall themselves, and gash gold-vermilion.

                                                    1877
                        Italian sonnet in "sprung rhythm"

EMMA LAZARUS

The New Colossus

Not like the brazen giant of Greek fame
With conquering limbs astride from land to land
Here at our sea-washed sunset-gates shall stand
A mighty woman with a torch, whose flame
Is the imprisoned lightning, and her name
Is Mother of Exiles. From her beacon-hand
Glows world-wide welcome, her mild eyes command
The air-bridged harbor that twin cities frame.
"Keep, ancient lands, your storied pomp!" cries she,
With silent lips. "Give me your tired, your poor,
Your huddled masses yearning to breathe free,
The wretched refuse of your teeming shore.
Send these, the homeless, tempest-tossed, to me.
I lift my lamp beside the golden door."

                                                    1883
                Italian sonnet (with only two rhymes in the sestet)

EDNA ST. VINCENT MILLAY

From "Sonnets from an Ungrafted Tree"

So she came back into his house again
And watched beside his bed until he died,
Loving him not at all. The winter rain
Splashed in the painted butter-tub outside
Where once her red geraniums had stood,
Where still their rotted stalks were to be seen;
The thin log snapped; and she went out for wood,
Bareheaded, running the few steps between

The house and shed; there, from the sodden eaves
Blown back and forth on ragged ends of twine
Saw the dejected creeping jinny-vine,
(And one, big-aproned, blithe, with stiff blue sleeves,
Rolled to the shoulder that warm day in spring
Who planted seeds, musing ahead to their far blossoming.)

c. 1923

English sonnet variation, with seven-foot
(heptameter) last line throughout the sequence

W. H. AUDEN

The Useful

From "The Quest"

The over-logical fell for the witch
Whose argument converted him to stone;
Thieves rapidly absorbed the over-rich;
The over-popular went mad alone,
And kisses brutalized the over-male.

As agents, their effectiveness soon ceased;
Yet, in proportion as they seemed to fail,
Their instrumental value was increased
To those still able to obey their wish.

By standing stones the blind can feel their way,
Wild dogs compel the cowardly to fight,
Beggars assist the slow to travel light,
And even madmen manage to convey
Unwelcome truths in lonely gibberish.

1940
Nonce sonnet

GWENDOLYN BROOKS

The Rites for Cousin Vit

From Annie Allen

Carried her unprotesting out the door
Kicked back the casket-stand. But it can't hold her,
That stuff and satin aiming to enfold her,
The lid's contrition nor the bolts before.
Oh oh. Too much. Too much. Even now, surmise,
She rises in sunshine. There she goes
Back to the bars she knew and the repose
In love-rooms and the things in people's eyes.
Too vital and too squeaking. Must emerge.
Even now, she does the snake-hips with a hiss,
Slaps the bad wine across her shantung, talks
Of pregnancy, guitars and bridgework, walks
In parks or alleys, comes haply on the verge
Of happiness, haply hysterics. Is.

1950

modified Italian sonnet with four rhymes in the octave

ALBERTO RÍOS

From "Second Grade"

At A. J. Mitchell Elementary School
where no one could speak English in the first
grade class and where the second grade got swat
for speaking Spanish, one guy named Raul
he spit and said he didn't care. Raul
was always suited up and wore a fist
in front like I-don't-know-but-kiss-my-ass
on-Sunday-and-I'll-show-you-Very-Cool.

He knew who everybody's hero was.
He said he was the last Pachuco left
and got expelled for saying so, and cause
he wore a flat-top with a perfect set
of wings, and when she asked us who had cussed
we never told, but that Miss Lee she guessed.

1978

Italian sonnet with closing couplet; fifth in crown of seven sonnets

Triolet:
Trippingly on the Tongue

KATHLEENE WEST

The triolet is a true word-bargain poem. Its two refrains account for five lines of the eight-line poem, giving the writer of this rondeau-relative a chance to meld strength and pithiness. There are challenges of course. Short poems force us to see the value in each word; there's no room for squandering. Therefore, it's harder for us to hide our deficiencies. Writing a short poem in a form as compact as the triolet reminds us of the discipline necessary in writing all poetry.

The triolet turns on only two rhymes and can result in a poem of vapid description—nature and love often being the culprits. Consider the first two lines of a triolet from Dylan Thomas's juvenilia: "The bees are glad the livelong day / And lilacs in their beauty blow." It may be unfair to mine a poet's junior poems for an example, but Thomas's reputation is solid and won't be hurt by it. Even in France, the home of the first triolet in the medieval era, eighteenth-century poets, noted for their dexterity, found the form too difficult and settled for writing short poems mildly influenced by the form. In the nineteenth century in England, Leigh Hunt, John Keats's good friend, wrote "Jenny Kissed Me," a likable poem, vaguely connected to the triolet form.

The triolet probably received its name because the first line appears three times in the poem. Here is the pattern shown against a Thomas Hardy triolet:

A	How great my grief, my joys how few,
B	Since first it was my fate to know thee!
a	—Have the slow years not brought to view
A	How great my grief, my joys how few,
a	Nor memory shaped old times anew,
b	Nor loving-kindness helped to show thee
A	How great my grief, my joys how few,
B	Since first it was my fate to know thee?

1902

The rhymes are all full and, except for "anew," monosyllabic; the refrain lines have no syntactic variation, except for the punctuation after refrain B: "Since first it was my fate to know thee!" and "Since first it was my fate to know thee?" Medieval triolets were often iambic pentameter; around the seventeenth century the lines shortened to iambic tetrameter, which persisted into the nineteenth century, as Hardy's triolet exemplifies.

Contemporary triolets are often (though not universally) syllabic. Although the monosyllabic full rhyme still persists, the reader will notice more double-syllable rhymes and half rhymes as well as a variation of the refrain lines. Sandra McPherson's "Triolet" varies the A refrains as follows: "She was in love with the same danger"; "she was in love. With the same danger"; "she was in love with that danger." McPherson's triolet also uses double-syllable and polysyllabic rhyme as well as half rhyme, providing an excellent example of the possibilities for the contemporary triolet. Other poets, like Barbara Howes in "Early Supper," have managed to remove the length restrictions by writing triolet sequences.

The triolet was invented in France in the late 1300s and remained a French form until the late nineteenth century and early twentieth century. Medieval French triolets often were five iambic feet and serious; in the seventeenth century they were a favorite form for political satire in four iambic feet. In the 1650s, an English monk named Patrick Carey wrote the earliest triolets in English, but the form languished in this language for more than two centuries until Robert Bridges made the form seem more approachable for poets writing in English.

Not a wildly popular form in contemporary English poetry, the triolet daunts poets with its strict form and brevity. In the juvenilia section of Sylvia Plath's *Collected Poems,* which shows her diligent practice with formal verse, there is only one triolet, "Bluebeard." The benefits of this form are evident for those who rise to the challenge. Wendy Cope, a British poet known for her irreverent verses in strict form ("*The Waste Land* Limericks"), as well as being considered for the poet laureate position after Ted Hughes, has written a witty triolet beginning, "I used to think all poets were Byronic— / Mad, bad, and dangerous to know. / And then I met a few."

It has remained an enduring fashion to entitle one's triolet "Triolet." This does serve to remind the reader what the poet is up against, but it also wastes the perfectly good opportunity of the title's language. Worse, are those narcissistic triolets that take their content from the form: "Easy is the triolet / If you really learn to make it!" are the refrain lines from W. E. Henley's "Triolet." Examples like these are mainly found in vintage poetry handbooks, but presenting these poems as worthy triolets devalues the form. Such poems are usually more pleasing to the poet than to the reader.

When writing a triolet, I find it's best to be as specific and as nongeneric as possible, avoiding abstractions at all costs. (Nevertheless, see McPherson's "Triolet" for a stunning triolet that includes the abstracts love and danger.) It's also a good idea to avoid a complete reliance on end-stopped lines. The first triolet I wrote was based on a reaction to a small news item in the *Seattle Times,* headlined "Electric Women to Meet." Although I soon realized this was directed at women employed by electric subcontractors, for a visionary moment, I imagined Seattle as a site for a convention of electric women.

Current Event

A	Static, shock, a surge of power—
B	Electric women converge on the town.
a	A battery of women coil like wire.
A	Static, shock, a surge of power.
a	Circuits open, smooth as flour,
b	Ever-ready, they'll never run down.
A	Static, shock, a surge of power—
B	Electric Women converge on the town.

Composition 1977, copyright 1994

The A refrain line doubles as an opening phrase followed by a dash as well as a sentence fragment. I used one half rhyme in the A/a rhyme scheme (wire, power). Although there is punctuation at the ends of lines, the dashes and comma move the language of the poem at the brisk pace, as well as the number of electric words. The meter of the poem moves from trochaic tetrameter to iambic tetrameter, a subconscious decision that contributes to the movement. This triolet uses two similes and relies on active verbs (converge, coil). The title and the Ever-ready are obvious puns, even verging on groaners, but they add to the humor, making this a lively poem to recite.

The triolet leads to other related forms—rondel, rondeau, and villanelle, expanding one's knowledge of formal verse and teaching the importance held by each word in the poem. Because of the musical structure of the triolet, it is an easy poem to know by heart for both composer and listener, emphasizing the oral roots of poetry, bringing together poet and audience in a moment of celebration.

CINDI HARRISON

Your Search for Independence

Time now for dimness and I'm spinning—
what you ask for is never easi-
ly done—well, easy, yes, like taking
time out for dinner or spending
a day lolling about. There's something
different, Love, about loneliness
now. Time for dinner. I'm spending
what you asked for. It's never easy.

1998

MOLLY PEACOCK

Food for Talk

The bird delights in human food,
claw clamped to the lip of the cup,
and I delight in human good
the way the bird delights in food,
soft and foreign to its beak, wooed
by something not its own abrupt
crack of the seed. So human good
is soft law to the sharp lip's cup.

1989

ROBERT BRIDGES

Triolet

When first we met we did not guess
That Love would prove so hard a master;
Of more than common friendliness
When first we met we did not guess.
Who could foretell this sore distress,
This irretrievable disaster
When first we met?—We did not guess
That Love would prove so hard a master.

1914

SANDRA MCPHERSON

Triolet

She was in love with the same danger
everybody is. Dangerous
as it is to love a stranger,
she was in love. With the same danger
an adultress risks a husband's anger.
Stealthily death enters a house:
she was in love with that danger.
Everybody is dangerous.

1978

LEWIS TURCO

Jasper Olson

From Bordello

I take my women any way they come—
I'm Jasper Olson, brother, hard and fast
I play this game. Though some folks think I'm dumb,
I take my women any way they come,
and come they do. There's no time to be numb
in this life—grab it now and ram the past.
I take my women any way they come.
I'm Jasper Olson, brother, hard and fast.

1968

WENDY COPE

Triolet

I used to think all poets were Bryronic—
Mad, bad and dangerous to know.
And then I met a few. Yes, it's ironic—
I used to think all poets were Bryronic—
They're mostly wicked as a ginless tonic
And wild as pension plans. Not long ago
I used to think all poets were Bryronic—
Mad, bad and dangerous to know.

1986

CARRIE FOUNTAIN

Lane's End

Tonight at the bowling alley, men slap
each other ten and their hands meet with a smooth beat.
This is a strike and this is its owner, shaking out his hand.
Tonight at the bowling alley, men's laps
are weighted with liquor like children, and the night drags
on, dying with the sound of pins crashing, shrinking
to late night at the bowling alley, while men continue to slap
each other ten, and their hands meet with a smooth beat.

1998

Gymnastics: The Villanelle

MAXINE KUMIN

Consisting of nineteen lines divided into six stanzas—five triplets and one concluding quatrain—the villanelle turns on two rhymes and builds on two refrains, which alternate. The first refrain recurs as the final line in triplets 2 and 4; the second refrain performs the same function in triplets 3 and 5. In the concluding quatrain, the penultimate line consists of the first refrain and the final line, the second refrain. Although some metric regularity is common, there is no set line length. The rhyme scheme runs A ^{1}bA^2 abA^1 abA ^{2} abA^1 abA^2 abA^{1}A^2. A^1 and A^2 stand for the two refrain lines.

The villanelle came to us from the Renaissance, arising in Italy in the mid–sixteenth century, often as a pastoral tercet with musical accompaniment. By the close of the century the form had migrated to France and in the hands of Jean Passerat evolved into the model we know today. Largely ignored in the seventeenth and eighteenth centuries, it was revived by Edmund Gosse, who published his pioneering villanelle, "Wouldst Thou Not Be Content to Die" in 1874. Oscar Wilde also contributed to this form.

The villanelle soon crossed the ocean and was taken up by James Whitcomb Riley, whose "The Best Is Good Enough," published in 1883, was the first villanelle to appear in the New World. In 1897, Edwin Arlington Robinson's "The House on the Hill" further legitimized the villanelle in English.

In *A Portrait of the Artist as a Young Man,* first published in 1916, James Joyce has Stephen Daedalus compose a villanelle, "Are You Not Weary of Ardent Ways," for his old girlfriend. But it was not until 1952 that the best known of all contemporary villanelles, Dylan Thomas's "Do Not Go Gentle into That Good Night," was published, just a year before the poet's death.

The fifties were a fine decade for the villanelle: Sylvia Plath, Theodore Roethke, W. H. Auden were all experimenting with the form. Contemporary villanelles by Elizabeth Bishop, Marilyn Hacker, Richard Hugo, Donald Justice, Carolyn Kizer, David Wagoner and others continue to resuscitate this form.

Repeated lines in any poem have an incantatory quality. In the villanelle they become almost hypnotic, particularly in poems that are rigidly end-stopped and that employ monosyllabic masculine rhymes, as in Robinson's "The House on the Hill," and the rather wooden examples by Wilde and Riley, cited below for their historical rather than poetic value. James Whitcomb Riley's sunnyside-up stoicism strikes us today as vapid; Wilde's heavyfooted reliance on classical allusion drives us to a dictionary of mythology in order to riddle his intent.

In Dylan Thomas's "Do Not Go Gentle into That Good Night" and Theodore Roethke's "The Waking," villanelles to be found in virtually any anthology, the end-stopped lines and monosyllabic rhymes, while still constraining, are employed to much greater emotional effect. Thomas's villanelle, hortatory and grieving, gathers power as it moves through one lyrical declamation after another. He calls up lightning and meteors, the expanse of ocean, the setting sun, all the while mourning, even raging that the close of day is at hand. To hear this poem archived in the poet's voice is to be made aware of the incantatory spell Thomas cast on his audiences.

Roethke's "The Waking," almost as famous, teases us with its seemingly guileless simplicity—*slow* and *go*; *there* and *stair*—surely with rhymes as simple as these we can find our way easily from line to line. But what are these dichotomies, these contradictions, how does one "wake to sleep," " think by feeling," "learn by going"? Gradually we come to realize that the poet's subject is essentially the same as Thomas's: the ultimate journey toward death. Roethke capitalizes *Ground, Tree,* and *Nature.* In a poem as brief and disciplined as a villanelle, we may read this as the poet's shorthand for deification.

Thomas's refrain, "Rage, rage against the dying of the light" may differ in tone from Roethke's "I wake to sleep, and take my waking slow" but the intent—the acknowledgment of our mortality—is the same.

Because English is a rhyme-poor language, many poets have resorted to the use of slant or approximate rhymes to extend their options. Some poets have taken liberties with the refrain lines, transmuting them subtly or ruthlessly, contributing a sometimes welcome elasticity to the form's challenging strictures. Hugo, in "The Freaks at Spurgin Road Field," cited below, has reversed the order of his concluding quatrain so that the first refrain line falls as line 2 of the stanza. Further, he has sidestepped the rhyme requirement of the triplets, contenting himself with some approximations: *night, heat, spastic, quake, worked,* and his line lengths vary between the iambic pentameter of his two refrain lines and looser lines that propel the narrative forward.

Elizabeth Bishop's justly famous "One Art," also reprinted here, takes extensive liberties with the second refrain line. She is content to reuse the rhyme word *disaster* and to bend the remainder of the line to her needs, lending a refreshing colloquial speech pattern to the poem. Her first refrain line, "The art of losing isn't hard to master," holds fast until the penultimate line of the poem, when it expands to "the art of losing's not too hard to master"; moreover, her selection of the polysyllabic words *master* and *disaster* presses her into interesting, surprising yet apt rhymes: *fluster; faster; last, or; vaster; gesture*. These so-called feminine or Italianate endings entice the poet to reach farther afield for unexpected equivalents that will provide an emotional tension to balance the otherwise lighthearted chime of double rhymes. Also, the strong caesuras in the first lines of the second, fourth, and fifth stanzas, to cite the most obvious ones, and the deceptively casual enjambments in the second lines of the first three stanzas, to note the most visible, accord this difficult and demanding form a casual, conversational tone. It is a very different voice from the priestly incantation of Dylan Thomas or the mysterious hypnotism of Theodore Roethke.

In my own double villanelle, "The Nuns of Childhood: Two Views," I've given myself considerable leeway with the refrain lines, repeating just the tag ends of them where it suited my uses. I've bent the rhymes almost to the breaking point, too, always with the intent of achieving an accessible narrative flow while still playing the game by my own amended rules. The sheer sport of rhyming *thimble, humble, shambled, scramble, preamble* and *brambles* within the story made this poem a delightful challenge. In the second part, I went much farther afield with approximate rhymes, allowing myself to move from the feminine slant rhymes of *wimples* and *example* to *vestal* and then to monosyllables that carried only the "l" sound forward: *lolled, child, gold*.

It's my thesis that we don't need to ossify these ancient French forms by slavish imitation. We can enliven and enhance them with our own approximations. By resorting to the ingenuities of our own time and place, American poets in the last fifty years have turned a stultifying and restrictive form into an elastic, even gymnastic one. Perhaps in the twenty-first century others will remake the villanelle in ways as yet unthought of.

EDWIN ARLINGTON ROBINSON

The House on the Hill

They are all gone away.
　　　The house is shut and still,
There is nothing more to say.

Through broken walls and gray
　　　The winds blow bleak and shrill.
They are all gone away.

Nor is there one to-day
　　　To speak them good or ill:
There is nothing more to say.

Why is it then we stray
　　　Around the sunken sill?
They are all gone away.

And our poor fancy-play
　　　For them is wasted skill:
There is nothing more to say.

There is ruin and decay
　　　In the House on the Hill:
They are all gone away,
There is nothing more to say.

　　　　　　　　　　　　　　　1921

JAMES WHITCOMB RILEY

The Best Is Good Enough

I quarrel not with Destiny,
But make the best of everything—
The best is good enough for me.

Leave Discontent alone, and she
Will shut her mouth and let *you* sing.
I quarrel not with Destiny.

I take some things, or let 'em be—
Good gold has always got the ring;
The best is good enough for me.

Since Fate insists on secrecy,
I have no arguments to bring—
I quarrel not with Destiny.

The fellow that goes "haw" for "gee"
Will find he hasn't got full swing.
The best is good enough for me.

One only knows our needs, and He
Does all of the distributing.
I quarrel not with Destiny:
The best is good enough for me.

1916

OSCAR WILDE

Theocritus: A Villanelle

O singer of Persephone!
      In the dim meadows desolate
Dost thou remember Sicily?

Still through the ivy flits the bee
      Where Amaryllis lies in state;
O singer of Persephone!

Simaetha calls on Hecate
      And hears the wild dogs at the gate;
Dost thou remember Sicily?

Still by the light and laughing sea
      Poor Polypheme bemoans his fate:
O singer of Persephone!

And still in boyish rivalry
      Young Daphnis challenges his mate:
Dost thou remember Sicily?

Slim Lacon keeps a goat for thee,
      For thee the jocund shepherds wait,
O singer of Persephone!
Dost thou remember Sicily?

1909

RICHARD HUGO

The Freaks at Spurgin Road Field

The dim boy claps because the others clap.
The polite word, handicapped, is muttered in the stands.
Isn't it wrong, the way the mind moves back.

One whole day I sit, contrite, dirt, L.A.
Union Station, '46, sweating through last night.
The dim boy claps because the others clap.

Score, 5 to 3. Pitcher fading badly in the heat.
Isn't it wrong to be or not be spastic?
Isn't it wrong, the way the mind moves back.

I'm laughing at a neighbor girl beaten to scream
by a savage father and I'm ashamed to look.
The dim boy claps because the others clap.

The score is always close, the rally always short.
I've left more wreckage than a quake.
Isn't it wrong, the way the mind moves back.

The afflicted never cheer in unison.
Isn't it wrong, the way the mind moves back
to stammering pastures where the picnic should have worked.
The dim boy claps because the others clap.

                                        1986

ELIZABETH BISHOP

One Art

The art of losing isn't hard to master;
so many things seem filled with the intent
to be lost that their loss is no disaster.

Lose something every day. Accept the fluster
of lost door keys, the hour badly spent.
The art of losing isn't hard to master.

Then practice losing farther, losing faster;
places, and names, and where it was you meant
to travel. None of these will bring disaster.

I lost my mother's watch. And look! my last, or
next-to-last, of three loved houses went.
The art of losing isn't hard to master.

I lost two cities, lovely ones. And, vaster,
some realms I owned, two rivers, a continent.
I miss them, but it wasn't a disaster.

—Even losing you (the joking voice, a gesture
I love) I shan't have lied. It's evident
the art of losing's not too hard to master
though it may look like (*Write* it!) like disaster.

1983

MAXINE KUMIN

The Nuns of Childhood: Two Views

1.
O where are they now, your harridan nuns
who thumped on young heads with a metal thimble
and punished with rulers your upturned palms:

three smacks for failing in long division,
one more to instill the meaning of *humble*.
As the twig is bent, said your harridan nuns.

Once, a visiting bishop, serene
at the close of a Mass through which he had shambled,
smiled upon you with upturned palms.

"Because this is my feast day," he ended,
"you may all have a free afternoon." In the scramble
of whistles and cheers one harridan nun,

fiercest of all the parochial coven,
Sister Pascala, without preamble
raged, "I protest!" and rapping on palms

at random, had bodily to be restrained.
O God's perfect servant is kneeling on brambles
wherever they sent her, your harridan nun,
enthroned as a symbol with upturned palms.

2.

O where are they now, my darling nuns
whose heads were shaved under snowy wimples,
who rustled drily inside their gowns,

disciples of Oxydol, starch and bluing,
their backyard clothesline a pious example?
They have flapped out of sight, my darling nuns.

Seamless as fish, made all of one skin,
their language secret, these gentle vestals
were wedded to Christ inside their gowns.

O Mother Superior Rosarine
on whose lap the privileged visitor lolled
—I at age four with my darling nuns,

with Sister Elizabeth, Sister Ann,
am offered to Jesus, the Jewish child-
next-door, who worships your ample black gown,

your eyebrows, those thick mustachioed twins,
your rimless glasses, your ring of pale gold—
who can have stolen my darling nuns?
Who rustles drily inside my gown?

1993

IV

Principles for Formal Experimentation

Organic Form

HILDA MORLEY

As my poetic style crystallized at a time when I was closely associated with the abstract expressionist painters in New York, I turned to some of their statements to see how they might shed light on my own perception of organic form in poetry. Mercedes Matter speaks of "the effect . . . which results from the order of correspondence that is true to my perceived experience." She goes on to speak of "the coherence of my experience, revealed as I work," that "guides me toward coherence in the painting." Commenting on Matter's work, the painter and critic Louis Finkelstein notes that "the balance between the openness and completeness of the entire painting . . . and the specification of completed shapes . . . is a precarious one." Both these statements stress the quality of process in the making of art as a paramount factor. So too the French poet, Paul Valéry, speaks of poetry as "the voice in action, the voice as direct issue of, or provoked by—things that one sees or that one feels as present" and of "the nature of that energy which spends itself in responding to what is" and "is profoundly related to the situation of the inner being." The challenge of discovery as the central thrust in the making of the poem relates closely to Denise Levertov's definition of organic form in poetry.

As Levertov sees it, form is to be discovered and revealed in the "inscape" (Gerard Manley Hopkins's term) of objects and their relationship. She quotes Thomas Huxley as using the term *organic* as an equivalent to "living."

It is the movement of the poet's process using various perceptions to get at the life of the poetic experience that gives rise to the measure, the movement of the metre. And because a process of discovery is involved, there is a degree of irregularity, of unexpectedness not found in "free verse," precisely because the poet does not take the experience for granted, being immersed in the density of the process. Thus, the experience itself is revealed to the poet step by step and often in the form of sudden brakes and shifts. In free verse the essential basic perception tends to be taken for granted and assumed from the beginning of the poem. Therefore the tone tends to be less personal, more public, more like the chanting of voices together, while the poem of organic form stays close to the poet's personal voice, that inward noise that makes use of intensely personal rhythms. This is why the use of breath is so important in the organic poem, while free verse tends to make use of a more public, or even official voice. The beat is basically regular, as in Whitman's "When lilacs last in the dooryard bloomed / and the great star early drooped in the western sky in the night / I mourned" or "Out of the cradle endlessly rocking / out of the mocking-bird's throat, the musical shuttle" lines with strong and weak beats alternating fairly regularly. Another aspect of free verse is its unusually declamatory public tone. What is being said is directed less to the single reader than to a large, public audience.

I am not making use of Ezra Pound as an example, despite the great variety of rhythms he uses, because to my ears his most moving lines tend to take a public tone and pentameter rhythm as (from the *Pisan Cantos*, LXXXI): "The ant's a centaur in his dragon world; / Pull down thy vanity, it is not man / Made courage, or made order, or made grace, / Pull down thy vanity, I say, pull down," which I sense as having the effect of a declamation, a chant, or a choral sound directed to a larger audience.

As I have noted, the movement of rhythms, stresses, and breaks in a poem in the organic form is the movement of a process, so that the shape of the poem follows stresses and breaks of the way in which the experience of the poem came about in the poet's perception, a process of discovery. This notion of a process of discovery is emphasized in Robert Creeley's statement, when he speaks of the intelligence that cannot propose the assumption of content prior to its experience of that content. The irregularity of the breathing rhythms in the poem of organic form can be as irregular as the shape of the process by which the poem comes about, depending as it does on the different levels of discovery within that process, instant by instant. The tendency of free verse to a fairly regular repetition of stresses creates a sense of relative detachment from the poet's own experience of discovery. The free verse poem becomes individualized largely in terms of pace, as in Whitman's "Out of the cradle endlessly rocking," where we can be fairly certain that the initial cadence will be confirmed in the lines following the opening. Thus the rhythm of the free verse poem is more even and level, without the unexpected drops, pauses, or knots of breathing that appear in the poem of organic form. In Charles Olson's words, "every element in an open poem (the syllable, the line, as well as the image, the sound, the sense) must be taken up as participants in the kinetic of the poem" and "a series of tensions made to hold and to hold exactly inside the content and the context of the poem which has forced itself into being." These tensions are expressed in "certain laws and possibilities of the breath, of the breathing of the man who writes as well as of his listenings." The "listenings" of the poet are the signs of what Levertov refers to when she speaks of the "discipline" of the poem of organic form, which "begins with the development of the utmost attentiveness." This type of poem "voluntarily places itself under the laws which are variable, unpredictable but nonetheless strict . . . discovered by instress." Therefore, she continues, "the sounds, acting together with the measure . . . imitate the feeling of an experience, its emotional tone, its texture." Thus, in the words of Paul Valéry, "the ear speaks for it; it is the vigilance of the poet's interior ear which finds the words, the language." The reader of a poem in organic form is forced to identify with this inner vigilance in a most particularized way so that every pause, extra space, extra emphasis, or break must find its precise echo in the reader's ear before the poem can breathe or be breathed. The more general reverberation of rhythms and emphasis may be sufficient in free verse, but are inadequate here. The poem in organic form requires that the pulse or pulses of the poetic experience be shared in a kind of fierce, unswerving intimacy, so that the reader's attention becomes the dense soil in which each step of the poem's progress is planted, for the poem of organic form molds its phrasing and spacing to conform to the pressures of the poetic content.

An early poem of mine, "Rome, 1970," took me by surprise as I was writing it. I discovered, as I came close to the ending, that I had to make the moon into a personage, so that instead of using the phrase *welcomes us,* which seemed weak and without any impact, I said, *a welcomer.* The poem reads:

> I lean out
> closing the shutters:
> fading trans-
> parent rose color along the
> rim of the sky
> Caught in the
> branches of the Roman pine the moon is
> just past the sickle
> stage
> loud cry of the hoopoe
> a sudden power
> breaks into
> early night
> The moon
> amazing in
> brightness, gaiety,
> a welcomer

As I immersed myself in the inner movement of the poetic experience, I realized that the image of opening the shutters was equivalent to the raising of a stage curtain, and the images that followed were aspects of a stage set in which a moment of dramatic action would occur—the moon offering a welcome. All this was not explicit but was embedded in the moving rhythm of the poem and the shift of the breath in the tenth and eleventh lines as well as in the sharp sound of "breaks," which creates a suspension, or intake of the breath, an instant of suspense, the level, full sound of "moon" affirmed that gap with the "i" sound of "brightness" releasing the tension and the gathered trisyllabic sound of "gaiety" becoming an equivalent to a ripple of laughter attendant to the moon. Focusing my attention on the thrust, the rhythmic curve, of the opening gave me the means to intensify the poetic perception and to discover which steps were essential to the life of the experience. The breaks in the line are there in order to stress the importance of the first word in the next line. The break in "transparent" is equivalent to the fading out of the rose color there.

The first examples of organic form that I have chosen are by the master, William Carlos Williams, beginning with "The Birdsong."

> Disturb the balance, broken bird
> the distress of the song
> cuts through an ample silence
> sweeping the trees.
>
> It is the trouble
> of the brook that makes it loud,
> the current broke to give
> out a burbling
>
> breaks the arched stillness,
> ripples the tall grass
> gone to heady seed, bows the heads
> of goldenrod
>
> that bear a vulgar happiness,
> the bay-berry,
> briars—
> break also your happiness for me.

1950

An example of Williams's extraordinary use of the three-line form he invented appear in a later poem, "View by Color Photography on a Commercial Calendar."

The church of Vice-Morcate
          in the Canton Ticino
                    with its apple-blossoms
Is beautiful
          as anything I have ever seen
                    in or out of
Switzerland.
          The beauty of holiness
                    the beauty of man's anger
reflecting his sex
          or a woman's either,
                    mountainous,
or a little stone church
          from a height
                    or
close to the camera
          the apple-tree in blossom
                    or the far lake
below
          in the distance—
                    are equal
as they are unsurpassed.
          Peace
                    after the event
comes from their contemplation,
          a great peace.
                    The sky is cut off,
there is no horizon
          just the mountainside
                    bordered by water
on which tiny waves
          without passion
                    unconcerned
cover the invisible fish.
          And who but we are concerned
                    with the beauty of apple-blossoms
and a small church
          on a promontory,
                    an ancient church—
by the look of its masonry
          abandoned
                    by a calm lake

in the mountains
        where the sun shines
                of a springtime
afternoon. Something
        has come to an end here,
                it has been accomplished.

1955

GEORGE OPPEN

The Forms of Love

Parked in the fields
All night
So many years ago,
We saw
A lake beside us
When the moon rose.
I remember

Leaving that ancient car
Together. I remember
Standing in the white grass
Beside it. We groped
Our way together
Downhill in the bright
Incredible light

Beginning to wonder
Whether it could be lake
Or fog
We saw, our heads
Ringing under the stars we walked
To where it would have wet our feet
Had it been water

1975

CHARLES OLSON

From For Sappho Back

II
As blood is, as flesh can be
is she, self-housed, and moving
moving in impeccability to be
clear, clear to be
as, what is rhythm but
her limpidity?
        She
who is as certain as the morning is
when it arises, when it is spring, when, from wetness comes
   its brightness
as fresh as this beloved's fingers, lips
each new time she new turns herself to
tendernesses, she
turns her most objective, scrupulous attention, her own
self-causing
        each time it is,
        as is the morning, is
        the morning night and revelation of her
        nakednesses, new
        forever new, as fresh as is the scruple of her eye,
          the accurate
        kiss

III
If you would know what woman is, want
strength the reed of man unknows, forever
cannot know, look, look in these eyes, look
as she passes, on this moving thing, which moves
as grass blade by grass blade moves, as
syllable does throw might on fellow syllable, as,
in this rare creature, each hidden, each moving thing
is light to its known, unknown brother,
as objects stand one by one eye another, so
is this universe, this flow, this woman, these eyes
are sign

        1953

DENISE LEVERTOV

Overland to the Islands

Let's go—much as that dog goes,
intently haphazard. The
Mexican light on a day that
"smells like autumn in Connecticut"
makes iris ripples on his
black gleaming fur—and that too
is as one would desire—a radiance
consorting with the dance.
                    Under his feet
rocks and mud, his imagination, sniffing,
engaged in its perceptions—dancing
edgeways, there's nothing
the dog disdains on his way,
nevertheless he
keeps moving, changing
pace and approach but
not direction—"every step an arrival."

                                        1960

The Vron Woods (North Wales)

In the night's dream of day
the woods were fragrant.
Carapaced, slender, vertical,
          red in the slant
          fragmented light, uprose
Scotch firs,
boughs a vague smoke of
green.
          Underfoot
                    the slipping
of tawny needles.

I was wholly there,
aware of each step
in the hum of quietness,
each breath.

                Sunlight
    a net
                of discs and lozenges, holding
    odor of rosin.

    These were the Vron Woods,
                    felled
            seven years before I was born,

            levelled,
                    to feed a war.

                                                1982

                    HILDA MORLEY

                    Sea Lily

        Inside the sea-lily light
    stirs
            a vibration.
                            The pulse
    of water nourishing the flower

                                        outward

    it moves fluting
    the petals upward
                    A shudder
    of impulse   shaking
    it into a cup,
                a cup
    of fullness
                    taking
    from whatever passes
                            giving
    itself away

                                    Eilat, Israel, 1969

Fractal Amplifications

ALICE FULTON

In the 1970s, the mathematician Benoit Mandelbrot found that certain structures once thought to be "chaotic" contained a deep logic or pattern. The occurrence of earthquakes; the way our neurons fire when we search our memories; patterns of vegetation in a swamp; price jumps in the stock market; turbulence in the weather; the distribution of galaxies; and the flooding of the Nile are examples of chaotic structures found to contain fractal designs. Mandelbrot coined the word *fractal* (from the Latin *fractus,* meaning "broken or fragmented") to describe such configurations. Just as fractal science analyzed the ground between chaos and Euclidean order, fractal poetics could explore the field between gibberish and traditional forms. It could describe and make visible a third space: the nonbinary *in between.*

Scientist John H. Holland writes that complex systems possess "a dynamism" that is different from the static structure of a computer chip or snowflake, which are merely complicated. Complex systems are balanced on the edge of chaos, where the components "never quite lock in place, and yet never quite dissolve into turbulence either." A rain forest, the immune system, the economy, and a developing embryo are examples of complex adaptive systems. In poetics, Holland's "dynamism" makes itself felt in eccentric forms that share broad similarities, in contrast to received forms with specific similarities. On the ground between set forms and aimlessness, a poem can be spontaneous and adaptive— free to think on its feet rather than fulfill a predetermined scheme.

In a departure from Romantic ideals, fractal aesthetics suppose that spontaneous effects can be achieved through premeditated as well as ad libitum means. Thus "spontaneity" does not refer to a method of composition but to linguistic gestures that feel improvisatory to the reader. Riffing and jamming, rough edge and raw silk—such wet-paint effects take the form of asides, digressions, and sudden shifts in diction or tone. By such means "spontaneity" becomes a structural component of the poem.

Complex adaptive systems do not seek equilibrium or try to establish balance; they exist in unfolding and "never get there." As Holland says, "the space of possibilities is too vast; they have no practical way of finding the optimum." Like complex systems, fractal poetry exists within a vast array of potentialities: it is a maximalist aesthetic. Moreover, while a fractal poem might offer transcendence at the local level—in a line, a phrase—it does not try to create a sublime optimum throughout. Its high lyric passages might be juxtaposed with vulgar or parodic sections; its diction can range from gorgeous to caustic.

Complex systems tend to recycle their components. A rain forest, for instance, captures and reuses critical resources as a means of enriching itself. Fractal poetry likewise makes use of recurring words, lines, or stanzas as a means of creating depth. Unlike the villanelle or sestina's recycling, fractal repetition does not appear at a predetermined place within a set scheme. The poem is more dynamic, more turbulent and surprising, because its repetitions have an element of ambush. Readers experience the rhymic consolation of pattern without being able to anticipate the moment of return. Such recycling, at once spontaneous and reassuring, can occur throughout a poem, book, or body of work.

Holland's *Hidden Order* notes that when reading formal structures we decide to call some aspects irrelevant. We agree to ignore them. "This has the effect of collecting into a category things that differ only in the abandoned details." The form of Petrarchan sonnets, for instance, differs only in those structural aspects we choose to overlook. We focus on the identical rhyme scheme, the iambic pentameter, the "turn" at line 8. We examine properties that define the sonnet and disregard properties that fall outside of this definition. Fractal poetics are composed of the discarded details. Diction, surface textures, irregular meters, shifts of genre, tonal variations, and punctuation are regarded as defining formal elements. Function words (articles, conjunctions, prepositions) take center stage and assume schematic importance. The gender of pronouns and the relation of foreground and background provide a formal means of addressing issues of power and hierarchy. The meanings of form—form's subversive or reactionary possibilities—are recognized rather than denied.

Poetry in received forms can be likened to standard mathematics (calculus, say, or linear analysis) in which the value of the parts adds up to the value of the whole. That is, the strength of a metered poem's lines add up to the poem's strength as a whole. The disjunctive shifts of fractal poetry, however, are akin to nonlinear interactions in which the value of the whole cannot be predicted by summing the strength of its parts. A fractal poem might contain purposely insipid or vulgar lines that would be low in value when decontextualized. When juxtaposed with other inclusions, however, these debased lines create a friction or frame that adds up to something more than their discrete presence would predict.

The form of complex adaptive systems is determined by internal models. In like fashion, the fractal poem's growth and resolution are activated by the poem's self-determined imperatives rather than by adherence to a traditional scheme. But how does the inner imperative of fractal verse differ from the organic form of free verse? Both organic and fractal form compare poetry to living creatures in the natural world. Organic form, however, extends this prizing of nature to replications of the "natural" speaking voice. Fractal poetry, in contrast, regards voice as a construct: a consciously made assemblage of dictions, meters, rhetorics, gestures, and tones. Organicism insists upon wholeness and smoothness of thought. Fractal poetry regards interruption, artifice, discontinuity, and raggedness as facets of its formal vocabulary. In practice, these differences mean that the textures of fractal poetry will be more various and colorful than those of organic free verse. A fractal poem might establish iambic pentameter only to break it with purposely discordant effects. It locates structure in disruption and allows new forms to emerge as the poem proceeds.

In organic verse, the poem's language is meant to vanish into transparency. In fractal verse, the surface is refracted in order to make its linguistic presence more evident. As free verse broke the pentameter, fractal verse breaks the poem plane. It does so by means of clashing dictions, tones, or meters; by effects of typography, lineation, or punctuation. In some cases, the poem's shifting densities create a linguistic screen that alternately dissolves and clouds. We gaze through transparent lines and are rebounded to the surface by more textured language. This modulating depth of field allows us to experience the poem as a construct of varying focal lengths.

The motion of reading is horizontal and vertical: our eyes skim across and edge down the flat planes of print. We experience the text in two dimensions. A fractal poem, however, can create depth perception by means of shifting linguistic plates. Transparent language becomes negative space, while textured effects have the solidity of positive space. Planes of varying textures move the reader into and out of the poem, as if it were a sculptural field of three dimensions. Such palpable architectonics also create an awareness of the poem as thing-in-itself rather than proxy for meaning.

As soon as one begins to analyze or dissect a poem's formal components, the poem is no longer organic or "whole." This is why organicism seems the antithesis of formalism. And it explains why organic free verse never developed a vocabulary with which to describe its formal properties. Although fractal poetry does not adhere to a predetermined scheme, it offers a terminology (planes, surface, textures, transparency, opacity, obverse, understory . . .) that is descriptive of its structure.

It is difficult to exemplify a maximalist poetics by means of short poems. The effect of recycling, for instance, might be apparent only over the entire span of a poet's work. (Dickinson's recurring vocabulary comes to mind.) Each of the following brief poems offers a partial illustration. Kathleen Halme insouciantly breaks the tonal range of the high lyric. Lawrence Joseph recycles, transposes genres, and refracts the language of commerce with Romantic transparency. Rather than the regular measures of formalism, W. D. Snodgrass composes a carnivalesque of swiveling rhythms and dictions that juxtapose Shakespeare to the blues, French courtly love to street rhymes. In C. D. Wright's "Girl Friend," halting caesuras favor the content and power of the splice over the resolve.

Yet rather than map existing territories, I hope these remarks might suggest future landscapes for fractal poetry. I leave the compass of its location to you.

KATHLEEN HALME

A Celibate Imagination

Hi! I don't care about your actual uncle
in his skull and sweet snuff,
the rat-eyed rat in his root cellar
and real spots on his beeches,
red spruces, and papery birches.
I, too, could love his ethnic ink.

Where does your imagination make love
with the world that's always anyway you?
When you abandon the restoration of the real,
wrap cords around the necks of power tools,
where does your imagination rain,
over Uncle Anton's miter box?

O sad times washed in acid!
You can't help but live inside your life,
even when you step outside
in stockings oily with lanolin
of the sheep that bore them,
even when you step outside in horror.

1995

LAWRENCE JOSEPH

Under a Spell

Now the governor of the Federal Reserve Bank
doesn't know how much more he can take
while my thoughts wander outside me and can't be grasped—
I'm under a spell. While the prisoners
on Death Row whose brain cells will reach
the point of boiling water during electrocution
receive blessings through cable television
and Presidents and Commissars devise
international house-cleanings
history won't recognize for years,
the precedence of language and image preoccupies me too
under the influence of a spell.
Under a spell you have to remember
Monday morning of the insurrection,
the body in the ruins of Stanley's
Patent Medicine Store on John R
a block away from Joseph's Market,
when we argued time and space and memory are the same,
worked at The Rouge or The Axle,
read essays by an activist monk on non-violence
unaware of the strains we placed on our souls,
skies always choked by gray clouds
moving at different speeds, slag piled
pink and black at the end of the streets.
Under a spell paradise opens again,
a labyrinth. The vistas down the cross streets
are slabs of sun. The confused time
we cried in each other's arms.
Returning at the end of the suffering
to myself who loves no one. Returning
years later to that smoky twilight, still easy to find,
the breezes and sea smells from the Hudson
unexpectedly surrounding us, your eyes
unusually blue. Only you—with whom I can't pretend—
see everything go through me. Nothing's said
when you turn and look through me.

1993

W. D. SNODGRASS

The Carnival Girl Darkly Attracts W. D.

O she does teach the torches to burn bright
    As a rich jewel in an Ethiop's ear.
        Romeo,
        Romeo,
      Ró me o-ver
      In the clo-ver
    Besides, what would I say to her?
Belle qui tient ma vie
In this capture of your eyes.
      And would her mother let her out?
        And then? And then? And then?
Even as a common Italian young woman
Loaned her fresh visage to the holy mysteries,
So here, St. Anne, who's next to the Madonna,
    Donna?—that has to maybe be her name.
A glove, that I might touch that cheek
      Ham and eggs
      Between your legs;
      Mine's got meat with gravy.
Je suis aymé by her whose beauty
Surpasseth all the wonders of the earth.
      She says she ain't nice
    And what she's doing here is working.
      hath Dian's wit
And in strong proof of chastity well armed . . .
      Two and two's four; five and four's nine.
    I can piss in yours; you can't piss in mine.
Beauty too rich for use, for earth too dear.
      They were only playing leapfrog
    So Nelly, keep your belly close to mine.

             1993

C. D. WRIGHT

Girl Friend

When I first saw her a few summers ago I felt.
            Her photogenic spit.
I was climbing a coruscating staircase.
In my flammable skin. To be so full of.
Everything. At her age. It is very difficult.
A singer manqué. Among a small host of poets.
            Noisier
than the men. Quaffing schnapps. No lens
could describe her.
            Shoulders. Hands.
Such longings: Errant. Verdant.
To have a good time. And dream. In one's own
country. The lack. Of. Everything.
The confusion. It is very difficult. One needs.
One's own set of golden books. What if.
A ladder were. Miraculous. Extended. Across
a nursery for new stars.
            And then.

for nina

1996

Performance Poetry

BOB HOLMAN

A blank page! now there's a performance poem! as into your ears the poem rushes. Head lifts, eyes follow sound, poet's in front of you, crazy motions in a costume with CD-playback blazing, on Rollerblades of course, fer shure: Performance Poem. Dissolve to eyes back to book, now text-covered.

Poetry began as an oral art, so one can only admire the success of the book in spreading the word. Otherwise, there would be a couple chapters in *this* book on "text poetry" and the rest devoted to the many forms of performance—there are at least as many kinds of "performance poetry" as there are of music, say, your classical, jazz, rock 'n' roll, blues, contemporary, mood, swing, country, western, and hip-hop, which is today's most influential form of performance poetry, the one that opened the ears of popular culture, allowing poetry that had always surrounded us to be heard as art. (See Raymond Patterson for blues, Tracie Morris for hip-hop, and DJ Renegade for rap.)

Of course, for the performance poetry "examples" we should include a CD or videotape or send you to a website. Or, drop by your house and read you the poem!

A performance poem is a poem written to be performed before an audience, Anne Waldman once told me, and I believe her. But as a poets' theater director who has taken as a challenge to produce the unproduceable play, such as Artaud's *Jet of Blood,* I must add: any poem deemed unperformable simply awaits the poet/performer with appropriate vision. And most of the poets who write what I would call performance poetry do not write exclusively for the stage, but do acknowledge the multitasking possibilities of a poem. As text, as performed live, as recorded on film or audio- or videotape, via HTML on the Net, it's still a poem, the poem. Those who scoff at performance poetry as simply using live performance skills to hide a poorly written poem haven't learned to trust their ears as much as their eyes.

The distinctions between performance poem and song; poem and performance art piece; performance, poem, and monologue are all debatable and generally have everything to do with the poet or performer's intent. Poetry's becoming an endangered species, I believe, had everything to do with the neglecting of live performance, and its current renaissance is due in large part to the acceptance of the live presentation of the poem as the performance twin of text. The moment when Allen Ginsberg, Jack Kerouac, Gregory Corso, Bob Kaufman, David Amram, and other Beats fueled a café culture with poetry readings was critical for the preparation of today's renaissance, but this is only one strand in a broad weave of performance aesthetics.

Unlike other forms in this book, the nature of performance makes the lineage impossible to trace. Perf is evanescent.

So, a few sitings of the invisible.

Say you start with Homer, great oral poet: "Bring on the blind guy," as Ed Sanders says. Indeed, many literary conceits that critics once saw as giving aesthetic dimension to *The Iliad* and *Odyssey* have been revealed as mnemonic devices to keep the poem flow. In *Poetry as Performance,* Gregory Nagy describes the process of texts altering as performance-driven oral practitioners improvised. Such evolutions from the "original" take on the dimensions of Darwin and the dynamics of the history of literature in its entirety. The troubadours of the Middle Ages passed on their epics in this fashion (of special interest is Meg Bogin's *The Women Troubadours*) as many oral bards of the Balkans still do.

Or start with the griot, or more properly, the jali traditions of African poetry. Here the poet is the chief's right-hand, power player: keeper of the history, still a way of life in many tribes. Yassou N'Dour, great pop singer, is in fact a Senegalese jali. The call-and-response of gospel, the boasting repartee of the dozens that underlies much of rap, the chants and drummings, all are elements of African oral poetry that live on in contemporary performance poetry.[1]

Perhaps begin with American Indian shamans, songmakers, healers, chanters—these poets, imbued with spirituality and trickster shenanigans, create with language as changer and keeper of the flame. Again, the move of the poet into ritual is common to many cultures, and continues today.[2]

In 1998, teahouse "rappers" in China were heard in Beijing again, accompanied by clacking sticks. China did not have an epic tradition, but Confucius collected *The Book of Songs* (trans. Waley, or Pound's *Confucian Odes*) as one of the five elemental texts, poems that were passed on orally in all regions of China.

During the First World War, poets who were stung with their inability to compete with the new technology's lock on absurdity (machine guns, tanks, bombs) used their own bodies as the art, or antiart. Modern performance poetry began. It was born of dada, which begat surrealism. The futurist performer poets of Russia would help bring on the Revolution; the futurist performer poets of Italy would hold the Fascists in highest regard. These avant-garde movements all broke down the classical/Romantic modes of poetry, and showed the way to modernism. Yet in the United States, in this century, the idea that poetry could exist in or as performance was so heretical that a whole genre, the performance art movement of the 1980s, occurred with no acknowledgment of the poets who had begun it.[3]

Now there are so many varieties of performance in orbit that I only have room for a list: strands of performance poetry in United States, not exhaustive I am sure, and many poets could be found in more than one position in the taxonomy:

- Music and Poetry. Let's start with The Last Poets and Gil Scott-Heron. With subsets of jazz (Amiri Baraka, Jayne Cortez, Sekou Sundiata, Quincy Troupe, Kenny Carroll, DJ Renegade), rock (Capt. Beefheart, Lou Reed, Patti Smith, David Thomas, Tom Waits, John Trudell, Maggie Estep, Jim Carroll, Jessica Hagedorn, Reggie Gibson, Wammo), pop/opera (Kenward Elmslie), country western (Paul Zarzyski), gospel (Carl Hancock Rux). The Cambodian poet U Sam Oeur has created his own style of singing in Khmer that seems to come straight from the statues at Angkor Wat. And any reading by Rev. Pedro Pietri, including appearances by his condom cross and his "Help Me! I Can See!" basket and his hymnlike sing-alongs have a one-of-a-kind musicality.
- Sound poetry/multivoice. Practitioners like Ernst Jandl, John Giorno, the 4 Horseman, Jaap Blonk, Jerome Rothenberg, Julie Patton, Floom, AWOL, Edwin Torres, whose work emanates from the dada-surreal-futurist nexus. Larry Goodell has been costuming himself for decades; Bern Porter's Found'n'-Sound are a direct link to Breton. Emily XYZ and Myers Bartlett, and Cyn Salach and Sheila Donohue, perform bravura duets in their own distinct styles.
- Dub poetry. A reggae poetics, from the Caribbean and particularly Jamaica, exemplified here by Linton Kwesi Johnson. Includes toasting. Michael Smith, Jean Binta Breeze, Benjamin Zephaniah, Mutabaruka, Everton Sylvester.
- Slam. The mock Olympics of poetry has created a form that clocks in under three minutes and penalizes the use of props and costumes—and, more importantly, a community of poets who have democratized an art that was suffocating under a false perception of elitism. Originated by Marc Smith at the

Green Mill Tavern in Chicago, this bare knuckles poetic for-
mat may be a form that includes such techniques as memoriza-
tion, raucousness, and powerful presentation. The wildwoman
humor of Beth Lisick, the rants of Justin Chin, the drop-dead
absurdity of Jeff McDaniel, the polished knife of Gayle Dan-
ley, all come at us from the dynamo that is slam.
- Cowboy. The Annual Cowboy Poetry Gathering in Elko,
Nevada, is the largest poetry festival in the United States.
Poets like Paul Zarzyski, Baxter Black, Wallace McRae, Sue
Wallis, Waddie Mitchell, and Vess Quinlan read before ten
thousand people. Through the art of recitation, these poets
make their history a living thing; indeed, the whole cowboy
way of life survives in their work.
- Audio, film, and video poetry. Translations to other media are
keeping poetry alive, and, in fact, inspiring the opposite arts to
get with the program. Kurt Heintz exemplifies a poet-with-a-
camera aesthetic. Jean Howard has also done amazing work in
this medium, as have the amazing collaborations of Cathy
Bowman/Andy Biskin and Walter Lew/Lewis Klahr and Cathy
Cook/Shakespeare. John Giorno, through his performances
and pioneering Dial-A-Poem label, began presenting audio po-
etries.
- Political Heart. The "straight" readings of Sonia Sanchez,
Adrienne Rich, Martin Espada, Luis Rodriguez, Sherman
Alexie, Jenny Lim, Michelle T. Clinton, Willie Perdomo always
blaze with performance. Is there a link? What if politicians
spoke poetry?
- ASL. Of course, to the Deaf, the only reading is a perfor-
mance, and the gestural language called American Sign re-
quires a video camera to publish. When Peter Cook, a deaf
poet, and Kenny Lerner, a hearing poet who signs, perform as
Flying Words, the worlds and words collide.
- Trance. A pure performance style, with practitioners as diverse
as Wanda Coleman, who uses a deep political scour, Janet
Hamill, whose hallucinatory work is reminiscent of Rimbaud,
and Saul Williams, who orbits hip-hop to land on his own
turntable globe.
- Personae. Slam champ Patricia Smith creates characters in her
poems—hear the voice of a white supremacist skinhead come
from the mouth of this black woman. Dael Orlandersmith
takes this a step further by creating solo plays of characters
linked by her poems as delivered by herself as poet.

• Web poetry. When you land on a website where the words dance, colors blaze, and meanings flip, I'd say we're in the realm of performance.

Anthropologists count as oral literature only that which has never been written down, when in fact, any time a poem is read aloud it is oral literature. Even that lovely past- and present-tense verb *read* contains both the act of "reading silently to oneself" and "reading aloud." It is performance, the acceptance of the poem aloud as the poem, not as a rendition of the poem, that is the driving force in the rediscovery of this art as a mainstay of our culture, not a game of Clue for footnote addicts.

How you decide to perform is up to you. But if you perform, the landscape of the poetry reading needs to be treated with the same focus that you apply to make the page a proper setting for text. Poetry will into the world, and when you read, you engage both the art and the world's eye and ear. Poetry says no censorship, no compromise with the art. Performance poetry, ultimately, is the missing link in MacLeish's "Ars Poetica" dictum that it not mean but be. Coleman Barks says he found Rumi when Robert Bly told him to "let him out of his cage." Unleashing a poem on stage should have the impact that a great poem has on you when you read it to yourself.

SAPPHO

Translated by Mary Barnard, 1958

Tell everyone

Now, today, I shall
Sing beautifully for
My friends' pleasure

KURT SCHWITTERS

Simultaneous Poem

kaa   gee   dee

kaa gee dee	take pak	tapekek
katedraale	take	tape
draale	takepak	kek kek
kaa tee dee	takepak	tapekek

| kateedralle | take | tape |
| draale | takepak | kek kek |

(all:)	oowenduumiir	
kaa tee dee	diimaan	tapekek
kateedraale	diimaan	tape
draale	diimaan	kek kek

didiimaan	————	didiimaan
	diimaan	
(all:)	aawanduumiir	

1919

PATRICIA SMITH

Skinhead

They call me skinhead, and I got my own beauty.
It is knife-scrawled across my back in sore, jagged letters,
It's in the way my eyes snap away from the obvious.
I sit in my dim matchbox,
on the edge of a bed tousled with my ragged smell,
slide razors across my hair,
count how many ways
I can bring blood closer to the surface of my skin.
These are the duties of the righteous,
the ways of the anointed.

The face that moves in my mirror is huge and pockmarked,
scraped pink and brilliant, apple-cheeked,
I am filled with my own spit.
Two years ago, a machine that slices leather
sucked in my hand and held it,
whacking off three fingers at the root.
I didn't feel nothing till I looked down
and saw one of them on the floor
next to my boot heel,
and I ain't worked since then.

I sit here and watch niggers take over my TV set,
walking like kings up and down the sidewalks in my head,
walking like their fat black mamas *named* them freedom.

My shoulders tell me that ain't right.
So I move out into the sun
where my beauty makes them lower their heads,
or into the night
with a lead pipe up my sleeve,
a razor tucked in my boot.
I was born to make things right.

It's easy now to move my big body into shadows,
to move from a place where there was nothing
into the stark circle of a streetlight,
the pipe raised up high over my head.
It's a kick to watch their eyes get big,
round and gleaming like cartoon jungle boys,
right in that second when they know
the pipe's gonna come down, and I got this thing
I like to say, listen to this, I like to say
"Hey, nigger, Abe Lincoln's been dead a long time."

I get hard listening to their skin burst.
I was born to make things right.

Then this newspaper guy comes around,
seems I was a little sloppy kicking some fag's ass
and he opened his hole and screamed about it.
This reporter finds me curled up in my bed,
those TV flashes licking my face clean.
Same ol' shit.
Ain't got no job, the coloreds and spics got 'em all.
Why ain't I working? Look at my hand, asshole.
No, I ain't part of no organized group,
I'm just a white boy who loves his race,
fighting for a pure country.
Sometimes it's just me. Sometimes three. Sometimes 30.
AIDS will take care of the faggots,
then it's gon be white on black in the streets.
Then there'll be three million.
I tell him that.

So he writes it up
and I come off looking like some kind of freak,
like I'm Hitler himself. I ain't that lucky,
but I got my own beauty.
It is in my steel-toed boots,
in the hard corners of my shaved head.

I look in the mirror and hold up my mangled hand,
only the baby finger left, sticking straight up,
I know it's the wrong goddamned finger,
but fuck you all anyway.
I'm riding the top rung of the perfect race,
my face scraped pink and brilliant.
I'm your baby, America, your boy,
drunk on my own spit, I am goddamned fuckin' beautiful.

And I was born

and raised

right here.

                                                                    1992

JEROME ROTHENBERG

A Poem about a Wolf Maybe Two Wolves

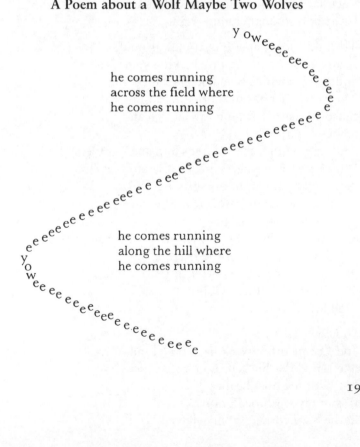

                                                                    1972

LINTON KWESI JOHNSON

Yout Scene

last satdey
I neva dey pan no faam,
so I decide fe tek a walk
doun a BRIXTON,
an see wha gwane.

de bredrin dem stan-up
outside a HIP CITY,
as usual, a look pretty;
dem a laaf big laaf
dem a talk dread talk
dem a shuv an shuffle dem feet,
soakin in de sweet MUSICAL BEAT.

but when nite come
policeman run dem dung;
beat dem dung a grung,
kick dem ass,
sen dem pass justice
to prison walls of gloom.

but de bredda dem a scank;
dem naw rab bank;
is packit dem a pick
an is woman dem a lick
an is run dem a run de WICKED come.

1975

BOB HOLMAN

Performance Poem

Voices. Voices. Listen, my heart, as only
saints have listened; until the gigantic call lifted them
off the ground; yet they kept on, impossibly,
kneeling and didn't notice at all:
so complete was their listening.

—Rilke

He's diving off the front of the stage!
You better bring the house lights up some
The audience can't see him.
He's still screaming, screaming and
Dancing and he's twirling the mic—
I dunno, should we turn off the mic?
I dunno, turn it up?
He's running around, he's twirling and
He's still like reading
The book is in his hands, sort of, the people
Seem to like it, they're into it
Maybe it's part of the act

If it's part of the act he shoulda told us
Now he's in the back of the house—he's
Still going strong. This is pretty
Amazing. I've never seen anything
Like this! He's running out
Of the theater—I can still hear him screaming
In the lobby. He's back in the house!
What's he saying—it's something about
It sounds like "lake snore freedom"
I dunno. "Breaking down reason"?
Oh shit! Oh shit oh shit—he's got a gun!

Christ! wait—oh shit, it's just one of those pop guns,
It shoots like firecrackers or popcorn or—
What about the hat? He's still wearing the hat.
Holy—he's dying now, I mean he's acting like that,
Like he's dying. This is it for poetry in this house man,
I've had it.

He's just lying there.
The audience is wailing, they're keening
You know, like at a wake. No, I do not think
He's dead. He's getting back up, see, I told
You, it's all part of the act.

It's all part of the end of the world.
What am I, the guy's father?
Come here! Look at the monitor yourself
He's ditched the mic somewhere,
Should I go get the mic?
Look! oh my God—he's, what's it called,

He's going up, he's levitating!
Holy shit! The roof, the roof is going up
Music is coming in
The crowd's up outta the chairs, man this is it
This is it I'm telling you,
Raising the fucking roof is what he's doing
Now he's back on the stage with his poetry stuff
Yeah heh heh yeah,

He never left the stage
It's what his poem was about
I'm just saying what he's saying
Through the headset
Yeah he's good
He's pretty good alright
But I could write something like that
Anybody could write something like that

NOTES

1. See CD and book *Jali Kunda: Griots of West Africa and Beyond* (Ellipsis Arts, 1996).
2. See Jerome Rothenberg, *Shaking the Pumpkin: Traditional Poetry of the Indian North Americas* (Albuquerque: University of New Mexico Press, 1991).
3. See Robert Motherwell, *The Dada Painters and Poets: An Anthology* (New York: Wittenborn, Schultz 1951); *Hans Richter, Dada: Art and Anti-Art* (New York: McGraw-Hill, 1965); Michael Kirby, *Futurist Performance* (New York: Dutton, 1971); Michael Benedikt and George E. Wellwarth, *Modern French Theater* (New York: Dutton, 1964).

Beyond Found Poetry

KEITH TUMA

It's all found of course, or none of it is, or not in the way the naive might believe, as if they'd stumbled into poetry, Bashō's frog come out of the pond and plop into their lap—or "ploop" as Frank O'Hara would have it. There it is, one can imagine somebody thinking, some language, a chunk of text, pithy or more likely absurd, announcing itself as "poem." Sure, we'll invent such a reader if we can't find her, somebody before or after concept, unprepared to see that what's at issue here are the conventions and frames of reading, of the poetic.

Found poetry would seem most often to refer not to a form but to an epiphenomenon of process and procedure. It signals, ironically or otherwise, the obdurate materiality of our creative and interpretive processes. As such, it is subject to, names as inevitable, historical contingency. What counts as "the poetic" is its only question, its triumph the dispersal of the question itself into occasion and context. What might have been taken for ordinary by somebody else turns out to be extraordinary, or is it the other way around? Intellectual slapstick hovering between irony-cum-condescension and the folky thumb in your sophisticated eye: this would outline only its most familiar shapes and effects, as in the work of Jonathan Williams.

One prime site for plundering language that is to be presented as if it were "found poetry" is the road sign. Another would be a mis-Englished advertisement. Often the genre shades into concrete poetry or, alternatively, other art forms altogether. It is as if one wants to resist the ephemerality of the sign that the genre recognizes and insists upon. So that, for instance, in a book by one Mason Williams including what I'd like to call failed or weak examples, a road sign is photographed. As if the poet said, "Just in case you don't believe that I found this incredibly banal pun here's a picture!" The words—"Frog Bayou Relief"—might have been enough.[1] Buy you relief indeed. Life is hard for the frog in Louisiana.

Now to exit quickly by pointing out the obvious and offering a qualification: this is in the spirit of the genre. All poetry's "found" in the sense that Virgil sits on Homer and Catullus on Sappho, but perhaps never have we been so self-consciously derivative or belated as in the vanished twentieth century, which had inclusiveness and historical pastiche among its signatures. With the museums and archives of other art forms stuffed full of collage and assemblage, musique concrète and sampling, poetry's relationship to the "found" in the twentieth century is hardly unique. But the "found" in poetry has shaded into textuality and intertextuality to such a degree that it hardly makes sense to identify "found poetry" except by the most stringent and ultimately arbitrary eliminations. The high seriousness of Pound's Malatesta Cantos or Peter Riley's *Excavations* includes the use of "found," nonpoetic material, as do many other poetic texts; cutting and pasting and in Riley's case the "treating" of preexisting, nonpoetic texts has everywhere been central to poetic innovation. And if it's something other than high seriousness you're looking for, you might ponder the found poem as purportedly overheard conversation. Consider Jonathan Williams's "Aunt Dory Ellis, of Penland, Remembers When She Fell in Her Garden at the Home Place and Broke Her Hip in 19 and 56":

> the sky was high,
> white clouds passing
> by, I lay
> a hour in that petunia patch
>
> hollered,
> and knew I was out of whack[2]

Williams will be seen to have worked these lines to bump up their sonic effects, their pacing and rhyming. I don't know anything about Aunt Dory, and there's no finding her anymore than there's any finding a "found poetry."

Nevertheless, one still hears tell of "found poetry," just as I am slipping into an idiom. Indeed, the words usually seem to refer to an idiom self-consciously represented as "other." Or sometimes what is meant seems to be the use of a "form" not first or often associated with the poetic, such as the grocery list or the things-to-do-on-ship Gary Snyder text. Even here, though, it is harder and harder lately to determine just when one is dealing with "found" text or, instead, with what one might call a "mock-found" text, or something "beyond found poetry." I am thinking for instance of one section of Charles Bernstein's "Emotions of Normal People" that appears to be a consumer survey run amok.[3] What is interesting about that poem is that some of its collage of idioms and (mostly but not entirely) "nonpoetic" forms and formulaic discourses— the aforementioned survey, the software manual—seem "left alone as found," while others are clearly inhabited as forms to be mocked and/or used. In the end I cannot say which if any are exactly found and which are created to sound like, say, the consumer survey. You don't have to be Jean Baudrillard to understand that a simple opposition between the real and the fictive, the poetic and the ordinary has been altogether trashed. For that reason—because of that destabilization, the collapse of the "reality effect" I associate with the most conventional found poetry, the disappearance of "reality" into multiple simulacra—it doesn't make sense to me to call the Bernstein poem "found poetry" any more than it does to call the Malatesta Cantos "found poetry."

The same might be said of the example I have included from section 13 of Randolph Healy's *Scales*. The language there seems obviously borrowed from an undertaker's manual. The heavy blocks of black ink interspersed among this language might be read any number of ways—as iconic representation of the inert body meeting the embalming process, or as indicating edited or rejected text. (Maybe these two among the options available are the same thing. This is not the place for a full or even preliminary "interpretation" of what is after all only a selection from a longer poem.) What interests me about this example in the context of a discussion of the "found" and the "treated" or the "beyond found" is the text's last line: "Some manuals suggest using Superglue to keep orifices closed." When I first read this, I was sure that this must be entirely fabrication, Healy's own grotesquely comic addendum. Now I am not so sure. Might it not instead indicate something suggested in manuals "like" the one seemingly used here? Alas, that "like" says it all. It is entirely possible that the foregoing text is not "found" at all but an "imitation" of the language of an embalming manual. These days, you never know what you've found. These days, you never know what's "found." Not much of a difference there. One might well be nostalgic for stricter definition. We will have to do without it.

JONATHAN WILLIAMS

**Three Graffiti in the Vicinity of
The Mikado Baptist Church,
Deep in Nacoochee Valley**

bulldogs
        stamp out
    dragon fire

•

PEACHES HEAR

•

pleeze
vot fer lindin

1985

ELIZABETH ALEXANDER

The Dirt-Eaters

"Southern Tradition of Eating Dirt Shows Signs of Waning"
—headline, New York *Times*, 2/14/84

tra
dition
wanes
I read
from North
ern South:
D.C.

Never ate
dirt
but I lay
on Great-
grandma's
grave
when I
was small.

"Most cultures
have passed
through
a phase
of earth-
eating
most pre
valent today
among
Southern
black
women."

*Geo
ghagy:*
the practice
of eating
earthy matter
esp. clay
or chalk.

(Shoe-
boxed dirt
shipped North
to kin)

The gos
sips said
that my great-
grand
ma got real
pale when she
was preg
nant:

"Musta ate
chalk,
Musta ate
starch, cuz
why else
did her
babies
look
so white?"

The Ex
pert: "In ano
ther gener
ation I
sus
pect it will dis
appear al
together."

Miss Fannie Glass
of Creuger, Miss.:
"I wish
I had

some dirt
right now."

Her smile
famili
ar as the
smell
of
dirt.

1990

RANDOLPH HEALY

XIII *from* Scales

The body is placed in the proper position with the arms laid over the stomach.

██████████ washed ████ disinfected.

██████ shaved ████████

The eyes are closed. A small curved plastic disc called an "eye cap" placed under the eyelid. Perforations in the cap ████ hold the eye lid in place.

The mouth is closed. (A specially designed "tack" is placed in the upper and in the lower jaw. Each tack has a fine wire attached. By twisting the two wires together, the jaw is thus closed and the lips are set to the natural lip line ███████
████████████████████

An incision is made over the carotid or the femoral artery.

A tube is inserted ████████ A slightly larger tube ██████
████████████████ to a hose to the sewer system.

The fluid is injected into the artery under pressure. As the blood is displaced ██████████ it is forced out ██████████ and disposed of. The pressure forces the embalming fluid into the capillaries and ██████ to the cells of the body. ████
██████████████████████████████████

(Never rush your work, as this can lead to swelling in the face which is impossible to fix and is frequently the cause of criticism from the deceased's relatives. Steady, low-pressure injection of embalming fluids, with frequent drainage is crucial.)

The tubes are removed and the incision sutured.

The thoracic cavity is filled with an approved cavity filler if the chest is sunken. The lungs are re-aspirated and the windpipe corked.

Pressure due to gaseous build up must be frequently relieved by opening the anal vent. (Ensure none of the mourners are present.)

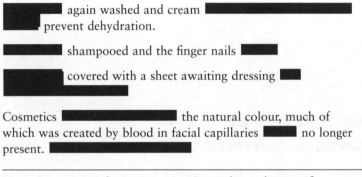

████████ again washed and cream ██████████████ prevent dehydration.

████████ shampooed and the finger nails ████

████████ covered with a sheet awaiting dressing ██

Cosmetics ████████████ the natural colour, much of which was created by blood in facial capillaries ████ no longer present. ██████████████

Note: Some manuals suggest using Superglue to keep orifices closed.

NOTES

1. See Mason Williams, *The Mason Williams Reading Matter* (New York: Doubleday, 1969).

2. See Jonathan Williams, *Blues and Roots/ Rue and Bluets: A Garland for the Southern Appalachians* (Durham, N.C.: Duke University Press, 1985).

3. "Emotions of Normal People" is in *Dark City* (Los Angeles: Sun and Moon, 1994). The passage or "consumer survey" I am discussing here as "found" begins as follows: "Which best describes your dress size? What brands of bar soap have been in your household in the past six months? Which of the following hypoallergenic products are currently being used in your household? Which of the following best describes the sensitivity of your skin?" While this language clearly seems lifted or found, perhaps edited and combined—the multiple-choice answers removed—the language from another section seems equally so until in the end we find one of Bernstein's favorite words inserted—"dysraphism," a technical term for a congenital disease that he has taken up and transformed as a word of his poetics, meaning in his lexicon a troubling of stress, pitch, and rhythm: "You don't have to be a victim of loneliness, depression, 'mid-life' crisis, indecisiveness, or regrets. Free up your ability to grow and change as you learn the emotional and social skills you need to be intimate and passionate. Write The Dysraphism Center for more Information."

The List Poem

DAVID LEHMAN

The poem in the form of a catalog or inventory has held a particular attraction for modern poets. With free verse triumphant over stanzaic forms and metrical restraints, poets needed new principles for organizing and unifying a poem. Walt Whitman's amazing list poems in *Leaves of Grass*—"The Sleepers," for example, and the section of "Song of Myself" beginning "The pure contralto sings in the organloft"—initiate an American tradition. ("It is only a list," Randall Jarrell wrote of that passage from "Song of Myself." "But what a list!") The list emerged as a form commensurate with Whitman's vision of American demographics and "democratic vistas." In Whitman's lists, diversity replaces hierarchy as a structural principle, while simultaneity substitutes for narrative cause-and-effect. Whitman favored parallel constructions for his long, loose lines:

> The groups of newly-come immigrants cover the wharf
>   or levee.
> The woollypates hoe in the sugarfield, the overseer views
>   them from his saddle;
> The bugle calls in the ballroom, the gentlemen run for their
>   partners, the dancers bow to each other;
> The youth lies awake in the cedar-roofed garret and harks to
>   the musical rain,
> The Wolverine sets traps on the creek that helps fill
>   the Huron,
> The reformer ascends the platform, he spouts with his mouth
>   and nose,

And again:

> The bride unrumples her white dress, the minutehand of the
>   clock moves slowly,
> The opium eater reclines with rigid head and just-opened
>   lips,

The prostitute draggles her shawl, her bonnet bobs on her
  tipsy and pimpled neck,
The crowd laugh at her blackguard oaths, the men jeer and
  wink to each other,
(Miserable! I do not laugh at your oaths nor jeer you,)
The President holds a cabinet council, he is surrounded by
  the great secretaries,
On the piazza walk five friendly matrons with twined arms;

1855

The syntax itself reinforces the governing idea of equality—the president no better than the opium eater, the prostitute equal to the bride ("For every atom belonging to me as good belongs to you"). The subordination of the field-workers to the overseer is reversed in the order of clauses. And the individual self is superior to the crowd, morally if not in force of arms. The freshness of childish wonderment informs Whitman's lists. As Jarrell exclaimed, "How inexhaustibly interesting the world is to Whitman!"

The modern popularity of the list poem should not obscure its lineage, which goes back to the Bible and Homeric epic. W. H. Auden once devised a test for critics. Only someone who likes—"and by like I mean really like, not approve of on principle"—Old Testament genealogies and the catalogue of ships in *The Iliad* could pass Auden's test. Rabelais's *Gargantua and Pantagruel* is an extravaganza of lists. The seventeenth-century poet Robert Herrick, in "The Argument of His Booke," uses the list poem to fulfill the function of a table of contents:

I sing of times trans-shifting; and I write
How roses first came red, and lilies white.
I write of groves, of twilights, and I sing
The court of Mab, and of the Faerie-King.

1648

The description of Belinda's toilette is a list poem embedded in Alexander Pope's *The Rape of the Lock*.

Christopher Smart's ode to his cat Jeoffry (often exerpted as "For I will consider my cat Jeoffry" from *Jubilate Agno*) is among the most beloved list poems in English literature. The poem illustrates the efficacy of anaphora (i.e., the repetition of an element, in this case the word *for*, at the beginning of each line) as a rhetorical device ideally suited to link the disparate clauses or images that make up a list:

For he is of the tribe of Tiger.

For the Cherub cat is a term of the Angel Tiger.

For he has the subtlety and hissing of a serpent, which in
   goodness he suppresses.

For he will not do destruction if he is well-fed, neither will he
   spit without provocation.

For he purrs in thankfulness, when God tells him he's a
   good cat.

For he is an instrument for the children to learn
   benevolence upon.

For every house is incomplete without him & a blessing is
   lacking in the spirit.

For the Lord commanded Moses concerning the cats at the
   departure of the Children of Israel from Egypt.

For every family had one cat at least in the bag.

For the English cats are the best in Europe.

                                                    1757–63

The list allows for points of view zoological, empirical, pedagogical,
biblical, and even nationalistic.

The special example of the Ten Commandments provides the model
for the satiric or ironic decalogues given by Lord Byron in *Don Juan*
(Canto 1, stanzas 205 and 206) and by W. H. Auden in "Under Which
Lyre." Byron's list of pleasures earlier in Canto 1 of *Don Juan* (stanzas
122 through 127) is a brilliant instance of lyric aria interrupting narra-
tive flow:

>   Sweet to the miser are his glittering heaps,
>   Sweet to the father is his first-born's birth,
>   Sweet is revenge—especially to women—
>   Pillage to soldiers, prize-money to seamen.
>
>   1819

Kenneth Koch championed the list poem in his writing classes at
Columbia and again in the public school classes that formed the basis
of his books on teaching poetry to children (such as *Wishes, Lies, and
Dreams* and *Rose, Where Did You Get That Red?*). Koch's "Taking a
Walk with You" (a catalog of the poet's "misunderstandings"),
"Locks," and "Thank You" were exemplary; the inventory became a
staple of New York School poetics. "Thank You," a list of invitations
the poet must refuse, turns the insincere letter of gratitude into a poetic

conceit. The poem is the vehicle of irony that permits the poet to transform aggression into jubilation. "And thank you for the chance to run a small hotel / In an elephant stopover in Zambezi, / But I do not know how to take care of guests, certainly they would all leave soon, / After seeing blue lights out the windows and rust on their iron beds."

The "Things to Do" poem, a form favored by James Schuyler and Ted Berrigan, is at heart an inspired variant of the list poem. So is Joe Brainard's *I Remember*—a book of prose recollections, every paragraph of which begins with the title phrase. A. R. Ammons's long poems (*Garbage*, for example) are packed with lists of particulars. They form the "many" in the "one / many" argument that has long been an obsession for him. Raymond Carver's "Fear" is a down-to-earth list of fears (of electrical storms, being late or arriving early, having to identify the body of a dead friend) culminating in the fear of death. Out of this inventory of fears emerges a self-portrait.

Carver's poem sets store by its sincerity, but the list is an invitation to be expansive, and it lends itself particularly well to comic or ironic purposes. In "Lineups" Charles North has discovered the rhetorical possibilities of the baseball lineup, a specialized list with unexpected applications beyond the diamond. In North's all-star lineup of tropes, for example, Pun leads off at shortstop followed by Paradox in left field, Metaphor in center, and Simile, the rightfielder, batting cleanup. (See *Ecstatic Occasions, Expedient Forms*.) Carolyn Creedon's love poem "litany," another notable recent example, is a list of entreaties the heroine of the poem directs at "Tom," along with his replies. (See *The Best American Poetry* 1993.) Paul Violi's list poems include "Exacta" (an account of a horse race), "The Totem Pole" (a list of decapitated people), "Triptych" (a spoof of *TV Guide* listings), and "Acknowledgments" (wherein Samuel Taylor Coleridge's poems are assigned to magazines—"The Rime of the Ancient Mariner," for example, to *Modern Bride*). Catherine Bowman's prose poem "No Sorry" is an inventory of weapons, escalating humorously (but with deadly point) from scissors and paring knife to "enhanced tactical neutron lasers emitting massive doses of whole-body gamma radiation."

Larry Fagin's *The List Poem: A Guide to Teaching and Writing Catalog Verse* (New York: Teachers and Writers Collaborative) is highly recommended for further reading.

WALT WHITMAN

From Song of the Exposition, *Leaves of Grass*

Silent the broken-lipp'd Sphinx in Egypt, silent all those
    century-baffling tombs,
Ended for aye the epics of Asia's, Europe's helmeted
    warriors, ended the primitive call of the muses,
Calliope's call forever closed, Clio, Melpomene, Thalia dead,
Ended the stately rhythms of Una and Oriana, ended the
    quest of the holy Graal,
Jerusalem a handful of ashes blown by the wind, extinct,
The Crusaders' streams of shadowy midnight troops sped
    with the sunrise,
Amadis, Tancred, utterly gone, Charlemagne, Roland,
    Oliver gone,
Palmerin, ogre, departed, vanish'd the turrets that Usk from
    its waters reflected,
Arthur vanish'd with all his knights, Merlin and Lancelot
    and Galahad, all gone, dissolv'd utterly like an exhalation;
Pass'd! pass'd! For us, forever pass'd, that once so mighty
    world, now void, inanimate, phantom world,
Embroider'd, dazzling, foreign world, with all its gorgeous
    legends, myths,
Its kings and castles proud, its priests and warlike lords and
    courtly dames,
Pass'd to its charnal vault, coffin'd with crown and
    armor on,
Blazon'd with Shakspere's purple page,
And dirged by Tennyson's sweet sad rhyme.

                                                1891

RACHEL LODEN

Headline from a Photograph by Richard Avedon

New York World-Telegram, November 22, 1963[1]

> *Epstein to give up on Tuesday,*
> Slocum to succumb on Wednesday.
>
> Snavely: smithereens by Thursday;
> Pottle buys the farm on Friday.

Saturday, Hadley-Smith eats dust.
Sunday's child is not discussed,

Pixley: the world will end in one day,
Not unlike this coming Monday.

Drabble's set his cap for doomsday;
Epstein to give up on Tuesday.

1999

CATHERINE BOWMAN

No Sorry

Do you have any scissors I could borrow? *No, I'm sorry I
don't.* What about a knife? You got any knives? A good
paring knife would do or a simple butcher knife or maybe a
cleaver? *No, sorry all I have is this old bread knife my
grandfather used to butter his bread with every morning.*
Well then, how about a hand drill or hammer, a bike chain,
or some barbed wire? You got any rusty razor-edged barbed
wire? You got a chain saw? *No, sorry I don't.* Well then
maybe you might have some sticks? *I'm sorry, I don't have
any sticks.* How about some stones? *No, I don't have any
sticks or stones.* Well how about a stone tied to a stick? *You
mean a club?* Yeah, a club. You got a club? *No, sorry, I don't
have any clubs.* What about some fighting picks, war axes,
military forks, or tomahawks? *No, sorry, I don't have any
kind of war fork, axe, or tomahawk.* What about a morning
star? *A morning star?* Yeah, you know, like those spiked ball
and chains they sell for riot control. *No, nothing like that.
Sorry.* Now, I know you said you don't have a knife except
for that dull old thing your grandfather used to butter his
bread with every morning and he passed down to you but I
thought maybe you just might have an Australian dagger
with a quartz blade and wood handle, or a bone dagger, or a
Bowie, you know it doesn't hurt to ask? Or perhaps one of
those lethal multipurpose stilettos? *No, sorry.* Or maybe you
have simple blow pipe? Or a complex airgun? *No, I don't
have a simple blow pipe or a complex airgun.* Well then
maybe you have a jungle carbine, a Colt, a revolver, Ruger,
an axis bolt-action repeating rifle with telescopic sight for

sniping, a sawed-off shotgun? Or better yet, a gas-operated
self-loading fully automatic assault weapon? *No, sorry I
don't.* How about a hand grenade? *No.* Shrapnel? *No.*
Napalm? *No.* Napalm 2. *No, sorry I don't.* Let me ask you
this. Do you have any intercontinental ballistic missiles?
Or submarine-launched cruise missiles? Or multiple
independently targeted reentry missiles? Or terminally guided
anti-tank shells or projectiles? Let me ask you this. Do you
have any fission bombs or hydrogen bombs? Do you have
any thermonuclear warheads? Got any electronic measures
or electronic counter-measures or electronic counter-counter-
measures? Got any biological weapons or germ warfare,
preferably in aerosol form? Got any enhanced tactical
neutron lasers emitting massive doses of whole-body gamma
radiation? Wait a minute. Got any plutonium? Got any
chemical agents, nerve agents, blister agents, you know, like
mustard gas, any choking agents or incapacitating agents or
toxic agents? *Well I'm not sure. What do they look like?*
Liquid vapor powder colorless gas. Invisible. *I'm not sure.
What do they smell like?* They smell like fruit, garlic, fish or
soap, new-mown hay, apple blossoms, or like those little
green peppers that your grandfather probably would tend to
in his garden every morning after he buttered his bread with
that old bread knife that he passed down to you.

1996

NOTE

1. In the photograph ("Times Square, New York, November 22, 1963")
a haggard-looking woman holds up the *New York World-Telegram* with ban-
ner headline "President Shot Dead."   A tiny headline above the fold reads
"Epstein Due to Give Up on Tuesday."—R. L.

Procedural Poetry: The Intentions of Nonintention

JENA OSMAN

All "forms" of poetry are written according to some kind of procedure; however, certain procedural poems are distinct in that they are written according to rules that seem to diminish or completely eliminate authorial intention. These poems use as their starting point a belief that systems of "constraint" (i.e. chance operations, sets of rules, etc.) can reveal something in language that our conventional usages might occlude. Thus procedural poems have the capacity to produce aesthetic platforms from which the reader can take part in an act of receptive invention. The result is that the poet becomes a kind of "mechanic," creating a language machine that is fairly independent in its activity, and the reader becomes a writer in working with the output. Probably the best-known explanation of how to create such a poem comes from Tristan Tzara's 1921 dada manifesto:

> Take a newspaper.
> Take some scissors.
> Choose from this paper an article of the length you want to make your poem.
> Cut out the article.
> Next carefully cut out each of the words that makes up this article and put them all in a bag.
> Shake gently.
> Next take out each cutting one after the other.
> Copy conscientiously in the order in which they left the bag.
> The poem will resemble you.
> And there you are—an infinitely original author of charming sensibility, even though unappreciated by the vulgar herd.

In the 1960s, the still-active Oulipo group introduced its own formulas for instant poetry. (See Nielsen on *Oulipo* in this book.) Writer Italo Calvino, in his book *If on a Winter's Night a Traveler*, explains the appeal of artificially constrained writing:

How well I would write if I were not here! If between the white page and the writing of words and stories that take shape and disappear without anyone's ever writing them there were not interposed that uncomfortable partition which is my person!

While the surrealists also relied on various systems of automatic text generation, they often did so as a means to unlock the unconscious. The rules of the Oulipo group seem more interested in freeing the writer as a means of freeing the reader.

More recent configurations of procedural poetry include John Cage's mesostics. Cage's mesostics are a means for "writing through" a source text according to a chance operation. A quotation or a name provides a center string (a row down the middle, as opposed to the acrostic format of a row down the left margin) that determines what words will be chosen from various source texts. An example of this can be found in his piece "Art Is Either a Complaint or Do Something Else" (1988), which works with the words of Jasper Johns as source. Cage uses various quotes from Johns as center strands. When the center strand is "I don't want my work to be an e[x]posure of my feelings," the mesostic begins

vIsual **but**
anD in '
thing Occurs
to differeNt kinds of space
in which we ' re
edge of **The** '

Cage selects the first word appearing in the source text that contains the first letter—but not followed by the second letter—of the center strand: "vIsual." If the word *video* had been found in the source text, it could not have been used because it does not answer to the rules of the procedure. The second line consists of the next word found in the source text that contains the second letter of the center strand not followed by the third, etc. The number of "wing words" appearing to either side of this chance-determined word varies according to authorial preference. Although this procedure sounds somewhat tedious, its results are quite rich with semantic possibility. Cage has described mesostics as "a way of writing that, though coming from ideas, is not about them but produces them." The mesostic procedure has been recreated by Mesolist, a computer program developed by Jim Rosenberg.

Another poet whose working procedures have been replicated by a computer program is Jackson Mac Low. The program Diastext (designed by Charles O. Hartman) re-creates the diastic form that he invented. A good example of how disastics work can be found in Mac Low's *Virginia Woolf Poems*. Here, Mac Low takes a phrase from Woolf's *The Waves* ("Ridiculous in Piccadilly") as the legend to "spell through." The first word is the first word in the book that uses the letter 'r,' the second is the next word where the second letter is 'i,' etcetera, until the entire phrase has been reinvented according to letter placement. Once the entire phrase has been spelled through, the cycle repeats. Unlike Cage, Mac Low is much less comfortable with the term *chance* to describe his procedures, preferring to use terms such as *nonintentional* and *deterministic* because they acknowledge that the work is the result of authorial intention (in regards to the device that generates the text) and unpredictability (the results generated from the device).

Whereas Cage and Mac Low's procedures were originally devised "manually," and were only later replicated by computer programs, other writers have been using the computer as the first step in making non-intentional work. Charles O. Hartman and Hugh Kenner recently took a grammar school book called *Sentences for Analysis and Parsing* and ran it through two computer programs, Travesty and Diastext. At this point, the authorial trace is getting weaker and weaker, to the point where the results rely entirely on the power of words to spin signification autonomously through various combinatory configurations. It could be asked if the complexity of the procedures found in the Hartman-Kenner "collaboration" reaps a rich enough material for the reader to work with. Although the primary text they have chosen to work with is amusing, it can't possibly offer the dialogic possibilities found in source texts used by someone like Cage. In addition to the fact that Cage's primary texts seemed to have a more lively "subtext" waiting to be exposed through chance, Cage's results were also the product of some very deliberate composition, as evidenced by the wing words he chose; his active and caring dialogue with the source texts he uses is very clear. In the case of Hartman and Kenner, the primary interest seems to be in the wonders of the machine, rather than the language of the source text. The conversation between the source text and the poet-technicians is almost nonexistent, which leads to much less generative results than we find in Cage and Mac Low.

It is clear that computer technology is making its mark when it comes to aleatoric poetic procedures. In the second volume of the anthology *Poems for the Millennium,* editors Pierre Joris and Jerome Rothenberg have included a section called "Toward a Cyberpoetics: The Poem in the Machine." This section includes work by Duchamp, Abraham Lincoln Gillespie, Steve McCaffery, as well as that of poets who use computers, such as Mac Low, Jim Rosenberg, and John Cayley. Poems that make use of random text generation are easily found on the Internet (some good examples can be found at <http://epc.buffalo.edu/e-poetry/>). These works all have an interest in allowing the reader to be a producer; however, it seems to me that many of them suffer from the same problems found in Kenner and Hartman's *Sentences*. By dismissing all authorial subjectivity, computer poetries can leave the reader in a dehumanized and nondialogic quandary. Conversely, computer poetry that makes use of flash technology—although providing a certain degree of reader interactivity essentially turns the reader into a passive video-viewer of predetermined authorial intentions. As with earlier proceduralists, the most provocative poems will be the result of procedural choices that complicate the conversation between author and primary text. A delicate balance between the machine and the human hand is what allows the reader to enter the poem.

There are a number of procedural writers who, although extremely interested in modes of science and technology, maintain closer "intentional" contact with their texts. Joan Retallack's poem "AFTERRIMAGES" can be found in her book of the same name published by Wesleyan Press in 1995. The book begins with four epigraphs, one of which recounts the detonation of the first atomic bomb at Alamogordo in 1945. Retallack's concern over this event is "performed" by the procedure of the poem.

The main text of "AFTERRIMAGES" appears as a split screen on the page. The top half of the screen is "intuitively composed" text (i.e. no chance operations), culled from Retallack's memories, from collection notebooks, from ideas and associations she had while writing. The bottom screen is the residual afterimage—what is left after the reaction of a chance procedure has eradicated most of the composed text. A look at Retallack's process reveals an attention to visual performance that is quite different from the procedural poems described above.

In the "AFTERRIMAGES" project I wanted something violent (as violent as a bomb or a natural disaster or history . . .) to happen to the text above the lines that would leave only fragments, as afterimages, below. (The two "r"s in afterrimages are there in order to accommodate both terra and terror, as well as error.) The "bombing" relates to the anniversary of the first atomic detonation at Alamagordo . . . I literally bombarded the top half of the page with an assortment of 13 paper clips having decided that the fragments that would remain below would be only those that appeared inside the border of the paper clips—those "clipped" out. I then had them appear in the corresponding spaces below as "afterrimages." I was very strict about only allowing those letters to remain that remained whole within the space of the paper clip. In some cases none of the text appeared within the clips; those poems have empty space after the line that divides the page. I felt that everything that remained, partly because it would be so minimal, would—in demanding a new quality of attention to the letters, a new way of apprehending their presence in that white space—take on a strange humor and intensity. They remain for any reader (including myself) to make of them what we can. They are very suggestive to me; I delight in them much more than what is above. They are the grace, the gift of what is present despite and beyond our control.[1]

Whereas Retallack's procedures function to reveal the "gift" of language lurking inside of language, they are also inherently linked to her own subjective concerns. Retallack's "poem-machines" cannot be separated from their inventor. Her utopian hopes for how her inventions might be used are clear when she writes

I've long had images—of a dicey aesthetic nature—in which I see all of civilization blowing up (in the wind?) and then falling back to earth in scattered shards and fragments out of which one (anyone left) must compose a new mosaic culture . . . Of course, on a far less dramatic scale, such fragmentations of memory and object and experience are occuring all the time.[2]

Provocative use of procedures, with varying degrees of intentionality, can be found in the work of Tina Darragh (*On the Corner to Off the Corner* uses actual dictionary pages as source text and guide), Robert Grenier (*Sentences* is structured as infinitely combinatory), Louis Zukofsky (*80 Flowers* works according to numerical limits for words and stanzas), Ron Silliman (*Tjanting* is based on the Fibonacci sequence), Lyn Hejinian (*My Life* is an "autobiography" made of forty-five sections, each of forty-five lines representing the author's age at the time of writing), and others. The work of procedural poets allows for the usually repressed (often disjunctive) activities of language to make their appearances. As opposed to perceiving the resulting poems as opportunities for decoding, the reader must recognize them as somewhat utopian meditations on semantic possibility: behind the use of procedures is the belief that if we can access the "other life" of language, perhaps we can find parallel methods to access similarly repressed elements in our immediate social context.

JOHN CAGE

From Art Is Either a Complaint or Do Something Else

2
vIsual **but**
anD in '
thing Occurs
to differeNt kinds of space
in which we ' re
edge of **The** '
i Would like my work to
A
itself' i thiNk
arTs
soMething
citY
of the things We like
tO have ' some vivid indication of
the tRaffic there ' some clear souvenir' a photograph'
thinK of
iT's very
different kinds Of space
it's in part mental and in part visual' But that's
thE mirror my experience of life is
form of plAy or
iN
foldEd or bent ' or stretched skin think of **the**
a form of exercise and it's in Part mental and
fOrm '
but that'S one of the things we like '
space being represented in it my work feeds Upon itself i think it is a
play oR
placE
tO be '
liFe is
accustoMed to thinking
it's verY
Form
souvEnir ' a photograph ' a
city and thE traffic there '
certain kinds of things occur and in another pLace '
I
city aNd the traffic there '
arroGant
differenceS

1988

JACKSON MAC LOW

From Ridiculous in Piccadilly[3]

1.
ridiculous
Piccadilly.

end stain
bookcase,
reassuring brutally
eating-house.

eating-house.

waitresses,
in and plates right
included.

prick contains forged
companion
pale-yellow
smooth-polished melancholy
rooted,
Rippling side.

hesitating consciousness
treasures ridicule sensations,
mysteriously eating-house
imbue entirely phrase with
pictures,
thick.

Written 1976; published 1985

CHARLES O. HARTMAN AND HUGH KENNER

From Sentences, XV

THEE

Sentences for cigars would hear the ship. We
were filled with joy and six years was too
anxious to learn. He was as diligence, he
leaped over the best apple might have more
excuses than who was said. I will take such
things as are thee, Captain.

Sentences hear
Sentences best apple
Sentences
Sentences
Sentences for would were
Captain.

cigars might cigars cigars things would joy would filled
    would hear
We years learn.

the than are
Sentences the ship.

leaped who
Sentences would hear were have for cigars filled apple

Sentences filled with six with might joy too joy and anxious
    and six diligence,
six years learn.

leaped over excuses who was was too to who as and six
    anxious anxious anxious excuses than for learn.

He leaped over learn.

He he who was was anxious as diligence,
might will anxious diligence,
excuses
Captain.

diligence,
diligence,
he leaped learn.

He leaped ship.

filled leaped over over the hear the ship.

1995

JOAN RETALLACK

From AFTERRIMAGES

"My Commedia" she called it

astride   alight   awash   afoul   agape

orange stuck with cloves or loose necked fowl
(no it wasn't that way at all)
regular rhythm that can collapse a stadium or a bridge
Dr. Heidi's grammar for a nuclear age
●●●

              ia"

                   awa

                   loves

       eid

                                              1995

RON SILLIMAN

From Tjanting, "The Figures"

Not this.
What then?
I started over & over. Not this.
Last week I wrote "the muscles in my palm so sore from halving the rump roast I cld barely grip the pen." What then? This morning my lip is blisterd.
Of about to within which. Again & again I began. The gray light of day fills the yellow room in a way wch is somber. Not this. Hot grease had spilld on the stove top.
Nor that either. Last week I wrote "the muscle at thumb's root so taut from carving that beef I though it wld cramp." Not so. What then? Wld I begin? This morning my lip is tender, disfigurd. I sat in an old chair out behind the anise. I cld have gone about this some other way.
Wld it be different with a different pen? Of about to within which what. Poppies grew out of the pile of old broken-up cement. I began again & again. These clouds are not apt to burn off. The yellow room has a sober hue. Each sentence accounts for its place. Not this. Old chairs in the back yard rotting from winter. Grease on the stove top sizzled & spat. It's the same, only different. Ammonia's odor hangs in the air. Not not this.
Analogies to quicksand. Nor that either. Burglar's book. Last week I wrote "I can barely grip this pen." White butterfly atop the grey concrete. Not so. Exactly. What then? What it means to "fiddle with" a guitar. I found I'd begun. One orange, one white, two gray. This morning my lip is swollen, in pain. Nothing's discrete. I straddled an old chair out behind the anise. A bit a part a like. I cld have done it some other way. Pilots & meteorologists disagree about the sky. The figure five figures in. The way new shoots stretch out. Each finger has a separate function. Like choosing the form of one's execution.
Forcing oneself to it. It wld've been new with a blue pen. Giving oneself to it. Of about to within which what without. Hands writing. Out of the rockpile grew poppies. Sip mineral water, smoke cigar. Again I began. One sees seams. These clouds breaking up in late afternoon, blue patches. I began again but it was not beginning. Somber hue of a gray day sky

filld the yellow room. Ridges & bridges. Each sentence
accounts for all the rest. I was I discoverd on the road. Not
this. Counting my fingers to get different answers. Four
wooden chairs in the yard, rain-warpd, wind-blown. Cat on
the bear rug naps. Grease sizzles & spits on the stove top. In
paradise plane wrecks are distributed evenly throughout the
desert. All the same, no difference, no blame. Moon's rise at
noon. In the air hung odor of ammonia. I felt a disease. Not
not not-this. Reddest red contains trace of blue. That to the
this then. What words tear out. All elements fit into nine
crystal structures. Waiting for the cheese to go blue. Thirty-
two. Measure meters pause. Applause.

1981

LOUIS ZUKOFSKY

From 80 Flowers

Heart us invisibly thyme time
round rose bud fire downland
bird tread quagmire dry gill-over-the-ground
stem-square leaves-cordate earth race horsethyme
breath neighbors a mace nays
sorrow of harness pulses pent
thus fruit pod split four
one-fourth *ripens* unwithering gaping

1978

LYN HEJINIAN

From My Life

When one travels,   It flies in the night. In that light it is
one might "hit"   obvious that you are related to your
a storm   mother. Boots, plows, cheese, burls.
   As for we who "love to be
astonished," the night is lit. Remarkably to learn to look. My
father would say I've a "big day" tomorrow. Words are not
always adequate to the occasion, and my "probably"
sounded hopeless. It's real, why, so, it's wrong. I mentioned
my face because I am made that way wonderfully like a
shadow I do not despise. But if I don't like the first dress I try

on, I won't like any. It is only a coincidence. Whose shadow
who's. At the circus the elephants were more beautiful than
the horses, more touching than the clowns, and more
graceful than the tigers trained to jump on their backs.
Physical education was required. At school, the choral
director described the torso in terms of the muscles of sound.
Always infinity extends from any individual life, but eternity
is limited between one's birth and one's death. Interpreting
such combinations of events, and the sort of mysticism on
which such interpretations are based, is what gives
coincidence its bad name. Religion is a vague lowing. I was
beginning to look for some meaning when I should have
been satisfied with events. It is hard to turn away from
moving water. For the time, being; twilight seen even full. I
mean to say "hopelessly" in a promising tone, as one would
say, "hopelessly in love," and mean, really, "very much,"
and, especially, "full of hope." In my "trouble with conflict,"
I was reluctant to be disconcerting, to cause discontinuity.
Panic versus crystallographic form. Knickknacks are for
browsers. There is some discomfort more active than
boredom but none more fatiguing. I had gone back to bed
and was pretending to sleep in order to avoid saying goodbye
to the friends who had been visiting, hiding from farewell's
display. The lives of which I read seemed more real than my
own, but I still seemed more real than the persons who had
led them. A sunlit winter's day lay thin, frozen to the
hummocks and rubble of mud in the cold but erotic
marshlands beside the Concord River. We have come a long
way from what we actually felt. But he remains aloof, saying
only that things *seem* familiar. The invisible but realistic
details of an ultimate monument. By hand, put together, with
hook and thread. Poco Bueno was buried, saddled, standing.
To do things for the sake of fame or other gain is selfish, but
to do them for your own pleasure is to do them generously.
One might become a volunteer down with the poor Italians.
At least, we shall solve the riddle presented by money, or so
he says. It seemed that we had hardly begun and we were
already there. Memory is the money of my class. What a
vast! what a business! The lowly cabbage strives and the
turnip in the garden yearns to be a person. You know, things
like that. Systems betray, or are, as in a "made place," made
betrayals. I was organized by addition and addiction. I found
a penny in a calla lily.

1987

TINA DARRAGH

From on the corner   to   off the corner

"legion" to "Lent" for "R"

"Lem" cuts a figure eight around "le ma" and "le me,"
generating the kind of fiber bands associated with "brain"
and "ribbon." The lower oval of the eight is uniformly
southern in including a Greek island, 14 variations of
lemon, money from Honduras and Roman exorcisms. The upper
oval far from the north has a gloss heading, lemming barks,
and a young hero sometimes helped by his mother.

"mobilizer" to "modern language" for "U"

The mobius strip is part of the "writing as carving"
tradition. First, the rectangle is held steady at
one end and given a sudden half twist at the other.
The ends then are taped or glued together resulting in
a one-sided figure where before there were two. This
180 degree turn is much like the suffix "mo" which—
after numerals or their names—indicates the number
of leaves made by folding a sheet of paper.

1981

NOTES

1. E-mail from author, March 10, 1997.
2. E-mail from author, June 16, 1998.
3. This is the first section of "Ridiculous in Piccadilly," from Mac Low's
The Virginia Woolf Poems.

Nude Formalism: A Sampler

CHARLES BERNSTEIN

With its doctrineless dogmatism—dogmatism for its own sake—Nude Formalism is perhaps the characteristic art movement of the fin de siècle. Though essentially hybrid in spirit, Nude Formalism excoriates all forms of hybridity. Early accounts of the movement suggest that it took its name from Marcel Duchamp's *Nude Ascending a Stairmaster* and that Nude Formalist poems were Duchampian bachelor machines—the groom stripped bare by his bachelorettes (maybe); but this account has been all but discredited by recent scholarship which suggests that *nude* was employed to suggest a *natural* or *brute,* in the sense of pure, unembellished, ur, in the current jargon, *essential* formalism.[1] However, this reading does not seem supported by close attention to the semantic features of the poems themselves; but perhaps this is a small matter in a project so large. While Nude Formalism seemed to appear on the poetics horizon as if out of the blue, and much has been made of its putative claims to be unprecedented, nonetheless a certain lineage can be traced. The supposed founder of the movement—if something stumbled on can be said to be founded— Algernon Charles Bernstein—had, for a time, been with the First Church, Poetic License; but it came to pass that he was defrocked and removed from his post, to which he nonetheless clung, even after being stripped of his vestments, for what we can now see, in retrospect, was an uncontrollable attraction to proto–Nude Formalist sound patterns. Unhinged from the mooring of his church, Algernon Charles went on to establish the Center for the Study of Dysraphic Phenomena, for which he assumed the title of director of research and development. It was during his time at the center that he unexpectedly discovered Nude Formalism, as the story is often told, in a dark and unattended corner of his laboratory.

It would be impossible to assemble an authentic representation of Nude Formalism since the movement never managed to attract any members and even its founder denies any affiliation with the group. What the present editor has assembled here, then, are a few works that suggest a possible, even if tangential, affiliation with the movement, in

an effort to give readers of this anthology the look and feel of Nude For-
malism, if not the thing itself.

—C. B.

Silver Bay, NY

July 1996

LEE ANN BROWN

Summery

An undone tropic fell too lush
A canyon climb a bird a thrush
A tea before the ending hitch
The sprite from hell said smoke the bitch

I wandered lonely in the midst
of poets conversing not quite kids
and many lovers ex and all
chasing through the water

Fall

As leaf to leave to lavish to laugh
A gape gaffed taped onto dinner mapped
I batter the dough of those who wert
pommeled to structures suturing work

A septet drunk on eating another
forked forgetting a pallid mother
Hence a fruit a bitter bother
Telling truths a ridden scholar

in

Winter

Pity me where the cold north throes
An arm on my cheek a windy pose
In my very bedroom no heat is there
Except when you climb in and dare

to

Spring

Where roses bud and violents bloom
In a circular saw, riding my room
Inscribed on behest   a back anew
Imploding such that she held my view

Oh spring is here and it's only Feb
How it comes to this impatient Reb
She sang invisibly—not this week
Held time enough for us to speak

1999

JENNIFER MOXLEY

When in Rome

No, I will not fondle you willingly centurial world
nor stroke your shred of decency, I hold no candles
or so you broadcast, ever since you kissed
by world weary decadence.
Hey soldier, go flaunt your swags and jabots elsewhere
this girl is bowing out, full to the glands with garlands
and Democrats, the truthful and bad will eventually see
    my way.
My webbing or weaving grows thick with all your
    travel plans
you tree trunk, you bile monger, you ghastly gewgaw
bereft of Metaphor, this time your ignorance will kill you
once and for all Centurion.
Didn't you notice your hundred years are up.

1996

JOEL KUSZAI

the dark
and time's consuming
  couldst think to flee
  ease my smart

    it is so with me
    off have I prest
Ah
  Lord
    what a Purchase will that be
            Ah
    what bright days were those
foolish Muse
  our murmurings
tread an endless maze
in deep sleep
                calm
as it was bright
  before must descend
at strife

                                        1998

CATRIONA STRANG

For all ease lent
it trods a gay tryst while folly cavorts
nor can it promote odd fires and due riot
not when mauled and plainly stung—
we're lit.

I'm vernant, knocked over, the, uh
fruit you pulsed for times renewed
and interminable rigid dolts.
Spate. Swank like lilacs
though a lewd calm might cap
this fulgid verging.

So forget ardour—
anxious choler swipes my high tread
once the fulcrum's veined.

                                        1993

LISA ROBERTSON

I SAW A DOG KILL TWO BIRDS IN A PARK
o little world approximate, all soft
things roar: each cruddy beast, each bloated hour
each hunger monstrous with tongues, the baroque
yawn of the avant garde, its purloined game
of solitaire and wielded branch pastoral
Curse its gilded milkteeth! Dedicate the
grave to nothing! Such splendid maggots swag
the lid; in suburban streets, suburban
speed, the pungent blackness moves as lettrist.
Now arcane weeping ceases. And I shall
abandoned the smudge-throated lawn. And I
shall defend what rhythm's touched. And I shall
live according to each resung cunt. As
it speaks! ad infinitum into the
grass! of how the quickened sea was
reddening roseate saffron-forced
rapid flecked with varied plume undulate
become all fine spun haunted growling
shaded to the tepid river. Multa!
Multa! I shall not translate
Some won't know better. What is that gleam?
It is radiating from a phoneme
a royal habit plucked from crux of
matted blade and brownish sky. But don't
sing to the border: Wars, captives; captives,
wars—the joke's torqued on the side of horses
and dust. I've fucked things up, but I'm awake.
I'll prompt no valour, turned no prow—my
story's slight, my task's opaque:
I just want to live according to that reasoned ache.

                                        1997

CHARLES BERNSTEIN

Pinky Swear

Such mortal slurp to strain this sprawl went droopy
Gadzooks it seems would bend these slopes in girth
None trailing failed to hear the ship looks loopey
Who's seen it nailed uptight right at its bearth
There's been a luring and a ladling lately
That swills the pitch and hiccups fates gone dim
With gumption and such buckle-bursting hurt
Allies with pomp paraded, permed and soapy
You'd guess the call was made by that same twerp
Destroyed the rig and left you almost dopey
        Let daze frequent a thought that's soft and gloopy
        Fluttering like a drill 'een here and earth
        Then skin a phrase spill a toast in verse
        Such swivel cups the sail of tusked whoopee

1995

NOTE

  1. The 23rd encyclical of The Nude Formalism, which survives only on
Styrofoam fragments, repudiates all social-constructivist formalisms and ar-
gues that even the social is not a social construction.

Oulipian Poetry

ALDON LYNN NIELSEN

Oulipo is not a form of writing, but a form of writers. An organization founded in 1960 in France, the Ouvroir de Littérature Potentielle might well be regarded as the research-and-development laboratory of international poetics. An avant-garde that assiduously studies the poetry and poetics of the past, a group of writers given to the writing of manifestoes who nonetheless cultivated for years what one of the founding members terms a "voluntary obscurity," Oulipo is among the few determinedly experimental groups of writers who can be said to have lived up to their potential, and who have made that potential available for poets everywhere.

Jean-Jacques Thomas has written that Oulipo rejected the exhibitionism of earlier avant-gardes and "has chosen the more arduous introverted path of research and experimentation." Originally a gathering of ten mathematicians and artists convened for a colloquium on the works of Raymond Queneau, Oulipo eventually grew to an official membership of twenty-five, including the American writer Harry Mathews and the noted Italian novelist Italo Calvino. Despite their deliberately small numbers, the work of this prolific group has had worldwide influence. The principal activities of the official organization have been devoted to the historical research into poetic forms of the past, particularly less well known forms, and the development of new forms for literary art.

As is true of all formalisms, Oulipian experiments develop algorithms and programs for generating and combining materials while operating under a set of predetermined constraints. The emphasis within Oulipo upon the potential unleashed by such formal operations might at first sound similar to the aleatory or chance operations frequently associated with such American poets as John Cage and Jackson Mac Low. The writers of Oulipo, however, are fundamentally opposed to aleatory art. In reality, the chance operations of most Cagean experiments are highly determinative of the outcome, and this may explain part of the Oulipian objection. Oulipo insists upon the "voluntary" or "conscious" aspect of composition. Thus, few literary readings involve quite so much "potential" as Raymond Queneau's *Cent Mille Milliards de poémes,* in which each line in each of ten sonnets is written in such a way that it can substitute for a line in the same position in one of the other sonnets, affording the reader the potential of reading 10^{14} sonnets. The book was published with the sonnets cut into strips, bound at the edge, so that readers could easily do the work of recombination. The exact number of potential sonnets was known in advance, and the finite possible readings are determinable; but no one reader could live long enough to produce all the possible readings.

Oulipian forms are equally simple in their description and equally complex in their realization. The S + 7 technique, one of the most frequently adopted by other writers, is practiced by taking an existing text and replacing each substantive with the seventh substantive following it in a given dictionary. The number seven is, of course, wholly arbitrary, and similar experiments may be accomplished using other numbers. Another common Oulipian technique with a long and honorable pedigree is the lipogram, a writing in which a particular letter of the alphabet is repressed. Georges Perec's *La Disparition* opens with its protagonist Anton Vowl suffering an odd sense that something is missing, and proceeds to its end without ever once using a word with the letter *e* in it. Gilbert Adair's masterful translation of this text into English, a language in which the *e* is seemingly unavoidable, provides the eerie *e*-less Ozymandias of our examples. Other Oulipian forms include "isomorphisms," in which texts are rewritten using the same phonemes or the same grammatical patterns to produce new poems that mirror the sound or structure of their antecedents. "Haikuization" of an existing poem involves erasing all but its rhyme words, as in the example from Queneau offered below, which is given in French to preserve its audible effects. Jacques Bens has devised "irrational" sonnets, in which the stanza length is determined by π.

There is an unmistakable resemblance between Oulipian poetry and the exercises often attempted in creative writing workshops, and given the Oulipo's focus upon the *work* of writing such a resemblance is not entirely accidental. Indeed, many workshop exercises have been derived from Oulipo's work, what Jacques Roubaud calls the public domain of "applied *Oulipo.*" The Oulipian work is done, as Queneau has said, for the benefit of its own members and for any other writers who might find this work useful. Still, the rigorous work of Oulipo should not be confused with the pedagogy of the creative writing workshop. Oulipo does not create its constraints as exercises to get the writer in the right frame of mind to be creative; indeed their resistance to a poetics of "inspiration" augurs against ready appropriation of their efforts as "springboard to creativity." Oulipo is serious fun, work undertaken to explore the potential offered by the fundamental functioning of language. As Roubaud has remarked, "one cannot respond to the question of 'utility' or to that of 'seriousness' if one is not already both useful and serious (and thus incapable of posing oneself that question)."

Perhaps the best source for English readers further interested in Oulipo is Harry Mathew's collection, *Oulipo: A Primer of Potential Literature*.

GEORGES PEREC

Translated from the French by Gilbert Adair, 1994

Ozymandias

I know a pilgrim from a distant land
Who said: Two vast and sawn-off limbs of quartz
Stand on an arid plain. Not far, in sand
Half sunk, I found a facial stump, drawn warts
And all; its curling lips of cold command
Show that its sculptor passions could portray
Which still outlast, stamp'd on unliving things,
A mocking hand that no constraint would sway:
And on its plinth this lordly boast is shown:
"Lo, I am Ozymandias, king of kings:
Look on my works, O Mighty, and bow down!"
'Tis all that is intact. Around that crust
Of a colossal ruin, now windblown,
A sandstorm swirls and grinds it into dust.

PBS, 1969

Liminal Poem
to Martin Gardnerà

O
t o
see
man's
stern
poetic
thought
publicly
espousing
recklessly
imaginative
mathematical
inventiveness,
openmindedness
unconditionally
superfecundating
nonantagonistical
hypersophisticated
interdenominational
interpenetrabilities.
Harry Burchell Mathews
Jacques Denis Roubaud
Albert Marie Schmidt
Paul Lucien Fournel
Jacques Duchateau
Luc Etienne Perin
Marcel M Benabou
Michele Metail
Italo Calvino
Jean Lescure
Noel Arnaud
P Braffort
A Blavier
J Queval
C Berge
Perec
Bens
FLL
RQ
•

1986

Presto

Sartre rasped, "Oulipo retops Aldine spares,
Repots Delian tropes, repads spared traces,
Retars rarest padres—reacts, Topers spread
Sparse drapes (presto—tropes!), arrest denial,
Repass rasped aspers. Nailed? Spared arrest.
Sartre-raters repost rarest: alined poster."

Denial presto. (Sartre? Sparse stoper! poster—
coster! Daniel-caster! Carets-, recast-spares-
passer! Traces rasped, alined tropes. Arrest
Sartre-raters! Sartre? Sartre recast, traces
Spared—nailed crates, drapes. Sparse denial:
Raters nailed, Oulipo reacts, spears spread.)

Oulipo, padres alined, caters rarest spread;
Raters parsed, drapes rarest parsed poster—
Repass, starer, arrest presto rasped denial,
Recast alined tropes! Aldine spader spares
Denial, parses carets, spares tropes, traces:
Caster-crates, stoper aspers, alined-arrest-

raters (Daniel arrest? Delian topers' arrest?
Passer arrest? padres' arrest?—arrest spread
Presto, arrest recast . . .). Oulipo spader traces
"Delian denial," Aldine lead-in," "Daniel Poster";
Spares Sartre; spares nailed starers; spares
Presto raters; spares Daniel; spares denial.

Oulipo spares denial, traces denial-denial;
Crates rarest traces recast, retops arrest
Spared; carets recast traces, tropes, spares.
Padres (topers!) repass rasped raters, spread
Rarest aspers. Aldine spader parses poster,
Spears parsed tropes, drapes alined traces,

Retops Delian padres, caters recast traces.
Oulipo spader: Daniel. Starer, repass denial!
Recast, rarest passer, repost, rarest poster,
Denial, Sartre, presto alined. Stoper, arrest
Rasped starer traces! Spared Daniel, spread
Tropes! Spears, Aldine padres' spader spares.

Passer (ô poilu!), Oulipo spares rarest traces—
Caster-spread presto alined. Rasped denial
Traces sparse arrest. Repost Delian poster!

1994

RAYMOND QUENEAU

"Haikuization" of Mallarmé

Onyx?
Lampadophore . . .
Phnix?
Amphore . . .

Nul Ptyx
Sonore
au Styx
s'honore

Un or?
le décor . . .
Une Nixe

encor
se fixe:
septuor

1986

Two American Verse Forms:
The Cinquain and the Quatern
ALLISON JOSEPH

I hold in my hands a slender hardcover book, its gilt-edged pages slightly browned with the passage of many years. The book, copyright 1915, is simply titled *Verse*. It was written by Adelaide Crapsey, an American poet born in 1878, whose promising career ended too soon when she died at age thirty-six in 1914. But during her brief poetic career, Crapsey was able to formulate an original verse form she called the cinquain—a five-line syllabic poem containing two syllables in line 1, four in line 2, six in line 3, eight in line 4, and two in the fifth and final line. With this syllabic scheme, Crapsey was able to create poems of great fragility and beauty. Perhaps this slender verse form was somewhat indicative of Crapsey's own personality—the anonymous introduction to *Verse* (signed only by the initials C.B.) describes her as "fair and fragile, in action swift, in repose still; so quick and silent in her movements that she never seemed to enter a room but to appear there, and on the stroke of some invisible clock to vanish as she had come."

A good cinquain, in my opinion, has the same ephemeral and startling quality. Crapsey's cinquain is not, as Myra Cohn Livingston cautions in her book, *Poem-Making: Ways to Begin Writing Poetry,* a "language-arts cinquain," which, she explains, "sometimes counts words instead of syllables and is nothing more than an exercise in identifying and writing nouns, verbs, adjectives, a sentence, a synonym and/or an antonym." According to Livingston, Crapsey's verse form allows poets to "express ourselves in some image or thought, using one or perhaps even two sentences. The twenty-two syllable pattern is just long enough to allow us room for our poem, yet helps us to be succinct, not to waste any words." Babette Deutsch, in her *Poetry Handbook,* defines the cinquain as "an American equivalent of the Japanese haiku or tanka," and it seems highly likely that Crapsey immersed herself in a study of those Japanese verse forms. One reference source even credits the cinquain to the Japanese, pushing Crapsey's legacy even further back into oblivion. But if we turn to Crapsey's own poems, we find ample evidence for the cinquain as a verse form capable of producing its own startlingly American effects.

Laurel in the Berkshires

Sea-foam
And coral! Oh, I'll
Climb the great pasture rocks
And dream me mermaid in the sun's
Gold flood.

The interjection after "coral," the "Oh" of surprised enthusiasm and discovery, and the reference to the "great pasture rocks" all locate this cinquain in a distinct American milieu. Among Crapsey's cinquains are ones that touch on the waters of Niagara Falls and the chasm of the Grand Canyon. As future generations of poets discover the form's potential, Crapsey's own poems will hopefully gain a renewed readership, and her short startling poems will be given new appreciation:

Triad

These be
Three silent things:
The falling snow.. the hour
Before the dawn.. the mouth of one
Just dead.

Another American poetic invention, the quatern, also deserves the attention of today's poets. The form, a variation of the kyrielle, was invented by a woman named Vivian Yeiser Laramore. It's a sixteen-line poem of four quatrain stanzas, in which the first line of stanza 1, used as a refrain, appears as the second line of stanza 2, the third line of stanza 3, and the last line of stanza 4. In describing the form in the 1943 edition of his *Unabridged Rhyming Dictionary*, Clement Wood states that Laramore used lines of four feet each. Here's an example of the form at work.

The Fitting

She wraps my form in red and gold,
in sacred cloth that she has made.
Her colors glimmer, growing bold,
a swirling weave of golden braid.

Her colors twist, a skilled parade.
She wraps my form in red and gold.
She knows how every stitch was laid
in winding skeins my eyes behold.

I watch her hands work with each fold—
her touch is light, and never staid.
She wraps my form in red and gold
and sings of light, then darker shades.

Her work is finer than brocade,
a whirl of russet, marigold.
May her creations never fade.
She wraps my form in red and gold.

Allison Joseph

When I discovered the quatern, I felt as if I'd stumbled upon a wonderful poetic secret. I'd never seen the form before, and have not seen it cited in many places other than Wood's dictionary. As I read his description, I realized that the term *fixed form* is a bit of an oxymoron—both Crapsey's and Laramore's contributions to the body of existing forms remind us that poets are inventors, constantly seeking new tactics for their visions. Learning about and writing in these two forms has given me the courage to invent forms of my own, and wisdom to know that real people, not so long ago, were engaged in the quest of finding shapes to fit the ideas and emotions of their times. Form is only fixed in the sense that Crapsey and Laramore have left us templates to use in crafting poems that fit the notions and sentiments poets have today.

The *Low Coup* as a Contemporary Afro-American Verse Form

AMIRI BARAKA

Although I have stated relentlessly that I have created the *Low Coup* as a contemporary buddy to the ancient revered Japanese haiku, I should be clear that *created* is a term of "propriety" but not precision. To be precise, the *Low Coup* is old Blood axiomatic speech. We is all heard of *the dozens,* the African Speech of Recrimination, &c, *12's, hikes, slips,* and even the odious *snaps* that Ru Paul and the commercial "Wooden Negroes" have appropriated to be solely on their own, as beings, &c. The *Low Coup* is not exactly the dozens; rather it is an insight, a penetration into what this all is, or ain't. But a penetration that carries its own "proof," so to speak, within the limited rigors of its form. Quick analysis with cymbals.

Why *Low Coup?* Having studied the classical Japanese haiku assiduously, I have always much valued the combined sensuousness and intellectual preciseness of its imagery. A seemingly small thing, yet like Kurosawa in *Yojimbo,* who describes a town beset by heathens in the first frames just by showing you a wild dog trotting through the town with a human hand in its mouth!

As well, obviously, the word *haiku,* I took into my own pun searching mental armament responding "automatically" (Yeh, fifty years after I heard it) to that sound parallel, but the deeper fix is that this seemingly cavalier looseness of response is directly akin to the proverbs and axioms the "old folks" dealt with so heavy as to pile them up past knowing here in the present.

So the *Low Coup* is proverb, axiom, saying, slogan, dagger (as in Lu Shun's description of his two kinds of essays, the Dagger, for quick work and the Javelin for heathens that wants to run). The *Low Coup* is obviously the dagger form. Brief, sharp, penetrating, meant to draw blood. Low because it can't "tear the whole playhouse down" as Son House and them used to sing, but it can put a hole where there ain't no

394

soul. The *Low Coup* is the kinda weapon Mikey Smith spoke of before the wooden negroes killed him. "Shd I joog him?" he asked. "Shd I joog him?" Obviously, he should have.

Monday in B Flat

I can pray
  all day
  & God
wont come.

But if I call
  911
  The Devil
    Be here

In a minute!

1994

The Paradelle

BILLY COLLINS

Note: The paradelle is one of the more demanding
French fixed forms, first appearing in the *langue
d'oc* love poetry of the eleventh century. It is a
poem of four six-line stanzas in which the first
and second lines, as well as the third and fourth
lines of the first three stanzas, must be identical.
The fifth and sixth lines, which traditionally re-
solve these stanzas, must use all the words from
the preceding stanzas and only those words. Simi-
larly, the final stanza must use every word from all
the preceding stanzas and only those words.

Despite the claims of this authentic-sounding note, which accompanied
my poem "Paradelle for Susan," the first paradelle was actually written
in 1996 by me. I invented the form (parody + villanelle = paradelle) in
order to produce a very badly written one. "Paradelle for Susan" was
the original, and I hope it will remain the most poorly executed exam-
ple of the form. My intention was to present a poem that would be rec-
ognized as the product of a technically incompetent and shameless poet
(not necessarily me) whose choice of the paradelle form put him well
outside the small realm of his ability.

That is why the paradelle carries two kinds of requirements. First,
there is the nearly mindless rule in the early stanzas of simply repeating
the first and third lines. This is what would have initially attracted our
hapless poet to the form. "Surely I can do that," he must have said to
himself as he sat down to compose. Unfortunately for him and the
poem, the next set of rules—the need to recycle all the previous words
in the stanza and later in the entire poem—is nearly impossible to fol-
low: thus all the remainder words at the ends of stanzas, the verbal de-
bris that resisted integration, and thus the gross failure of the whole
poem.

I figured that some readers would be amused by the poem and oth-
ers would find themselves not amused. I was not prepared for what ac-
tually happened when "Paradelle for Susan" went public, first in the
American Scholar and later in a book of poems titled *Picnic, Lightning*.

It didn't take long for three kinds of readers to emerge. Group A, we might call it, consisted of readers who got quickly into the spirit of the spoof. They recognized in the ineptness of the poem a parody of badly written formal poetry, and in that parodic mood, they accepted the footnote as part of the joke. Group B managed to get only half the put-on. They enjoyed the "badness" of the poem, but they took the footnote seriously, despite their failure in some cases to find any mention of the paradelle in dictionaries of literary terms. Group C—alas—bought the whole package—hook, poetic line, and sinker. Among this group was a subscriber to the *American Scholar* (a Phi Beta Kappa member no doubt) who wrote a letter to the editor bemoaning the low literary standards that would have allowed such a shoddy poem to appear in such a distinguished journal.

I never foresaw such a diversity of reactions, but more surprising to me was the news that other poets had begun writing their own paradelles. I even heard that a few teachers of creative writing were assigning their classes the paradelle as an exercise. Most amazing was that some of these paradelles, which began to appear in the mail, were actually rather good. Take Henry Taylor's "Paradelle: Nocturne de la Ville" for example. Later I found myself in contact with a young professor-poet who was interested in compiling an anthology of paradelles, a work currently in progress. How shortsighted of me to think that the history of the paradelle would begin and end with "Paradelle for Susan."

All this fallout reminded me that the ability to recognize humor is not possessed equally by all. But it also seemed to reveal among poets a true hunger for new forms. As silly as "Paradelle for Susan" was meant to be, the large number of serious efforts to write a decent paradelle shows that poets are eager to accept whatever difficulty is required in order to play the high and challenging game of form.

Paradelle for Susan

I remember the quick, nervous bird of your love.
I remember the quick, nervous bird of your love.
Always perched on the thinnest, highest branch.
Always perched on the thinnest, highest branch.
Thinnest love, remember the quick branch.
Always nervous, I perched on your highest bird the.

It is time for me to cross the mountain.
It is time for me to cross the mountain.
And find another shore to darken with my pain.
And find another shore to darken with my pain.
Another pain for me to darken the mountain.
And find time, cross my shore, to with the it is.

The weather warm, the handwriting familiar.
The weather warm, the handwriting familiar.
Your letter flies from my hand into the waters below.
Your letter flies from my hand into the waters below.
The familiar waters below my warm hand.
Into handwriting your weather flies letter the from the.

I always cross the highest letter, the thinnest bird.
Below the waters of my warm familiar pain,
Another hand to remember your handwriting.
The weather perched for me on the shore.
Quick, your nervous branch flies from love.
Darken the mountain, time and find my into it with is to.

1997

HENRY TAYLOR

Paradelle: Nocturne de la Ville

Somewhat behind, rather than
After, Villiers de l'Isle-Adam

An empty chair inhabits a troubled dream.
An empty chair inhabits a troubled dream.
Hoisted to light from wells of unknown depth,
hoisted to light from wells of unknown depth.
Hoisted from an unknown chair to dream of light,
a troubled depth inhabits empty wells.

The lamp says he feels it's slow use his way.
The lamp says he feels it's slow use his way.
"Around the street here I'm no drunk prisoner.
Around the street here I'm no drunk prisoner."
The drunk feels his slow way around the street lamp.
"It's no use," he says, "I'm a prisoner here."

Leaves fall from trees, moths fly to city lights.
Leaves fall from trees, moths fly to city lights.
On thin ice skaters flash across the dark.
On thin ice skaters flash across the dark.
Ice leaves the city to flash on fall trees;
Thin skaters fly from moths across dark lights.

It's fall. The city around feels slow to light.
No thin trees fly, flash a chair from ice;
a hoisted lamp lights moths. Across the street
from here an empty drunk leaves skaters troubled;
his unknown prisoner inhabits depths of dream.
"I'm on the way to use dark wells," he says.

                                                      2000

Predetermined
Avant-Garde Forms

MARK WALLACE

Throughout the twentieth century, American avant-garde poets were highly skeptical of predetermined forms. When Robert Creeley announced in the early 1950s that "form is never more than an extension of content," he defined what became for the following half century the core attitude of American avant-garde poets toward the issue of literary form. Creeley's comment needs to be understood as a reaction against the dominant modernists of the 1930s and 1940s, such as W. H. Auden and Allen Tate, who had rejected the more radical poetic experiments of older modernists like Pound, Williams, and Stein in favor of a return to traditional European forms and rhyme schemes. For modernists such as Auden and Tate, whom many American avant-garde poets regard as countermodernists, returning to traditional forms was a way of containing the chaos of actual experience through a controlled literary language that relied on irony, self-contained complexity, and the supposed unity of the poetic object. However, for Creeley and many poets featured in Donald Allen's 1960 anthology *The New American Poetry*, the goal of poetry was not to control experience by distancing oneself from it through formal devices, but to engage experience more openly and directly. Rather than seeing form as something that existed prior to the poem, such poets believed that the shifts and disruptions of the moment of composition should determine form.

It remains true that most current avant-garde poems have what might be called "discovered forms," that is, forms created in the act of composition. Still, some avant-garde poets have continued to work in predetermined forms, although rarely relying on the traditional European variety. The poems in this section all feature predetermined self-created forms that have been created for reasons as various and complex as the writers who have created them. Each poet was also asked to provide a short statement on the rationale and/or methodology of the particular form he or she uses.

Predetermined self-created forms raise a number of interesting questions. Is it true that predetermined forms really control the act of composition, or that such control is, in all instances, a bad thing? Is it possible to write a poem without having some prior assumptions about the form of poetic language? How can such predetermined forms, however self-created, avoid controlling the poem that they help generate? Or if they do not avoid that control, how can they be seen as other than an attempt to use form to contain and distance the complexities of experience? One answer might be that since language structures exist prior to their users, working in predetermined forms reveals the condition that all language users already occupy. Poets creating such forms are making changes in preexisting language structures, thus showing the limits of those structures and how such limits might be altered.

Mainstream poets, of course, often say that they find traditional forms valuable for similar reasons—that such forms allow poets to create new variants within predetermined formal limits. The difference is that predetermined self-created forms allow form to continue as a problem for which new solutions can be invented, rather than as a problem for which answers are already known. That is, predetermined self-created forms allow writers to reveal their skepticism about the notion that any single form, or even group of forms, can offer a final solution to the problem of form in poetry, while making it clear that they understand that language structures exist prior to the act of composition.

JACKSON MAC LOW

Statement about "154 Forties"

"154 Forties" was begun on October 12, 1990, during an automobile trip from New York to Buffalo with Petr Kotik, leader of the S.E.M. Ensemble, in a concert of which—in the performance space Hallwalls—I was about to participate as a composer and performer. I continued writing the poems' first drafts until February 1995 and have been continually revising them before and after that time. Each of the Forties poems is written in the following "fuzzy verse form": eight stanzas, each comprising three rather long lines followed by a very long line (usually occupying more than one typographical line) and then a short one. What "rather long," "very long," and "short" mean varies from poem to poem and stanza to stanza. The words, phrases, etc., in the poems' first drafts were gathered liminally ("intuitively") from what I thought of, saw, and heard while I was writing those drafts, which were and are often revised in many ways, prosodical and sometimes lexical, often involving changes of emphasis and/or hyphenated syntactical or grammatical connections between contiguous words.

The Forties include a number of "prosodic devices": nonorthographic acute accents indicating stresses (a usage borrowed, of course, from Gerard Manley Hopkins); simple compound words, indicated by unspaced hyphens, e.g., "patent-tally-córks," which are to be spoken somewhat more rapidly than other words but never hurried, and "sloweddown" compounds, indicated by spaced hyphens, e.g., "bírdie-aporia," which are to be spoken more slowly than other words though never dragged; and "caesural spaces" indicating silences and/or prolongations (of final phonemes or syllables) of several lengths, typically including that of an unstressed syllable, that of a stressed syllable or beat, and/or that of two beats (other lengths sometimes occur). These are described in endnotes, which also give the times and places the poems were written and revised. These devices make for continually changing rhythms, tempi, and rests when the poems are spoken aloud. The poems often seem quasi-metrical and are sometimes reminiscent of what Hopkins called "sprung rhythm," including paeons and other hypersyllabic feet, but the actual number of *beats* in the lines varies between and within poems and stanzas.

When published as a book, "154 Forties" will be entitled *Unannounced without a Name: 154 Forties.*

New York
July 21, 1998

GUIDE FOR READERS OF FORTIES POEMS

Caesural spaces: durations of silence and/or prolongations of final phonemes or syllables:
4 letter spaces [   ] = 1 unstressed syllable; 8 letter spaces [   ] = 1 stressed syllable or beat. None occurs between typographical lines. Breath pauses at verse-line endings ad lib.

Nonorthographic acute accents indicate stress rather than vowel quality. Each hyphenated compound is read as one extended word: somewhat more rapidly than other words, but never hurried. [-] indicates a slowed-up compound. Indented typographical lines continue verse lines begun above them.

Deciduous Lips

Forties 117

Deciduous bishops enjoy   salacious errata in unpleasurable
   artworks
riddled with doubt   Tschaikowskian orchestras play on
   the ocean
wrong-headed homesteaders   saddled-with-sod-hoúses
   rising from generous straps
only connéct   rage & greed   Kíerkegaard - dotty their
   onomatophilia cracks paratactically crossbred codes
musical textures of Grosseteste

Canting revolutionaries trifle with lives of saints &
   bullshitters
voicing silences of prolix revísionists in peplum léotards
forcing their Béowulf-calls on ex post facto masses
performing in the afternoons in Álbany   dancers asleep
   savagely tranquil   rushed to the rim of the canyon wide
   and deep
for a new lease on life   in jeans

We ate all we wanted   mostly peppery pies with chocolate
   sauce & tequila
Sri Lankan risottos with watercress mousse   wrapped in
   Malibu lace
won the alphabet licenses   for Marcel Duchamp's   dreams
children with toó-many gene-spliced limbs looked up in
   history open to Russian
dances   with no-beans-befóre & the image
   of nothingness
polishing-off-Pernód & péanut butter

Green sauce & lemon juice functioned as truth & beauty
   & good
as a policeman reached for a solitary outlook over
   Persian bees
busy as fragmentary embryos enlívened by electric shocks
scheduled as selfless names   ridiculed by Hilton & Clive in
   perfect wéather amid the mimosas guarding the lakeside
   wintertime víllas
devoted to further performance

The act of reading to fulfill our commitments to eyes & ears
in another solar system going-into-infinite-régress
gracefuly retreating to principles based on triads & margins
attracted by raspberries and cándy-bars enveloped in-Swiss -
    chéese as they confiscated our tickets   we explained we
    buttered our cuffs
closer to salads than confusion

Interrupted by bothersome opportunities & pomegranate
    seeds
we worried the soil for potatoes & grains   measuring
    success
by accretion of boredom revealed to be interesting they said
hiding the hole in his shirt with a formal jacket in a puddle
    luscious as pickles &
thistles   Milarepa ate what he had to to float
like a transitory theory in New England

Light & delightful as butane or notes   decried by
    Krishnamurti
ancient keepers of poker-faced-silences-bróthels-imposed
when lingering microtones   forced the birds to scream
    in Kansas
emptied glasses of corny liquor destroying our laundry
    goodbye to all that & no more parades whatever
    else happens
surrounded by mémory islands

Aware of momentary ringing in the ears at noon & sunset
simple as music & living this way in a disciplined structure
ecstacy trained us like horses   with sugar-cubes & apples
to near-macrocosmic-accéptance   but who can welcome
    everything that comes from the tangled surround   or
    passes-through-the-mínd
or the líps
                    written 1994–99, from "154 Forties," 1990–99

JOAN RETALLACK

Note for A I D /I/ S A P P E A R A N C E

In 1993 I was asked to write a poem for a special issue of *Object* being published as a memorial to Stefan Fitterman, who had recently died of AIDS. I wanted to make a form that would replicate—in the reading experience—both the proximal form of contagion and the literal disappearance of the person as this disease moved him toward death. The disappearance moves through the letters of the alphabet, and the text, in this way: Beginning with letters A I D S, it spreads to (and deletes from the text) adjoining letters B H J C E R T, then F G K Q U, then L P V, then M O W, then N X, and finally Y.

Part of the text in the first stanza is from "The Atomic Theory and the Fundamental Principles underlying the Description of Nature" in *The Philosophical Writings of Niels Bohr*.

A I D /I/ S A P P E A R A N C E

for Stefan Fitterman

1. in contrast with the demand of continuity in the
   customary description
2. of nature the indivisibility of the quantum of action
   requires an essential
3. element of discontinuity especially apparent through the
   discussion of the
4. nature of light she said it's so odd to be dying and laughed
   still it's early
5. late the beauty of nature as the moon waxes turns to
   terror when it wanes
6. or during eclipse or when changing seasons change
   making certain things
7. disappear and there is no place to stand on and strangely
   we're glad

A I D S
for tefn Fttermn
1. n contrt wth the emn of contnuty n the cutomry ecrpton
2. of nture the nvblty of the quntum of cton requre n eentl
3. element of contnuty epeclly pprent through the cuon of the
4. nture of lght he t o o t be yng n lughe tll t erly

5. lte the beuty of nture the moon wxe turn to terror when
   t wne
6. or urng eclpe or when chngng eon chnge mkng certn thng
7. pper n there no plce to tn on n trngely we're gl

B H J C E R T
fo fn Fmn
1. n on w mn of onnuy n uomy pon
2. of nu nvly of qunum of on qu n nl
3. lmn of onnuy plly ppn oug uon of
4. nu of lg o o yng n lug ll ly
5. l uy of nu moon wx un o o wn wn
6. o ung lp o wn ngng on ng mkng n ng
7. pp n no pl o n on n ngly w gl

F G K Q U
o n mn
1. no n w m no on ny no my pon
2. o n nvly o nm o on n nl
3. lm no onny plly pp no on o
4. no l o o yn nl ll ly
5. l y o n moon wx no own wn
6. o n l pow n n n no n n mn n n
7. pp n no pl o no n n nly w l

L P V
o n mn
1. no n w m no on ny no my on
2. o n ny o nm o on n n
3. m no onny y no on o
4. no o o y n n y
5. y o n moon wx no own wn
6. o now n n no n n mn n n
7. n no o no n n n y w

M O W
n
1. n n n n n y n y n
2. n n y n n n n
3. n n n y y n n
4. n y n n y
5. y n n x n n n
6. n n n n n n n n
7. n n n n n n y

N X

1. y y
2. y
3. y y
4. y y
5. y
6.
7. y

Y

1.
2.
3.
4.
5.
6.
7.

                                                    1998

FORREST GANDER

NOTES ON THE FORM OF "THE BLUE ROCK COLLECTION"

My first degree and career was in geology. Each of the poems in "The Blue Rock Collection" is structured according to properties inherent to the rock, mineral, or geological concept specified by the title. For instance, the following poem, "yellow quartz" appears in the section "Crystals":

> Men cruising
>   the park. Dogs
>   barking.
>   In the
>   Highrise,
>   Lights.

Because quartz crystals are hexagonal, the poem occurs in six lines. Because quartz is ellucid, the poem's scenario includes a description of the passage of light. The three pairs of linked sounds ing/ing, park/bark, high/lights enact at a phonic level the paired facets of the crystal face. While the subject material ostensibly has nothing to do with geology (unless one considers, after George Oppen, "the mineral fact" revealed in the act of perception), the form generates another level of meaning that, whether or not it is recognized, influences all the meanings of the poem.

From The Blue Rock Collection

IGNEOUS

granite (slab)

They will slaughter you
pray for you and wish you peace
but there is something wrong with this.

gabbro

Scarecrow
in the field
with a bow
and arrow.

lava

I wake on
the futon,
a stream
of ants shining
to the baseboard from
the cut in my palm.

moon

moon

Winter 1992–93

DAN ZIMMERMAN

On Isotopes

I see these new pieces, which I call Isotopes, as the first examples of a new form, virtually impossible without computers, yet not a form of "computer poetry," any more than poetry written with a felt-tip pen becomes "felt-tip poetry." Less difficult, perhaps, than a sestina—though more pizzicato—each Isotope presents one of potentially hundreds of by-products resulting from the fractional distillation of a wordsquare's anagrammatical factors. One might post a "wordsquare of the month," invite gold rushes, issue a call to Isotopian prospectors, some striking it rich, others going bust working the lode, but all bitten by the bug. I also see these wordsquares as mountain ranges hiding small patches of arable land—rice paddies, vineyards, mushroom caves, boulder fields of edible lichen epaulets, wild onion tufts. Machu Picchus. Angkor Wats.

a noun knew her best.
then a new sun broke,
a known Thebes rune,
to be shrunken anew.
she knew a non-brute
seek a newborn, hunt
a known ten-use herb,
know serene Bhutan.
he went, a broken sun,
he bent a known ruse,
a here unbeknownst,
a bee-shrunken town.
the new sun, on break,
knew her, a neon bust.

1997

no lie is not known,
so on, like a non-twin,
I, a known stone lion,
now link one to a sin.
a silken notion now,
no lotion, a new skin,
a tension low on ink,
no oil in a news knot.
I skin no town alone,
know no one in a list.
I ink a sonnet, no owl,
ink sown onto a line,
a sonnet Loki won in.

1997

TINA DARRAGH

Ames Distorted Room Transcriptions of Puns in "Scale Sliding"

To critique/expose the "blind spots" in my narrative "Scale Sliding," I borrowed figures used in visual perception experiments and literally drew them on dictionary pages. One figure I used was the Ames Distorted Room. A. Ames (painter/psychologist) used two straight lines and a sloping line to create a room with a "false" corner. If a viewer stationed outside looked in the room at two strangers of equal height, they appeared different in size. But if the viewer knew one of the participants, she wondered what was wrong with the room. I "put some puns in an Ames Room" by transcribing their dictionary locations in that form, leaving an opening for the "viewing point."

volcanic tuff

ur
mit
mals, re
tan of an
la rae mi a
called deer f
ley first foun
mic, *adj.*

la ro sa (too, la
(1960).

(too le; Sp. too le
f two large bulrushes
lifornicus, found in C
dated lands and marshes.

le ar (Fr. ty la ar), n. a
50 (1960).

le perch. See under perch[2]

l, ya), n. a town in North Ame

ip (too lip, tyoo —), n. any lil
Tulipa, cultivated in many varie
showy, usually erect, cup-shaped
wers of various colors. 2. a bu
(earlier tulipa   > NL apar. back
It. *tulipano* (taken as adj.)
a fancied   RBAN

viewing
point

Bibliography: Sources for Further Reading

Attridge, Derek. *Poetic Rhythm*. Cambridge: Cambridge University Press, 1995.

———. *The Rhythms of English Poetry*. New York: Longman, 1982.

———. *Well-Weigh'd Syllables: Elizabethan Verse in Classical Meters*. Cambridge: Cambridge University Press, 1974.

Bate, W. Jackson, and David Perkins. *British and American Poets: Chaucer to the Present*. New York: Harcourt, Brace, 1986.

Behn, Robin, and Chase Twitchell, eds. *The Practice of Poetry*. New York: HarperPerennial, 1992.

Benedikt, Michael. *The Prose Poem: An International Anthology*. New York: Dell, 1976.

Beum, Robert. "Syllabic Verse in English." *Prairie Schooner* 31 (1957): 259–75.

Bogin, Meg. *The Women Troubadours*. New York: Paddington Press, 1976.

Bridges, Robert. *Milton's Prosody*. Includes "Classical Meters in English Verse," by William Johnson Stone. Oxford: Clarendon, 1901.

Brown, Davis, and Lee Brown, eds. *The Negro Caravan*. New York: Dryden Press, 1941.

Cable, Thomas. *The English Alliterative Tradition*. Philadelphia: University of Pennsylvania Press, 1991.

Cage, John. *Musicage: Cage Muses on Words, Art, and Music: John Cage in Conversation with Joan Retallack*. Wesleyan Press, 1996.

Calvino, Italo. *If on a Winter's Night a Traveler*. Trans. William Weaver. New York: Harcourt Brace Jovanovich, 1981.

Cohen, Helen Louise. *Lyric Forms from France: Their History and Their Use*. New York: Harcourt Brace, 1922.

Dacey, Philip, and David Jauss, eds. *Strong Measures: Contemporary American Poetry in Traditional Forms*. New York: HarperCollins, 1986.

Daryush, Elizabeth. "Note on Syllabic Meters." *Collected Poems*. Manchester: Carcanet New Press, 1976.

de Banville, Théodore. *Petit Traité de Poesie Française*. Paris: Librairie de l'Echo de la Sorbonne, 1872.

deFord, Sara, and Clarinda Harriss Lott. *Forms of Verse*. New York: Appleton, Century, Crofts, 1971.

Delville, Michel. *The American Prose Poem: Poetic Form and the Boundaries of Genre*. Gainesville: University Press of Florida, 1998.

Deutsch, Babette. *Poetry Handbook: A Dictionary of Terms*. New York: Funk and Wagnalls, 1974.

Ellison, Ralph. "Richard Wright's Blues." In *Shadow and Act*. New York: Random House, 1964.

Emanuel, Lynn. "Language Poets, New Formalists, and the Techniquization of Poetry." In *Poetry After Modernism*. Ed. Robert McDonell. Ashland, Ore.: Story Line Press, 1991.

Fagin, Larry. *The List Poem: A Guide to Teaching and Writing Catalog Verse*. New York: Teachers and Writers Collaborative, 1991.

Finch, Annie. *The Ghost of Meter: Culture and Prosody in American Free Verse*. Ann Arbor: University of Michigan Press, 1993.

———, ed. *A Formal Feeling Comes: Poems in Form by Contemporary Women*. Ashland, Ore.: Story Line Press, 1994.

———, ed. With Susan Schultz. Multiformalisms: Postmodern Poetics of Form. Edited book in progress.

Fredman, Stephen. *Poet's Prose: The Crisis in American Verse*. Cambridge: Cambridge University Press, 1983.

Frost, Robert. *Collected Poems, Prose, and Plays*. New York: Library of America, 1995.

Fuller, Roy. *Owls and Artificers: Oxford Lectures on Poetry*. London: Andre Deutsch, 1971.

Fussell, Paul. *Poetic Meter and Poetic Form*. New York: Random House, 1965.

Gorey, Edward. *Amphigorey*. New York: G. P. Putnam, 1972.

Gross, Harvey, and Robert McDowell. *Sound and Form in Modern Poetry*. 2d ed. Ann Arbor: University of Michigan Press, 1996.

Hass, Robert, ed. *The Essential Haiku: Versions of Bashō, Buson, and Issa*. Hopewell, N.J.: Echo Press, 1994.

Henderson, Harold G. *An Introduction to Haiku: An Anthology of Poems and Poets from Bashō to Shiki*. Garden City, N.Y.: Doubleday Anchor, 1958.

Higginson, William J., and Penny Harter. *The Haiku Handbook: How to Write, Share, and Teach Haiku*. New York: McGraw-Hill, 1985.

Holland, John H. *Hidden Order: How Adaptation Builds Complexity*. Reading, Mass.: Addison-Wesley, 1995.

Hollander, John. *Rhyme's Reason: A Guide to English Verse*. New Haven: Yale University Press, 1981.

———. *Types of Shape*. New Haven: Yale University Press, 1991.

Kellogg, David. Canonical Drift and Poetic Reproduction. Manuscript in progress. <http://www.duke.edu./~kellogg/research.htm American Poetic>.

Kiernan, Victor, trans. *Poems from Iqbal*. London: John Murray, 1955.

Lammon, Martin, ed. *Written Water, Written in Stone: Twenty Years of Poets on Poetry*. Ann Arbor: University of Michigan Press, 1996.

Lanier, Sidney. *Science of English Verse*. New York: Scribner, 1898.

Lehman, David. *Ecstatic Occasions, Expedient Forms: 65 Leading Con-*

temporary Poets Select and Comment on Their Poems. 2d ed. Ann
Arbor: University of Michigan Press, 1996.

The Limerick—Book Two. New York: Greenleaf Classics, 1967.

Livingston, Myra Cohn. *Poem-Making: Ways to Begin Writing Poetry.* New
York: HarperCollins, 1991.

Mathews, Harry. *Oulipo: A Primer of Potential Literature.* Trans. and ed.
Warren F. Motte Jr. Lincoln: University of Nebraska Press, 1986.

McAuley, James. *Versification: A Short Introduction.* East Lansing: Michigan State University Press, 1966.

Merrill, James. "Education of the Poet." *Envoy* (Academy of American
Poets) 51 (1988).

Monroe, Jonathan. *A Poverty of Objects: The Prose Poem and the Politics
of Genre.* Ithaca, N.Y.: Cornell University Press, 1987.

Mother Goose's Melody, or Sonnets for the Cradle. Windsor, Vt.: Jessie
Cochran, 1814. Reprint New York: American Antiquarian Society,
1979.

Murphy, Margueritte S. *A Tradition of Subversion: The Prose Poem in English from Wilde to Ashbery.* Amherst: University of Massachusetts
Press, 1992.

Nagy, Gregory. *Poetry as Performance: Homer and Beyond.* Cambridge:
Cambridge University Press, 1996.

Nicholas, A. X., ed. *Woke Up This Morning: Poetry of the Blues.* New
York: Bantam, 1973.

Opie, Iona Archibald, comp. *The Oxford Nursery Rhyme Book.* New
York: Oxford University Press, 1955.

Piper, William Bowman. *The Heroic Couplet.* Cleveland: Press of Case
Western Reserve University, 1969.

Preminger, Alex, and T.V.F. Brogan, eds. *The New Princeton Encyclopedia
of Poetry and Poetics.* Princeton, N.J.: Princeton University Press,
1993.

Rothenberg, Jerome. *Shaking the Pumpkin: Traditional Poetry of the Indian North Americas.* Albuquerque: University of New Mexico Press,
1991.

Sackheim, Eric, ed. *Blues Line: A Collection of Blues Lyrics.* Hopewell,
N.J.: Ecco Press, 1993.

Smith, Clara. "Freight Train Blues." *Women's Railroad Blues.* Rosetta
Records 1301.

Stewart, George R. *Techniques of English Verse.* New York: Henry Holt,
1930.

Thompson, John. *The Founding of English Metre.* New York: Columbia
University Press, 1961.

Turco, Lewis. *The Book of Forms: A Handbook of Poetics.* New York:
E. P. Dutton, 1968.

———. *The New Book of Forms.* Hanover: University Press of New England, 2d ed., 1986, 3d ed., 2000.

Tzara, Tristan. *Seven Dada Manifestos and Lampisteries*. Trans. Barbara Wright. London: Calder Publications, 1992.

Untermeyer, Louis, and Carter Davidson. *Poetry: Its Appreciation and Enjoyment*. New York: Harcourt Brace, 1934.

White, Gleeson, ed. *Ballades and Rondeaux*. New York: Appleton, 1884.

Whitman, Walt. *An American Primer*. Boston: Small, Maynard, 1904.

Williams, Miller, ed. *Patterns of Poetry: An Encyclopedia of Forms*. Baton Rouge: Louisiana State University Press, 1986.

Williams, William Carlos. Introduction to *The Complete Works of François Villion,* trans. and ed. Anthony Bonner. New York: David McKay, 1960.

Wood, Clement. *Unabridged Rhyming Dictionary*. New York: World Publishing Company, 1943.

Contributors

Agha Shahid Ali's seven collections of poems include *The Half-Inch Himalayas* (Wesleyan), *A Nostalgist's Map of America* (Norton), and *The Country Without a Post Office*. His compilation, *Ravishing DisUnities*, an anthology of real ghazals in English with contributions by over 50 poets, was published by the University Press of New England in 2000.

Amiri Baraka, poet, critic, teacher, political activist, and a driving force behind the Black Arts Movement, is the author of nearly fifty book-length works of poetry, fiction, and drama. *The Leroi Jones/Amiri Baraka Reader,* a comprehensive overview of his forty years of writing, appeared recently from Thundersmouth Press. He has won numerous awards, including the 1987 American Book Award for Lifetime Achievement and was recently inducted into the American Academy of Arts and Letters.

Judith Barrington is the author of two volumes of poetry: *Trying to be an Honest Woman* (1985) and *History and Geography* (1989), as well as *Writing the Memoir: From Truth to Art* (1997). Her most recent book, *Lifesaving: A Memoir,* was a finalist for the PEN/Martha Albrand Award and winner of a Lamda Literary Award in 2001. Her third collection of poetry, *Horses and the Human Soul,* is forthcoming from Story Line Press.

Charles Bernstein is the author of more than twenty collections of poetry and essays. His most recent books include *With Strings* and *My Way: Speeches and Poems,* both from the University of Chicago Press, and *Republics of Reality: 1975–1995,* from Sun & Moon Press. Bernstein is the editor of *Close Listening: Poetry and the Performed Word* (Oxford University Press) and Executive Director of the Electronic Poetry Center (epc.buffalo.edu). He is also the Director of the Poetics Program at SUNY-Buffalo.

Michelle Boisseau's second volume of poems, *Understory* (1996), won the Samuel French Morse Prize from Northeastern University Press. Her first, *No Private Life* (1990), was published by Vanderbilt University Press. She has received fellowships from the NEA and the Kentucky Arts Council and prizes from the Poetry Society of America. Coauthor of the textbook, *Writing Poems,* she teaches at the University of Missouri-Kansas City.

Maxine Chernoff is the author of many prose poems included in six collections of poetry. Her most recent collections are *Japan* (1988), *Leap Year Day* (1991), and *World* (2001). She has also published three collections of short stories and three novels. Chernoff chairs the Department of Creative Writing at San Francisco State University, where she co-edits the journal *New American Writing.*

Jean Hyung Yul Chu has published two books of poetry, *Premonitions* and *Writing Away Here.* She is a doctoral candidate studying American and Asian American poetry at the University of California in Berkeley.

Billy Collins is the author of six books of poetry, including *The Art of Drowning* (1995), *Questions About Angels* (1991), and most recently *Sailing Alone Around the Room: New and Selected Poems* (Random House, 2001). He has received fellowships from the New York Foundation for the Arts, the National Endowment for the Arts, and the Guggenheim Foundation. He is a professor of English at Lehman College, City University of New York and is currently the Library of Congress's Poet Laureate Consultant in Poetry.

Michel Delville is co-founder of the Liège-based Simulated Trauma poetry-jazz project. His performance works, created with Andrew Norris, include *The Mad Queen Simulated Trauma* (1995) and *The Wrong Object* (2001). He teaches at the University of Liège, Belgium, where he directs the newly-founded Centre Interdisciplinaire de Poétique Appliquée. His book, *The American Prose Poem: Poetic Form and the Boundaries of Genre* (Florida, 1998) won the SAMLA Studies Book Award.

Thomas M. Disch is a poet, novelist, playwright, and critic. His collection of essays, *The Castle of Indolence: On Poets, Poetry, and Poetasters,* was a finalist for the National Book Critics Circle Award in Criticism in 1996. A new collection, *The Castle of Perseverance: Job Opportunities in Contemporary Poetry,* is forthcoming soon.

Annie Finch's books of poetry include *Eve* (Story Line, 1997); *Marie Moving* (forthcoming, 2002); and *Brutal Flowers* (a 2000 National Poetry Series finalist). Her translation of the complete poems of renaissance poet Louise Labé is forthcoming from the University of Chicago Press. She is also editor of several anthologies, including *A Formal Feeling Comes: Poems in Form by Contemporary Women,* and the book on poetics *The Ghost of Meter.* She teaches at Miami University (homepage: <http://www.miavx1.muohio.edu/~finchar/>).

Alice Fulton's most recent book of poems is *Felt* (W. W. Norton). A longer version of "Fractal Amplifications," as well as her 1986 essay on fractal form, are reprinted in her collection of essays, *Feeling as a Foreign Language: The Good Strangeness of Poetry,* which was published by Graywolf Press in 1999. A recipient of a John D. and Catherine T. MacArthur Foundation Fellowship, she is Professor of English at The University of Michigan, Ann Arbor.

Dana Gioia has published three books of poetry, *Daily Horoscope* (1986), *The Gods of Winter* (1991), and *Interrogations at Noon* (2001), as well as a critical collection, *Can Poetry Matter?: Essays on American Poetry and Culture* (1992). He co-edits (with X. J. Kennedy) a series of college anthologies, including *An Introduction to Poetry.* His book on contemporary British poetry, *The Barrier of a Common Language,* will appear soon from University of Michigan Press.

Vince Gotera teaches at the University of Northern Iowa, where he serves as Editor of the *North American Review.* He has published a collection of poems, *Dragonfly,* and a literary study, *Radical Visions: Poetry by Vietnam Veterans,* as well as numerous poems in journals and anthologies. Gotera is listowner of FLIPS, an e-mail discussion list for Filipino writers <flips@uni.edu>.

R. S. Gwynn is the author of six collections of poetry, most recently *No Word of Farewell: Selected Poems* 1970-2000, and the editor of *The Advocates of Poetry: A Reader of American Poet-Critics of the Modern Era* (1996), *Poetry: A Longman Pocket Anthology* (1998), and *New Expansive Poetry* (1999). He is University Professor of English at Lamar University.

Marilyn Hacker is author of nine books, including *Presentation Piece,* which won the National Book Award in 1975; *Winter Numbers,* which won both a Lambda Literary Award and the Lenore Marshall Award of *The Nation* magazine and the Academy of American Poets in 1995; the verse novel, *Love, Death and the Changing of the Seasons;* and *Squares and Courtyards* (2000). Her *Selected Poems* won the Poets' Prize in 1996.

Rachel Hadas is Professor of English at the Newark campus of Rutgers University. Her twelfth book, *Halfway Down the Hall: New and Selected Poems,* was published in 1998, and a collection of her critical prose was published in 2000 by the University of Michigan Press. A new book of poems, *Indelible,* is out this fall (2001) from Wesleyan University Press.

Rob Hardin began piano lessons at the age of six and prosody lessons with poet Betty Siegel at the age of ten. He is the author of a novel, a volume of poetry and an unapologetically ornate collection of short stories, *Distorture,* which won the Firecracker Award in 1997. He has played keyboards on over forty albums. He is currently at work on a new novel and on *The Accursed Nursery,* an album of songs for string trio and *hautes-contre.*

Penny Harter has published fifteen books of poems, six since 1994: *Shadow Play: Night Haiku, Stages and Views, Grandmother's Milk, Turtle Blessing, Lizard Light: Poems From the Earth* and *Buried in the Sky.* She has won awards from the New Jersey State Council on the Arts, the Geraldine R. Dodge Foundation, and the Poetry Society of America. In connection with her contribution to *American Nature Writing 2002,* she received the first William O. Douglas Nature Writing Award.

Charles O. Hartman has published five books of poems, most recently *Glass Enclosure* and *The Long View* (Wesleyan University Press), as well as *Free Verse: An Essay on Prosody* (Princeton, reprint Northwestern 1996), *Jazz Text,* and *Virtual Muse: Experiments in Computer Poetry.* He is Professor of English and Poet in Residence at Connecticut College.

Anthony Hecht is a recipient of the Tanning Prize in Poetry (1998); the Eugenio Montale Award in Poetry (1984); and the Pulitzer Prize (1968). From 1982–84 he was Consultant in Poetry to the Library of Congress.

William J. Higginson's books on traditional Japanese poetic forms include *The Haiku Handbook: How to Write, Share, and Teach Haiku,* with Penny Harter; *The Haiku Seasons: Poetry of the Natural World,* and *Haiku World: An International Poetry Almanac.* He has published four collections of poems, including *Paterson Pieces: Poems 1969–1979.* He is currently a Toshiba Fellow with the Japanese Text Initiative at the University of Virginia.

Jan D. Hodge, Professor Emeritus of English, Morningside College, Sioux City, Iowa, grew up in a letterpress print shop in small town Michigan. His poems have appeared in *Negative Capability, The Beloit Poetry Journal, South Coast Poetry Journal, Defined Providence, the North American Review,* and elsewhere. His "Carousel," a carmen figuratum written in dactylic meter, won the 1997 WordArt Esme Bradberry Prize, and his *Poems to be Traded for Baklava* was the Onionhead Annual chapbook for 1997.

John Hollander has published 17 books of poetry, the most recent being *Figurehead* (Knopf, 1999); his seven books of criticism include *The*

Work of Poetry and *The Poetry of Everyday Life,* and the handbook of verse form, *Rhyme's Reason.* He has been awarded the Bollingen Prize and a MacArthur Fellowship, and is Sterling Professor of English at Yale University.

Margaret Holley is the former director of the Creative Writing Program at Bryn Mawr College. Her books include *The Poetry of Marianne Moore: A Study in Voice and Value* (Cambridge University Press 1988) and four books of poems, most recently *Kore in Bloom* (Copper Beech 1998).

Bob Holman has published in many venues including *Aloud! Voices from the Nuyorican Poets Cafe* (Henry Holt); *The United States of Poetry* (PBS/Abrams); *In with the Out Crowd* (Mouth Almighty/Mercury); *The Peoples Poetry Gathering* (<www.peoplespoetry.org>); and *The World of Poetry* (<www.worldofpoetry.org>). He teaches at Bard College as a Visiting Professor of English.

Paul Hoover is author of seven books of poetry including *Rehearsal in Black* (Salt Publications), *Winter(Mirror)* (Flood Editions), *Totem and Shadow: New & Selected Poems* (Talisman House), *Viridian* (U. of Georgia Press), and *The Novel: A Poem* (New Directions). He is also editor of the anthology *Postmodern American Poetry* (W. W. Norton) and the literary magazine *New American Writing.*

Allison Joseph is the author of three books of poems: *What Keeps Us Here* (Ampersand Press, 1992), *Soul Train* (Carnegie-Mellon UP, 1997) and *In Every Seam* (U of Pittsburgh P, 1997). She currently teaches at Southern Illinois University in Carbondale, Illinois.

X. J. Kennedy has written verse (including *Nude Descending a Staircase* and *Dark Horses),* textbooks (among them *An Introduction to Poetry,* co-authored with Dana Gioia), and seventeen children's books. *The Minimus Poems* (published by Robert L. Barth) is a collection of his epigrams. He lives in Lexington, Massachusetts, in a partially old house next to the Minuteman Bikepath.

Maxine Kumin is the author of thirteen books of poems, most recently *The Long Marriage* (Norton), four novels and three collections of essays. A former Poet Laureate of New Hampshire, she has won the Pulitzer Prize, the Aiken Taylor Award, The Poets' Prize, and the Ruth E. Lilly Award.

David Lehman's most recent of four collections of poems is *The Daily Mirror* (Scribner, 2000), and his most recent critical book is *The Last*

Avant-Garde. He is the general editor of the Poets on Poetry Series for the University of Michigan Press, which published his anthology *Ecstatic Occasions, Expedient Forms*, and he initiated *The Best American Poetry* in 1988. His many awards include a Guggenheim Fellowship in poetry.

Pat Mora writes poetry, nonfiction and children's books. She has published five poetry collections, most recently *Aunt Carmen's Book of Practical Saints* and *Agua Santa: Holy Water*. She has received awards from the National Endowment for the Arts and the Kellogg National Leadership Fellowships. A native of El Paso, Texas, she divides her time between the Southwest and the Cincinnati area.

Hilda Morley published several books of poetry during her lifetime, including *A Blessing Outside Us, What Are Winds & What Are Waters, To Hold in My Hand: Selected Poems, Cloudless at First*, and *The Turning*, which was published by Asphodel Press in 1998. Her poems have appeared in many journals, most notably *The New Yorker, The Paris Review, New American Writing, Pequod*, and *The American Voice*.

Tracie Morris's awards include: National Haiku Slam Championship, Lila Wallace Arts Partnership Grants, ASCAP special award, and Franklin Furnace's artist-in-exile grant. Morris has participated in eight recording projects and has been published in dozens of magazines. She is the author of *Intermission* (Soft Skull Press, 1999) and *Chap-T-Her-Won: Some Poems by Tracie Morris*.

Aldon Lynn Nielsen's books of poetry include *Heat Strings, Evacuation Routes, Stepping Razor*, and *Vext*. Among his works of criticism are *Reading Race, Writing between the Lines, Black Chant: Languages of African-American Postmodernism*, and *C.L.R. James: A Critical Introduction*. He has recently edited the critical collection *Reading Race in American Poetry: An Area of Act*. He teaches at Penn State University.

John Frederick Nims, beloved poet, editor, and translator, was an inspiration to many during his lifetime. He translated two plays of Euripides, the poems of St. John of the Cross, a variety of poems in *Sappho to Valéry*, and *The Complete Poems of Michelangelo* (University of Chicago Press, 1998). All of these translations dealt with the metrical forms of the originals. He also published eight volumes of poetry, and four editions of *Western Wind: An Introduction to Poetry*.

Jacqueline Osherow's most recent book is *Dead Men's Praise* (Grove, 1999). She has received fellowships from the Guggenheim Foundation, the NEA, the Poetry Society of America, and the Ingram Merrill Foundation, and has been awarded the Witter Bynner Prize by the American Academy and Institute of Arts and Letters. She is Professor of English at the University of Utah.

Jena Osman is an Assistant Professor of English and Creative Writing at Temple University. Her book, *The Character,* won the Barnard New Women Poets prize in 1998 and was published by Beacon Press. She is co-editor of the award-winning interdisciplinary arts journal, *Chain,* with Juliana Spahr. She has received grants from the NEA, the New York Foundation for the Arts, and the Fund for Poetry.

Raymond Patterson once wrote of himself that he fell into the blues in the 1980s and has been working his way out ever since. He authored *26 Ways of Looking at a Black Man and Other Poems,* and *Elemental Blues,* a collection of blues poems. For many years he taught at the City College of New York, where he co-founded and directed its annual Langston Hughes Festival.

Carl Phillips is the author of five books of poetry, most recently *The Tether* (FSG, 2001). A sixth book, *Rock Harbor,* will be published in the winter of 2002. Phillips teaches at Washington University, St. Louis.

DJ Renegade is a former Hip-Hop DJ, who lives in DC, works for WritersCorps teaching poetry in underserved communities, is a nationally known performance poet, and has published in various places including the recent anthologies *Catch the Fire* and *Poetry Nation.*

John Ridland has taught writing and literature courses at the University of California in Santa Barbara since 1961. His books included *John the Valiant,* an English version of Sándor Petőfi's Hungarian folk epic János Vitéz (Budapest: Corvina Press, 1999); *Life with Unkie* (Santa Barbara: Mille Grazie Press, 1999) and *Palms* (Santa Barbara: Buckner Press, 1993).

Grace Schulman's poetry collections include *For That Day Only, Hemispheres, Burn Down the Icons, The Paintings of Our Lives,* and, forthcoming, *Days of Wonder: New and Selected Poems.* She is a recipient of the Delmore Schwartz Memorial Award for Poetry, and is represented in *The Best American Poetry* and *The Best of the Best American Poetry.* A Distinguished Professor of English at Baruch College, C. U. N. Y., she is Poetry Editor of the *Nation.*

W. D. Snodgrass's latest book is *De/Compositions: 101 Good Poems Gone Wrong* (2001) from Graywolf Press. Other recent publications include *After-Images: Autobiographical Sketches* (1999), *Selected Trans-*

lations (1998) and *The Fuehrer Bunker: The Complete Cycle* (1995) all from BOA.

Timothy Steele's collections of poems include *The Color Wheel* and *Sapphics and Uncertainties: Poems 1970–1986*. He has also published two books of literary criticism, *Missing Measures* and *All the Fun's in How You Say a Thing: An Explanation of Meter and Versification*. He is as well the editor of *The Poems of J.V. Cunningham*.

Felix Stefanile's books of poems include *The Country of Absence* (Bordighera, 2000), *A Fig Tree in America* (1970), and *The Dance at St. Gabriel's: Poems* (1995). He is the first recipient of the newly established John Ciardi Award for lifetime achievement by an Italian American poet and a professor emeritus at Purdue.

Keith Tuma's essays and a scattering of performance texts and poems have appeared in numerous print and electronic journals. His *Fishing by Obstinate Isles: Modern and Postmodern British Poetry and American Readers* (Northwestern UP) and the co-edited *Mina Loy: Woman and Poet* (National Poetry Foundation) were published in 1998. *The Oxford Anthology of 20th Century British and Irish Poetry* appeared in 2001.

Lewis Turco has won many awards including the Bordighera Bilingual Poetry Prize for *A Book of Fears* in 1997 and the John Ciardi Award for lifetime achievement in poetry in 1999. His books include *Dialogue, A Socratic Dialogue on the Art and Craft of Writing Dialogue in Fiction* (Writers Digest Books, 1989), now in its ninth printing; *The Book of Literary Terms*; and *The Book of Forms, A Handbook of Poetics*.

Mark Wallace's books of poetry include *Nothing Happened and Besides I Wasn't There* (Edge Books); *The Sonnets of a Penny-A-Liner* (Buck Downs Books); and New American Poetry Prize winner *Temporary Worker Rides a Subway* (Sun and Moon Press). He is co-editor of *A Poetics of Criticism*. With Steven Marks he edited *Telling It Slant: Avant Garde Poetics of the 1990s* (U of Alabama Press 2001). He lives in Washington, D.C., where he writes reviews for *The Washington Review* and runs The Ruthless Grip Art Project Poetry Series.

Rosanna Warren's most recent book is a verse translation of Euripides' *Suppliant Women* (with Stephen Scully, Oxford UP, 1995). Her books of poetry include *Stained Glass* (Norton, 1993, winner of Lamont Prize for Academy of American Poets), *Each Leaf Shines Separate* (Norton, 1984), and a chapbook, *Snow Day* (Palaemon Press, 1981). A Fellow of the American Academy of Arts and Sciences, and a Chancellor of the

Academy of American Poets, Warren teaches comparative literature at Boston University.

Kathleene West is Poetry Editor of *Puerto del Sol.* She has published nine books and chapbooks of poetry and fiction. She received the Kenneth Patchen Memorial Award for her unpublished fiction manuscript *The Summer of the Sub-Comandant.* A Fulbright fellow at the University of Iceland in 1983–85, she is now professor of English at New Mexico State University in Las Cruces.

Gail White is co-editor (with Katherine McAlpine) of *The Muse Strikes Back,* an anthology of women's poetry. She also edited a 4-woman collection, *Landscapes with Women,* now nearing publication. She lives in Breaux Bridge, Louisiana, with Arthur and Yellow Cat.

Nancy Willard teaches in the Department of English at Vassar College. Her books include *Swimming Lessons: New and Selected Poems* (Knopf) and a book of essays on writing, *Telling Time: Angels, Ancestors, and Stories.*

Grateful acknowledgment is made to the following authors, publishers, and journals for permission to reprint previously published materials.

Alcaeus, "Fragment Q L," translated by Denys Page, from *Sappho and Alcaeus*. Copyright © 1955. Reprinted with the permission of Oxford University Press, Ltd. Elizabeth Alexander, "The Dirt-Eaters" from *The Venus Hottentot*. Copyright © 1990 by the Rector and Visitors of the University of Virginia. Reprinted with the permission of The University Press of Virginia. Agha Shahid Ali, ghazal ["Where are you now? Who lies beneath your spell tonight"] from *The Country Without a Post Office*. Copyright © 1997 by Agha Shahid Ali. Reprinted with the permission of W. W. Norton & Company, Inc. Dante Alighieri, excerpt [12 lines] from *The Divine Comedy*, translated by Felix Stefanile. Reprinted with the permission of the translator. Julia Alvarez, "Bilingual Sestina" from *The Other Side* (New York: Dutton, 1995). Copyright © 1995 by Julia Alvarez. Reprinted with the permission of Susan Bergholz Literary Services, New York. Anonymous, excerpt from "Beowulf," translated by Tim Murphy and Alan Sullivan. Reprinted with the permission of Tim Murphy and Alan Sullivan. Guillaume Apollinaire, excerpt from shaped poem ["This sad tie that you wear . . . ," translated by Jan D. Hodge. Reprinted with the permission of the translator. W. H. Auden, "The Quest XIII" (originally titled "The Useful") from *W. H. Auden: Collected Poems*, edited by Edward Mendelson. Copyright 1941 and renewed © 1969 by W. H. Auden. Reprinted with the permission of Random House, Inc. and Faber and Faber, Ltd. Amiri Baraka, "Monday in B Flat" (1994). Copyright © 1994 by Amiri Baraka. Reprinted with the permission of Sterling Lord Literistic, Inc. Bashō, Kyorai, Boncho and Fumikuni, excerpt [verses 1–6, 25–36] from "Kite's Feathers," translated by William Higginson, from *Monkey's Raincoat*. Reprinted with the permission of the translator. ["stillness—the cicada's cry / drills into the rocks"]; ["deep autumn"]; and ["even in Kyoto"], translated by Robert Haas, from *The Essential Haiku: Versions of Bashō, Buson and Issa*, edited by Robert Haas. Reprinted with the permission of the translator. Robyn Bell, "Visitation" from *Small Potatoes* (Kalamazoo, Mich.: Buckner Press, 1996). Reprinted with the permission of the author. Bruce Bennett, "Mack the Epigram" from *Taking Off* (Washington, DC: Orchises Press, 1992). Reprinted with the permission of the author. Edmund Clerihew Bentley, "Sir Christopher Wren" and "Cervantes" from *The Complete Clerihews*. Copyright the Estate of E. C. Bentley. Reprinted with the permission of Curtis Brown, Ltd., London, on behalf of the Estate of E. C. Bentley. Charles Bernstein, "Pinky Swear" from *Republic of Reality: 1975–1995* (Los Angeles: Sun & Moon Press, 1999). Reprinted with the permission of the author. Elizabeth Bishop, "One Art" and "Sestina" from *The Complete Poems*. Copyright © 1979, 1983 by Alice Helen Methfessel. Reprinted with the permission of Farrar, Straus & Giroux, LLC. Cathy Bowman, "No Sorry" from *Rock Farm* (Layton, Utah: Gibbs Smith, 1996). Reprinted with the permission of the author. Gwendolyn Brooks, "We Real Cool" and "Rites for Cousin Vit" from *Blacks* (Chicago: Third World Press, 1991). Copyright © 1991 by Gwendolyn Brooks Blakely. Both reprinted with the permission of the author. Lee Ann Brown, "Summery" from *Polyverse* (Los Angeles: Sun & Moon Press, 1999). Reprinted with the permission of the author. Yosa Buson, haiku ["The petals fall"], translated by Robert Haas, from *The Essential*

Haiku: Versions of Bashō, Buson and Issa, edited by Robert Haas. Copyright © 1994 by Robert Haas. Reprinted with the permission of HarperCollins Publishers, Inc. "The horse's tail," translated by R. H. Blyth, from *Haiku, Volume IV*. Reprinted with the permission of The Hokuseido Press, Japan. John Cage, "Art Is Either a Complaint or Do Something Else" (excerpt) from *MUSICAGE: Cage Muses on Words, Art and Music: John Cage in Conversation with Joan Retallack*. Copyright © 1996. Reprinted with the permission of Wesleyan University Press. Fred Chappell, "Conservative" from C (Baton Rouge: Louisiana State University Press, 1993). Reprinted with the permission of the author. Maxine Chernoff, "How Lies Grow" *Leap Year Day: New and Selected Poems* (Chicago: Another Chicago Press, 1990 and Jenson Daniels, 1998). Reprinted with the permission of the author. Kaga No Chiyo, "The morning glory!," translated by Jane Hirshfield, from *Women in Praise of the Sacred* (New York: HarperPerennial, 1994). Copyright © 1994 by Jane Hirshfield. Reprinted with the permission of the translator. C. W. Christian, "The Anaconda." Reprinted with the permission of the author. Billy Collins, "Paradelle for Susan" from *Picnic, Lightning*. Copyright © 1998. Reprinted with the permission of the University of Pittsburgh Press. Jane Cooper, "Wanda's Blues" from *The Flashboat: Poems Collected and Reclaimed* Copyright © 2000 by Jane Cooper. Reprinted with the permission of W. W. Norton & Company, Inc. Wendy Cope, "Triolet" from *Making Cocoa for Kingsley Amis*. Copyright © 1986 by Wendy Cope. Reprinted with the permission of Faber and Faber, Ltd. Alfred Corn, "Sapphics at a Trot" from *Present*. Copyright © 1997 by Alfred Corn. Reprinted with the permission of Counterpoint Press, a member of Perseus Books L.L.C. Wesli Court, "The Obsession" from Lewis Turco, *The Little Book of Forms: A Handbook of Poetics* (Hanover, NH: University Press of New England, 1986). Reprinted with the permission of Lewis Turco. J. V. Cunningham, "Epigram #76" from *The Collected Poems and Epigrams of J. V. Cunningham*. Excerpt from "There is a ghosttown of abandoned love" from *The Poems of J. V. Cunningham*, edited by Timothy Steele. Both reprinted with the permission of Ohio University Press/Swallow Press, Athens, Ohio. Tina Darragh, "'legion' to 'lent' for 'R,'" "'mobilizer' to 'modern language' for 'U',", "volcanic tuff," and "ludicrous stick" from *on the corner to off the corner*. Copyright © 1981 by Tina Darragh. Reprinted with the permission of Sun & Moon Press. "Ames Distorted Room Transcriptions of Puns in 'Scale Sliding'." Reprinted with the permission of the author. Elizabeth Daryush, "Still Life" from *Collected Poems*. Copyright © 1976 by Elizabeth Daryush. Reprinted with the permission of Carcanet Press, Ltd. L. A. Davidson, excerpt from "Paper Flower Unfurling" ["church usher"] from *Frogpond* XV:2 (Fall-Winter 1992). Reprinted with the permission of the author. Dick Davis, "Into Care" from *Touchwood*. Copyright © 1996 by Dick Davis. Reprinted with the permission of Anvil Press Poetry, Ltd. Lydia Davis, "The Fish" from *Break It Down* (New York: Farrar, Straus & Giroux, 1986). Copyright © 1986 by Lydia Davis. Reprinted with the permission of International Creative Management, Inc. Lope de Vega, "Los Pastores de Belén," translated by Aurelio Espinosa, from *Folklore of Spain in the American Southwest*. Copyright © 1985 by the University of Oklahoma Press. Reprinted with the permission of the publishers. Emily Dickinson, #709 ["Publication—is the Auction"] and #1595 ["Declaiming Waters none may dread—"] from *The Complete Poems of Emily Dickinson*, edited by Thomas H. Johnson. Copyright 1951, © 1955, 1979 by the President and Fellows of Harvard College. Reprinted with the permission of The

Belknap Press of Harvard University Press and the Trustees of Amherst College. Tom Disch, "Rondeau for Emporio Armani." Reprinted with the permission of the author. Rita Dove, "Soprano" from *Poetry* (January 1998). Copyright © 1998 by Rita Dove. Reprinted with the permission of the author. Russell Edson, "The Optical Prodigal." Reprinted with the permission of the author. Kenward Elmslie, "Amazon Club." Reprinted with the permission of the author. Annie Finch, "Watching the Whale" from *Thirteenth Moon* (Spring 2000). "Lucid Waking" from *Eve* (Brownsville, Oregon: Story Line Press, 1998). Both reprinted with the permission of the author. Carrie Fountain, "Lane's End" (1998). Reprinted with the permission of the author. Robert Frost, "For Once, Then, Something," "Acquainted with the Night," and "Nothing Gold Can Stay" from *The Poetry of Robert Frost,* edited by Edward Connery Lathem. Copyright 1951, © 1956 by Robert Frost. Copyright 1923, 1928, © 1969 by Henry Holt and Company, LLC. Reprinted with the permission of Henry Holt & Company, LLC and Jonathan Cape, Ltd. Forrest Gander, "Notes on the form of 'The Blue Rock Collection'." "The Blue Rock Collection" from *Deeds of the Utmost Kindness* (Hanover, New Hampshire: Wesleyan University Press, 1994). Both reprinted with the permission of the author. Amy Gerstler, "Bitter Angel" from *Bitter Angel* (Berkeley: North Point Press, 1990 and Pittsburgh: Carnegie Mellon University Press 1998). Copyright © by Amy Gerstler. Reprinted with the permission of the author. Dana Gioia, "Vampire's Nocturne" from *Nosferatu* (St. Paul: Graywolf Press, 2001). Copyright © 2001 by Dana Gioia. Reprinted with the permission of the author. Vince Gotera, "Chain-Letter Pantoum." Reprinted with the permission of the author. Thom Gunn, "Word for Some Ash" from *The Man With Night Sweats.* Copyright © 1993 by Thom Gunn. Reprinted with the permission of Farrar, Straus & Giroux, LLC and Faber & Faber, Ltd. Max Gutman, "Alice." Reprinted with the permission of the author. R. S. Gwynn, excerpt (9 lines) from "The Dream Again" from *No Word of Farewell: Selected Poems 1970–2000* (Brownsville, Oregon: Story Line Press, 2000). "Two Views from a High Window." Both reprinted with the permission of the author. Marilyn Hacker, two rondeaux from *Love, Death and the Changing of the Seasons* (New York: W. W. Norton & Company, 1986). Copyright © 1986 by Marilyn Hacker. Reprinted with the permission of the author. Rachel Hadas, "On That Mountain" from *Halfway Down the Hall: New and Selected Poems* (Hanover, New Hampshire: Wesleyan University Press, 1998). Copyright © 1998 by Rachel Hadas. "Greek Gold" from *The Empty Bed* (Hanover, New Hampshire: Wesleyan University Press, 1995). Copyright © 1995 by Rachel Hadas. Both reprinted with the permission of University Press of New England, Hanover, NH. Daniel Hall, "Souvenir." Reprinted with the permission of the author. Kathleen Halme, "A Celibate Imagination" from *Every Substance Clothed.* Copyright © 1995 by Kathleen Halme. Reprinted with the permission of The University of Georgia Press. Rob Hardin, excerpt from "Justine Variations." Copyright © 1998 by Carnographies, Limited. Thomas Hardy, "The Voice" from *The Complete Poems of Thomas Hardy,* edited by James Gibson. Copyright © 1976 by Macmillan London Ltd. Reprinted with the permission of Macmillan Press, Ltd. Cindi Harrison, "Your Search for Independence." Reprinted with the permission of the author. Charles O. Hartman and Hugh Kenner, "XV" from *Sentences* (Los Angeles: Sun and Moon Press, 1995). Copyright © 1995 by Charles O. Hartman and Hugh Kenner. Reprinted with the permission of the authors. Randolph Healy, "XIII" from *Scales* (Bray, Ireland: Wild Honey Press, 1998).

Reprinted with the permission of the author. Lyn Hejinian, excerpts from *My Life*. Copyright © 1987 by Lyn Hejinian. Reprinted with the permission of the author and Sun & Moon Press. William J. Higginson, Penny Harter and Connie Meester, "Triangle of Snow." Reprinted with the permission of the authors. Jan D. Hodge, two versions of a shaped poem ["the / grace of / the dancer / the rays of / the flame"]. Reprinted with the permission of the author. John Hollander, "Catamaran," "Self-Descriptive Hendecasyllabics," and Ghazal ["For couplets the ghazal is prime; at the end"] from *Rhyme's Reason, Second Enlarged Edition*. Copyright © 1989. "Swan and Shadow" from *Types of Shape*. Copyright © 1991. All reprinted with the permission of Yale University Press. Margaret Holley, "C.ner Countries." Reprinted with the permission of the author. Bob Holman, "Performance Poem" from David Lehman and Star Black, eds., *The KGB Bar Book of Poems* (New York: Harper/Perennial, 2000). Reprinted with the permission of the author. Paul Hoover, "How did you get the Elephants here?" (1987). Reprinted with the permission of the author. A. D. Hope, "Coup de Grace" from *Collected Poems* (New York: Viking, 1966). Copyright © 1966 by A. D. Hope. Reprinted with the permission of Curtis Brown (Aust) Pty Ltd., Sydney. Horace, "Ode I, 9," translated by James Michie, from *The Odes of Horace* (Harmondsworth: Penguin, 1964). Copyright © 1964 by James Michie. Reprinted with the permission of the translator. Richard Hugo, "The Freaks at Spurgin Road Field" from *Making Certain It Goes On: The Collected Poems of Richard Hugo*. Copyright © 1984 by The Estate of Richard Hugo. Reprinted with the permission of W. W. Norton & Company, Inc. Lawson Fusao Inada, "Just as I thought" from *drawing the line* (Minneapolis, Minn.: Coffee House Press, 1997). Reprinted with the permission of the author. Kobayashi Issa, "only one guy and," translated by Cid Corman, from *One Man's Moon*. Reprinted with the permission of Gnomon Press. Elizabeth Jennings, "Answers" from *Selected Poems* (Manchester: Carcanet Press, 1979). Copyright © 1979 by Elizabeth Jennings. Reprinted with the permission of David Higham Associates, Ltd. Linton Kwesi Johnson, "Yout Scene" from *Dread Beat and Blood* (London: Bogle-L'Ouverture Publications Ltd, 1975). Copyright © 1975 by Linton Kwesi Johnson. Reprinted with the permission of the author. Allison Joseph, "The Fitting." Reprinted with the permission of the author. Lawrence Joseph, "Under a Spell" from *Before Our Eyes*. Copyright © 1993 by Lawrence Joseph. Reprinted with the permission of Farrar, Strauss & Giroux, LLC. Rafique Kathwari, "Jewel House Ghazal." Reprinted with the permission of the author. X. J. Kennedy, "Old Man Pitching Horse Shoes" and "On Someone Who Insisted I Look Up Someone" from *Cross Ties: Selected Poems* (Athens: The University of Georgia Press, 1985). Copyright © 1985 by X. J. Kennedy. Reprinted with the permission of the author. Kris Kondo, excerpt from "Blooming Street" ["transcribing"] [unpublished renku written in Belmont, CA, February–August 1992]. Reprinted with the permission of the author and the Association for International Renku. Maxine Kumin, "The Nuns of Childhood: Two Views" from *Looking for Luck*. Copyright © 1992 by Maxine Kumin. Reprinted with the permission of W. W. Norton & Company, Inc. Joel Kuszai, ["the dark / and time's consuming"] from "*A Miscellany*" (San Diego: MeowPress, 1998). Reprinted with the permission of the author. Elizabeth Searle Lamb, excerpt from "The Split Moon" ["a happy little boy"] from *Haiku Magazine* 6: 3 (1976). Reprinted with the permission of the author. Denise Levertov, "Overland to the Islands" from *Collected Earlier Poems 1940–1960*. Copyright © 1958, 1979 by Denise Levertov.

"The Vron Woods (North Wales)" from *Candles in Babylon*. Copyright © 1958, 1979 by Denise Levertov. Excerpts from "Psalm Concerning the Castle" from *Poems 1960–1967*. Copyright © 1966 by Denise Levertov. All reprinted with the permission of New Directions Publishing Corporation. Janet Lewis, "A Cautionary Note" from *The Dear Past* (Edgewood, Kentucky: R.L. Barth, 1994). Reprinted with the permission of Daniel Lewis Winters, Literary Executor for Janet Lewis. Shirley Geok-Lin Lim, "Pantoum for Chinese Women" from *Monsoon History: Selected Poems* (London: Skoob Books, 1994). Copyright © 1994 by Shirley Geok-Lin Lim. Reprinted with the permission of the author. Rachel Loden, "Headline from a Photograph by Richard Avedon" from *Hotel Imperium*. Copyright © 1999 by Rachel Loden. Reprinted with the permission of The University of Georgia Press. Jackson Mac Low, "Ridiculous in Piccadilly" from *The Virginia Woolf Poems* (Providence: Burning Deck Press, 1985). Copyright © 1985 by Jackson Mac Low. "Statement About *154 Forties*." Copyright © 2000 by Jackson Mac Low. "Deciduous Lips (Forties 117)" from *154 Forties*. Copyright © 2000 by Jackson Mac Low. All reprinted with the permission of the author. Estella Majozo, "The Malcolm Calling Blues" from *Jiva Telling Rites* (Chicago: Third World Press, 1991). Martial, excerpt from "Preface," translated by William Matthews, from *Selected Poems and Translations, 1969–1991*. Copyright © 1992 by William Matthews. Reprinted with the permission of Houghton Mifflin Company. All rights reserved. Masaoka Shiki, "A lightning flash," translated by Harold Henderson, from *An Introduction to Haiku: An Anthology of Poems and Poets from Basho to Shiki*. Copyright © 1958 by Harold G. Henderson. Reprinted with the permission of Doubleday, a division of Random House, Inc. David Mason, "Song of the Powers" from *The Country I Remember* (Ashland, Ore.: Story Line Press, 1996). Copyright © 1996 by David Mason. Reprinted with the permission of the author. Harry Matthews, "Liminal Poem" from *Oulipo: A Primer of Potential Literature,* translated and edited by Warren F. Motte, Jr. (Lincoln, Neb.: University of Nebraska Press, 1986). "Presto" from *New Observations* 99 (January/February 1994). Copyright © 1994 by Harry Matthews. Both reprinted with the permission of the author. Paul McCallum, "A Vertical Reflection" (previously unpublished). Reprinted with the permission of the author. Michael McClintock, excerpt from "The Split Moon" ["the photo album"] from *Haiku Magazine* 6: 3 (1976). Reprinted with the permission of the author. Sandra McPherson, "Triolet" from *The Year of Our Birth*. Copyright © 1973, 1974, 1975, 1976, 1977, 1978 by Sandra McPherson. Reprinted with the permission of The Ecco Press. Peter Meinke, "Atomic Pantoum" from *Liquid Paper: New and Selected Poems*. Copyright © 1991 by Peter Meinke. Reprinted with the permission of the University of Pittsburgh Press. Edna St. Vincent Millay, "Sonnet I" ["So she came back into his house again"] from "Sonnets from an Ungrafted Tree" from *Collected Poems* (New York: HarperCollins). Copyright 1923, 1951 by Edna St. Vincent Millay and Norma Millay Ellis. All rights reserved. Reprinted with the permission of Elizabeth Barnett, literary executor. Marianne Moore, "A Grave," "The Mind Is an Enchanting Thing" (excerpt), and "The Fish" from *The Complete Poems of Marianne Moore*. Copyright 1935, 1944 and renewed © 1963 by T. S. Eliot and Marianne Moore, © 1972 by Marianne Moore. Reprinted with the permission of Simon & Schuster, Inc. and Faber & Faber, Ltd. Richard Moore, "Overheard at a Feminist Conference" from *Bottom is Back* (Washington, DC: Orchises Press, 1994). Reprinted with the permission of the author. Pat Mora, "Santa Teresa de

Ávila" from *Aunt Carmen's Book of Practical Saints*. Copyright © 1997 by Pat Mora. Reprinted with the permission of Beacon Press, Boston. Hilda Morley, "Sea Lily" from *To Hold in My Hand*. Copyright © 1983 by Hilda Morley. Reprinted with the permission of Sheep Meadow Press. "Rome, 1970" from *The Turning* (Wakefield, Rhode Island: Asphodel Press/Moyer Bell, 1999). Copyright © 1998 by Hilda Morley. Reprinted with the permission of Moyer Bell. Jennifer Moxley, "When in Rome" from *Imagination Verses* (New York: Tender Buttons Press, 1996). Reprinted with the permission of the publishers. Paul Muldoon, excerpt [LXXXVIII] from "Hopewell Haiku" from *Hay*. Copyright © 1998 by Paul Muldoon. Reprinted with the permission of Farrar, Strauss & Giroux, LLC. Jonathan Musgrove, "Sara's Ghazal." Reprinted with the permission of the author. Patricia Neubauer, excerpt from "Paper Flower Unfurling" ["the clairvoyant's cat"] from *Frogpond* XV:2 (Fall–Winter 1992). Reprinted with the permission of the author. Terence Nicholson, "Don't Run," "Darkcide," and "My Cipher Go Way Back." Copyright © 1999 by Terence Nicholson. Reprinted with permission of the author. John Frederick Nims, from "Niagara" [excerpt, "Section III"] and "Water Music" from *The Six-Cornered Snowflake and Other Poems*. Copyright © 1990 by John Frederick Nims. Both reprinted with the permission of New Directions Publishing Corporation. "Critic: Coterie Review of Books" from *Zany in Denim* (Fayetteville: University of Arkansas Press, 1990). Copyright © 1990 by John Frederick Nims. Reprinted with the permission of Bonnie Nims. Charles Olson, "For Sappho, Back" from *The Collected Poems of Charles Olson: Excluding the Maximus Poems*. Copyright © 1987 by the Estate of Charles Olson. Reprinted with the permission of the University of California Press. George Oppen, "The Forms of Love" from *Collected Poems*. Copyright © 1975 by George Oppen. Reprinted with the permission of New Directions Publishing Corporation. Jacqueline Osherow, "London, Before and After the Middle Way" from *With a Moon in Transit*. Copyright © 1996 by Jacqueline Osherow. Reprinted with the permission of Grove/Atlantic, Inc. Dorothy Parker, "The Actress" (Part VI of "Tombstones in the Starlight") from *The Portable Dorothy Parker*. Copyright 1928 and renewed © 1956 by Dorothy Parker. Reprinted with the permission of Viking Penguin, a division of Penguin Putnam Inc. and Gerald Duckworth, Ltd. Linda Pastan, "Because" from *Carnival Evening*. Copyright © 1978 by Linda Pastan. Reprinted with the permission of W. W. Norton & Company, Inc. Raymond R. Patterson, "Computer Blues" from *Elemental Blues* (Merrick, NY: Cross-Cultural Communcations, 1989). Reprinted with the permission of the author. Molly Peacock, "Food for Talk" from *Take Heart*. Copyright © 1989 by Molly Peacock. Reprinted with the permission of Random House, Inc. Georges Perec, "Ozymandias," translated by Gilbert Adair, from *A Void*. Copyright © 1969 by Editions Demoël. English translation copyright © 1994 by HarperCollins Publishers. Reprinted with the permission of The Harvill Press. Bob Perelman, "Chronic Meanings" from *Virtual Reading* (New York: Roof Books, 1993). Reprinted with the permission of the publishers. Gloria Procsal and Frederick Gasser, excerpt from "Windswept Walk" from *Frogpond* XV:I (Spring–Summer 1992). Reprinted with the permission of Frederick Gasser and the Haiku Society of America. Raymond Queneau, "'haikuization' of Mallarme" from *Oulipo: A Primer of Potential Literature*, translated and edited by Warren F. Motte, Jr. Copyright © 1986 by the University of Nebraska Press. Reprinted with the permission of the University of Nebraska Press. T. M. Ramirez, excerpt from "A Distant World" ["up the stairs from the bubway"] [unpublished renku written by correspondence, 1995]. Reprinted with the permission of the author. Dudley Randall, "The Southern Road." Reprinted with the permission of the author. Ishmael Reed, "Oakland Blues" from *New and Collected Poems* (New York: Atheneum Publishers, 1988). Copyright © 1988 by Ishmael Reed. Reprinted with the permission of the author. Joan Retallack, excerpt from *Afterrimages* (Middletown, Conn.: Wesleyan University Press, 1995). Copyright © 1995 by Joan Retallack. Excerpts from email messages (March 10, 1997 and June 16, 1998). "AID/I/SAPPEARANCE" from *How To Do Things With Words* (Los Angeles: Sun & Moon, 1998). All reprinted with the permission of the author. Lisa Robertson, "I Saw a Dog . . ."from *Debbie: An Epic* (Vancouver: New Star Books and London: Reality Street Editions, 1997). Copyright © 1997 by Lisa Robertson. Reprinted with the permission of the author. Jerome Rothenberg, "A Poem About a Wolf, Maybe Two Wolves" (after Seneca) from *Shaking the Pumpkin: Traditional Poetry of the Indian North Americas* (New York: Doubleday, 1972). "The Killer" [after Cherokee] from *Technicians of the Sacred* (Garden City, New York: Anchor Books, 1969). Both reprinted with the permission of the author. Maurice Sagoff, "Monet" from *Light*. Reprinted with the permission of Charlotte Sagoff. Sonia Sanchez, "my bones hang to" from *Like the Singing Coming Off the Drums: Love Poems* (Boston: Beacon Press, 1998). Reprinted with the permission of the author. Ursula Sandlee, excerpt from "A Distant World" ["in quiet desperation"][unpublished renku written by correspondence, 1995]. Reprinted with the permission of the author. Sappho, "Tell Everyone," translated by Mary Barnard, from *Sappho: A New Translation*. Copyright © 1958 by The Regents of the University of California, renewed 1984 by Mary Barnard. Reprinted with the permission of the University of California Press. Kurt Schwitters, "Simultaneous Poem" from *Poems, Performance Pieces, Proses, Plays, Poetics*, edited and translated by Jerome Rothenberg and Pierre Joris (Philadelphia: Temple University Press, 1993). Copyright © 1993 by Jerome Rothenberg and Pierre Joris. Reprinted with the permission of the translators. Ichiyo Shimizu, Mary Conley and Shinku Fukuda, excerpt from "Morning Fog." Reprinted with the permission of the authors and the Association for International Renku. Ron Silliman, "The Figures" from *Tjanting* (Great Barrington, Mass.: The Figures Press, 1981). Reprinted with the permission of the author. Patricia Smith, "Skinhead" from *Big Towns, Big Talk* (Cambridge, Mass.: Zoland Books, 1992). Copyright © 1992 by Patricia Smith. Reprinted with the permission of the author. W. D. Snodgrass, "The Carnival Girl Darkly Attracts W.D." from *Each in His Season* (Rochester: BOA Editions, 1993). Copyright © 1993 by W. D. Snodgrass. Reprinted with the permission of the author. Gary Snyder, "Hitch Haiku" from *The Back Country* (New York: New Directions Publishing Corporation, 1957). Copyright © 1957 by Gary Snyder. Reprinted with the permission of the author. Sor Juana, "Having had a portrait of Her Ladyship, the Countess de Paredes, painted on a ring, she tells why" and "On the same subject," translated by Alan Trueblood, from *A Sor Juana Anthology*. Copyright © 1988 by the President and Fellows of Harvard College. Reprinted with the permission of Harvard University Press. A. E. Stallings, "Arachne Gives Thanks to Athena" from *Archaic Smile* (University of Evansville Press). Originally published in *The Beloit Poetry Journal* 46 (Winter 1995–1996). Reprinted with the permission of the author. Timothy Steele, "Summer" from *Sapphics and Uncertainties: Poems 1970–1986*. Copyright © 1979 by Timothy Steele. Reprinted with the permission of the University of Arkansas Press. Alan Stephens,

"The Morning of Glen Gould's Funeral" from *The White Boat* (Kalamazoo, Mich.: Buckner Press, 1995). Reprinted with the permission of the author. Wallace Stevens, "Metaphors of a Magnifico" from *Collected Poems*. Copyright 1954 by Wallace Stevens. Reprinted with the permission of Alfred A. Knopf, a division of Random House, Inc. and Faber & Faber Ltd. Pamela Stewart, "Punk Pantoum" from *Crazy Horse* (1979). Reprinted with the permission of the author. Mark Strand, "From a Litany" from *Selected Poems*. Copyright © 1979, 1980 by Mark Strand. Reprinted with the permission of Alfred A. Knopf, a division of Random House, Inc. Catriona Strang, ["For all ease lent"] from *Low Fancy* (Toronto: ECW Press, 1993). Reprinted with the permission of the author. May Swenson, "Four-Word Lines" from *The Love Poems of May Swenson*. Copyright © 1991 by the Literary Estate of May Swenson. Reprinted with the permission of Houghton Mifflin Company. All rights reserved. James Tate, "Peggy in the Twilight." Reprinted with the permission of the author. Henry Taylor, "Berryman," "Judas," and "Cixous." Reprinted by permission of Louisiana State University Press from *Brief Candles: 101 Clerihews* by Henry Taylor. Copyright © 2000 by Henry Taylor. Lewis Turco, "Jasper Olson" from *Pocoangelini: A Fantography and Other Poems* (Northampton, Mass.: Despa Press, 1971), and in *Bordello, A Portfolio of Poem-Prints*, with George O'Connell (Oswego, New York: Grey Heron Press, 1996). Copyright © 1971, 1996 by Lewis Turco. Reprinted with the permission of the author. Tristan Tzara, excerpt from *Seven Dada Manifestos and Lampisteries*, translated by Barbara Wright. Copyright © 1992 by Barbara Wright. Reprinted with the permission of Calder Publications, Ltd. Cor van den Heuvel, excerpt from "Net Renga" ["the neon goes out . . ."] from *Haiku Magazine* 6, 3 (1976). Reprinted with the permission of Cor van den Heuvel. Anita Virgil, excerpt from "Net Renga" ["when WHIZ! Go the pinwheels"] from *Haiku Magazine* 6:3 (1976). Reprinted with the permission of the author. Ellen Bryant Voigt, "Ravenous" from *Five Points* II, no. 3 (Spring/Summer 1998). Reprinted with the permission of the author. Kathleene West, "Current Event" from *Water Witching*. Copyright © 1984 by Kathleene West. Reprinted with the permission of Copper Canyon Press, P. O. Box 271, Port Townsend, WA 98368-0271. Gail White, "Epitaph on a Minor Poet," and "Edmund Clerihew Bentley" from *Light*. Both reprinted with the permission of the author. Richard Wilbur, "Thyme Flowering Among the Rocks" from *Walking to Sleep and Other Poems*. Copyright © 1969 by Richard Wilbur. Reprinted with the permission of Harcourt, Inc. Jonathan Williams, "Aunt Dory Ellis, of Penland, Remembers When She Fell in Her Garden at the Home Place and Broke Her Hip in 19 and 56" and "Three Graffiti in the Vicinity of / The Mikado Baptist Church, / Deep in Nacoochee Valley" from *Blues & Roots/Rue & Bluets* (Durham, North Carolina: Duke University Press, 1985). Reprinted with the permission of the author. Paul O. Williams, excerpt from "Blooming Street" ["in the empty house"] [unpublished renku written in Belmont, CA, February-August 1992]. Reprinted with the permission of the author and the Association for International Renku. Sherley Anne Williams, "Any Woman's Blues" from *The Peacock Poems*. Copyright © 1975 by Sherley Anne Williams. Reprinted with the permission of Wesleyan University Press. William Carlos Williams, "Spring and All" and "View by Color Photography on a Commercial Calendar" from *The Collected Poems of William Carlos Williams, Volume II, 1939–1962*, edited by Christopher MacGowan. Copyright © 1955 by William Carlos Williams. Reprinted with the permission of New Directions Publishing

Corporation and Carcanet Press, Ltd. C. D. Wright, "Girl Friend" from *Tremble*. Copyright © 1996 by C. D. Wright. Reprinted with the permission of The Ecco Press. Richard Wright, "no. 31" from *Haiku: This Other World*. Copyright © 1998 Ellen Richard Wright. Reprinted with the permission of Arcade Publishing, New York, New York and John Hawkins & Associates, Inc. William Butler Yeats, "Among School Children" from *The Poems of W. B. Yeats: A New Edition,* edited by Richard J. Finneran. Copyright 1928 by Macmillan Publishing Company, renewed © 1956 by Georgie Yeats. Reprinted with the permission of Simon & Schuster, Inc. and A. P. Watt, Ltd. on behalf of Michael Yeats. Daniel Zimmerman, "On Isotopes," "a noun knew her best," and "no lie is not known." Reprinted with the permission of the author. *Every effort has been made to trace the ownership of all copyrighted material in this book and to obtain permission for its use.*

Index of Names

1884